39th ANNUAL EDITION

SONGWRITER'S MARKET

2016

Cris Freese, *Editor*

Andrea Williams, *Contributing Editor*

WRITER'S DIGEST
BOOKS
WritersDigest.com
Cincinnati, Ohio

SONGWRITER'S MARKET. Copyright © 2015 by F+W Media, Inc. Published by Writer's Digest Books, an imprint of F+W Media, Inc., 10151 Carver Road, Suite #200, Blue Ash, OH 45242. Printed and bound in the United States of America. All rights reserved. No other part of this book may be reproduced in any form or by any electronic or mechanical means, including information storage and retrieval systems without permission in writing from the publisher, except by a reviewer, who may quote brief passages in a review.

Publisher: Phil Sexton

Writer's Market website: www.writersmarket.com
Writer's Digest website: www.writersdigest.com
Writer's Digest bookstore: www.writersdigestshop.com

Distributed in Canada by Fraser Direct
100 Armstrong Avenue
Georgetown, Ontario, Canada L7G 5S4
Tel: (905) 877-4411

Distributed in the UK and Europe by F&W Media International
Brunel House, Newton Abbot, Devon, TQ12 4PU, England
Tel: (+44) 1626-323200, Fax: (+44) 1626-323319
E-mail: postmaster@davidandcharles.co.uk

Distributed in Australia by Capricorn Link
P.O. Box 704, Windsor, NSW 2756 Australia
Tel: (02) 4577-3555

ISSN: 0161-5971
ISBN-10: 1-59963-939-4
ISBN-13: 978-1-59963-939-0

Attention Booksellers: This is an annual directory of F+W Media, Inc.
Return deadline for this edition is December 31, 2016.

Edited by Cris Freese
Cover designed by Alexis Brown
Page layout by Claudean Wheeler
Production coordinated by Debbie Thomas

fw

a content + ecommerce company

CONTENTS

MANAGEMENT & MARKETING

MARKETS

RESOURCES

INDEXES

FROM THE EDITOR

As *Songwriter's Market* approaches its 40th anniversary, I felt it necessary to take this edition back to the basics: the craft of songwriting. At the heart of any song that stands the test of time is good writing. And it can be a difficult task for songwriters: There's only so much time and so many words to tell a story. That's where this edition comes into play.

Within the revamped opening section, Getting Started, you'll find a craft-based article on diagnosing what makes a song a hit. The articles on avoiding rip-offs and pitching your songs have also been rewritten, thanks to the help of talented contributing editor Andrea Williams. Andrea also provided brand new material for the Music Business Basics, including a quick primer on PROs, a state of the industry report, and interviews with six different songwriters who have paved their way to a career in the industry.

In the new Craft section, you'll find articles on discovering your voice, editing and rewriting for alliteration and assonance, and mining your personal experiences for quality ideas. In Interviews, you'll find a special article featuring a sit-down with four award-winning songwriters who share their experiences on craft and honing your writing.

We also asked Pat Pattison, a professor at Berklee College of Music, to share a webinar. In this unique video, Pat walks his students through word choice, point of view, and creating a rhythm for a stronger song. Find more about this exclusive piece at www.writersmarket.com/sm16-webinar.

With this new focus and content, and of course the many listings, *Songwriter's Market* will be your trusted guide in traversing any point of your career.

Cris Freese
Associate Editor, Writer's Digest Books

HOW TO USE *SONGWRITER'S MARKET*

Before diving into the *Songwriter's Market* listings, it's a good idea to take time to research—you want to be in the best possible position for success before submitting. As you read through the articles and advice in this book's opening sections, ask yourself if you currently have what it takes to succeed: strong songs, a well-recorded demo, a professional presence both online and in person, the ability and desire to network, the patience to learn new technologies and skills, and, perhaps most important, the commitment to your craft and to researching the business aspects of the music industry. By educating yourself and constantly assessing your needs and skills, you'll be better prepared when you actually do submit your songs.

Now, let's take a look at what is inside *Songwriter's Market*, why these articles were put into the book in the first place, and how they can help your career.

THE LISTINGS

Beyond the articles, which we highly encourage you to read first, there are eight market sections in this book, including Music Publishers, Record Companies, Contests & Awards, and Managers & Booking Agents. Each section begins with an introduction detailing how the different types of companies function—what part of the music industry they work in, how they make money, and what you need to think about when approaching them with your music.

These listings are the heart of *Songwriter's Market*. They are the names, addresses, and contact information of music business companies looking for songs and artists, as well as descriptions of the types of music they are looking for.

So how do I use *Songwriter's Market*?

The quick answer is that you should use the indices to find companies that are interested in your type of music; then read the listings for details about how they want the music submitted. For support and help, join a songwriting or other music industry association (see the Organizations section at the back of this book). Also, read everything you can about songwriting (see the Publications of Interest section), and talk to other songwriters. Always conduct your own research (using this book is a great starting point), especially since businesses can change contact information and location between a book's publication and when you pick it up. The industry moves fast!

How does *Songwriter's Market* work?

The listings in Songwriter's Market are packed with information. It can be intimidating at first, but they are structured for ease of use. Take a few minutes to get used to how the listings are organized, and you'll save time in the long run. For more detailed information about how the listings are put together, read the section: "Where Should I Send My Songs?"

The following are general guidelines about how to use the listings:

READ THE ENTIRE LISTING to decide whether to submit your music. Please *do not* use this book as a mass mailing list. If you blindly send out demos by the hundreds, or e-mail links to your website or social media profile at random, you'll waste a lot of time and annoy a lot of people.

PAY CLOSE ATTENTION TO THE "MUSIC" SECTION IN EACH LISTING. This will tell you what kind of music the company is looking for. If they want rockabilly only and you write heavy metal, don't submit to that company. That's just common sense.

FOLLOW THE SUBMISSION INSTRUCTIONS shown under How to Contact. A lot of listings are particular about how they want submissions packaged. If you don't follow their instructions, your submission will probably be discarded. If you are confused about a listing's instructions, contact the company for clarification. Some companies will also list their submission instructions on their website.

IF IN DOUBT, CONTACT THE COMPANY FOR PERMISSION TO SUBMIT. Some companies don't mind if you send an unsolicited submission, but others may require you to get special permission prior to submitting. Others still may be currently closed to unsolicited submissions, in which case they are legally forbidden from even listening to your music. Pay attention to these guidelines and act accordingly. Contacting a company first is also a good way to determine its latest music needs, while also briefly making contact on a personal level—you'll be more likely to get a response to your submission if you've already been in contact with someone at the company.

BE COURTEOUS, BE EFFICIENT, AND ALWAYS HAVE A PURPOSE to be in touch with your personal contact. Don't waste a contact's time. If you call, always have a legitimate reason: seeking permission to submit, checking on guidelines, following up on a demo, etc. Once you have someone's attention, don't wear out your welcome, and always be polite.

CHECK FOR A PREFERRED CONTACT. Some listings designate a contact person after the bolded Contact heading. This is the person you should contact with questions or to whom you should address your submission. Again, you may want to use the listing as a starting point and then look up the company online to verify that the contact person is still there. Double-checking never hurts!

READ THE TIPS SECTION. This part of the listing provides extra information about how to submit or what it might be like to work with the company.

FREQUENTLY ASKED QUESTIONS

How do companies get listed in *Songwriter's Market*?

No company pays to be included—all listings are free. The listings come from a combination of research the editor does on the music industry and questionnaires filled out by companies who want to be listed (many of them contact us to be included). All questionnaires are screened for known sharks and to make sure they meet our requirements.

Why aren't other companies I know about listed in this book?

There are many possible reasons. Perhaps they did not reply to the questionnaire we sent, were removed due to reader com-

plaints, went out of business, specifically asked not to be listed, could not be contacted for an update, or were left out due to space restrictions.

What's the deal with companies that don't take unsolicited submissions?

In the interest of completeness, the editor will sometimes include listings of crucial music companies and major labels you should be aware of. We want you to at least have some idea of their policies. And, you never know: Their submission policies may change.

A listed company claimed that it accepts unsolicited submissions, but my demo came back unopened. What happened?

Needs can change rapidly. This may be the case for the company you submitted to. That's why it's a good idea to contact a company before submitting.

So that's it. You now have the power and resources at your fingertips to begin your journey. Let us know how you're doing. Drop us a line at marketbookupdates@ fwmedia.com and tell us about any successes you have had thanks to the materials in this book.

WHERE SHOULD I SEND MY SONGS?

This question depends a lot on whether you write mainly for yourself as a performer or if you want someone else to pick up your song to record (often the case in country music, for example). These two types of songwriters may have different career trajectories, so it's important to assess whom you'd like to write for and what you'd like to write. This is important for figuring out what kind of companies to contact, as well as how you contact them.

What if I'm strictly a songwriter/lyricist?

Many well-known songwriters are not performers. Some are not skilled instrumentalists or singers, but they understand melody, lyrics, and harmony and how those elements go together. They can write great songs, but they need someone else to bring their words to life through skilled musicianship. This type of songwriter will usually approach music publishers first for access to artists looking for songs. Music publishers are to songwriters what literary agents are to authors. They take great songs and find homes for them while managing the rights and money flow for you. Some producers and record companies may also seek out songwriters directly, but music publishers might be your best bet. Additionally, you can reach out to artists directly—especially indie artists—and offer your songs for their upcoming projects. (For more details on the different types of companies and the roles they play for songwriters and performing artists, see the section introductions for Music Publishers, Record Companies, Record Producers, and Managers & Booking Agents.)

What if I am a performing artist/songwriter?

Famous songwriters can also be famous performers. They are skilled interpreters of their own material and know how to write to their own particular talents as musicians. In this case, songwriters' intentions are usually to sell themselves as performers in the hope of recording and releasing an album. They could also have an album

Songwriter's Market lists music publishers, record companies, producers, and managers (as well as advertising firms, play producers, and classical performing-arts organizations) along with specifications about how to submit your material to each. Trade publications such as *Billboard* and *Variety*, available at most local libraries and bookstores, are great sources for up-to-date information. These periodicals list new companies as well as the artists, labels, producers, and publishers for each song on the charts.

Band websites, social media pages, and album liner notes can also be valuable sources of information, providing the name of the record company, publisher, producer, and usually the manager of an artist or group. Use your imagination in your research, and be creative with your results—any contacts you make in the industry may help your career as a songwriter in some way. See the "Publications of Interest" section for more details.

already recorded and simply be trying to find gigs and people who can help guide their careers. After working independently to maximize opportunities in their local markets, these songwriters will likely benefit from the assistance of booking agents and managers.

However, a music publisher can still be helpful for this kind of artist, especially in managing a catalog of music and securing licensing opportunities in TV, film, and advertisements. Some music publishers in recent years have also taken on the role of developing artists as both songwriters and performers, or are connected to a major record label, so performing songwriters might go to them for these reasons, too.

How do I use *Songwriter's Market* to narrow my search?

Once you've identified whether you are primarily interested in getting others to perform your songs or want to perform your own songs and get a record deal, etc., there are several steps you can take:

IDENTIFY WHAT KIND OF MUSIC COMPANY YOU SHOULD APPROACH. As mentioned earlier, deciding whether you're a performing artist or strictly a songwriter will affect who you want to contact. Songwriters may wish to contact a music publisher for a publishing deal first. Performing artists may prefer to first contact record companies, managers, and record producers in order to find a record deal or record an album, and reaching out to music publishers might be a secondary, though still important, option.

CHECK FOR COMPANIES BASED ON LOCATION. Maybe you need a manager located near you. Maybe you need to find as many Nashville-based companies as you can because you write country music and that's where most country publishers are. You can also recognize Canadian and foreign companies by the icons in the listing (see A Sample Listing Decoded within this section).

LOOK FOR COMPANIES BASED ON THE TYPE OF MUSIC THEY WANT. Some publishers want country. Some record labels want only punk. Read the listings carefully to make sure you're maximizing your time and submitting your work to the appropriate markets.

LOOK FOR COMPANIES BASED ON HOW OPEN THEY ARE TO BEGINNERS. Some companies are more open than others to beginning artists and songwriters. If you are a beginner, it may help to approach these companies first. Some music publishers are hoping to find that wild card hit song and don't care if it comes from an unknown writer. A good song is a good song no matter who writes it. Maybe you are just starting out looking for gigs. In this case, try finding a manager willing to help build your band's career from the ground up.

BEWARE OF FALSE ADVERTISEMENTS. It is important to note that some companies out there are actually service companies for songwriters and not actual "markets." For example, many demo-recording companies that charge songwriters to professionally record their demos are legitimate, but there are others that may present themselves misleadingly as potential "markets" and over-promise exposure. Make sure you perform appropriate research before committing to any company for any reason.

TYPES OF MUSIC COMPANIES

MUSIC PUBLISHERS evaluate songs for commercial potential, find artists to record them, find other uses for the songs (such as in film or TV), collect income from songs, and protect copyrights from infringement.

RECORD COMPANIES sign artists to their labels, finance recordings, promotion, and touring, and release songs/albums to radio and TV.

RECORD PRODUCERS work in the studio and record songs (independently or for a record company), may be affiliated with a particular artist, sometimes develop artists for record labels, and locate or co-write songs for artists who do not write their own.

MANAGERS & BOOKING AGENTS work with artists to manage their careers, find gigs, and locate songs to record for artists who do not write their own.

A SAMPLE LISTING DECODED

What do the symbols at the beginning of the listings mean?

These icons give you quick information about a listing with one glance. Here's what they mean:

Openness to Submissions

○ means the company is open to beginners' submissions, regardless of past success

◑ means the company is mostly interested in previously published songwriters or well-established acts, but will consider beginners

● means the company does not want submissions from beginners, only from previously published songwriters/well-established acts

⊘ means the company only accepts material referred by a reputable industry source

Other Icons

◔ means the market is Canadian

◓ means the market is located outside of the U.S. and Canada

⊕ means the market is new to this edition

⊛ means the market places music in film/TV

EASY-TO-USE REFERENCE ICONS →

E-MAIL AND WEBSITE INFORMATION →

TERMS OF AGREEMENT →

DETAILED SUBMISSION GUIDELINES →

WHAT THEY'RE LOOKING FOR →

INSIDER ADVICE →

○ RUSTIC RECORDS

6337 Murray Lane, Brentwood, TN 37027. (615)371-8397. Fax: (615)370-0353. E-mail: rusticrecordsam@aol.com. Website: www.rusticrecordsinc.com. President: Jack Schneider. Executive VP & Operations Manager: Nell Schneider. VP Publishing and Catalog Manager: Amanda Mark. VP Marketing and Promotions: Ross Schneider. Videography, Photography, and Graphic Design: Wayne Hall. Image consultant: Jo Ann Rossi. Independent traditional country music label and music publisher (Iron Skillet Music/ASCAP, Covered Bridge/BMI, Old Town Square/SESAC). Estab. 1979. Staff size: 6. Releases 2-3/year. Pays negotiable royalty to artists on contracts, statutory royalty to publisher per song on record.

DISTRIBUTED BY CD Baby.com and available on iTunes, MSN Music, Rhapsody, and more.

HOW TO CONTACT Submit professional demo package by mail. Unsolicited submissions are OK. CD only, no MP3s or e-mails. Include no more than 4 songs with corresponding lyric sheets and cover letter. Include appropriately sized SASE. Responds in 4 weeks.

MUSIC Good combination of traditional and modern country. 2008-09 releases: *Ready to Ride*—debut album from Nikki Britt, featuring "C-O-W-B-O-Y," "Do I Look Like Him," "Long Gone Mama," and "I'm So Lonesome I Could Cry."

TIPS "Professional demo preferred."

DEMO RECORDINGS

What is a "demo"?

The demo, shorthand for demonstration recording, is the most important part of your submission package. Demos are meant to give music-industry professionals a way to hear all the elements of your song as clearly as possible so they can decide if it has commercial potential.

What should I send?

Some music-industry people will still want CDs or DVDs, but most now request digital files or MP3 files via e-mail, a Dropbox account, etc. Others accept submissions through a contact form on their website, rather than giving out an e-mail address. You should also consider having your songs avaialble on a streaming site, such as YouTube, which allows you to easily share your music via a link, without sending any materials. Some companies would prefer to receive a link to a YouTube video, rather than physical (or digital) files. If a listing isn't specific, contact the company or check their website for details. For more details, see the next chapter, "How Do I Submit My Demo?"

How many songs should I send, and in what order and length?

Anywhere from three is enough, but the number varies. Most music professionals are short on time, and if you can't catch their attention in three songs, your songs probably don't have hit potential. Also, put at least three complete songs on your demo, not just snippets. Make sure to put your best, most commercial song first. An uptempo number is usually best.

Should I sing my own songs on my demo?

If you can't sing well, you may want to hire someone who can. There are many resources for locating singers and musicians, including songwriter organizations, music stores, and songwriting magazines. See the Organizations section of this book for potential songwriter organizations. Some aspiring professional singers will sing on demos in exchange for a copy they can use as a demo to showcase their talent.

Should I use a professional demo service?

Many songwriters find professional demo services convenient if they don't have the time or resources to hire musicians on their own. For a fee, a demo service will produce your songs in their studio using in-house singers and musicians (this is fairly common in Nashville). Many of these services advertise in music magazines, songwriting newsletters, and bulletin boards at music stores. Perform thorough research before selecting a service. Make sure to listen to samples of work they've done in the past, and look for reviews of the service online. Some are mail-order businesses—you send a rough recording of your song or the sheet music, and they produce and record a demo within a couple of months. Be sure to find a service that will allow some control over how the demo is produced, and tell them exactly how you want your song to sound. As with studios, look for a service that fits your needs and budget. Some will charge as low as $300 for three songs, while others may go as high as $3,000 and boast a high-quality sound. Shop around and use your best judgment!

Should I buy equipment and record demos myself?

If you have the drive and focus to learn good recording techniques, yes. Digital multitrack recorders are readily available and affordable, and many artists can set up a passable home studio using just some software, a laptop, and some basic recording equipment. If this is not something you feel comfortable doing yourself, it might be easier to have someone else do it, thus a demo-recording service becomes handy. For performing songwriters in search of record deals, the actual sound of their recordings can often be an important part of their artistic concept. Having the "means of production" within their grasp can be crucial to artists pursuing the independent route. But if you don't know how to use the equipment, it may be better to utilize a professional studio.

How elaborate and full should the demo production be if I'm not a performing artist?

Many companies listed in *Songwriter's Market* tell you what types of demos they're looking for. If in doubt, contact them and ask. In general, country songs and pop ballads can often be recorded with just a vocal plus a guitar or piano, although many songwriters in those genres still prefer a more complete recording with drums, guitars, and other backing instruments. Up-tempo pop, rock, and dance demos usually require a full production. If you write for a chorus, you will need a number of vocalists to help you create your demo.

What kind of production do I need if I'm a performing artist?

If you are a band or artist looking for a record deal, you will need a demo that is as fully produced as possible. Many singer/ songwriters record their demos as if they are going to be released as an album. That way, if they don't get a deal, they can still release it on their own. Professionally pressed CDs are also now easily within reach of performing songwriters, and many companies offer graphic-design services for a professional-looking product.

What should I send if I'm seeking management?

Some companies want a video of an act performing their songs. Check with the companies for specific requirements. If they don't list this on their website, send them an e-mail through their contact form.

HOW DO I SUBMIT MY DEMO?

You have three basic options for submitting your songs: submitting by mail, submitting in person, and submitting over the Internet.

SUBMITTING MATERIAL BY MAIL

Should I call, write, or e-mail first to ask for submission requirements?

This is always a good idea, and many companies require you to contact them first. If you call, be polite, brief, and specific. Also, be sure to check the company's website before calling. Companies will often indicate whether they wish to hear from a potential artist via phone or not. If you send a letter, make sure it is typed and to the point. Include a typed SASE (self-addressed stamped envelope) for reply. If you send an e-mail, again, be professional and to the point. Proofread your message before you send it, and then be patient. Give them some time to reply. Do not send out mass e-mails or otherwise overload their e-mail account with repeated requests.

What do I send with my demo?

Most companies have specific requirements, but here are some general pointers:

- Read the listing carefully and submit *exactly* what they ask for. It's also a good idea to check online in case they've changed their submission policies.
- Listen to each demo to make sure it sounds right and is in the right order (see the previous section, Demo Recordings).
- Enclose a *brief*, typed cover letter to introduce yourself. Indicate what songs you are sending and why you are sending them. If you are pitching your songs to a particular artist, say so in the letter. If you are an artist/songwriter looking for a record deal, you should say so. Be specific.
- Include *typed* lyric sheets or lead sheets, if requested. Make sure your name, address, and phone number are on each sheet.
- Neatly label each CD with your name, address, e-mail, and phone number,

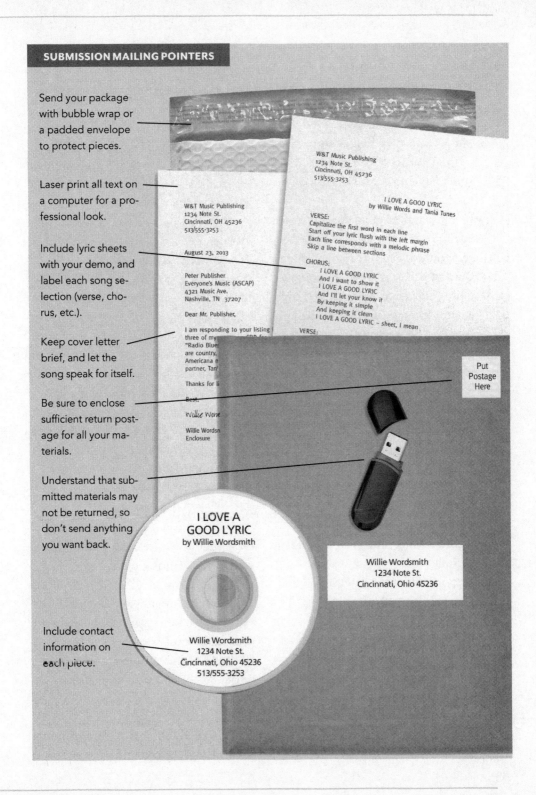

SUBMISSION MAILING POINTERS

Send your package with bubble wrap or a padded envelope to protect pieces.

Laser print all text on a computer for a professional look.

Include lyric sheets with your demo, and label each song selection (verse, chorus, etc.).

Keep cover letter brief, and let the song speak for itself.

Be sure to enclose sufficient return postage for all your materials.

Understand that submitted materials may not be returned, so don't send anything you want back.

Include contact information on each piece.

W&T Music Publishing
1234 Note St.
Cincinnati, OH 45236
513/555-3253

August 23, 2013

Peter Publisher
Everyone's Music (ASCAP)
4321 Music Ave.
Nashville, TN 37207

Dear Mr. Publisher,

I am responding to your listing
three of my _____ CD for
"Radio Blue_____
are country,
Americana n_____
partner, Tan_____

Thanks for li_____

Best,

Willie Words

Willie Wordsn
Enclosure

W&T Music Publishing
1234 Note St.
Cincinnati, OH 45236
513/555-3253

I LOVE A GOOD LYRIC
by Willie Words and Tania Tunes

VERSE:
Capitalize the first word in each line
Start off your lyric flush with the left margin
Each line corresponds with a melodic phrase
Skip a line between sections

CHORUS:
I LOVE A GOOD LYRIC
And I want to show it
I LOVE A GOOD LYRIC
And I'll let your know it
By keeping it simple
And keeping it clean
I LOVE A GOOD LYRIC – sheet, I mean

VERSE:

Put
Postage
Here

I LOVE A
GOOD LYRIC
by Willie Wordsmith

Willie Wordsmith
1234 Note St.
Cincinnati, Ohio 45236
513/555-3253

Willie Wordsmith
1234 Note St.
Cincinnati, Ohio 45236

along with the song names in the order they appear on the recording.

- Include a SASE with sufficient postage, and make sure it's large enough to return all your materials. **WARNING:** Many companies do not return materials, so read each listing carefully. Be sure to double check information on their website.
- If you submit to companies in other countries, include a self-addressed envelope (SAE) and International Reply Coupon (IRC), available at most post offices. Make sure the envelope is large enough to return all of your materials.
- Pack everything neatly. Clearly type or print your company's address and your return address so they are clearly visible. Your package is the first impression a company has of you and your songs, so neatness counts!
- Stamp or write "First Class Mail" on the package and the SASE you enclose.
- Do not use registered or certified mail unless requested. Most companies will not accept or open demos sent by registered or certified mail for fear of lawsuits.
- Keep records of the dates, songs, and companies you submit to.

Is it okay to send demos to more than one person or company at a time?

It is usually acceptable to make simultaneous submissions. One exception is when a publisher, artist, or other industry professional asks you to put your song "on hold."

What does it mean when a song is "on hold"?

This means they intend to record the song and don't want you to give the song to anyone else. This is not a guarantee, though. Your song may eventually be returned to you, even if it's been on hold for months. Or it may be recorded and included on the album.

How can I protect my song from being put "on hold" indefinitely?

One approach is to establish a deadline for the person who asks for the hold, e.g., "You can put my song on hold for three months." Or you can modify the hold to specify that you will still pitch the song to others but won't sign another deal without allowing the person with the song on hold to make you an offer. Once you sign a contract with a publisher, they have exclusive rights to your song and you cannot pitch it to other would-be publishers.

SUBMITTING MATERIAL IN PERSON

Do I need to visit to New York, Nashville, or Los Angeles in order to submit in person?

A trip to one of the major music hubs can be valuable if you are organized and prepared to make the most of it. You should have specific goals and set up appointments before you go. Some industry professionals are difficult to see and may not consider meeting out-of-town writers a high priority. Others are more open and even encourage face-to-face meetings. By taking the time to travel, organize, and schedule meetings, you can appear more professional than songwriters who submit blindly through the mail.

What should I take?

Take several copies of your demo and typed lyric sheets of each of your songs. More than one company you visit may ask you to leave a copy for them to review. You can expect occasionally to find a person has canceled an appointment but wants you to leave a copy of your songs so they can listen and contact you later. (Never give someone the only [or last] copy of your demo if you absolutely want it returned, though.)

Where should I network?

Coordinate your trip with a music conference or make plans to visit ASCAP, BMI, or SESAC offices while you are there. For example, the South by Southwest Music Conference in Austin and NSAI Spring Symposium in Nashville often feature demo listening sessions, where industry professionals listen to demos submitted by songwriters attending the seminar. ASCAP, BMI, and SESAC also sometimes sponsor seminars or allow aspiring songwriters to make appointments with counselors who can give them solid advice.

How do I deal with rejection?

Many good songs have been rejected simply because they were not what the publisher or record company was looking for at that particular point. Do not take it personally. If few people like your songs, it does not mean they are not good. On the other hand, if you have a clear vision for what your particular songs are trying to convey, specific comments can also teach you a lot about whether your concept is coming across as you intended. If you hear the same criticisms of your songs over and over—for instance, the feel of the melody isn't right or the lyrics need work—give the advice serious thought. Listen carefully, and use what the reviewers say constructively to improve your songs.

SUBMITTING MATERIAL OVER THE INTERNET

Is it okay to submit over the Internet?

More and more, this is becoming a standard practice, but many companies still require regular mail submissions, so make sure you verify which process the company prefers. Web-based companies like Songspace.com and TAXI, among many others, are making an effort to connect songwriters and industry professionals over the Internet. The Internet is proving important for networking. Garageband.com has extensive bulletin boards and allows members to post audio files of songs for critique. Some companies also just include a contact form through which songwriters should submit their material. This eliminates the possiblity of someone sending spam or a virus via an e-mail attachment.

If I want to try submitting over the Internet, what should I do?

First, send an e-mail to confirm whether a music company is equipped to stream or download audio files properly (whether MP3 or streaming at Bandcamp, Soundcloud, etc.). If they do accept demos online, it is possible to use sites such as Dropbox to set up an online folder for sharing. Many e-mail services also have larger maximum file sizes for attachments than they used to, making it easier to e-mail songs. Another strategy is to build a website with audio files that can be streamed or downloaded, or make YouTube videos using just a band photo or album cover image, or better yet, a memorable video. (For those companies that just have contact forms, just the link to your YouTube videos may be sufficient.) Then, when you have permission, send an e-mail with links to that website or to particular songs. All they have to do is click on the link, and it launches their web browser to the appropriate page. Do not try to send MP3s or other files as attachments if the company doesn't accept them or doesn't request them—this is an almost sure-fire way to receive an immediate rejection.

THE ANATOMY OF A HIT

....

Andrea Williams

///

These days, country superstar Blake Shelton is everywhere—from coaching a cadre of talented vocalists on NBC's *The Voice*, to co-hosting the Academy of Country Music Awards and walking red carpets with his equally successful country-crooning wife, Miranda Lambert.

Shelton's also no stranger to the *Billboard* charts, with recent songs like "Boys 'Round Here" and "Doin' What She Likes" dominating the country market. It hasn't always been that way, though. At the turn of the century, Shelton was just another wannabe in Nashville—signed to a record deal but struggling to stand out among the crowds of other aspiring stars constantly flooding country music's Mecca. Then, in 2001, Giant Records released "Austin" as Shelton's debut single. The result was a hit that stayed atop the *Billboard* Hot Country Songs chart for five weeks.

The song was born when, inspired by a fellow songwriter who was struggling to get over the girlfriend who left him and moved to Austin, Texas, Kirsti Manna partnered with co-writer David Kent to turn the tale of lost love into music.

It's been a while since Manna penned the song that would introduce the now-ubiquitous Shelton to the world, but she's still very active in Nashville, working on new songs every day. Luckily, for those who'd like to try to follow in her chart-topping footsteps, she's also teaching everything she knows. With numerous resources, including a series of YouTube videos, workshops, and her Songwriter Girl Camp for female artists of all ages, Manna is committed to mentoring the next wave of writing talent.

Here, Manna shares her thoughts on what it takes to write a hit and break out as a songwriter.

PLAN AHEAD, BUT BE SPONTANEOUS

It is difficult to write great song lyrics, and one of the biggest mistakes new writers make is to start rhyming before they know where the song is going. I think it is important to figure out a road map for the song. Decide, with your co-writer if you are working with someone, how the characters in the song interact, what their relationship is with each other, etc. We have all heard stories of songs being written in thirty minutes and later becoming hits, but most songs take a little longer than that!

I love to start songs with a title. I'm a need-to-know kind of person, so I like working out the details before I get rolling, always keeping my options open. For me, it's like planning a trip and then letting spontaneity have its moment, too.

I think it's important to know who you are as a writer and what gets you "in the zone" in the most efficient way. But, then again, it's smart to challenge yourself and change it up. Be open to starting the song with only a melody idea or even a beat. I also think it is a good idea to write without your instrument. Sometimes a new writer's songs will all sound the same, and the reason may be that they only know a few guitar chords, so every time they write a song, they end up playing what is familiar.

I usually am fixing lyrics on my songs up to the minute we record the vocal, and I sometimes do tweaks in the session. I try to listen to the song as if I've never heard it before, thinking about any holes in the story, if the tenses are correct, whether it all ties up, and if the chorus is being set up correctly.

Kirsti Manna, who co-wrote with David Kent "Austin," the song that catapulted Blake Shelton to country music fame.

LEARN THE BASICS

The key components of every song are a great melody, catchy lyrics (whether thought provoking or just ear candy), and a hook. In Nashville, the hook also means the title, but the hook can be an instrumental lick or repetitive lyric that is catchy and makes the song memorable.

Another key component is the story of the song—in other words, where is it taking listeners? How can listeners relate to the song? Do they care about the characters in the song (especially if it is a story song)?

We all know that words and music make up a song, and in today's world, production can play a big part in what makes or breaks a song's success. But if we are talking purely about the core of a song, I think it is vital to have a melody that is undeniably moving, inspiring, or exciting in some way. How many times have we heard songs that have a simple title, and the song

> The key components of every song are a great melody, catchy lyrics (whether thought provoking or just ear candy), and a hook.

is better in many ways than the title? One I always think of is "I Will Always Love You," written by Dolly Parton. The title is repeated over and over in the chorus, yet the song is so perfect in its simple way. I love great melodies, so maybe I am partial, but melody is what captures people's hearts and moves them.

But with that said, one part of the song should not be responsible for polishing the other. Every element needs to be spot-on. The lyrics need to marry with the melody. It drives me crazy to hear a song where the lyrics don't seem to exactly fit the melody. Maybe the writer wanted to say the lyrics a certain way but didn't take time to make the melody work its magic, too.

Every writer starts a song in a different way. Some writers hear the melody first and that's what drives them, while others may start with a lyric idea or a hook. To get practice making sure each song element is great, I think it is a good exercise for writers to start a song in a different way than they usually write. In other words, if you're a writer who always starts with lyrics, try coming up with a melody first. For me, the melody usually changes as the lyrics fall into place and vice versa. When every part of the song is "tighter than a hat band," it has the makings of a classic.

PERFECT YOUR FORM

In general commercial music, one of the most commonly used song forms is ABABCB, where A refers to a verse, B refers to the chorus, and C is usually a bridge, though it can act as a musical break, too.

This form is very listener and radio friendly because, as writers like to say, it gets to the "money," or chorus, very quickly.

There are other song forms, however. AABA is a song form that was used until around the 1960s. A good example of this is "Somewhere Over the Rainbow." In this case, the A section is the main melody, or chorus, of the song.

AABABA started to become popular in the 1960s, and a good example of this is "A Hard Day's Night" by The Beatles. It is like the AABA form but with an additional bridge, or B section, and a final verse.

I think song form is really based on the current style. We don't hear many commercial songs in the AABA style now, though I do love ballads in that form. But songs can also be very powerfully delivered in the ABABCB form. Most listeners have become accustomed to hearing music in the ABABCB form for many years now, so I think that all genres, tempos, and styles seem to work well and get the point across in this current, most popular form.

SHARE A STORY

It's important to think about how a personal story or experience can relate to listeners. Is it a story everyone would be interested in hearing over and over? Is it a subject a recording artist would want to sing about? There may be a way to write about one element of the story or experience and base the entire song on that one moment or emotion. In the case of "Austin," the chorus says something different each time, so we can perceive the passing of time and build the case for how much he loved her, to the point that he would leave this very personal message on his answering machine.

No matter what, any songwriter who is writing an emotional song wants to hook the artist they are pitching with a message that is universal and moving. The song may be about something as simple as love but written with a different spin on the subject. If the artist is moved, his fans will be moved, and the song has a good chance of becoming a hit!

So how can you write about a familiar topic in a fresh way? Here are a few tips:

- Write with people who are younger than you. Each generation has its own lingo, attitude, and way of looking at life and the world. Tap into that!
- If you are co-writing, have a conversation first and talk about the song's options and how you can express its meaning without ever saying the typical word attached to that subject. (I'm thinking of the word *love*, which is actually a difficult word to rhyme in a song, but also a subject we never get tired of hearing about.)
- Take classes, go to workshops, and study! When I started to write songs I

Write with people who are younger than you. Each generation has its own lingo, attitude, and way of looking at life and the world. Tap into that.

read *The Craft of Lyric Writing* by Sheila Davis. It is a must-read, as is studying music of all genres and all eras. Make time to get out of your comfort zone and absorb art in many forms. Let it inspire you to look at the world differently and to express your deepest feelings in a conversational way.

KEEP IT SIMPLE

My mantra for writing a hook that sticks in the minds of listeners is KISS. As in, Keep It Simply Singable.

Sometimes a "hooky" line that isn't the title becomes how a listener remembers the song. (A great example of this is Tim McGraw's hit "Something Like That," which a lot of fans call "Barbeque Stain" because of the line in the song about one on his white T-shirt.) As a commercial songwriter, it's important to remember who you are ultimately writing for—the person who is driving to work listening to the radio, the fan who loves to sing along in the audience … you get my meaning. I always remind writers to be objective about their work.

So play your melodic idea for others and see if they can sing along, remember it, and love it! I think it is important to also study hit melodies. What makes them resonate? What is the phrasing like? Is it repetitive? (Repetition is key.)

It is also possible that you aren't a great melody writer and need a co-writer who is.

BEAT WRITER'S BLOCK

I have written quite a few newsletters on this subject, and I always close them with

"Whatever you do, stay inspired." I think inspiration is all around us, and there are some good ways to stay in the zone. I personally believe that writer's block is based on fear—fear of not being good enough, fear of only being as good as your last hit, fear of running out of ideas ... the list goes on and on.

In Nashville, and in other music centers, songwriters co-write most of the time. So, if you get stuck, you usually have a co-writer in the room who can help pull you out of your dry moment. But that doesn't mean you have to succumb to writer's block if you're writing alone. Here are some of my tricks:

- **CHANGE THE SCENE.** Sometimes the best thing a writer can do is to leave the writing space, take a quick break from himself and/or his co-writer, and clear his mind for a few minutes. I've done this in co-writing appointments, and it can help spark a great new idea or direction. Take a short walk, hang out on your porch for a moment, or stretch out and take a few deep breaths.
- **LISTEN TO SOME INSPIRING MUSIC.** I know this sounds like a crazy idea, but a song or piece of music that moves you can help you get re-motivated. Think of other artists or athletes who listen to music to pump themselves up for a winning performance. A songwriter can do the same with a few minutes of inspiration.
- **MOVE YOUR BODY.** This goes along with changing the scene. If you've been sitting in the same room for sev-

> No matter what, any song-writer who is writing an emotional song wants to hook the artist they are pitching with a message that is universal and moving.

eral hours, just moving your body and getting your blood pumping can rejuvenate your mind and spirit.
- **KEEP WRITING.** Sometimes the best thing to do when you encounter writer's block is to keep pushing on through. Creating any piece of art takes work, determination, and commitment.

BE OBJECTIVE

There is just something undeniable about a song that has the "hit" factor. There are so many songs that are popular but, in my opinion, are not great songs. There is so much that goes into a song, but when it is stripped down, without all the bells and whistles and production, is it a song that can be sung with only simple accompaniment and still move the listener? It needs to have this one true quality to be a classic.

But let's face it—every song we write is not a hit. To paraphrase a famous saying: Write a hundred songs; throw them out, and then start over. We all have to write a lot of songs to get to the great ones and to be objective about our work. That is a huge part of becoming a great songwriter, in my humble opinion.

I don't think songwriters are naturally good at self-evaluation. We are all too interested in knowing what others think of our ideas and message. One of the best things a songwriter can do is find a mentor. In working with someone who is objective and offers constructive criticism, I think it's possible to get to a place of self-evaluation and, more important, self-validation.

And every songwriter can "test market" her own songs with friends, family, or other writers. If you have a song that people keep gravitating to, then you know you probably have something special.

ANDREA WILLIAMS is an author, celebrity ghostwriter, and journalist living in Nashville, Tennessee. She has written hundreds of articles for numerous publications, including CNNMoney.com, *Pregnancy and Newborn* Magazine, USNews.com, *Vegetarian Times*, and MediaBistro.com, and she has several books in various stages of publication with traditional and independent publishers. Along the way, Andrea has interviewed everyone from stay-at-home moms and multimillionaire entrepreneurs, to megachurch pastors and award-winning athletes—and she's always on the lookout for the next great story.

Though currently residing in the South with her husband and four children, Andrea's heart will always remain in her hometown of Kansas City, Missouri—constantly feasting on Kansas City Royals baseball and Gates & Sons Bar-B-Q. Follow her online at AndreaWillWrite.com.

HOW DO I PITCH MY SONGS?

....

Andrea Williams

Once you've learned how to write hit songs and how you'll get paid from them, the next step is to get them in the hands of people who can record them and generate income for you. While every pitch is different based on the recipient and his specific needs (see the listings in the back of this book for more info), there are some pitching tips that are universal. Follow these suggestions to ramp up your chances for success.

DON'T BE AFRAID TO START SMALL

When songwriter/producer, sound engineer, and instrumentalist Kevin Kadish started co-writing with a young, unheard-of Meghan Trainor, he had no way of knowing that their collaborations would become

the uber-successful "All About That Bass" and "Lips Are Movin." As it turns out, some of the most successful songs are born this way, so if you want the chance to write with pop music's next big star, your best chance of doing so is actually *before* she becomes a star. "In your neighborhood or in your state is probably the next Carrie Underwood or Christina Aguilera," says Sheree Spoltore, founder and president of the Global Songwriters Connection. "You find the up-and-coming talent and you grow together and learn together. And that's how these circles form around the artists where other people are trying to get in, but it's too tight at that point. They've already been working with those writers and producers, and they know one another and have that relationship."

GLOBAL SONGWRITERS CONNECTION

For more on Global Songwriters Connection, see the "Organizations" section in this book. Mention *Songwriter's Market* in an e-mail to Sheree Spoltore (sheree@globalsongwriters.com) and receive a free PDF of her class on earning additional income through indie artist cuts.

Not sure how to find the Christina Aguilera in your neck of the woods? Try

> The key for success in these markets ... is sounding similar without being copycat or derivative. And the only way to achieve that is by studying what's already out there.

checking out ReverbNation.com, Splotore suggests. ReverbNation is an online platform developed to help artists and bands connect with fans and promote live shows. It's also a way for songwriters to find acts to write for. "A lot of people are putting their music up on ReverbNation, but they never think of it as a pitch sheet," she says. "The cool thing about the site is that it ranks all these great performers, so you can look and hear the voices of the people you want to pitch to, and you can search it by your state. There's some incredible up-and-coming talent on ReverbNation, and if someone is doing twenty-five or thirty dates a year, you need to be pitching to them because not only could you get a cut, but you could also get paid every time they perform your song."

DELIVER THE BEST QUALITY

Grabbing your acoustic and pressing record on your iPhone might work for a rough demo of a song, but when it comes to pitching, quality is everything. You'll have to use professional software like Pro Tools or Log-ic Pro, and you may need to pay a producer and/or engineer who can record your demo for you. If you feel you can't be completely objective about whether your songs meet commercial standards, enlist the help of a focus group who will tell you the truth. Just don't take the chance of sending out anything that's less than great because you may never get a chance to redeem yourself.

"In most cases, songs need to be fully produced and delivered at a level that is commensurate with the songs you hear on the radio," says Aurora Pfeiffer, co-founder of the Los Angeles-based artist and song-writer management firm Rolen Music Group. "Managers, publishers and A&R's listen to thousands of songs a year, and every song you send is in competition with the song next to it. The same artist you are submitting to is most likely one of the same artists that the top 5% of songwriters in the world are submitting to as well."

Quality can also refer to your ability to meet the exact needs of the market you're pitching. Obviously, a song you write for a teenage Disney pop star will be vastly different from a song you want to pitch for a beer ad. "Watch TV shows, movies, trailers, and ads, and play video games," says Jennifer Yeko of Beverly Hills' True Talent Management. "Pay careful attention to the type of music that is being used in these mediums. Of course, you should write what inspires you, but I often tell songwriters to make an album that just speaks to you, and then write another EP or album with songs and lyrics specifically geared towards licensing."

The key for success in these markets, says Yeko, is sounding similar without being copycat or derivative. And the only way to achieve that is by studying what's already out there. "Songwriters will think that's selling out, but it's really just being savvy about the type of music that gets used in these formats," she says. "It needs magic and creativity without losing the edge. There is definitely a certain style of songwriting and song that gets licensed, and either you're able to create that or you aren't."

BRING SOMETHING TO THE TABLE BESIDES YOUR MUSIC

We've talked a lot about how competitive the music industry is for songwriters right now, even for those with great songs. And while that reality should certainly cause you to take your craft more seriously and keep working to reach your full potential, it shouldn't leave you fearful or worried. There are still plenty of songwriters getting album cuts and signing publishing deals. The key differentiator between those who are getting opportunities and those who aren't is that successful writers bring value to the table. It is the music *business*, after all, so if you can communicate how a potential buyer will benefit from working with you, your odds of landing a deal or a cut will increase exponentially.

Case in point: From early 2006 to early 2014, Nashville-based Big Loud Shirt Music Publishing didn't sign any new writers who

hadn't previously signed at least one other publishing deal. That's *eight years* of only signing veteran songwriters. Unfortunately, many executives just can't afford to take risk, explains Seth England, Big Loud Shirt's creative manager. The company finally did, though—but only because it was a good business decision that minimized the level of risk.

As England explains, one of the major costs of doing business for publishers is the recording of demos. And he says it's one of the quickest ways writers can get upside down in their deals—that is, when the publisher is continuing to front the money for the demos, yet the writer hasn't earned any money from which to recoup. So when England met with a talented songwriter who was also able to produce his own demos, the decision to sign him came easy. "It's just smarter business," England says. "And the demos end up coming out better sometimes, too, because he can produce the feel of the song he had in his head, and he's talented enough to play multiple instruments and understand rhythms and melodies."

If you want an advantage over your competition when pitching, determine what sets you apart and push that with fervor.

BUILD YOUR BRAND

Many songwriters who are not also artists fail to take the time to establish their personal brand. But with the Internet at your fingertips and numerous free platforms at your disposal, there's no reason for you *not* to do so—and, in fact, it can make all the difference in your career.

"It's always best to have a strong social media presence across all platforms," says Pfeiffer. "You don't need to have a website, but it does add value to your brand if you do. There's so much competition in this business, it's best to utilize as many platforms as you can to make yourself visible. Sound-Cloud is a great platform to share music on and can easily be linked to a website if you choose to create one."

Yeko agrees about the importance of establishing a brand and encourages songwriters to define their niche. "Songwriters should absolutely brand themselves because, like it or not, people get known for writing a certain type of song very well, whether it's pop or rock or country," she explains. "Focus on becoming amazing in one genre first, before branching out into others."

Another tip from Pfeiffer when you're setting up shop on the Internet: "Be careful to not publicly put out any songs that you plan on placing with other artists in the future, as most artists want songs that were never previously released or shared with others."

GET HELP

The act of writing songs can be a lonely venture, but getting them out to potential buyers shouldn't be. Actually, bringing a professional on board to help you pitch your songs can generate more success for your efforts. "Having a manager helps connect the dots, and it keeps a songwriter organized and on track," explains Pfeiffer. "A manager helps filter talent and put her client in the right rooms. The right manager works with the songwriter, not *for* the songwriter. They help bring opportunities to the table, and negotiate and close deals. They build a strategy and execute ideas together."

By now, you've no doubt experienced the uncertainty and heartbreak of reaching out to a contact via e-mail and never hearing anything back. Well, the secret to getting on a manager's radar and best positioning yourself for possible representation—and a return e-mail—is to have someone refer you and vouch for your work, says Pfeiffer. When that isn't possible, you should still reach out, but you must remember that first impressions are everything. "When approaching via a cold e-mail, the best way is to reach out with a product that's undeniable," Pfeiffer says. "It's all in the way your e-mail is worded. You need to learn how to sell yourself and make an undeniable pitch that makes the recipient intrigued to know more."

Even if you can't convince a manager to work with you, Pfeiffer says having a third party reach out on your behalf is still possible—just recruit a friend or family member in a manager's stead. "I know a few writers who pursue this route, and both parties seem to learn as they go if they don't have a music business background," she says. "If you don't have the luxury of having a close friend or relative representing you, then a clever way around that is to create an e-mail [address] just for pitches ... I've seen that route also [taken] before, and it can open up doors if it's done right."

AVOIDING THE RIP-OFFS

....

Andrea Williams

Since you're reading this book, there's a high likelihood that you're one of the thousands, if not millions, of songwriters looking to ramp up their careers. And as you may or may not have realized thus far, there are tons of shady outfits at the ready to prey on your ambition. Luckily, getting ripped off as a naïve, unsuspecting songwriter is not a forgone conclusion. There are, in fact, specific steps that you can follow to help you preserve your dignity—and your earning potential—on your way to stardom.

GET SOME LEVERAGE

Most songwriters are dreaming of days when they can live fabulously off of fat advances and ever-streaming royalty checks, relishing in the luxury of working (that is, writing songs) only because they want to—not because they *have* to. The reality, however, is that it takes years for songwriters to reach that elite status, if they ever do. In the meantime, bills still need to be paid, and there is nary a collector who will accept "proof of potential fame and riches" as suf-

ficient payment. In short: Don't quit your day job.

You may have already been advised to keep a steady income while you're building your music career so that you can sleep on an actual mattress and have a full belly at night. That's most important, but there's another issue at stake: When you're worried about keeping the lights on in your dingy apartment, you aren't in the best state of mind for negotiations. All of a sudden, $250 seems perfectly reasonable for five cuts on an indie album, or you're willing to sign over all your authorship for a publishing deal that may only net a $10,000 advance.

That's not to say you won't have to work for little or nothing in the early stages of your career, because you probably will. But there's a difference between strategically pursuing opportunities that provide little present value but have a major upside in the long run versus signing the first deal that comes along because you feel you have to—or, worse, you're *desperate*. It comes down to being in a position of power in business deals. In that sense, power doesn't mean that you have more money, or clout, or influence than the other party. It means, simply, that you understand your value and worth as a songwriter (even if you're just starting out) and don't need to accept any offer that dangled before you. Entertainment attorney Barry Chase, of Miami, Florida-based ChaseLawyers, says it like this:

> *If the other party—a producer, publishing company, artist, or business seeking a jingle; let's call them the "buyer"—has approached the songwriter, rather than vice versa, that suggests that something about the songwriter's previous work or personality has specially appealed to the buyer. Or, if some higher-up on the buyer's side has already recommended the songwriter, that also equalizes the bargaining leverage somewhat. The worst situation, from the point of view of the songwriter's bargaining leverage, is one where the songwriter approaches the buyer, hat-in-hand, desperate for a gig. It is almost impossible to maintain one's rights and respect when you need to pay the rent tomorrow.*

So how can you avoid begging for opportunity and instead entice music industry big-wigs to come knocking on your door? The answer, says Chase, is to launch your own career, DIY-style. As our State of the Industry report in the next section mentions, in the history of recorded music, there has never been a time greater than today to be a songwriter. Yes, there's more competition than ever, and incomes across the board have decreased. But no longer are

songwriters beholden to the merciless gatekeepers who've historically cherry-picked those they deemed worthy enough to have a career. Now, more than ever, you can get started, do some co-writes, put your songs out, and build your own brand. Ultimately, if you've also taken time to hone your skills and refine your craft, bigger doors may start to open. And if they do, you'll have evidence of your talent and drive—which you will be able to effectively communicate—and could be offered a deal that honors that.

INVEST IN YOURSELF— BUT DO IT WISELY

If you're going to get serious about launching your career independently (at least to start), you need to be aware that you'll have to spend some cash along the way. That's not a bad thing—after all, where there's no risk, there's no reward. And if you aren't willing to bank on your own songwriting ability, it's unlikely that anyone else will be, either. Unfortunately, coming to terms with that reality isn't as difficult as determining where you can actually invest your hard-earned money to reap the greatest return in your career.

From third-party A&R companies that screen songs and claim to forward those that pass muster on to record labels, producers, ad agencies, and other buyers looking for music, to song pluggers who promise to use their connections to secure album cuts and licensing opportunities for writers, a quick Internet search will yield numerous opportunities to spend cash in hopes of furthering your career.

Some experts believe that while newbie songwriters should generally expect to pay some dues when starting, those dues shouldn't necessarily be in the form of hundreds of dollars spent upfront for a service. "I would avoid altogether or, at the very least, tread extremely carefully in any situation where someone is requesting large sums of upfront money to review or pitch your work," says Atlanta-based entertainment attorney John Seay. "You should pay attention to the exclusivity of the service. Is it open to pretty much anyone, or is the client list curated? If someone has reached out to you, have they demonstrated legitimate interest in your work or was it a form e-mail? If the service is not very exclusive and no one has expressed legitimate excitement about your music, then do you really think they're going to spend much time pitching your songs? In my experience, if someone thinks you can make them money, they are much more willing to work for a piece of the back end versus charging a fee upfront."

That said, not all industry veterans condemn upfront fees. "There are many legitimate song pluggers in Nashville and in other major music centers," says Steve Weaver, an entertainment attorney in Music City with more than thirty years of experience representing songwriters. "A few pluggers work on a percentage only, but the top pluggers charge a retainer and sometimes bonuses and/or a percentage, depending on certain measurable levels of success of a song placement."

At *Songwriter's Market*, we believe every songwriter's situation is unique and should be treated as such. If you're siphoning from your trust fund and have cash to burn, signing up for one of these services may not be a terrible option. It certainly won't hurt your career, and you may land some decent opportunity in the process. Before you start, though, ask around and get an objective take on the individual or business, and if something doesn't feel right, go with your gut. "The contract for these services should have clear ways to measure and determine the efforts of the plugger or other service and an easy way to terminate the contract if the service or plugger is not performing as agreed," Weaver adds.

For those songwriters who are tight on cash and can't afford to invest in an A&R service or professional song plugger without guarantee of success, we advise caution. It is those who are caught between a rock and a student loan (or phone, or gas, or credit card) bill who will most likely feel cheated or ripped off should things not pan out. And there are safer investments for your money anyway. Songwriting organizations like Nashville Songwriters Association International and Global Songwriters Connection charge fees, but there are so many guaranteed benefits built into the membership plans (including networking events, opportunities to pitch to publishers and other decision makers *directly*, and educational resources that teach the ins and outs of the music business) that the costs are more than worth it.

DO YOUR HOMEWORK, AND KNOW WHEN TO HIRE HELP

You've heard about unscrupulous car mechanics who take advantage of little old ladies who don't know the difference between a carburetor and a carport. Well, the same ruthless behavior happens all the time in the music industry. In the end, the best protection against rip-offs is education.

Become well versed in the usage of split sheets when working with co-writers. "Remember," says Seay, "in the absence of a written agreement to the contrary, under United States copyright law, each writer of the song automatically owns an undivided interest in the entire song. That could get messy if a writer only contributed to a small part of the song, but nevertheless claims an equal share to the royalties generated from the song." And get a good grasp on independent contractor and work-for-hire agreements, whether you're executing one with a session musician or producer you're hiring or if you, yourself, are brought in as a work-for-hire songwriter (which means, basically, that you forfeit all ownership rights to the song).

Once you've started putting songs out for the public, research and register with one of the performing rights organizations to ensure no one can use your work without your permission. And, perhaps more important, be savvy enough to understand when you need to recruit the services of an attorney.

"Although you may not need to hire a lawyer early on in your career, it might be a good idea to consult with one initially," says Seay. "Regardless of whether you take advantage of an early consultation, though, you should absolutely consider consulting with an attorney as soon as a contract is introduced into the equation. Remember that many contracts last forever, or for so long that it might as well be forever. An attorney can help you draft, review, and negotiate those agreements. I speak from experience saying that it's much better and cheaper for you to address any potential issues on the front end than it is to hire an attorney to try to extricate you from, or enforce, a bad deal."

The key, adds Weaver, is to hire your own attorney who is experienced in the entertainment industry and intellectual property matters. "It should go without saying, but a writer should never rely on the producer's or publisher's lawyer to tell them that the contract is okay," he explains. "I have seen writers do this and the end result was never good. And the attorney should be an entertainment attorney—not a generalist or attorney with some other specialty. Sure, the writer's father's business attorney can read a publishing contract and tell the writer what it says. But it is not likely that the non-entertainment lawyer will know if its terms are acceptable. And, more important, the non-entertainment lawyer probably will not know what is *not* in the contract that should be there."

Finally, it also helps to research the typical career trajectory of a songwriter in your chosen genre. How long does it typically take for someone to "make it"? We'd like to believe that you are the exception and not the rule—and you may very well be. But just in case, having conserva-

tive expectations for your career will save you the heartache of being bamboozled by some sleazy suit who promises you the world two weeks after you've penned your first full song.

"Be realistic about the fact that you are trying to make a living in a way that almost everyone on Earth would like to if they could," says Chase. "You shouldn't expect to get Paul Simon's deal until you have demonstrated that you are a bankable talent. At the end of the day, I'm afraid it's a business, and the sooner a new talent reconciles herself to that ugly fact, the better."

STATE OF THE INDUSTRY

....

Andrea Williams

Bart Herbison, the executive director of the National Songwriters Association (NSA), fondly remembers how Harlan Howard, the legendary songwriter who penned the country hits "Heartaches By the Number" and "I Fall to Pieces," used to mentor young writers. As an inductee in the Nashville Songwriters Hall of Fame (1973) and the Country Music Hall of Fame (1997), Howard was bubbling over with tricks of the trade, and as a Nashville import himself, he was all too willing to share his advice with starry-eyed kids who'd moved to Music City to make their dreams come true.

"But at one moment," Herbison explains, "Harlan's tone would change. And he'd look at that writer, and he'd say, 'Nashville didn't send for you. Nobody called and said, "We've gotta have you." They didn't send for me; they didn't send for Willie Nelson. They didn't send for Johnny Cash. We came to town; we learned how it worked and we dug it out.'"

NSA is the world's largest nonprofit trade association for songwriters, with more than 140 chapters and about five thousand members across the globe. Herbison's been the executive director for eighteen years, and in that time—what amounts to a lifetime in music years—the industry has changed drastically, with the Internet and digital technologies becoming both a blessing and a curse. So while songwriters now have the resources to record and release songs faster than ever, competition has exploded, and standing out is more difficult. Meanwhile, the glut of often free music in the marketplace (along with other factors) has significantly impacted songwriter earnings.

So even today, thirteen years after his death, Harlan Howard's admonition for wannabe writers to learn the business and "dig it out" is still relevant. And as the lure of chart-topping success burns bright, so, too, does the necessity for ample amounts of creativity, diligence, and perseverance.

When Napster launched in 1999 and pioneered the now ubiquitous peer-to-peer file sharing model, record label execs were literally trembling in their corner offices. How could they maintain their chokehold of the industry—and profits—if fans could get music without paying for it? It seemed, then, that any respite from the thievery would be a more favorable option, and as the first decade of the new millennium came to a close, that option was streaming music sites. Pandora (which operates more like a traditional radio station, in that listeners only choose the genre of music they want to hear, not specific songs) had been around since 2000, but it was the more interactive streaming sites like Spotify (which allow listeners to choose the exact songs they want to hear), that completely shook the game.

Now, rabid fans need only log in to their favorite streaming site—with a free account, mind you—and they have unlimited and unfettered access to their favorite songs from their favorite artists. In order for the sites to host the music, they have to enter into licensing deals with the labels, but, unfortunately, very little of that revenue is kicked back to the songwriters.

It helps to get some background to understand how this has become an issue. As explained by Herbison, songwriters get paid under two sets of government rules. The first is the mechanical royalty, which pays artists and songwriters anytime there is a purchase of physical CDs or legal downloads. "Those rules are from 1909," he says, "and they were created for player piano rolls. They've never worked effectively, and they certainly don't work in the digital era." The second set of rules is related to performance royalties, which are paid whenever a song is played on terrestrial radio (local stations), in a bar or restaurant, in any live venue, or on the aforementioned streaming services. Those rules, while not *as* dated, still go back to 1941.

In both cases, the royalty rates are set by the federal government—mechanical royalties are reset once every five years by a Copyright Royalty Board (CRB) in something similar to a trial, while performance royalties are set by a rate court. The problem, explains Herbison, is that once rates are set, songwriters are under a compulsory license, which means they have to license songs for the rates the government sets, whether they agree or disagree with the terms. And most don't.

"So here's the result of all that, as it relates to the streaming sites," says Herbison. "If you get a song played on a regular radio station, it averages five to six cents every time it spins, for the songwriter and the music publisher. When it plays on a streaming service, it's eight ten-thousandths of a penny."

That wouldn't signal as big of a crisis if the digital streams had only supplemented an already robust industry. But as Zack O'Malley Greenburg, a senior editor at *Forbes*, noted in an article in the magazine's May 2015 issue, the industry has never really recovered from the days of piracy. Total US albums sold hit a peak of 785 million in 2000, the year after Napster's launch. But, Greenburg writes, "By 2008, annual album sales had plummeted 45 percent. Between then and now, even as the labels reined in illegal downloading, sales dropped another 40 percent to 257 million. That means, at $15 per album, the industry is currently taking in $7.9 billion less in annual retail sales than it was a decade and a half ago."

Currently, Herbison spends much of his time in Washington, DC, lobbying on Capitol Hill for more favorable royalty rates for songwriters. He's confident that things will change and that the arcane rules dictating songwriter incomes will finally be updated. "But that doesn't mean that we're going to go back to where we once were, and it's still going to take a few years," he says.

In the meantime, while Herbison works to fix the current system, others, like Graham Alexander, president of the newly reformed Radio Corporation of America, see opportunity in the brokenness. "What's the best model for songwriters? There isn't one yet, and the old model wasn't that great either," he says. "Your best bet is to take advantage of every opportunity. Labels are in the industry of investing in products that appear to be profitable in the short and long haul. The days of labels and publishers signing hundreds of staff writers are essentially dead; however, it is not the be-all and end-all of the modern writer. There are many writers handling their own publishing and licensing on a day-to-day basis."

Still, Graham doesn't completely eschew the industry as a whole—provided songwriters understand how to navigate it on their terms. "The remaining record labels can be excellent partners in a songwriter's business relationships, but times have changed," he adds. "Songwriters are luckily not prevented from making such arrangements with clients on their own accord. Historically, the phrase 'gatekeepers' applied to the entire recording industry; however, these days there are simply too many modern platforms that poke holes—and have even opened their own gates."

No matter what journalists and industry experts say about the future of record labels, streaming sites, and all the other individual factors that, when combined, make up the larger music *business*, one thing is certain: Music, itself, will live on forever. And in a world of cubicles and time clocks, there's something to be said for the rebel music maker who's willing to buck the status quo and forge his own path. Call him a dreamer; call him frivolous or impulsive, or crazy, even—because, to a certain degree, he has to be.

But given today's harsh realities, says Herbison, songwriters must also be realistic. He speaks of Plan Bs in a way that is sure to rankle any hard-core creative, but he does it in a way that compels you to listen closely, as if your very career depends on his choice words.

"In Nashville, we've gone from needing twelve to thirteen thousand songs a year in the late 1990s—that many songs were actually released on records—to three hundred or four hundred that the artist is not involved in writing," Herbison explains. "We've gone from three or four thousand publishing deals, to three or four hundred. So it's awfully hard to break into the professional ranks as a songwriter."

In addition to paltry digital royalties, Herbison notes several other factors that converged in a storm so perfect and vicious that it upended the entire music industry as we knew it a of couple decades ago. First, he says, there are many fewer record labels putting songs out. Then, those that are released stay on the charts much, much longer, further diminishing the need for songs. Oh, and there's also the fact that many artists have gotten hip to 360 deals (in which labels now get a piece of *all* of their income streams) and lower royalties, so they're more actively participating in the writing of their songs in order to keep more of their publishing revenue.

The result, Herbison says, is opportunities and total incomes that are 80 percent to 90 percent lower for songwriters who are not also artists. "Let's remember this," he adds, "Songwriters don't sell concert tickets; they don't sell T-shirts; they don't get product endorsements on TV. It's simply royalties. So it's awfully, awfully, tough." It's especially tough for writers whose primary focus is on landing cuts with artists signed to major labels. But for writers willing to look beyond the charts, there is an alternative.

If the idea of writing songs for a local stage play or regional commercial spot is your idea of "selling out," it's time to come to terms with the realities of today's industry and the fact that if you don't diversify your efforts and revenue streams, your songwriting career will likely meet an inglorious and impoverished end.

And while Herbison may call the pursuit of alternative songwriting markets a backup plan, Sheree Spoltore, founder and president of the Global Songwriters Connection, calls it smart business. Spoltore's industry experience covers the gamut from staff writer to song plugger and several management roles. She also worked

... In a world of cubicles and time clocks, there's something to be said for the rebel music maker who's willing to buck the status quo and forge his own path.

for seven years as the assistant executive director of the Nashville Songwriters Association International under Herbison, so she, too, has seen the transformation of the industry up close. And as a songwriter who has pivoted quite gracefully within her own career with the founding of her own songwriters organization in 2013, she is wholly committed to helping writers find their own niche and establish fruitful careers that are carefully suited to their unique strengths and interests. It's a path that, in the end, can be much more fulfilling than the chase for number ones.

"A lot of times songwriters have tunnel vision at the major artist pitch sheet," Spoltore says. "However ... in that music is generating income every day outside of radio and major markets. So the first thing is being willing to look outside of the normal parameters."

And, interestingly enough, this road less traveled can actually lead back to the most desired destination. "Let's take a songwriter from Kansas City. If he comes to Nashville, and his résumé shows [he] had 25 indie cuts last year, six independent film and TV placements, and four jingles, what do you think an industry professional's perception is going to be of that person?" she asks. "He just positioned himself to succeed by showing industry professionals that if they choose to work with him, they have a partner, because he's actually out there making things happen. He's not looking for someone to wave a magic wand, and industry professionals don't have time to be waving that magic wand anyway. They've got to be working with somebody who understands the process."

Ah, yes. It goes back to the sage wisdom of Harlan Howard. So whether you curse the Internet as the ultimate obstacle standing in the way of you and your destiny, or you praise it as the launching pad that will get you there faster, there is but one truth: You're going to have to hustle. Period.

"I see too many people who think *Oh, I'm going to play some publisher a song, and they're going to discover me and I'm going to be the next star.* You're not," Herbison says flatly. "A lot of people want to know the secret to success in the music industry, and there is a secret. It is the exact same secret to success in any pursuit. The people who work the hardest, know the most about it, and make their own opportunities—those are the ones who succeed."

IN THE KNOW ABOUT PROs

....

Andrea Williams

Finally, you've written some songs that someone other than your mother and best friend will hear. Perhaps you've landed a cut on a hot new indie artist's album, or maybe you've taken up writing songs for a local band's revamped live show. Either way, you're excited that someone is singing your songs on stages across the country, or that a new radio station is plugging your music into heavy rotation every day. The reality, though, is that, for the first time, you have no way of knowing exactly when and where your songs are being played—or "performed," in industry speak. Consequently, that also means you have no way to track your earned royalties. And that's where performing rights organizations come in.

Performing rights organizations, or PROs, serve three main purposes in the careers of their affiliated songwriters. First, they track the performances of their songs, including any domestic terrestrial radio spins (online radio royalties are paid by SoundExchange), live venue, or otherwise public performances/broadcasts, and TV/film broadcasts. The PROs then collect the appropriate licensing fees from the users of the songs, and, finally, distribute royalties (minus administrative fees) to the songwriters. While there are three different PROs in the United States—the American Society of Composers, Authors and Publishers (ASCAP), Broadcast Music, Inc. (BMI), and the Society of European Stage Authors and Composers (SESAC)—they each serve this basic function.

As a songwriter, you may have heard that affiliating with a PRO is your first step to becoming a professional, but that may not actually be the case. In fact, Tim Fink, SESAC's VP of writer/publisher relations at the organization's Nashville headquarters discourages writers from signing on with a PRO too early. "If you're thirteen years old, you probably don't need to go buy a car," he says. "You don't have your driver's license yet, and there's just no need for it. And it's the same thing with performance rights organizations. Most people can't tell you why they joined, and they don't realize that they've actually entered into a contract with that organization."

Obviously, if you fit the example above and know that artists are recording or performing your songs, you also know that you need to sign with a PRO if you expect to get paid. If you're not at that point in your career, however, Fink suggests you really consider your goals and plans as a songwriter. Are you a hobbyist, or are you serious about writing songs professionally? If the latter is true, you may derive some value from a PRO, even before you land your first cut.

"We provide tools and services for up-and-coming songwriters to meet their evolving needs, including educational panels, workshops, networking opportunities, and more," says Nicole George-Middleton, ASCAP's VP of rhythm & soul/urban membership. "We teach about the business, how to manage your money, and the art of songwriting, so when you're a new writer and you join ASCAP, you have access to all of these resources."

Indeed, each of the PROs offers some level of career development to its member songwriters that extends beyond their main function of collecting and disseminating royalties. But *how* each organization interacts with its writers and helps to nurture their careers can vary substantially. SESAC, for example, may offer fewer workshops and conferences for budding writers than ASCAP, but Fink believes the main benefit of affiliation with his organization is the hands-on, personal attention offered to writers, which is made possible by the fact that SESAC is, by far, the smallest of

the three PROs. "At SESAC, there are only 30,000 members [compared to ASCAP's and BMI's 525,000 and 650,000, respectively], and that's by design," he says. "The relationship comes first and the contract comes later, and it's the relationship that helps you get in the door."

Ultimately, it's up to songwriters to research each PRO and choose the organization that best suits their needs. It's certainly not a decision you want to enter into blindly, nor should you automatically choose the PRO that your favorite artist or songwriter is affiliated with. With that in mind, we've done some of the legwork to help you determine whether ASCAP, BMI, or SESAC is right for you.

ASCAP

WEBSITE: www.ascap.com
YEAR LAUNCHED: 1914
NUMBER OF MEMBERS: 525,000
LOCATIONS: New York, Los Angeles, Nashville, Atlanta, Miami, London, Puerto Rico
HOW TO JOIN: Sign up online with your social security number. A one-time processing fee of fifty dollars is required.
NOTABLE MEMBERS: Alicia Keys, Katy Perry, Pharrell Williams, Bill Withers
NOTEWORTHY FACTS:

- ASCAP is the only PRO that offers a one-year contract term to members.
- The ASCAP board of directors consists solely of songwriters and publishers.
- The annual ASCAP EXPO is the organization's flagship event, which draws thousands of attendees and puts up-and-coming songwriters in the same

room as high-profile, successful writers and composers, all in the name of education and networking.

BMI

WEBSITE: www.bmi.com
YEAR LAUNCHED: 1939
NUMBER OF MEMBERS: 650,000
LOCATIONS: New York, Los Angeles, Nashville, Atlanta, Miami, London, Puerto Rico
HOW TO JOIN: Sign up online for free.
NOTABLE MEMBERS: Taylor Swift, Lady Gaga, Eminem, Willie Nelson
NOTEWORTHY FACTS:

- BMI was initially established to compete against ASCAP, which, until that point, had full market dominance. BMI offered music users lower licensing fees and offered to pay new songwriters a fixed fee per performance, as opposed to ASCAP's two-tier structure that penalized less established writers.
- BMI became the first PRO to represent songwriters in marginalized or less popular genres, including jazz, gospel, country, R&B, and blues.

SESAC

WEBSITE: www.sesac.com

YEAR LAUNCHED: 1930
NUMBER OF MEMBERS: 30,000
LOCATIONS: New York, Los Angeles, Nashville, Atlanta, Miami, London
HOW TO JOIN: Fill out the free online form with introductory information about your life and songs, and submit music samples. Upon submission, a writer representative will review all materials before scheduling a meeting or conference call. At that point, the rep will decide whether to extend an offer for representation.
NOTABLE MEMBERS: Mariah Carey, Natalie Grant, Lady Antebellum, Rico Love
NOTEWORTHY FACTS:

- Because of the personal nature of SESAC representation, writer reps are often able to closely assist in the career development of songwriters, including helping to arrange meetings with co-writers and publishers.
- SESAC is the only PRO that pays songwriters monthly royalties for domestic terrestrial radio plays. Those twelve disbursements are in addition to the quarterly royalty payments for all other performances.
- SESAC was the first PRO to pay live performance royalties to songwriters.

FOR THE LOVE OF THE MONEY

....

Andrea Williams

On June 30, 1997, hip-hop mogul Sean "Diddy" Combs (then known as Puff Daddy) released "All About the Benjamins," a single from his debut album *No Way Out*. It was a slicked-out rap anthem professing love, not for Benjamin Franklin himself, but for the one-hundred-dollar bills that bear his image—and, of course, all the wonderful things they can buy. Then, the very next day, on July 1, Diddy's Bad Boy Records dropped the second single from rapper The Notorious B.I.G.'s posthumous *Life After Death* album. The title? "Mo Money Mo Problems."

Since the dawn of recorded music, there has been no shortage of songs dedicated to all things green, and, still, the contradiction that Bad Boy illuminated back in the late 1990s lives on. It's most evident, perhaps, in the careers of the very people behind the music, the songwriters who pour everything into their search for the elusive hit that will sell millions of copies and, presumably, bring lots and lots of cash. But those same songwriters have heard the horror stories of their predecessors who didn't

Barry Shrum is an entertainment lawyer who has been practicing law in the intellectual property, music, entertainment, and business industries for more than twenty-five years.

understand the business of their craft and, as a result, could relate to The Notorious B.I.G.'s hit all too well.

As an entertainment attorney with more than 25 years' experience, Nashville's Barry Shrum is acutely aware of how important it is that songwriters understand the value of their intellectual property, as well as how to protect and leverage it. In fact, he's been lead counsel on major copyright infringement cases that ultimately won six-figure verdicts for his clients. Here, Shrum details everything you need to know about earning money as a songwriter so you can get paid—without going to court.

Once a songwriter writes a song, how, exactly, does he get paid?

As they often say in Music City, "It all begins with a song." But while that may be true, the *value* of a song is only as much as someone is willing to pay for it. A songwriter receives royalties when he (or the publisher) *licenses* one or more of the first five exclusive rights granted by Section 106 of the Copyright Act: distribution, reproduction, adaptation, display, and performance.

A writer receives income from distribution and reproduction rights, for example, when a record label "mechanically reproduces" the song and distributes it for sale. That mechanical royalty is prescribed by law and is called a *statutory royalty*. Currently, that is 9.1 cents per record. The songwriter is also paid this mechanical royalty when a song is downloaded from the Internet on iTunes, Amazon Music, or Google Play. It is important to distinguish "streaming" from downloading, in that streaming implicates the payment of royalties for licensing the digital performance in a sound recording—not the mechanical royalty referenced above. The royalties for that activity are collected by SoundExchange and distributed to the owner of the sound recording copyright and the artists/musicians that performed on the track, and any implicated performance rights for those streams are paid to the songwriters by the traditional performance rights organizations (PROs): ASCAP, BMI, and SESAC.

The performance royalties paid to songwriters are less defined than statutory royalties paid under the Copyright Act. In the US, the songwriters and publishers are generally affiliated with one of the performance rights organizations. Under the authority of non-exclusive agreements with the songwriters, these organizations license out their performance rights to various venues and organizations. Each organization has its own proprietary formula for calculating performance royalties that are due to each songwriter/publisher based on various factors. These formulas are generally defined on each PRO's website.

Finally, there are other royalties to which a songwriter may be entitled. When Don Schlitz licensed the rights to his Kenny Rogers hit, "The Gambler," to a television production company for the [television] mini-series of the same name, he received a royalty payment for the adaptation rights (as the song was "adapted" [for television]). If the lyrics to the song were subsequently used in a paperback book about the movie, the publisher of the book would obtain a license to "display" the lyrics and pay Mr. Schlitz an additional royalty for that use. Finally, if the television company wanted to use a recording of the song in the movie (either Kenny's version or their own recorded version), that would require an additional license, commonly called a synchronization license, to "sync" the copyright with audiovisual content.

When a songwriter finishes a song, or a collection of songs, the first thing to be done is to register the copyrights on the US Copyright Office's eCo site (copyright.gov/eco). Next, I would

> When a songwriter finishes a song or a collection of songs, the first thing to be done is to register the copyrights on the U.S. Copyright Office's eCo site (copyright. gov/eco).

recommend that the songwriter investigate the offerings of ASCAP, BMI, and SESAC and choose one with which to affiliate. That way, if the songwriter anticipates that the song will be used commercially, she can submit the appropriate forms to her selected PRO to notify the organization of the impending use. Once alerted to the possibility of performances, the PRO will collect the writer's royalties. Also, the PRO has people who are

dedicated to helping writers find affiliated publishers, who may advocate for the songwriter and help her seek out other uses for the song.

Is it mandatory that a songwriter register his copyright?

The Copyright Act clearly states that a copyright exists from the moment that an original expression is fixed in a tangible format. For the songwriter, this means that a copyright exists from the moment the song is created and [recorded] in some way (paper, tape, CD, digital, etc.). This ownership of the copyright is distinct from registering the copyright with the Copyright Office, which is not a required step, but it is very beneficial because it gives the creator certain additional benefits, not the least of which is statutory damages up to $200,000 if a willful infringement occurs. This is well worth the small registration fee.

For years, there has been this folklore surrounding the infamous "poor man's copyright," where the songwriter mails a copy of the song to his address so that the postmark serves as proof of creation. The problem is, it's neither copyright nor proof. A good lawyer can easily disprove this kind of evidence. It is better for the songwriter to keep an accurate journal of his activity, including dates and times when possible. This kind of evidence is more useful when it comes to proving who created the song.

What if there is more than one writer on a song? How do the co-writers ensure they are both (or all) paid fairly?

A *split sheet* is a very rudimentary written document pertaining to one specific song. It can be completed by collaborating songwriters before, during, or immediately after a writing session. The document identifies the song and the percentages of revenues agreed to by each of the songwriters. Remember that, in the eyes of the law, each songwriter is said to have an equal and undivided 100 percent interest in the copyright itself, regardless of [the writers'] respective perceived contributions. Therefore, if there are two songwriters, the typical split of revenue would be 50/50. However, if the songwriters feel that the original creator of the melody and lyrics should get a higher percentage of revenues, say 70 percent, then the splits would be identified as 70/30. Often, split sheets will also contain additional information, such as the names of publishers and performance rights affiliation.

Examples of these documents are abundant on the Internet, but [it is important] to understand the legal implications. Having a signature on a split sheet is a good start toward a written collaboration agreement, but the songwriter should be careful: Signing off on a split sheet for less than an equal share of the revenues may have significant implications on a songwriter's future income. [Any concerns should be discussed in consultation] with a qualified attorney. In one case involving the writer of the hook in the Garth Brooks song "Two of a Kind, Workin' on a Full House," there was not a written split sheet, and the publisher ended up giving the contributor a lesser share. He had to file a lawsuit in order to enforce his rights.

Aside from a split sheet, what are the most common contracts that a songwriter would encounter, as well as the key terms and conditions of each?

A songwriter who is lucky enough to land a deal with a successful publishing company that has active writers will generally encounter two basic types of contracts: the single-song agreement (SSA) and the exclusive writing agreement. The exclusive agreement may be one of two kinds, depending on a number of factors.

The first thing a songwriter should know about these agreements is that *all of them* transfer some or all of the ownership in their copyrights to the music publisher, depending on the type of deal. Remember, ownership of the copyright is distinct from the revenues received from the copyright. Think of the revenues generated by the copyright as a pie that is split in half, with one side being the "publisher's half" and the other being the "songwriter's half." This will aid in visualizing the royalties a songwriter will receive from each deal.

The single-song agreement is just that—an agreement that transfers the copyright to *one song* to the music publisher. In exchange for that transfer, the songwriter receives the support of the publisher in exploiting that composition. Generally, all single-song agreements transfer 100 percent of the copyright to the publisher, although a successful songwriter may be able to negotiate different terms. As for revenues, the songwriter will receive 50 percent of everything the publisher receives, minus certain deductions such as any demo expenses and advances. Typically, these types of agreements are used when a publisher has an interest in the writer but still has some reservations. For the publisher, it locks down the song without tying up resources.

The exclusive songwriting agreement involves more of a commitment from the publisher. Like the name says, the songwriter is agreeing to write "exclusively" for the publisher for a period of time, usually in exchange for a monthly salary. Like the single-song agreement, the exclusive songwriting agreement, the songwriter is transferring 100 percent of all copyrights to the music publisher, often including songs written *before* the contract in addition to all of those written during the term. Although all copyrights are transferred, there are usually additional requirements that the songwriter deliver a minimum number of commercially viable songs during the term, usually twelve to fifteen. Similar to the single-song agreement, the writer is paid 50 percent of revenue after the typical deductions; in this case, that would definitely include the salary.

The co-publishing agreement is another type of exclusive agreement [stipulating that] the songwriter only transfers 50 percent of the copyright to the music publisher. Obviously, these kinds of agreements are typically reserved for the songwriters who have a track record of producing hits. Since the songwriter is only transferring half of the copyright, she receives 75 percent of the royalties after deduction of expenses (50 percent of the so-called "publisher's half" and 100 percent of the "songwriter's half" of the royalties). The critical term to consider in this type of agreement is who administers the copyright; i.e., who is entitled to license and collect the royalties. A songwriter should seek to obtain a portion of the administration rights, or least have them revert back after the term.

Finally, once a songwriter has an established catalog of material, he may encounter what is called an "administration deal" in which a company only *administers* the copyrights for a fee, which ranges from 10 percent of gross on up. For this, the administration company generally collects and distributes the royalty streams from existing copyrights, and nothing more.

In today's entertainment environment, there are many variations on these types of agreements. Sometimes publishers will want to start with some sort of development deal to work with the songwriter to hone their talents before committing to something more serious. I have also seen hybrid publishing and recording agreements that not only transfer song copyrights to the publisher, but also include some recording commitments so that the music publisher can essentially pitch the songwriter to the recording labels as an artist.

How much can a songwriter earn in today's industry?

Revenues in the songwriting industry have decreased over the last decade as a result of the decline in sales of physical product. However, a songwriter can certainly still establish an incredible income stream from the creation of songs. If a new songwriter enters into a writing agreement with an independent or small music publisher, a conservative salary from would be in the range of fifteen to thirty thousand dollars per year. The salary is, by definition in the agreement, a recoupable advance against royalties, meaning that the publisher will deduct the salary from future earnings paid to the songwriter, but the songwriter will not have to repay the advance if there aren't any earnings.

The salary is small potatoes compared to revenue streams, however. If the stars align and lightning strikes, and the music publisher successfully places a song with Taylor Swift, for example,

the game changes entirely. Let's say, optimistically, that the songwriter's cut is on Swift's *1989* album that sold more than one million copies when released. In mechanical royalties alone, the songwriter's music publisher would receive a check for $91,000 (based on the mechanical royalty of 9.1 cents per record) from Big Machine Records during the next accounting period, of which the songwriter would be entitled to her $45,500 (in a traditional exclusive songwriting agreement that transfers 50 percent of all royalties to the publisher). Since the album ultimately went double platinum, the publisher would receive another check for $91,000 to split with the artist.

Now, let's say that a songwriter or music publisher is affiliated with SESAC. The performance royalties for a double-platinum song will likely be around the half-million mark, if not double that, depending on a number of factors. Of course, the songwriter would only receive half of that because of his publishing deal, so let's conservatively say that he will receive $300,000 in performance royalties. That money is paid directly to the songwriter and music publisher, respectively, so songwriters often refer to it as "mailbox money."

Now for the fun part. A song this successful is a likely candidate for inclusion in movies and advertisements, so if the publisher does her job correctly and has an in with several music supervisors, the real money can begin to pour in. Use of the full song as an opening theme in a movie can bring six figures. As the use becomes more obscure, the number goes down dramatically. Synchronization royalties are negotiated on an *ad hoc* basis, so there are no standards. For example, let's imagine that the song is placed in two movies at $750,000 each and one commercial for $500,000. The songwriter would receive half of the total, or $1 million.

So, our dream number now has risen to $1,391,000 for one song ($1 million

....

Find a receptive music supervisor and submit relevant material for consideration. There is no requirement that the submissions come from a music publisher ...

....

in synch royalties for the movies and commercial; $300,000 in performance royalties for any time the song is played or performed in a public venue, including radio spins; and $91,000 for mechanical royalties). These numbers are, of course, based on speculation, and your results may vary.

What are some nontraditional revenue streams that songwriters should consider outside of the traditional album cuts, and what is the earning potential of those?

I'll answer this with an example. Gavin Heaney is a singer/songwriter known professionally as the "Latch Key Kid." Gavin creates his own style of music, in his basement, by playing all of the instruments on his recordings. In 2008, he wrote a song called "Good Times," which was picked up by DreamWorks Pictures for the opening scene of its movie *I Love You, Man*. It was also included as a song on the soundtrack. His Australian publisher then pitched the song to be used in commercials for the Australian TV show *Packed to the Rafters*. The song was seemingly on a snowball's run downhill at that point, because its next synchronization was in a commercial for Coca-Cola called "Jinx," which aired during Super Bowl XLII. The commercial exposed the already popular song to more than 97 million viewers. The song was also featured in trailers for other movies, television commercials for Liberty Mutual, in-flight radio shows for Continental Airlines, and a one-minute short film titled *Dave Knoll Finds His Soul*.

I use this song as an example of nontraditional revenue streams. Heaney started this journey with a clever collaboration with a publishing company, Experience Records, and his love for action sports. The collaborative effort landed him licensing deals and credits on television shows such as *The Amazing Race* and *Survivor*, which in turn led to the aforementioned string of successes.

If there is one arena that a songwriter can exploit independently, it would be that of licensing out rights for these types of uses. Find a receptive music supervisor and submit relevant material for consideration. There is no requirement that the submissions come from a music publisher, and these types of individuals often scout YouTube for resources when looking for material for particular scenes. Do your research. If you have a favorite nighttime drama, research the genre and style of songs used in the show and attempt to replicate [the sound]. Someone out there may be looking for his next big find.

What do songwriters need to know about paying taxes on their earnings? Is it important to work with an accountant who specializes or has experience in the entertainment industry?

Like any other small business, a songwriter pays income tax on the revenues she receives after deducting allowable expenses and credits. As soon as practical and affordable, a songwriter should consider, with qualified legal counsel, what kind of entity to use to operate the business: sole proprietorship, limited liability company, or some type of corporation. This decision should also involve the opinion of a qualified accountant who specializes in the entertainment industry and has a working familiarity with songwriter splits and copyrights. By doing this early on, the songwriter can have a team in place to handle and distribute any revenues that come rolling in.

CAREER SONGWRITERS

Andrea Williams

If you've been writing songs for any reasonable amount of time, you may be ready to trade one of your kidneys for a "hit" song that lands on the charts and establishes you as a legitimate talent. But while a charting hit here or there is nice, for real professionals, longevity—via opportunities *and* cash flow—is the ultimate goal. And it's possible, too. There's a bevy of hardworking songwriters out there who may never draw paparazzi attention on Sunset Boulevard but who've racked up an impressive stack of gold and platinum records (and regular paychecks) nonetheless.

With more than 170 years of combined experience, the following songwriters know what it takes to write songs that make money *and* careers.

> Just keep working and keep enjoying what you do, and branch out into mastering the writing of songs in all sorts of styles and genres.

in a wide range of genres, including pop, R&B, rock, country, jazz, and musical theater, and she is a three-time Grammy nominee. Aretha Franklin, Whitney Houston, Selena, Anne Murray, Peabo Bryson, Reba McEntire, The Jacksons, and Gladys Knight are just a few of the artists who've recorded Oland's songs, and Frank Sinatra commissioned her to write the song "Barbara" as an ode to his wife.

Oland's hit musical *Soldier of Orange* is the most successful musical in Dutch history and is in its fifth year of a sold-out run at the TheaterHangaar in Amsterdam, with more than 1.6 million tickets sold. The cast album spent seventeen weeks on the Dutch pop charts, topping at number seven.

PAMELA PHILLIPS-OLAND

CITY: Los Angeles
YEARS ACTIVE: 32
BIO: Oland has had more than 500 songs recorded

PHOTO CREDIT: Patricia Steuer

Recent cuts include the single "Forever," co-written by Ralphie Rosario and featuring Frankie, which is, at the time of this publication, number eight on the UK Music Week chart and number seven on Billboard's UK Dance chart. Oland also penned "Liquid Ice," a charting single for *Britain's Got Talent* phenom Charlie Green; six songs on the noted jazz album, *Hotel Souza*, of Argentinean star Karen Souza; the popular Danish single "Don't Stop" with Jørgen Thorup; and rock alternative cuts with White Apple Tree, Simon Lynge, and Michael Learns to Rock.

Oland's film and TV projects include opening and closing themes for Disney's *102 Dalmatians*, the Genie Award-nominated "Center of My Heart" from *Blizzard*, and songs in *Gideon*, *Coming to America*, *I'm Gonna Git You Sucka*, *JAG*, *The Sopranos*, *Xena: Warrior Princess*, *Crayola Kids Adventures*, and dozens of others.

ON PERSISTENCE: "I didn't choose my career; it chose me. I believe [in the old adage] that if you love what you do and do what you love, you will never work a day in your life. Becoming discouraged means you have no faith in your talents. Of course there were times I cried my eyes out—it happens to everyone! For me it was when I got three rejections in one week. I remember crying and saying, 'I'll never write another song! I'll never write another song ...' And then I used 'I'll never write another song' as the first line of a song, and my tears turned to a sort of hysterical laughter! Never give up is my motto, because the one

song you will for sure never get recorded is the one you never write."

ON THINKING OUTSIDE THE CHARTS: "Only a few people get to write the hit songs on the charts. I've had many times where I write many things and nothing happens with any of them. But I continue to write things all over the place stylistically. I spent two years writing commercials, and I wrote my fourteen musicals mostly without compensation, just to learn how to do it. There are many fields of music to pursue, from classical to theater, commercials to TV, infomercials to movie trailers, and even greeting card jingles. My advice to songwriters is not just for beginners, but to anyone who wants to sustain a career writing songs: Just keep working and keep enjoying what you do, and branch out into mastering the writing of songs in all sorts of styles and genres. Don't obsess about writing for the charts—most of those songs are written by the artists and their producers. Pitch finished masters to film and TV music supervisors. Try to co-write wherever you can, and your talented co-writers will help double your chances of success. Always support your collaborators' efforts. Their brilliance will see you in good stead."

NINA OSSOFF

CITY: Briarcliff Manor, NY
YEARS ACTIVE: 22
BIO: Nina Ossoff is a multi-genre, multiplatinum songwriter with recent releases that include cuts with

Daughtry, Orianthi, Shinedown, Theory of a Deadman, Emphatic, The Maine, Chemistry, and Love to Infinity. International credits include cuts with a winner of Spain's version of *American Idol*, Sandra Polop; Japan's number one-selling artist, Koda Kumi; and South Africa's Jonathan Butler; as well as a number one single with the UK's Judy Cheeks.

Ossoff's film and TV credits include songs in *Before I Go to Sleep, Miss Congeniality, Bring It On* and *Bring It On Again, Center Stage, The Powerpuff Girls, Barbershop, Cadet Kelly, Joan of Arcadia, The Young and the Restless, Entertainment Tonight, All My Children, Lizzie McGuire, The Cheetah Girls, The Hot Chick, Cathouse: The Series, Soul Food, The Barbie Diaries, Bratz, Good Morning America*, and many others.

ON LANDING PLACEMENTS: "During the very beginning of my career, I placed my own songs, as I constantly met with publishers, managers, and A&R people. However, after a while I just wanted to spend most of my time writing and less time in meetings. I ultimately began a very fruitful relationship with an independent publisher/song plugger. The fact that she lives in Los Angeles is great because she has access to film and television music supervisors. To date, she is the reason that so many of my songs landed in a variety of projects. This was a kind of alternate/independent route for me in a traditional way of doing business. I don't know that this way is right for everyone, and I think younger songwriters are placing things on their own without tying the songs up in lengthy contracts. In this new, stripped-down industry, it might be better for fledgling songwriters to make their own connections and work their own songs."

ON THE SECRETS TO SUCCESS: "My advice to songwriters today who are seeking a long-term career is to take advantage of every opportunity that comes your way. It's to write, write, write, *for* artists, *with* artists, for TV, film, commercials—anything that comes your way that intrigues you and sparks your creativity. My advice is also to network, network, network. You never know where even one connection will lead you. And it's to fully immerse yourself in the art, craft, and business of music. I think that is the only way. A career in the arts is so difficult to begin with that if you don't go full tilt, it will not happen for you. And you have to reinvent, reinvent, reinvent. Once the talent and love for music and writing is there, that's the only way to make it financially possible!"

SHELLY PEIKEN

CURRENT CITY: Los Angeles
YEARS ACTIVE: 29
BIO: The Grammy-nominated Peiken has been a prolific, behind-the-scenes force in the music business for more than two decades, during which time her songs have sold in excess of fifty million records. She is best known for penning culturally resonant, female-empowerment anthems, such as Christina Aguilera's number one hit "What a Girl Wants" and the Meredith Brooks' smash "Bitch."

Peiken's experiences and accomplishments, and the circles in which she has

Get to the city where the songwriting business is abuzz. Sure, with modern technology you can press "send" and get your songs anywhere. But nothing substitutes for relationships. Go out. See shows. Go everywhere you're invited. Ask to be someone's intern. Perform anywhere you can.

traveled, give her a unique perspective on the music business—that of a professional woman who fought her way into a highly competitive industry, found a way to succeed, balanced a thriving career and a family, and saw firsthand the technological changes that have recently turned that industry upside down. All the while she has stayed committed to her first true love: The often elusive but always immensely satisfying act of writing a great song. She published her memoir, *Confessions of a Serial Songwriter*, in the summer of 2015.

ON MAKING MONEY: "Because of the lack of actual sales, and because of the advent of digital streaming (songwriters aren't paid adequately when songs are streamed), the music business has taken a huge hit. Where publishers once signed writers simply because they believed in their work, today, one needs to have revenue already in the pipeline. So, financially, it's more challenging. On the other hand, there are actually far more songwriters than ever before, as one does not need to play a live instrument or write complete lyrics in order to *be* a songwriter. And there are usually more creators in the room for any given song, in which case, there's more room for you!"

ON DIVERSIFICATION: "There is more revenue in a top-five hit than ever before. Having said that, *without* that big hit, making a living is harder. In the 1990s, there was a gold rush in album and CD sales, and a songwriter was able to earn revenue from album cuts. Presently, there are few album cuts that generate substantial income, as albums are not selling. It's important to understand this and perhaps put some eggs in other baskets until you have your hit."

ON BREAKING IN: "Get to the city where the songwriting business is abuzz. Sure, with modern technology you can press 'send' and get your songs anywhere. But nothing substitutes for relationships. Go out. See shows. Go everywhere you're invited. Ask to be someone's intern. Perform anywhere you can. You could also sing demos or engineer. That also gets you in the room where songwriting is happening; perhaps they'll invite you to co-write the next one. Trade skills. For example, you could help an independent publisher with marketing with your social media prowess in exchange for song pitching. Be present online. Start a YouTube channel. Make a Facebook page. Find workshops and hone your craft. Put one foot in front of the other. Write another song every day. Live the life."

JODY GRAY

CURRENT CITY: New York (also Los Angeles and Nashville)

YEARS ACTIVE: 33

BIO: Jody Gray is an award-winning composer, lyricist, arranger, music producer, and educator. He has written for artists as wildly diverse as Judy Collins, the late Ray Charles, Grace Jones, the television series *Clifford the Big Red Dog*, Skid Row, Jimmy Fallon, and Rachel Dratch.

Gray's work has been featured on HBO, NBC, ABC, multiple cable stations, *Sesame Street*, Cartoon Network, and Netflix. In addition, he has composed major sports theme songs for CBS and Fox, as well as music and songs for advertisements and video games.

Gray is currently the musical director/composer/co-lyricist for the award-winning, animated public television series *Space Racers* and a new Disney project called *Prudence and the Imps*. He is also co-writing lyrics for the 2016 album release of Italian metal act *KLOGR*, in addition to co-writing the theme song, which will be performed by the legendary Judy Collins, for the upcoming feature film *Drawing Home*.

ON WRITING—A LOT: "It would be great if they were, but not every song needs to be a hit. Getting your music out there, on whatever platform, is imperative! I compose scores for film and TV series, so about 90 percent of the time, I'm also hired for my songwriting chops and usually end up penning a whole lot of songs for a given project. I also co-owned a boutique music library

company and, through the company, had material licensed to everything from *Sex and the City* to *The Tonight Show with Jay Leno*.

"In season one of my current TV series, *Space Racers*, there are about fifteen songs in total. Six have been released digitally. A physical album, with additional songs, will follow during season two.

"When it comes to building a career and having long-term success, you need to build relationships—on both the creative and business sides. Find like-minded collaborators. Embrace folks who technically and/or creatively fill in any gaps in what you do, and work with them. And write like crazy to get as many of your songs in front of as many people as you can."

DANA CALITRI

CURRENT CITY: Bloomfield, New Jersey

YEARS ACTIVE: 25

BIO: As a top session singer and multiplatinum-selling songwriter, Dana Calitri has appeared on more than twenty-five million records.

....

... work on your craft, build your network of musicians, artists, fellow songwriters, and music business folks, and learn as much as you can about the "business" of being a songwriter ...

....

She can be heard all over the world on radio and TV, and in film, video games, and toys. Dana has worked with acclaimed artists, such as Celine Dion, Elton John, Marc Anthony, Fergie, and Train, and has appeared on *Saturday Night Live*, *The Today Show*, and *Good Morning America*. She also performed with Richard Gere, Renée Zellweger, and Catherine Zeta-Jones in the Miramax movie *Chicago* and on the soundtrack. Dana has sung commercials for every product imaginable, including Folgers, Coca-Cola, Dr Pepper, Stouffer's, Pillsbury, and Sears.

After recording deals with Virgin and Universal Records, Calitri began writing songs for other artists and landed her first cut with *NSYNC, which went on to sell more than five million records. In 1999, Dana signed with Notation Music Publishing, writing songs for acclaimed international artists and winning more gold and platinum awards with Bad Boy Records group Dream and country singer Jessica Andrews. In 2005, she began working with BOK-Music, and her song "Crashed" appeared on the highly successful, self-titled Daughtry debut, which was the top-selling album of 2007. The song, a hit at rock radio, was licensed repeatedly for commercials and TV sports events and was even used in the Super Bowl.

In 2010, her hit single "I Get Off" put Atlantic recording artist Halestorm on the map and was one of the top-five rock singles of the year. In 2014, Dana added another gold record to her collection with Shinedown's "Amaryllis."

ON SMALL BEGINNINGS: "I started my professional career as a singer, singing back-

When it comes to building a career and having long-term success, you need to build relationships—on both the creative and business sides. Find like-minded collaborators.

ground vocals behind many high-profile artists and in jingles for every product you can think of. After a little stint as a recording artist, I got my first cut as a songwriter with *NSYNC. I had no idea who they were. I had written "All I Want Is You This Christmas" for Celine Dion, but it ended up being cut by them. I cannot complain, however, because it went on to sell five million records."

ON WORKING SMARTER: "I think a new writer has to go after everything. Yes, by all means, go after the 'big fish,' but you have to know how the business works. It's pointless, in my opinion, to write for a major artist unless you have an 'in.' Sending off a song without some kind of connection is like playing the lottery—the odds are definitely against you. Most artists have 'camps' consisting of producers, songwriters, and A&R people who are the 'go-to' people for their creative work. If you can find a way in, though, you should absolutely try to place your song.

"I write for all kinds of projects—TV shows, commercials, film, video games, toys, corporate industrial shows, etc. It's much, much harder to make money from record sales, so in order to survive, you have to have a lot of songs out there in as many markets as you can. In the meantime, work on your craft, build your network of musicians, artists, fellow songwriters, and music business folks, and learn as much as you can about the 'business' of being a songwriter so you can make wise choices for your career."

ALEX FORBES

CURRENT CITY: Wingdale, New York

YEARS ACTIVE: 30

BIO: With numerous *Billboard*-charting singles, more than 120 releases, and millions of album sales under her belt, Alex Forbes exudes a contagious passion on the subject of songwriting. Her material has found a home on major and indie labels, and in feature films, TV shows, and an Off-Broadway show. Overseas, Forbes's songs have been hit singles for artists in Europe, Australia, and Asia.

Forbes's first hit was the now-classic dance song "Too Turned On," performed by Alisha. This success led to a series of hit singles, including Taylor Dayne's massive hit "Don't Rush Me," which landed at number two on the Pop charts, number three on Adult Contemporary, and number six on Dance. It also led to a multiplatinum-selling album and an ASCAP Pop Award. Recent successes include co-writing "Where Will the Giants Roam" for the Global March for Elephants and Rhinos song competition—it won first prize, a $30,000 photo safari in Africa. Other placements include "Melt Away" in the Denzel Washington film *Déjà Vu,* and songs in *Dance Moms, Make It or Break It,* and the final episode of *Nurse Jackie.* New Zealand superstar Hayley Westenra's recording of Forbes's "You Are Water" appeared on her classical/pop album *Odyssey,* which spent more than a year on the *Billboard* charts.

ON TODAY'S MUSIC INDUSTRY: "These days, some aspects of 'breaking in' are easier. You can collaborate over Skype, meet potential colleagues in online communities, submit material to far-flung places, and educate yourself about the quirks of music publishing, licensing, and performing rights. It's also easier than ever to create a fantastic master recording of your song using the digital tools at your fingertips—or at the fingertips of a genius producer—provided you first have an absolutely killer song and a decent budget.

"What's harder nowadays is being heard above the 'noise.' Since everyone and their cousin is cranking out an album (or ten), you have to discover and express what makes *your* music special. Then, someone in a position of power has to believe that it's about to earn big bucks and/or inspire a zillion clicks. That generally means you need a hit single or a ridiculously license-able song, combined with some genuine artistry. Even in a stuffed-to-bursting marketplace, these are still rare and wondrous beasts.

"Meanwhile, since a majority of the music on major labels is supplied by already-established acts or producer-writer-artist camps, it's up to *you* to make music that goes above and beyond what they can create in-house. It still all boils down to *the song.* Depending on your level of talent and commitment, that's either good news or bad news."

ON THE WINNING FORMULA: "My best advice for up-and-coming writers is to polish your skills and write your heart out. You definitely need both. A song with all heart and no skills makes for a tough slog. And all skills and no heart … haven't we heard enough of those to last a lifetime?

"Next, learn about the business side of the music business. There's no excuse for ignorance when so much knowledge is available free online and through a wide variety of songwriting organizations. Finally, success as a music-maker is a function of successful relationships; i.e., *friendships*. Without our friends to play with and play for, this would be a lonely path indeed!"

FINDING YOUR VOICE

How Writing and Listening Can Help You Stand Out

....

Kelly Henkins

Voice is the key by which any piece is defined—the nuance that makes your lyrics stand out from the myriad of other songwriters out there. Voice should not be confused with style. In fact, style stems from a songwriter's voice.

Whether writing a song or a novel, each person has an individual voice. Just as you know a James Patterson novel when you begin to read, there are certain notes or cadences within a song that keep the listener downloading MP3s and buying CDs by specific artists. Fans often choose their favorite songs by those they can relate to ... songs that touch them in some way. The biggest question is how do you find your voice?

Like anything else at which you want to become proficient, you have to practice. In the early stages, you should not presume to know your voice. Your voice will change as you learn more about the process and who you are as a person. Award-winning songwriter and recording artist W.C. Jameson says, "Every songwriter/per-

former has the potential to be unique, but finding that uniqueness takes lots of stage time, lots of work."

The foundation of who you are as a songwriter will remain the same, but growth is a process. As you mature as an artist, you will build on that foundation.

To grow you must do several things. One is to study other songwriters. Who do you admire and why? What is it about their songs that make you think *Man, that is just cool the way they did that?* In the early stages of your journey, it is also important to not allow current radio play to influence your nurturing process. "If you're writing songs, you are better off not listening to what's happening on the radio. It has a way of creeping into the stuff that you're doing," Nashville recording artist Mark Chapman suggests. He also points out that what is popular today will have become something different six months down the road.

Shows like *The Voice* and *American Idol* are always looking for a unique artist.

So while the contestants may sound like Beyoncé or Carrie Underwood to the untrained ear, the judges are listening for that something different that defines the individual artist. "Performers tend to mimic their influences to a large degree—most of us have done that; it's part of the natural evolution," says Jameson. Write a great song like your idols, but make sure it is *your* voice that comes through when you are finished. While styles may be similar to other artists', it is only when you discover what makes yours different that you are closer to finding your voice.

Billy Dean is a country recording artist and the founder of Billy Dean Writers Block (www.billydeanwritersblock.ning.com). He describes the key element in finding your voice like this: "Courage. Taking the editor off. Stream of consciousness is where the magic is. Soul search. Be aware of when your logical side of your brain wants to take over and shut him down. Allow the creative side of your brain to come through. The ideas are abstract and you have to trust that process even though it doesn't make any sense. Get original thought down and go from there."

Another element in finding your voice is to write *every day*. Days when nothing seems to make sense are the most difficult but may also be the most important. Scribble anything down that comes to mind. While those words may not become chart toppers, they do act as weights for keeping your songwriting muscles toned and your voice strong. Like any other exercise, the results only come from a daily routine.

For example, hundreds of thousands of writers spend one month out of every year following this same process. National Novel Writing Month (www.nanowrimo.org) takes place throughout November. For thirty days, writers are encouraged to turn off the "infernal" internal editor and just get their story down. Writers of all genres, including songwriters, take part in this great event.

While some might think writing 50,000 words is a daunting or even impossible task, the exercise in itself allows the author's voice to come out. Many first-time authors are amazed at the discoveries about themselves and the craft during this period. Scientific studies have shown that phenomenal results occur when we do something on a regular basis. This is how habits are formed, and habits can produce results. Writing has to be a habit for you to find your voice.

"I believe physically writing with a pencil and paper as opposed to a keyboard is the way to go in that first process," Billy Dean says. We have become accustomed to the backspace or delete key, but, unlike an electronic version, if you have the words written down and then scratch through them as your mind whirls, the words are still there, peeking through, taunting you to remember that what you wrote might be a gem after all. You will also begin to physically see patterns. That's your voice.

While you may not want to pigeonhole your style to a specific genre, there will be specific keys that showcase your style, your signature—your voice. As you grow, you will begin to notice your voice in the way you construct your lyrics. You may not recognize this in the beginning, but over time cadences and tones become clear; for example, how you structure your verses, or where you place the conceptual point of your song within the confines of the lyrics (such as using the chorus as your opening, a tag at the end of each verse, or a repetitive word or phrase). You may also find that you are better when it comes to structuring a chorus over the melody or vice versa. Though these individual points are often considered style, they originate within your voice.

Once you have found your voice, and one that connects with a recording artist, you may find yourself writing with a specific person in mind. Knowing where you might potentially market your material is good business. A songwriter can make an artist. Think of who your favorite recording artist is. What was their first big hit? Was it something they wrote, or were those chart-shattering words written by someone else? Further research may show they recorded other songs by the same songwriter.

Just as fans know what they look for in their music of choice, so does a performer. Recording artists are searching for the same tug when poring through files looking for their next big hit. They know what their fans expect from them, and it is their job to deliver. The perfect marriage comes when an artist and a songwriter feel that same chord. Oftentimes, when an artist scores big with a song, he will look to that songwriter's catalog for similar potential hits. The artist grasps the concept of what could be a perfect relationship between him and the songwriter. He can hear the voice.

"My voice emanates from my sheer love of music and songwriting. I love to create stories from different stimuli. If my song connects with an artist enough that she wants to cut my song, then I've accomplished a goal. There is always someone somewhere that will connect with the story and meaning of the song," explains Larry Migliore, New York regional director of the Independent Country Music Association.

Mark Chapman says his voice is about "trying to take something in my life that means something and trying to make sure to keep it honest and keep it real—make it so it's about everybody, or something they can all relate to."

The old adage "practice makes perfect" applies to songwriting, like everything else in life. If you want your voice to be heard, you have to practice—and perfect—your craft.

KELLY HENKINS is a full-time writer and artist. She is a trusted online voice for Texas music and spends most of her daytime networking with singers and songwriters all over the country. She lives in the rural Ozarks. She blogs onine at kellyscountry.blogspot.com, and you can also follow her on Twitter (@kellyscountry) or contact her at kellyscountry@missouri.usa.com.

EDITING BY SOUND

Using Alliteration and Internal Rhyme to Improve Your Songwriting

....

Scarlet Keys

People love the sound of alliteration—having a string of words all begin with the same consonant. Maybe it started from the time we learned "Peter Piper picked a peck of pickled peppers." We also love when we hear assonance, the repetition of vowel sounds, such as these lyrics from hit writer Monty Powell's song *One More Christmas to Remember*: "*Fake spray* snow *flakes* from a can" or "Their *eyes* so *bright* their *mind* renewed." His entire song is full of assonance, as well as alliteration, adding proof that "art stands on the shoulders of craft," and that the best writers make use of these tools.

To the average listener, it's just plain fun to sing along with, but a neuroscientist would tell us that the brain loves patterns and feel-good chemicals are released when we hear alliteration or assonance. One of the things that makes hip-hop so irresistible is this use of alliteration and assonance; it's also one of the things that makes Jason Mraz so fun to listen to.

Clearly these lyrical devices can trigger a response and make us feel good. But they also serve as a memory device, creating a smoother flow, and can drive content.

For most beginning songwriters, it's better to not overthink the process so that you can focus on what you want to say, rather than how you want to say it. You don't want to think about how to use the tools during the process itself.

After you write your song, read and sing through it to see how the lyrics flow. Some word choices will feel clunky and obstruct the fluidity of the line. That's where the tools of alliteration and assonance can become powerful. Typically, choosing one word over another is a matter of deciding what it is you want to say. Content can be discovered along with the right sound that helps with the flow of the lyrics, and most often, you get a more interesting word if you think about it for awhile.

For example, I co-wrote a song with Mark Shilansky titled "Every Goodbye Ain't

Gone." Take a look at the first draft of our first verse:

When there's no proof that love was ever here
When you can't even remember when you
*   cried that last tear*

It works perfectly fine, but after reading through line two, we changed *when* to *why* because of the internal rhyme connection between *why/cried*:

When there's no proof that love was ever here
When you can't even remember <u>why</u> you
<u>cried</u> that last tear

What does the change from *when* to *why* do for the content? It takes away an element of time and brings the listener more intimately into the emotion of the song. No longer concerned about *when* you cried, you focus on *why* you cried, and now you have better content along with a better flow.

Then, looking through line two again to further smooth it out, we changed *remember* to *recall*, creating alliteration between *can't* and *recall*: can't/recall. We also removed *even*, since it crowded the line. In doing so, we never compromise content because *remember* and *recall* are synonymous.

When there's no proof that love was ever here
When you can't recall why you cried that
*   last tear*

Also, *remember* has three syllables, which clutters the line. This makes it more difficult to sing, so choosing *recall* with its two syllables provides alliteration *and* smoothes our clunky line.

Choosing one word over another based on its alliterative or rhyming qualities be-

came a sonic thesaurus where we maintained our meaning, yet streamlined the flow of our line.

In another song I co-wrote with Mark Simos (with the alliterative title "Starve the Spark"), we made several edits to add alliteration and internal rhyme, streamlining the flow. As you read through the first draft, notice the flow of the words and note where it's jarring or awkward to say certain words together.

The original verse was:

Starve the spark
From the fire's kiss
For I can<u>not</u> go <u>on</u> like this
If I won't be consumed by the heat of the
*   blaze*
Then I can't hold my hands in the warmth
*   of the flames*

Lines three and five felt the most awkward to sing. Although there is a connection in the internal sound not/on, we wanted to smooth it out even more and, by doing so, we ended up with better content.

Here's the rewrite, with added emphasis highlighting the changes made for alliteration and internal rhyme:

Starve the Spark
From the fire's kiss
Save my fevering heart from beating like this
If I can't be consumed by the blue of the blaze
Then I won't warm my hands in the glow of
*   the flames*

Note the changes:
1. We kept the alliteration between *s*tarve/*s*park as well as the internal rhyme **ar/ar**.

2. We kept the alliteration between *f*rom/*f*ire.

3. We used internal alliteration between sa*v*e/fe*v*ering and the internal rhyme fe*ver*/b*eat*. *Save* connects to *fever*; *fever* connects to *beat*—we instantly have a more cohesive line.

4. We used alliteration between *c*an't/*c*onsumed and *bl*ue/*bl*aze with the internal rhyme cons*umed*/bl*ue*. The alliterative connection keeps the parallel structure we have throughout the verse, maintains our content, and appeals to the listener by linking internally.

5. We changed *won't* to *can't* for a better flow of alliteration between *w*on't/*w*arm. If you stop to say *can't/hold*, you can feel the clunkiness like an unpaved road. There's no sonic connection; there are no common consonants or vowels. Now read or say *w*on't/*w*arm, and you feel like you've just gotten on the highway.

This subtle change in line five also adds deeper meaning to the song. With *won't*, we have a verb that is more interesting and adds more meaning to the song. *Can't* implies an inability to do something like in line four. *Won't* connotes a refusal on the part of the singer, giving her a stronger sense of urgency in the song. Add in the internal rhyme between *won't/glow* and the faint hint of alliteration between war*m*/fla*m*es, and the line dramatically shifts the content of the song, making it more vivid and tangible for the listener, with a smoother chain of sound.

As with all editing, adding these elements works best after you've written the song. Otherwise, we risk our song feeling contrived, and we can lose heart, forcing alliteration or rhyme where it may not yet belong. Once the song is in a more polished form, we can comb through it and consider this technique while not compromising feel or content.

When using this technique for finding content, we sometimes end up with better ideas than when we started. Added to our understanding of the chemicals triggered in the listeners' brains, we can see how these tools affect listeners, increase the feel of a song, and lead to a deeper grasp of content. When we take the time to find sonic connections between our lyrics, we find the rocks to walk across the river.

SCARLET KEYS is an associate professor in the songwriting department at the Berklee College of Music. She has experience as a staff writer for Warner/Chappell Music culminating in a gold record and several national commercials. She has also worked with such artists as Golden Globe nominee Monty Powell, Chris Stapleton, and Gretchen Wilson. Scarlet has mentored thousands of students, including Charlie Puth, Charlie Worsham, and Betty Who. Scarlet has been published in Pat Pattison's books *Writing Better Lyrics* and *Songwriting Without Boundaries*.

MINING PERSONAL EXPERIENCE

Using Emotion and Universal Appeal to Improve Your Writing

....

Charlene Oldham

Early in his musical career, Peter Himmelman arrived home on the eve of Father's Day without a new dress shirt or tie to give his terminally ill dad.

"So I wrote him a song on what would be his last Father's Day," he recalls.

Himmelman couldn't make it through the first take without breaking into tears, but that's the tape he played at the party celebrating his father. The rough recording brought the songwriter and his father closer than ever and also netted the musician his first solo record deal.

He sometimes shares that story and a snippet of the tape of "This Father's Day" at his Big Muse seminars, where Himmelman works with teams from organizations like McDonald's, Gap, and Pandora to help them discover their creative powers through the conventions of songwriting. From there, he gives audience members just one minute and forty-five seconds to tap out a meaningful message to a loved one.

"When I play that ['This Father's Day'] for the audience, that is sort of me going into the water first, showing how you would make this very open, very vulnerable connection to someone you love, and there's great power to it all," he says.

And all songwriters can learn to swim in that same sea if they are willing to jump into the depths of their own emotions and explore—without exploiting—the lives, loves, and losses of those around them.

To get started, Himmelman recommends doing what he did twenty years ago and still does today. The singer, songwriter, and son-in-law of Bob Dylan says when he writes a song, he almost always has a particular muse in mind.

"If it's going to be an emotional song, think of who in the world you would like to hear it. Picture yourself giving that person that song," he advises. "When I write, I usually write for one of about six people. It's not like I'm writing to a whole mass crowd.

They are very specific. They are not anonymous at all."

UNIVERSAL APPEAL

Musician Brad Williams also often draws inspiration from particular places and people around him. And though "Another Day in a Small Town" was featured in an episode of the Sundance Channel program "Rectify," as well as in the indie film "Valley Inn," the place that inspired the tune is far from fictitious. The tiny burg of Tyronza, Arkansas, just a few miles away from where he grew up, informed Williams's lyrics, proving the axiom that it's best to write what you know.

But the fact that Williams's songs have been featured in television episodes, feature films, and a yet-to-be-released documentary shows that he isn't the only person who was shaped by the small-town speed traps and countrified characters of his youth.

"If you grew up in a small town, there's a good chance your small town is going to be a lot like any other small town in America," says Williams, whose current band, The Salty Dogs, was named best original band in Arkansas in 2003 by the *Arkansas Times*. "If you are truthfully writing about something, I think that's going to touch a chord with someone."

Williams still keeps an open ear and notebook whenever he visits his hometown of Marked Tree. And it was his ninety-one-year-old grandmother's take on a feisty family member, combined with some of his personal experiences, that inspired one of his recent songs, "Too Old to Fight."

"When I go back, it seems like everyone is so country bumpkin. Whether it's right or wrong, it's always honest," he says of his grandmother's assessment of the world. "If I were to offer a recommendation, it would be: Don't be afraid to claim inspiration from other people, and don't feel like you have to have all the answers."

Reflecting on his family and childhood, while on a trip between Nashville and his native Michigan, also inspired songwriter and professor James Elliott to pen "My Redeemer Is Faithful and True." The verse and chorus came to him during the long drive, but it was performer Steven Curtis Chapman who eventually put the finishing touches to the tune by adding the bridge.

"He really liked it and connected with it as well, so that song was on his very first record," says Elliott, who added that Chapman recently recorded an acoustic version of the song for Cracker Barrel Restaurant's in-house record label.

Megastar Miranda Lambert also heard her own story in "The House That Built Me," a song co-written by Allen Shamblin and Tom Douglas, a friend of Elliott's.

"That was a song, when they first wrote it, they couldn't get any traction with it," Elliot says.

An article Shamblin read, which ignited memories about his own childhood home, was the original inspiration for the song. But it took about seven years for the pair to simplify the story into the chart-topping hit fans know today.

"It's basically one person's story, but Miranda Lambert really connected with it," says Elliott, chair of Belmont University's songwriting program. "So many people found themselves in that story that it became a number one hit."

Even in its streamlined form, the song is filled with sense-based details that appeal to listeners—even if they never buried a beloved dog and grew up two thousand miles from Texas or the nearest live oak tree. Elliott encourages his songwriting students

... the key is to be open enough to others—and yourself—to let those feelings show in song.

to use the same writing techniques because listeners react to songs driven by detail and authentic experience.

"The more specific, the more relatable, somehow. You don't get it all, but you're drawn into it," he says. "They feel like they find themselves in your story. People want to be moved by the songs they hear. People desperately want to feel something, whether it's happy or sad. And it's fun when that happens and you see that connection."

USE TRAPS AND TOOLS

For Elliott, connections start with conversations, and he tells his songwriting students working on collaborative writing projects to start with a few meaningful ones before they even pick up a pen or peck at a keyboard. He also recommends researching songs they love. Pick them apart, learn to play them, and examine what works about their lyrics, production, and performance.

"You just study great songs," he says. "Really study those songs like you are studying for a test that matters to you."

And don't be afraid to use some of the same reference materials as you would when studying for an important exam, says Williams. Consulting a rhyming dictionary or thesaurus during the writing process isn't cheating and doesn't compromise the creativity or emotional appeal of a song. At the same time, he doesn't hesitate to abandon material that just doesn't work.

"If I can't go any further with it, I just leave it there. I don't make a research paper out of it or anything," he says. "The true country music is a lot about life and truth and ups and downs. It's something I don't try to press too much."

It's true that the best way to mine personal experience is to just start digging, says Himmelman, who will sometimes set his smartphone timer for seven minutes and just sit down to write. If he comes up with ideas worth saving, he has the seeds for a song. If not, the struggle is at least short-lived, he says.

Himmelman also employs other tricks to beat writers' block. "I create these traps, I call them, where I book a studio date maybe a couple of months in advance, not in my home studio, but in somebody else's that I actually have to pay for. Maybe it's out of my home state so I have to buy a flight, and maybe I've booked musicians in advance so that I am on the hook for it. So that pressure, that structure, both in time and otherwise, that structure that I've created, helps pull this nebulous, emotional, musical information into the real world."

SHARED EMOTIONS

Struggling songwriters who might not have the resources to book fights and back-up bands can create their own traps. Himmelman suggests imposing everyday deadlines, like deciding to write a song for your mom's birthday, to overcome the difficulty that comes with truly tapping your deepest feelings and fears. Considering conventional science only identifies six emotions and recent research shows that number may actually be closer to four, giving personal experiences universal appeal seems a little less daunting for songwriters. Nearly everyone's fallen in love, fallen out of love, and been happy, sad, surprised, afraid, disgusted, or angry, sometimes all within the same day. So the key is to be open enough to others—and yourself—to let those feelings show in song.

People want to be moved by the songs they hear. People desperately want to feel something, whether it's happy or sad. And it's fun when that happens and you see that connection.

"If you are truthfully infusing some emotion, some insight, then it will be universal. After all, people don't have that many emotions. So it's pretty easy to be universal with these things," Himmelman says. "It's not a question of having emotions. Everyone does. It's a question of reducing your fear to allow those emotions or that native creativity to just appear."

CHARLENE OLDHAM is a teacher who currently focuses on college-level journalism courses, a music promoter who has helped clients attract media attention from newspapers and radio stations around the country, and a freelance writer whose recent work has appeared in national print and online outlets, including *SUCCESS* and Catster.com. She blogs about writing and life at www.charleneoldham.com.

THE PUBLISHER'S PERSPECTIVE

An Interview with Jorge Mejia of Sony/ATV Music Publishing

....

John Anderson

Jorge Mejia is the executive vice president, Latin America & US Latin, for Sony/ATV Music Publishing. He oversees a department with offices in six nations and operations across Latin America and the US Hispanic market. Sony/ATV has become a dominant force, winning top industry awards in its sector annually. The company handles the copyrights for household names like The Beatles, Taylor Swift, Shaki-ra, Ricardo Arjona, Pitbull, and many others. Among his many recognitions, Mejia was named to Billboard's 40 Under 40 in 2012, and he is also on the board of the Latin Songwriters Hall of Fame.

Music was always a part of Mejia's life growing up—his mother was a singer, songwriter, and recording artist in their native Colombia. But Mejia was a late starter for a classical pianist, taking up the instrument at the age of fifteen after a severe leg fracture required him to refrain from many activities.

He scrambled to catch up, regularly-practicing eight to ten hours a day. It wasn't long before he so impressed the music faculty at the New World School of the Arts (a Miami-based performing arts high school and college, which recently inducted him into its Miami Dade College Hall of Fame) that they admitted him midyear. He went on to study at the New England Conservatory of Music and then graduated with a piano performance degree from the University of Miami.

After college, rather than pursuing a career in performance, Mejia began working with Sony Music, quickly moving into the music publishing division, where he has been ever since.

Mejia recently completed recording a set of twenty-four piano preludes that he wrote, which he will be releasing later this year. He lives in Miami Beach with his wife, Amanda, and his two dogs.

Songwriter's Market spoke with Mejia, a nineteen-year veteran of the industry, on the state of songwriting publishing from the perspective of a large music publisher.

How did you get into the music industry, and what path have you taken to get where you are today?

I got in the music industry through an internship I did at Sony music, and that was straight out of college, where I did a piano performance degree. My brilliant plan was that I was going to learn as much as possible about the music industry while my band, The Green Room, took off. So I started that internship in sales and marketing. One day, the music publishing portion of the department asked if they could borrow me for the day. At that time, I had no clue what publishing was. Maybe they printed stuff, leaflets, I don't know. They borrowed me for one day, and that day turned into another, and I don't think I ever went back to sales and marketing. I finished that internship, and a few months later they called me for a job. And eighteen years later,

here I am, basically doing the job of the person I was first interning for.

What different roles did you play along the way?

I started out as an assistant to the vice president of Latin America. ... Within that role, I had the opportunity to delve into every single area of the publishing business. Interesting enough, as an assistant, I got to see all the admin portion of the music publishing industry. I was also involved in the synch portion of the industry, and the A&R components. When I finished being an assistant, the first thing I did was synchronization: the synch and TV and film part for Latin content here in the US ... I was responsible for ensuring that our repertoire would get synched in as many commercials, movies, and TV shows as possible. And the new business part was real interesting, because it allowed me to have a hand in the new technologies that were coming in the day, which back then were ringtones. So I got to broker some of the first deals for ringtones, both here in the US Latin portion of the market, as well as for Latin America. After doing synch and new business, I went straight from that into running the region.

Why did you choose the publishing side, and how does it differ from other areas of the music industry?

The publishing side kind of chose me; it was serendipitous really. And that's actually nice because my mom is a singer/songwriter. She had an album out back in the day in Colombia where I'm from originally. It's actually poetic that I ended up [working with] songs and songwriters. My mom actually had a TV program called *Componga, Cante y Gane*, which translated means *Write, Sing and Win*. So songwriters would sing their songs and be judged by a panel and win prizes, which is kind of what I do.

[Publishing] really is the backbone of the music industry. Nothing happens without a song; it's all about the song. An artist is successful through the songs they sing.

How has the industry changed for songwriters since you began your career in music publishing?

The industry has really changed for songwriters. Before, when I started, the main source of income would be album and CD sales. Nowadays, the main source of income is really performance, and when they get a big placement: synch income. Basically

> [Publishing] really is the backbone of the music industry. Nothing happens without a song; it's all about the song.

album sales have become less and less dominant as far as a revenue source. So songwriters are looking not just to place a song on a CD or album, but

also for that song to be the chosen single, the one that gets pushed on the radio and TV and so on. That's a big shift. Now, other than that, there's the shift into digital. There's Pandora, Spotify ... there's all these digital formats providing income to the songwriter—still not enough. But the digital shift is here to stay.

How does Latin music publishing differ from other music publishing genres?

First of all, it's language. I believe the definition for a Latin Grammy is 51 percent of the song needs to be in Spanish or Portuguese. One of the things about the Latin genre that's amazing is its immense and growing appeal. The number of artists crossing over is only rising. ... Artists like Pitbull, Shakira, Ricky Martin, all are mainstream artists now, and all started singing in Spanish. I think the ability to cross over has to do with the fact that Latin music is essentially universal music.

What types of songwriters do you work with, and what avenues are available for songwriters who want to build up their careers?

I work with all types of songwriters, from starting songwriters to well-established and culturally iconic songwriters. Some of the songwriters I work with are Pitbull, Enrique Iglesias, Ricardo Arjona, Ricky Martin, Mario Domm ...

Nowadays there's more avenues than ever. The great thing about this digital shift in the music industry is that there's more music now than there has ever been before. By the same token, it's harder to get above the noise than ever before. But now there's YouTube, Vine, all kinds of platforms where you can make your music heard as a songwriter.

You've worked with a number of Grammy-winning songwriters. What qualities and habits do you see that make for a successful songwriting career?

I would say there's a little bit of magic to every successful artist, and by artist I mean songwriter, but I also mean creative person. But that little bit of magic is definitely in the minority percentage when it comes down to work ethic and perseverance. At the end of the day, it's somebody who wakes up every day, striving for that goal. Focus is the key word.

Streaming versus downloads: Where do you see the music industry going in this regard, and how does it affect songwriters now and in the future?

The music industry is definitely going toward streaming: The streaming increase of late has been tremendous, whereas downloads are going ever downhill. So it's clear that streaming is here to stay and that's going to be the model of the future. As far as songwriters getting compensated, they're still not getting compensated in the way that they should be. I believe it's a matter of time, particularly as companies like ours make it their

commitment to fight for the fair compensation of songwriters. In fact, our chairman, Marty Bandier, has stat-

> Nowadays there's more avenues than ever [for songwriters]. The great thing about this digital shift in the music industry is that there's more music now than there ever has been before.

ed this is one of his life goals at this point in his career, and there's not much more he can do as a publisher. But fair compensation of songwriters as far as streaming is what he wants as a cornerstone of his legacy.

What do music websites like Pandora and Spotify mean for songwriters?

They mean great, great opportunity, fantastic reach. They also mean a place where better compensation should be attained. Songwriters need to be compensated fairly, and they're not being compensated as well as they should be, yet.

What do you foresee as a better system for the future?

I just foresee the rates and negotiations changing ever so slightly in the favor of the songwriter. Right now, the songwriters are receiving a lot less than the labels and the artists as far as royalties from these places, and that needs to shift.

With digital formats such as Spotify or Pandora, the margins are small. Is it still the same split with the publisher?

It depends on the type of income. Within digital, it could be streaming income, which would fall under our performance splits, or it could be download income, which would fall under our mechanical splits. And those are different royalty splits within the contract, which could be 80/20 or whatever. It just depends on the type of the agreement. Depending on the use, the different splits would apply.

As a music publisher, what are your needs, and what are you looking for in songs and songwriters?

At its most basic level our needs are for those great songs that symbolize certain periods in our lives—we all have them—those songs when we hear them we remember what was going on in our lives and what we were doing, songs that transform and enrich our lives. That's what we're looking for in songs. And that's easy to say. But if we all knew what made up those songs, what the ingredients were, we would just do it. There's a lot of magic, there's a lot of timing, there's a lot of things we can't put on a spreadsheet that make up those songs. But that's what we're looking for all the time. And also, as a publisher, we're looking for catalogs as well, timeless catalogs. Our company has purchased several catalogs, like the Motown catalog, which embody these fantastic periods of music.

Explain your process for finding new songwriters?

Songwriters do approach us. Obviously because of the company we are, our policy is to do business with someone we've already done business with. That's just the way to filter a little bit. We do scout for new songwriters … Sometimes we're lucky enough to have awesome talent just come to us, like this Brika artist/songwriter [recently signed by Sony] who came through a producer with whom we've done business. And do we lure established songwriters? Absolutely. We basically kill each other as far as competition, which is fierce with other publishers.

What are the challenges and obstacles for songwriters who aspire to work with a major music publishing label such as Sony?

The first part of that answer is honing the craft. The songwriter craft is truly an art form that needs to be practiced and worked. And [that's] what it takes for a song to get above the noise to be great. … To be great doesn't necessarily mean great in the traditional sense, but maybe it's a song that hits a chord with the times, a song that says something differently, the melody is different, or the way that it's produced. And that takes a lot of work. Writing a good pop song is one of the hardest things to do. It's a difficult thing but it's also the craft, and the joy of songwriting is in honing that craft.

The next challenge, and it all kind of goes hand in hand, is access. Getting access to fellow songwriters, great fellow songwriters, with whom you can co-write; a lot of great songs come as collaborations. Getting access to managers and artists who can help you place those songs, or help you get those songs heard by the right people. And ultimately also getting access to great publishers who can help you work on your craft. All of this is a perseverance game. To work with a big publishing company, it's going to take making a little bit of noise somehow, whether they've written songs for a big artist, or they're a singer/songwriter and have millions of views on YouTube, or maybe they're already on the charts somehow. Just because of the sheer volume of songwriters out there, and songs, publishers and A&R at major companies are relying more and more on some sort of noise or buzz happening. Or sometimes you'll take something because it comes from a trusted source, but it needs to blow your socks off.

For a songwriter who has just written a song or series of songs and wants to get them published, what actions or steps do you recommend she take?

For new songwriters, there has to be something that needs to happen so that the song or the songwriter, or the singer/songwriter, gets heard

above the noise. Maybe that song gets a lot of exposure on YouTube or any of the social media sites and that leads to people being interested. Usually songs that get a lot of exposure, there's

> All of this is a perseverance game. To work with a big publishing company, it's going to take making a little bit of noise somehow, whether they've written songs for a big artist or they're a singer/songwriter and have millions of views on YouTube ...

something to them, there's something that's happening. Sometimes it's inexplicable like *The Fox* song [by Ylvis], but even that song has that charming quality of like *I didn't expect that*. I mean, they're established producers and they did this as a joke. But sometimes it's serendipitous like that. So there is no roadmap. ... The one constant that I do see, that whatever you choose, just focus on it, and keep at it ... and eventually a break happens. ...

Do you work directly with songwriters on their craft?

Yes, and that's a delicate one. It's a case-by-case basis. There are songwriters you would obviously never dream to suggest changing one word because they're iconic and established, and honestly, what do you know. But there are songwriters who actively look for some form of creative guidance, and you do your best, and obviously it's a delicate thing, because songs are very much like children. You have to be careful if you're going to call somebody's baby ugly, careful how you word it. But for the most part we work with pretty established people, so a lot of the time it will not be at that level where we're saying, "Look, make sure the chorus comes in faster," or something like that. But every once in a while we do.

JOHN ANDERSON has written extensively on the South Florida music scene for various publications, including the *Miami New Times* and *Miami Herald*.

JACK OF ALL TRADES

A Q&A with Joe Escalante,
Record Label Owner, Musician, and Lawyer

....

Vanessa Herron

Joe Escalante was born and raised in Long Beach, California. He's a musician, entertainment lawyer, record label owner, and media personality. Since he was a teenager, Escalante has been a member of the long-running punk rock band The Vandals. Escalante still performs with The Vandals all over the world, and the band is currently signed to his label, Kung Fu Records, which has released more than fifty CDs and twenty-five concert and low-budget feature films. As a CBS executive in the 1990s, Escalante supervised the production of programs like *Walker, Texas Ranger, Rescue 911*, and *Everybody Loves Raymond*. Aside from the Vandals, Escalante is best known for his

years as the indie rock morning host on Indie 103.1 FM in Los Angeles, where his team included director David Lynch as the daily weatherman. He currently provides free entertainment legal advice on his weekly LA radio show, *Barely Legal*. Escalante lives with his wife, Sandra, in Seal Beach, California, where he's an avid stand-up paddle surfer in his spare time. In his earlier days, he also enjoyed an amateur bullfighting career but has retired from the ring, saying it's a young man's game and "In today's world, nobody likes a matador."

Who writes songs for The Vandals?

At this point, mostly our guitar player, Warren Fitzgerald. When we first started, I did most of it, but he took over because his juices were flowing more. I went to law school, which kills 98 percent of your creative juices. Your mind is filled with problems no one wants to hear about in music.

Your songs weren't very political. You had more fun with lyrics.

Yeah, I believe you can write a song with cuss words in it, or you can work harder and have something better. We were influenced by The Dickies and Evo, who wrote silly songs. There was intelligence, but they were nonpolitical or had hidden messages.

I remember on *The X-Files* there was an episode where the character wore a Vandals T-shirt. Did product placements come from your connections at CBS?

I got a few songs on CBS shows like *Walker, Texas Ranger*, but *The X-Files* was from knowing the show's creator, Chris Carter, since childhood. That episode needed music to play in a murderer's head. Back then, they didn't glamorize evil people like today's shows. Chris thought he'd have trouble finding a band to be identified with this killer, so he called me. He told me his concerns and asked if we would do it, and I didn't think twice. Definitely, that episode and being on the Tony Hawk video game led a lot more people to find out about us than anything else.

That and the Warped Tour, right?

Yeah, but that's a lot of work. Forty shows in the hot sun … you earn those one fan at a time, but being in front of eighteen million people watching *The X-Files* …

How did The Vandals get started?

We started in 1981. I joined at eighteen. I replaced the drummer, who hated the singer. Then the bass player quit because he hated the singer, and

the other bass player quit because he hated the singer. Then I moved to bass. The guitar player kicked the singer out, and in 1984 we got a new singer who's still with us. For twenty-six years, it's been the same four guys.

That's commitment.

Or lack of it. [laughs] The band sticks around, because you can go off and do whatever you want and come back … or maybe we'll just replace you for a show.

Oh yeah, you were replaced by Keanu Reeves!

One night, yes.

Did you feel threatened?

I did! My friend was getting married, but we had a gig. They said, "Hey, Keanu says he can play some of our songs, so you can stay at the wedding."

Was Keanu any good?

You don't have to be that good to play with The Vandals. [laughs] But he was good. He likes music and loves to play bass. We've kept in touch. He's a good guy.

Did your desire to be in music come before being a lawyer?

I dreamed of being in a band as a kid watching *The Partridge Family*, but I was practical and wanted to be a lawyer. After undergrad, I put off law school and toured with the band. After a while, I felt time running out and went on to law school. The band became a business later.

How'd you end up at CBS?

I had friends at CBS and got an internship by writing a paper about CBS's legal fight with ASCAP and BMI.

Speaking of litigation, why were you sued by *Variety*?

Variety magazine has a logo they feel is very precious, and if you do a parody of it, they come after you. So they came after us. I think they thought we had more money than we did. We settled, but years later they came after us again because kids were posting songs on YouTube using our old album cover. ... They spent probably a million dollars suing us again, and they lost, but it was terrible for us.

How many albums has the band sold over the years?

Probably 500,000. Our biggest album sold 200,000, and others sold between 100,000 and 150,000.

Why did you decide to start your own record label?

Punk rock became big business in 1984, and labels offered our band money and bribes to take new bands on tour with us. JVC Electronics owned a label and offered us televisions to let a band be our opening act. The band wasn't that good, but I was amazed that our opening slots became so valuable overnight. My friend Fat Mike from NOFX said to me, "You've gotta do this." You know the market's good when a competitor says, "You're going to make a lot of money and you'll be good at it." We

thought, *Why just take a television set? Why not create our own label, put our own bands out, and reap rewards someone would have paid us a television to get?* I just thought there was something here, and it worked out.

How can performers or songwriters get attention with no A&R execs?

You have to become a phenomenon that gets noticed by the few labels still signing bands or people finding you online. It's beneficial for the consumer, because no one gets to the top without good songs. Before, somebody could pour money into you and say, "I like the look, and songs will come later,"

> If people aren't talking about you or fighting to represent you, your songs aren't good enough. Make better songs, join a scene where people help each other find good lawyers, labels, good spots to play, and you'll have success.

and shove that down people's throats.

If people aren't talking about you or fighting to represent you, your songs aren't good enough. Make better songs, join a scene where people help each other find good lawyers, labels, good spots to play, and you'll have success.

Is it worth it for an artist to get on Spotify and Pandora?

Yes. The only person who can deny those platforms is someone like Taylor Swift, who can say, "The hell with you people. I'll make more without you, because you're a rip-off." Fine, but they're defining the new distribution platforms.

The old platforms were a rip-off, too. You need Spotify, Pandora, and others to get your songs out there.

Do you have to be on a record label to get on those platforms?

No, you can put your records out through TuneCore, which aggregates your songs into a digital platform, and get them on iTunes. You have to upload your songs on Pandora yourself. It's weird. I don't know how Spotify gets music, but they do pay for it.

How much do they pay for every song?

It's negligible … like .0001. We get checks every month or quarter, and it's going up every period. It won't replace CD sales, but what can you do? That's why, in this climate, I would not start a record label. My label has great distribution, I know what I'm doing, and there are good bands out there. I don't sign bands now because the numbers don't add up. By the time you've recorded, promoted, and paid for CDs and vinyl, an indie label can't make that back right now.

Is it because the industry hasn't found that next big technological discovery or revenue stream?

I think promotion costs got too high. Maybe the business model of charging fifteen to seventeen dollars a CD was overcharging and the Internet corrected that, but I cannot make a record sound good and make a profit off it. So, obviously I wasn't overcharging. Some bands spend their own money and bring us a finished record that we release. The band pays for CDs to sell at shows. My label handles marketing and gets digital distribution, and it's still not worth it.

The Vandals are still in demand after decades of playing.

Yeah. We sell fewer records, but make more on tour. Ticket prices are higher, attendance is higher, opportunities are larger, and that's why we're still in the business. Instead of new albums, we trickle out songs here and there.

How do you protect your rights as a songwriter?

Put your songs on CD, register them with the copyright office for thirty five dollars, and it's done! If you hear it on the radio, tell a lawyer your work is validly registered. That means the other side can pay attorney's fees—but you must have that registration.

What was the first song you ever wrote?

I was five years old at a movie theater; they asked if anyone wanted to perform. I went up and sang a song I wrote. I can sing it right now, if you want.

Let's hear it!

(Singing to tune of *The Beverly Hillbillies* theme song) Oh, let me tell you a story about a man named Noilet/ He took Ellie Mae and flushed her down the toilet/ Then, one day he was fishing in the sea/ And guess what he caught? Ellie Mae going pee.

[Laughs] Hey, it rhymed, and it was publicly performed.

Is it copyrighted?

No, but it's a derivative work, since I used *The Beverly Hillbillies*.

Final advice for emerging songwriters?

If two or more people aren't fighting over your songs, they need more work. Go back, write better songs, and keep going.

VANESSA HERRON is an optioned screenwriter with fifteen years of professional experience. She also has several film and television projects in various stages of development. Vanessa was a 2012 Guy Hanks and Marvin Miller Fellow and ranked in the top 20 percent of the 2012 Nicholl Fellowship. She is a freelance journalist, and works as an executive producer and news editor for iHeart Media in Los Angeles. Vanessa lives with her family in Thousand Oaks, California.

IT'S ALL FOR THE SAKE OF THE SONG

A Conversation with Four Award-Winning Songwriters

David McPherson

Get a handful of award-winning songwriters talking about their craft and you'll no doubt get a variety of answers and advice. Just like asking someone what's the trick to being a good lawyer or teacher, there are some universal proven tips to each profession, but each individual must discover what works—and what doesn't work. Some songwriters scribble words and phrases on bar napkins or in tattered old journals. These ideas might not make it into a finished lyric until years later. Others like to travel alone and meet people to get inspiration—writing character-driven narratives is more akin to fiction and poetry for them.

There are songs about planes and songs about trains. Songs about cars and songs about bars. Songs about love and songs about the tough times. Then, there are songs that make the perfect companion to play at 10 while you chase the white line down the highway. To write songs that linger long, you need to be a good listener. There is a bit of the lightning strikes—

the muse thing—but you have to be ready to grab hold of these a-ha moments when they come. Enough of my rambling. Let's let the following songwriting masters reflect on their craft—three veterans and one up-and-comer—Tom Cochrane, Steve Earle, Bruce Cockburn, and Del Barber.

STORYTELLER TOM COCHRANE WAITS UNTIL HE FEELS THE URGE TO WRITE

Tom Cochrane is an award-winning Canadian musician best known for hit songs "Life Is a Highway," "Lunatic Fringe," "Human Race," and "I Wish You Well." Cochrane fronted the Canadian rock band Red Rider and has won seven Juno Awards. He is a member of the Canadian Music Hall of Fame and an officer of the Order of Canada. He writes storied songs and only writes when the urge is strong.

"Some artists put out a record once every year or two, but that was never me," says Cochrane. "I could put out more records, but are they going to be good? You've also got to be motivated, and you've got to feel you are doing something that needs to be done and needs to be said. Finally, like a bird feels the urge to fly south, the instinct just takes over and it's time to make a record."

Cochrane's last record (*Take it Home*, 2015) featured his usual batch of eleven storied songs. "I can't pinpoint it. Just one day I felt the urge to write," Cochrane says about the muse hitting him. "I can't remember exactly, but the first songs I wrote for my last record were 'Can't Stay Here,' which leads off the disc, and 'Pink Time,' which is one of my favorite songs. When it comes time, the songs just flow. It's always work, but it's also always a balance between work and inspiration. There were things that needed to be said."

What moves Cochrane to write? Travel is one inspiration, and then there's everything else that compels him, "What you are reading, things you are going through, reflection … and unfinished business," he explains. "One song from my last record, 'Diamonds,' for instance, I wrote for Bill Bell, who co-produced the record with me. It was written quite a few years ago, and actually written for his wife when they broke up. Bill, being the mercenary that he is, said, 'Why don't you do "Diamonds."' I said, 'Man, I wrote that

for your wife when you guys broke up … we will just modify it.'

"Another one I love off my last record is 'A Prayer for Hope,' which happened seven years ago on a trip to Kenya during an HIV initiative. It's about a boy I met, and it hit me really hard, so I wrote that song.

> "When it comes time, the songs just flow. It's always work, but it's also always a balance between work and inspiration. There were things that needed to be said."

"There is also some unfinished business. 'Back in the Game' has that Texas swing thing; it talks about getting knocked down and getting back up and not letting things get to you. 'Pink Time' is about a couple living on Georgian Bay, which I love. It's a magical place for them; she got Alzheimer's and he didn't want to put her into a home, so he took her down to the Bay and that was it … he drowned both of them. That was a powerful story that touches on a lot of issues. Alzheimer's is such a tragic thing, but it's a beautiful song."

When I told Cochrane the song reminds me a lot of John Prine's classic "Hello, in There," he responds, "You know your stuff. You like Johnny Prine? He's one of the greatest storytellers ever.

"I like to tell stories," he adds. "I like writing songs that touch people in whatever way. It's important to reach people through your music as opposed to just putting stuff out for the sake of putting it out … it's got to mean something."

STEVE EARLE TEACHES WHAT HE PREACHES

Steve Earle began his career as a songwriter in Nashville and released his first EP in 1982. His breakthrough album was *Guitar Town* (1986). Since, Earle has released sixteen other studio albums (his most recent, the bluesy *Terraplane*, 2015). Earle's songs have been recorded by Johnny Cash, Waylon Jennings, Travis Tritt, Vince Gill, Shawn Colvin, Emmylou Harris, and Bob Seger. Camp Copperhead—a four-day immersion songwriting camp led by Earle—debuted in 2014 in upstate New York and immediately sold out. In 2015, Camp Copperhead took place again in Big Indian, NY, located in the Catskill Mountains just north of the Big Apple. What does the three-time Grammy winner teach to these aspiring artists?

"I teach songwriting the way that I do it," Earle explains. "I can't make anybody a songwriter, but I can show you what I do and why. It's about how I write, and

it's about input. There are exercises we do. We write haiku, and we read and listen to Shakespeare. I wrote 'You Are the Best Lover' [a song on *Terraplane*] at Camp Copperhead in 2014. Everybody saw it on the board every day. I wrote it on the chalkboard, so the students could see what my process is like."

Earle says his approach to songwriting has changed over the years. "I've learned not to be married to any particular routine or process … whatever it takes. As you get older, you get busier. I now have a five-year-old son. I can't say, 'I write in the morning,' as I don't always have that luxury. I write when I have the time."

Earle's older son Justin Townes Earle, named after revered Texas songwriter Townes Van Zandt, from whose songs the elder Earle learned a lot about the craft in his younger days, offers this final piece of songwriting advice he received from his dad:

"My father told me some very important things. I didn't listen to him early on, especially because he was a reasonably new person in my life. But, I've always remembered a couple of things he told me, about writing songs, right before I left home on my own when I was about 15. He told me, 'Never write about anything that you don't know.' That's a very simple thing to say, and you say it to people, they think what's the big deal, but that has meaning. If you don't understand that, then don't write songs. Keep it simple. There are very few people like Bob Dylan who can write a song about the Leopard Skin Pillbox Hat."

BRUCE COCKBURN TAKES A METHODICAL APPROACH TO SONGWRITING

Canadian Bruce Cockburn, best known for memorable songs such as "Pacing the Cage" (1995), "If a Tree Falls" (1988), "If I Had a Rocket Launcher" (1984), "Lovers in a Dangerous Time" (1984), and "Wondering Where the Lions Are" (1979), is an award-winning songwriter whose life and music have been shaped by politics, protests, romance, and spiritual discovery. He has released thirty-one albums spanning five decades. I caught up with Cockburn by phone at home in San Francisco, where he's on a brief break from promoting his recently penned memoir *Rumours of Glory*.

When asked about providing advice to aspiring songwriters he says, "I'm not sure how articulate I can be on the subject, but ask away!"

We proceed to chat for thirty minutes about his process for penning songs. "There is not a lot of deliberation that goes into the process in terms of people ... you haven't asked the question, but people do: 'Do you have any advice for aspiring songwriters?' Not really. Do what you think you should do," he says with a laugh.

"It's not quite that simple," he continues. "There are things I can say, but it's very subjective. Everybody I've talked to has different approaches to doing it. Some are very methodical; others aren't at all. I guess I would fall into the latter category."

I ask Cockburn whether the muse strikes and it's a waiting game, or whether something he reads or people he meets inspire him to write a song.

"It's more like the latter," he says. "It's a matter of waiting for the idea. The muse? I did go through a phase way back in the early days where I said, 'I should try and do what real writers do and write something every day, and keep the gears moving.' I found after a year or so of doing that, I had about the same number of useable songs as I would have had if I had just sat around and waited for the songs to come, so I dropped that practice.

"What you hope to do though is seize the idea when it comes," Cockburn continues. "The hope part of it comes in, if you don't have the time and space to seize an idea and run with it ... it will leave you. I keep a notebook and I write down things when they come to me. Sometimes an idea doesn't produce a whole song. It's just a standalone thing, and I have to wait for some other idea to make it useable. I keep those ideas on file in a notebook. If you don't have time to grab onto these things, they just evaporate."

Like most songwriters, Cockburn is also a voracious reader and advocates that anyone who aspires to write songs should read daily. "I would definitely recommend this. Especially for songwriting. It's good to read poetry; it's also good to read other things just because it's all about language. There is always room for furthering one's understanding about language," he says, "but there is also the inspiration you get from reading something that is exciting or touches you in some way. It's not as powerful a motivator as an actual, physical experience might be, but it's a source of encouragement and a source of ideas—not that you are stealing, but when you read others' ideas, you interpret them as your own."

Rarely, however, does Cockburn feel as if he falls into the Woody Guthrie tradition of a rambling man on the road, meeting characters and then chronicling their plight in song.

"My songs, for the most part, are not so much driven by characters, but more by situations … things that happen to people. It's not so much about the person. Take 'If I Had a Rocket Launcher,' for example. I suppose if I had been Woody Guthrie, I could have written about an individual refugee and his or her experiences, but what struck me in the powerful way that produced the song was the overall situation and all the people in it, and I wrote that song. … That's more typical of what gets to me than being able to draw interesting character portraits."

Cockburn, at age sixty-nine, hasn't changed his approach over the years. At least not to the extreme. "Part of learning the craft is that you learn as you grow," he says. "I've been doing it for a long time, so a lot of what I have to say, I've already said. Unless I can think of a newer and better way

to put it, [with] certain ideas. It happens now and then an idea will pop up and I think, 'That's a great idea.' Then I realize I wrote a song about that twenty years ago, so there goes that one. It gets harder as time goes on. I'm just more—not self critical, I've always been that—but more picky about what I put into a song and whether it's exactly the right thing. I guess the bar is just a bit higher now."

I ask Cockburn whether he ever fears the songs will stop coming; one day, will the muse decide not to visit anymore? He admits that at the end of the 1980s, he went for a year and a half without writing a song, and it was scary.

"I thought maybe this is over, that's the end of the run, I'll have to go back and re-educate myself for some other activity, but then I thought it had been a pretty crazy decade, and maybe I was just burnt out and I should take a year off," Cockburn recalls.

"Within a week of officially having taken a year off, I started writing songs again. In that case, it was burn out, and it was remedied by just taking all of the pressure off. There is always that fear, though. Having lived through that once, it's not as scary subsequently. It's always possible it will be gone; I don't take any of it for granted. It all depends on having the idea. If you don't have the idea, there is nothing to write."

One key to keeping ideas handy? Don't throw out those old notebooks. Many songwriters have stories of scribbles in a notebook collecting dust in the back of a nightstand drawer from years before that become the genesis for songs years later.

"It works like that to some extent," Cockburn says. "It hasn't happened to me a whole lot. But especially with phrases or images that sometimes I'll be stuck in a song I'm working on, I'll go back to my notebooks and see if there is something in there that never got used. That's happened rarely.

"On one occasion, it happened that a set of verses and lyrics for a song sat in my notebook for thirty years before I kind of came back ... had gone back to look at it now and then and never could make it work. Then, one day I went back to it and the idea was there for this chorus. There's a song called 'Celestial Horses' from around 2000, but those verses were written back in the 1970s. I can't say it doesn't happen, but it's not common. Usually my ideas are used up as they go by."

DEL BARBER FISHES FOR SONGS

Del Barber grew up in the Canadian Prairies. The landscape is as much a part of him and his songs as the people he has met along the way. From the fertile Red River Valley to the pastures of the west, straight onto the factory floors and into the slaughterhouses of the city, Barber's fourth album, *Prairieography* (2014) was born out of a love for his home, its people, and their stories. It was nominated for a Juno Award in the Roots & Traditional Album category for a solo.

Barber is the son of a draft dodger. He grew up in southern Manitoba, balanced on the line that separates town from country. His heroes yielded hockey sticks and fishing rods. He's worked in fifteen states and eight

Part of learning the craft is that you learn as you grow.

provinces. Barber has held jobs as a mountain guide, a janitor, a construction worker, a groundskeeper, a landscaper, a farmer, a counselor, an ice maker, a teacher's assistant, a driver, a roofer, a fisherman, and more.

"People want to know how I started, and it wasn't by design," he says. "I didn't go to my folks and say, 'This sounds crazy: I want to be a songwriter.' It was something that basically trickled towards me and slowly, slowly gained momentum, and whatever momentum I have is what I live on now for better or worse. I can definitely say this is my job (I don't have any other income) now, but I never made the decision to become a musician ... that seems like a silly idea."

Barber was raised around music fans and especially songwriting fans. "My parents are both huge fans of narrative," he says. "They demanded my attention when songs like that came on the radio—they wanted to play them for me and always asked if I got them. My favorite Dylan quote is something like 'It's taken me a long time to get this young.' It sounds pompous, and a little bit ego driven, but I think what it really means is it takes a long time to realize how little you really know.

"When I was younger, just starting out, I wrote a lot about myself, tried to wax about love and relationships. It's really hard not

> See [writing] as a muscle you are exercising rather than waiting for this bolt of lightning to strike down. Those moments do actually exist ... but if you don't practice, you are not going to be ready or aware when that moment comes.

to write stuff that ego driven when you are white middle class. You are very important at least in your own mind."

These days, that is the last thing Barber wants to write about. "More and more I'm looking back at that catalog of songs that raised me. All those people were interesting because they were writing parables. Even using the 'I,' you could tell it wasn't necessarily their experience. That's a pretty freeing place to be when you want to be considered a writer that has teeth—to be able to tell stories and use narrative in a way that you can even make soft political statements. You don't have to come right out and take a side ... I don't think I know how to anyway, but just to point at things in the world that

are unjust through a character and still have choruses people can hold on to ... that's the goal for me. I don't know how to do that well enough yet, but that's what I want."

The songs Barber writes are generally based on someone he's met in his travels. "I'm thoroughly an introvert, but traveling alone makes me want to crave human contact," he explains. "At shows, everyone treats you too importantly, so you don't get to have conversations with people that are anything but extremely positive. Those are good. They feed your ego. But if you go out to the all-night diners and talk to the waitresses of the world, they don't know who you are, and they don't care, and you actually get to have a conversation—as long as you offer to buy coffee—give them some explanation of your loneliness. Bartenders are the same, and so are smokers."

Barber says his goal these days is to be a part of the tradition of songwriters who write about working-class people—especially in a country that, in a way, is losing its working class. "That whole aesthetic framework is the sort of thing I want to be writing about," he says. "It's the same thing as writing about rural versus urban Canada and what that notion is all about—all sort of subjects that I can't get away from and I want to be known for."

Barber is also trying to be less vague these days, exercising his writing muscles by creating songs that tell stories people can understand. "How can I be more accessible and write songs that are in that folk and country tradition where people can understand it right from the first listen? Even in a crowded bar, there is character or a story, even a few lines that you can hear over the din that is going to move you in some way. It's an exercise in not alienating people," he says.

When it comes to other advice, Barber says to see writing as something you are practicing, no different than a hockey player shooting a thousand pucks a day. "See it as a muscle you are exercising rather than waiting for this bolt of lightning to strike down," he says. "Those moments do actually exist where there is a muse or creative force that you get trapped up in, but if you don't practice, you are not going to be ready or aware when that moment comes."

Barber spends more than two hundred days per year on the road. His therapy is fishing, and it's where many of these ideas germinate. "I bring a fly rod with me on tour in the fairer months," he says. "That's my thing. I will always seek out people and places to fish wherever I am. Those are the greatest places for me to interact with my muse and take stock with who I've met in the last six months and what stories I need to tell and what pictures stick with me. I always think of Tom Waits, who says you are just trying to write little movies … think about songs as these little pictures and try to give people these cutouts of a person's life."

The coolest part of being a songwriter to Barber is how he is constantly interacting with people from all walks of life. "One day you are at the Sheraton or The Ritz and the next you are at the Motel 6," he says. "You are walking between classes all the time. You play a bar one night and a theatre the next. Todd Snider has this line in one of his songs that says, 'There is a guy at the bar hogging one tooth all to himself.' I met that guy a lot of times, then the guy with the $3,000 suit that buys your record and you are engaging with him daily."

DAVID MCPHERSON, a Canadian writer and editor, believes music is the elixir of life. For years, he's written poetry on bar napkins, but he's yet to pen a song. In the interim, he lives vicariously through the award-winning songwriters he's been fortunate enough to interview over the past twenty years as a music writer. With more than 17,000 songs on his iPod, and an ever-growing vintage vinyl collection, it's a joy for him to discover new music, and he loves sharing these discoveries with his wife and two children. David is a regular contributor to *Words + Music*, *Hamilton Magazine*, *No Depression*, and *Penguin Eggs*. Over the years his writing on music has also appeared in *Paste*, *Performing Songwriter*, *American Songwriter*, *Bluegrass Unlimited*, *Exclaim*, *Canadian Musician*, and *Chart*. Reach him at: david@mcphersoncommunications.com and follow him on Twitter (@mcphersoncomm).

PROJECT MANAGEMENT FOR SONGWRITERS

How to Be Successful with Every Songwriting and Recording Session

....

Jonathan Feist

How long does it take you to write a song? How much does it cost? What resources do you need?

These answers will vary greatly, from songwriter to songwriter, and from project to project. A professional songwriter's answers will differ from a hobbyist's. If you are co-writing and planning to pitch to another artist's producer, your project will require different work than it would if you were an independent artist writing for yourself, or a teacher writing a song to teach preschoolers the alphabet. Yet, we are all songwriters, working on more or less similar projects.

The first step in understanding the true work required in songwriting is to clarify what you are creating and why. As with any project, to understand the work, you have to break it down. What are you creating? And besides actually writing the song, what work and resources are required for this endeavor?

FIVE *W*'S AND AN *H*

Answering the standard questions, who/what/where/when/why/how, is a good place to start, if your goal is to understand the project and the work and focus required to make it a success. Some of the more probing questions these words might inspire:

- **WHO** is the writer, performer, producer, band, listener, copyright holder, client? Who will own the master, get paid as a worker for hire, and have ultimate artistic control? Who decides if it's good enough?
- **WHAT** is the song about? What's the genre, instrumentation, delivery media, and length? What notation is needed? What creative constraints must be considered?
- **WHERE** will you write it, rehearse it, record it, perform/release it?

- **WHEN** will you work on it, receive your team's feedback, and finish the recording?
- **WHY** are you writing it? Are you writing for art's sake, for your next album, for another performer, for your students to sing, for a TV commercial? Are you writing to make money, to delight your grandchildren, or to gain easy YouTube hits?
- **HOW** will you record, pitch, and store it? How will you measure its success, or know whether it's good enough?

These probing *w*'s and that *h* can greatly clarify what effort your project requires. Then, you need a practical tool to keep your project organized, to help you track all this information and keep up on all of the details.

You need a checklist. Let's look at a process for creating one.

WORK BREAKDOWN STRUCTURES

Start by organizing all that good information you've uncovered into a hierarchical diagram. This helps you get a good look at your overall work process. One particular type of flowchart—called a "work breakdown structure" in formal project management parlance—can be helpful in breaking down the complexities of a song, or any other project. You start at the top by listing the most general dimensions of the work, and then "elaborate" them into their smaller component parts. For a song project that culminates in a recording, your breakdown might include the music's creation, rehearsals, recording, and various paperwork. Here's an example.

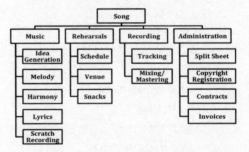

Whether it is quickly scrawled on the back of a napkin or generated cleanly and professionally with software, this kind of chart is an intuitive way to sketch out what your project will be, and how the various components interrelate. The important thing is to uncover a realistic view of what you need to accomplish. As your project evolves, more details will become clear, and the chart can grow.

Eventually, though, flowcharts become cumbersome to maintain, and it will be easier and more practical to render this information as text. It might look like the following list:

The important thing is to uncover a realistic view of what you need to accomplish. As your project evolves, more details will become clear, and the chart can grow

Song
    Music
        Idea Generation
        Melody
        Harmony
        Lyrics
        Scratch Recording
    Rehearsals
        Schedule
        Venue
        Snacks
    Recording
        Tracking
        Mixing/Mastering
    Administration
        Split Sheet
        Copyright Registration
        Contracts
        Invoices

Now, we're using tabs to illustrate the hierarchy, and the flow is from left to right, rather than top-down. It's not as intuitive as the chart, but text is more practical as the itemization of our work becomes more complex.

A great benefit of this text format is that you can convert it into a chart and store more information with each item. So, the work-breakdown structure serves double duty as a master checklist and project status sheet, which will then help us to track all the essential details required to bring each component into being.

Logically, there are now two different types of information on the breakdown chart. First, there are nouns—the individual components of the project that must be created. At a point, it becomes more helpful to start listing verbs—the tasks that need to get executed to make sure that the deliverable is accomplished.

The next step, and ultimate organizational goal, is to convert this information into a project chart/checklist to track all the project's essential information: who is responsible for completing the task, what it will cost, what the status is, what the next step will be to move it forward, when it will be completed, and so on.

While you can use a pencil and paper for this kind of checklist, software can be particularly helpful. I like to use a project management tool called Smartsheet (www.smartsheet.com), which was used to create the graphic below. Among Smartsheet's many benefits is that it lets us "collapse" some of the components so that we don't have to look at all the details at once (such as "Music" above). Instead, we can focus on just the area that I'm currently puzzling

Deliverable	Assigned To	Cost	Time (Days)	Status	Recent Progress	Next Action	Completion Date
⊟ Song							
⊞ Music			20				1/25
⊟ Rehearsals			6				
Schedule	Marci			In Progress	3/5 confirmed by all except Sue	Announce final date	3/15
Venue	Sue	200		Complete	Cost confirmed	At the studio, room 4B	
⊟ Snacks	Mark	80		In Progress			
Finalize menu/budget	Shane		1	Complete	Agreed to do snacks, not lunch		2/2
Buy stuff	Wendy		1	Assigned	W has list	W will get it night before	3/14
Clean Up	Val		1	On Track			
⊞ Recording			1800	13	In Progress		Must finalize date	
⊞ Administration			180		In Progress			

Project management tools, such as this one from Smartsheet, can make all the difference when you're parsing a multitude of steps in a project.

out—in this case, organizing the snacks for the rehearsal. Such tasks might seem frivolous, but these minor dimensions of a project require time and money. You

> The key to a successful outcome is to list all the work you have to do—from the obvious tasks like recording the demo to the subtler ones ...

can also use it to calculate how much total time and money the project will require by adding up various columns and setting up task times in relation to each other to arrive at a reasonable total.

If your goal is to have a realistic sense of what a project truly requires, in terms of time, money, resources, and so on, you need to consider them at this level of detail.

A comprehensive chart like this will be a great help in organizing the project's details and making sure they're completed. The key to a successful outcome is to list all the work you have to do—from the obvious tasks like recording the demo to the subtler ones, such as making sure that you have sufficient snacks on hand to fuel a productive rehearsal.

PROJECT LIFECYCLE

Another way to help ferret out the tasks of a project is to imagine what happens during the course of its life, step by step, looking for components of the work: anything that requires significant time, money, thought, etc., to bring about. A way to

bring additional order into the process is by considering what happens during the five large stages of a project's lifecycle, as described typically by project managers.

Let's consider each phase and what typical songwriting activities might occur during them.

Initiation

The *initiation* phase of a project is the beginning, where the idea is initially considered. It usually begins with someone's flash of inspiration. If inspiration comes from someone else (a client, a producer, an executive, etc.), there must be some conversation with them regarding exactly what is needed—how long, what style, the artistic vision, etc. Resources need to be discussed. How much money will you get paid, and in what timeframe? Who owns the copyright? Will you have a co-writer? What's the instrumentation? Who performs and records the track? Who gets to decide if it is acceptable? Exactly what should you deliver: a scratch recording, a lead sheet, or a score and parts for an arrangement? In a commercial songwriting context, these are all existential questions about the song project that need to be addressed before the actual lyrics and melody can get crafted.

This phase of the project concludes at a formal decision to move forward, such as a contract being signed.

Planning

Once you've committed to writing the song, you can plan how the process will unfold.

It's time for strategic *planning*. The task now is to look at what you've promised to deliver and arrange how to set that in motion. Again, consider those five *w*'s and the *h*, and come up with a realistic plan and resourcing scheme for finishing the song.

Now is the time to set a schedule and budget, as realistically as you can. You set a team in place and clarify everyone's roles. You might sign some more contracts or a split sheet. You might need to clear some copyrights if the song is going to include some material created by someone else, such as a cover, remix, or parody. It may be the time to determine what gear you'll need for the session. When you go off to that cabin in the woods, which guitar will you bring? What recording gear? If Randy Newman is coming over to your house for a co-write, you might get the Steinway tuned the day before. If production is part of your songwriting process, you might need to get some loops or tracks in order to prepare and make sure that you've got room on your hard drive or can set up a Pro Tools session.

Do all you can so that you won't have to fuss with technology during what should be well-protected creative time. Planning is cheaper than making and fixing mistakes, so take it as far as you can without spending too much time or money. Preparing your checklist now, as you read this article, is actually part of the planning process.

Execution

The *execution* stage is the actual writing process—when you finally grab your ukulele, your co-writer grabs her fiddle, and you lock the door, sit yourselves down, crack your knuckles, and bang that sucker out.

You might also need to take walks, have dinner, play other music, and glance at a songwriting how-to book to keep yourself focused and inspired. Playing loops and recording takes over them could also be a part of your process. Think about how you like to write and what you'll need to support that. There are no wrong answers.

Also, there might be some paperwork to handle during the session—lead sheets, co-writer split sheets, photo release forms. A checklist can help you remember to bring these along.

Monitoring/Controlling

During execution, you may want to *monitor* the song's progress and nudge it back towards a certain direction (*control*) if it starts to stray. Say you're writing that alphabet song for your preschoolers. Your co-writer keeps inserting curse words into the lyrics. Someone has to pay attention and put a stop to it—to whap the guy upside the head and get him to refocus. Hilarious as they may be, such digressions from the agreed-upon scope may be wasting precious time.

You might want to test some ideas, periodically reviewing recordings or getting feedback from others, such as a "typical listener" or a client. Making scratch recordings, passing them around, and gathering/considering feedback can be a part of execution/monitoring/controlling, as well. It's important to try different keys, tempos, and instrumental density, then listen back and determine what works best. Also try different song or arrangement forms—perhaps with a four-line chorus versus a three-line or five-line version. This is a great reason to have home recording capabilities: You can quickly and easily test iterations of a song, during the writing process, and listen to what works best.

Closing

After the creative work is done, there still may be tasks associated with the song. Generally, the *closing* tasks, including tidying up the mess you made during execution and preparing the song for its next phase of existence. You might need to register its copyright, send scratch tracks to your band, or deliver masters to a client. You might want to archive your DAW session files, add your song to a comprehensive list you maintain of all songs you've written, and file associated paperwork to make them easily accessible later on.

WORKFLOW: CREATIVITY TO PRACTICALITY

These different project lifecycle phases happen roughly sequentially, though it's common to backtrack, do a little revised planning, and then continue with execution. You might revisit an early decision to change the song's timing, for example, or the instrumentation, which could affect the budget and thus force a need to revisit the project approval process. But the phases happen more or less sequentially.

Again, imagining all these dimensions of the work will help you make sure you don't miss any details and get a realistic grasp of what's truly involved in "writing a song." Then, you will arrive at a project checklist that truly helps you track what you must do. That checklist makes your good planning work actionable.

It can be daunting the first time you look at the process in this level of depth. It gets easier, though, and you'll make fewer mistakes and waste less time overall as a result. You'll reuse much of your work from one songwriting project to the next, and the checklist will evolve and become an increasingly useful tool to track your progress, maintain focus, keep better control of quality, and take some of the flying-by-the-seat-of-your-pants guesswork out of the process.

Ultimately, you'll have more control over those pesky details that can be so draining. Hopefully, this will give you more creative bandwidth to focus on your art.

JONATHAN FEIST is the author of *Project Management for Musicians* (winner of the 2015 International Book Award for Performing Arts), several other books, and hundreds of articles about music. He is editor in chief of Berklee Press, the book publishing department of Berklee College of Music, where he also teaches online.

SONGWRITING ON THE GO

Make the Most of Electronic Songwriting Tools

....

Jennifer Billock

We've all been through it. You're out at the grocery store, the mall, the park, wherever, when suddenly … *bam!* Inspiration strikes. An amazing lyric, chord progression, or melody pops into your head. But with no paper or pencil in sight to write it down, you file it away in your mind and hope by the time you get home it's still there.

Maybe this was the case in the 1980s, but it shouldn't be anymore. We live in a tech-savvy world, and with mobile devices at our disposal every day, the options for jotting down a delicious bit of musical genius stretch far and wide.

GET BACK TO BASICS

One of the greatest things about modern mobility is the constant ability to capture a moment in time. Today's phones almost all have a note-taking app or voice recorder built in, and that's something Brenda Watkins, a Chicago-based songwriter, swears by.

"I always have my cell phone with me, and while it's not particularly fancy, it does have a voice memo feature," she says. "If

lyrics or a bit of a tune come to me while I'm out walking, I'll pull out my phone and talk, sing, or hum into it. If I can sit down, I'll type the lyrics into the phone's notepad.

"I also like to carry a small memo pad and a mechanical pencil with me—always handy for jotting down ideas."

Dean Massalsky, a songwriter based in the Detroit area, follows a similar method. He ditched his archaic system of sticky notes and scraps of paper for the more modern conveniences of his cell phone. If he can't use his Notes and Voice Memos apps on his phone, he'll still find a way to take down what he needs, even if it means taking pen to paper.

"On the odd chance I can't get what I need into Notes, I will write it down," he says. "But I will also take a picture of it with my iThing and e-mail it to myself with the subject 'lyric.'"

A LITTLE TECH GOES A LONG WAY

The preloaded apps on a phone are all well and good, but for collaborations and a few

ADVICE FROM THE PROS

This article features pros at recording on the go. Here, Hebert and Watkins share their best advice for getting everything down right when inspiration strikes.

JESSICA HEBERT: Just do it. Seriously. I don't know how many songs I've lost because I've written them on napkins, scrawled them in a notebook I then lost, or just plain didn't get them down at all. Get them in an electronic medium with other things you access and revisit every now and again. The PDX Broadsides' "The LEGO Song" took me over a year to write from initial idea to full conception, but I had it in a place where I could keep seeing it, tweaking it, and it became this beautiful nerd madrigal that crowds love. Just get it down, because sometimes those little glimmering ideas turn out to be gold.

BRENDA WATKINS: Use whatever is close at hand and is most comfortable. Also, when you're writing a song, save any lyrics or chord patterns that you discard along the way—you never know when they'll fit into another song later on. I also keep a pad and pencil on my bedside table. Never trust your brain to remember that great line that came to you at 3:00 a.m. Write it down!

more features and flexibility, it helps to embrace other methods. Google Drive, for example, works across all platforms and is the perfect tool for accessibility among a group of songwriters.

Jessica Hebert, a Portland, Oregon-based singer-songwriter and member of the bands The PDX Broadsides and PDXYAR, says Google Drive is hands-down the best portable program for not only songwriting, but also collaborating with other musicians while she's on the move.

"I've used Drive on people's Macs, my iPad and computer, and Droids, and my bandmates use it on iPhone," she says. "App-wise, I'm dependent on Google Drive for songwriting. It's so easy to share, and then the material is ubiquitous. I have docs for songs in progress, songs that are developed but need tweaking, things that are just snippets that I want to develop, and collab-

orative pieces with my bandmates, or other artists. And they're all with me, no matter where I go. It's invaluable."

Hebert's other app recommendations are KeyChord, a mobile keyboard app loaded with chords and scale configurations, and RecForge, an advanced voice recorder that creates .wav files.

According to Massalsky, the Garage-Band app is the ultimate in recording on the go because it's flexible, the file formats are accepted across the industry, and it's widespread throughout the music universe. The only downfall, he says, is that it's only available for Apple products. He also uses On-Song, an app with interactive digital chord charts, and iMaschine, a beat-making app.

MOBILE-FRIENDLY WEBSITES

Mobile Web browsers aren't left out in the cold, either. They're the perfect vehicle to find that perfect word when you're trying to write a song away from your studio. Hebert also likes the mobile-friendly wikirhymer.com: The site locates perfect rhymes, near rhymes, and slant rhymes. Watkins sticks with Wiktionary.org to make sure everything fits definition-wise, and thesaurus.com when another word might fit even better.

Of course, as far as jotting down lyrics and ideas, some people just hope for the best. Like a waiter quickly memorizing an order instead of writing it down, Jonathan Aronson, a prolific songwriter with more than three hundred original songs out in cyberspace, uses "a little blind faith that, if it came to me while at the market or the laundromat, it will come to me again someday."

In a way, Aronson lets all his creativity build up to a single-source outlet.

"I record direct onto my BR-900CD multitrack digital recording studio," he says. "In fact, I write my songs as I record them. That is my personal style, writing live."

And truth be told, with the wealth of tools readily at hand, you don't even need to be home to write.

JENNIFER BILLOCK is an award-winning writer and bestselling author. She has worked with such publications as the *New York Times*, *Playboy*, *National Geographic Traveler*, *Condé Nast Traveler*, Yahoo Travel, FreeStyle Cruiser, *Midwest Living*, and *Taste of Home*. She is the author of four books (two cookbooks and two history). Jennifer also owns a boutique content marketing company focusing on food and travel. Check out her website at www.jenniferbillock.com, and follow her on Twitter (@jenniferbillock).

SOCIAL MEDIA MARKETING

Defining Your Story and Ideas via Social Media

....

Charlene Oldham

As half of the folk and roots duo The Aching Hearts, Kelly Wells has discovered that spending a little time—and money—on social media marketing is a wise investment on both counts.

In the last year or so, The Aching Hearts has paid to sponsor more posts on Facebook to reach a targeted list of people who don't yet "like" the band's page in the virtual world, but might like their music in the real one. Wells has found the promoted posts to be an effective way to drive traffic to the band's websites, often offering a free download that sparks music lovers' interest in other songs.

"We've seen our mailing list increase tenfold by this method, and we've reached many people who wouldn't have known about us otherwise," she says. "We have learned that, while random updates across all platforms of social media can be [somewhat] effective, really honing some specific posts goes a very long way to creating actual engagement—not just likes, but shares, comments, traffic back to our website, mailing list sign-ups and video views."

Taking the time to define the story The Aching Hearts wants to tell through social media and to study the technology and the band's target audience has reaped rewards. And it hasn't compromised the duo's craft, creativity, or their authentic connection with fans.

"I think, if anything, social media has gone a long way toward our art reaching more people, giving us better ways to keep in touch and engage, and ways to tell our own story," Wells says.

Snickers can employ digital tricks to insert actor Steve Buscemi into Jan Brady's role as the jealous middle sister on *The Brady Bunch*. Anheuser-Busch has its Clydesdale and puppy pitchmen starring in ads that garner millions of views long after the Super Bowl. But should all songwriters be selling themselves through blogs, YouTube videos, Twitter feeds, Instagram photos, and Facebook fan pages? Marketers and musicians say the answer is almost always yes, whether it's a well-known artist like Taylor Swift or an unknown who hasn't sold a single song.

"Social media is the best way to market for me because the store is open twenty-four hours a day, seven days a week, 365 days a year," says Rick Barker, Swift's former manager and founder of Music Industry Blueprint, which offers artists advice and tools to help build their online presence. "You can reach an international audience without leaving your bedroom."

But before finding your voice and your audience, you have to write, perform, and maybe even record that first album. It's also helpful to surround yourself with other talented artists who can help you define your style and your story, says musician Aynsley Saxe.

"When you are first starting out as a songwriter, it's difficult to know what your voice is and what your brand is and what your authentic way of sharing music is," she says. "Sometimes you don't know that until you've released an album. Then, finding your brand may be an evolution."

But there are tons of talented singers out there, and many can even pen a catchy song. So, to evolve beyond the level of a teenage dreamer who wants to sell out arenas, musicians should have a larger purpose behind performing. Isolating a meaningful narrative makes sharing their story through social media a lot simpler.

"Once you can identify your core purpose, the second part will fall into place," says Ariel Hyatt, founder of Cyber PR. "All of your stories will tie into your main signature story—your mission—the backbone of why you do what you do. If you get clear on that, what you will share as 'mini stories' around it will come to you easily."

Once musicians define their mission, they then need to analyze their audience. Songwriters should start by looking over their mailing lists and roster of Facebook and Twitter followers. Then, they should use the analytical tools available within social media platforms to help them drill down into demographic data.

Are most fans male or female? How old are they? What do they do for a living and, on average, how much money do they make per year? What activities, hobbies, or interests do they have? Now look over the answers and align your own mission with five themes that you observe within your audience, advises Hyatt, who offers additional specifics in her book *Music Success in Nine Weeks*.

"Choose five themes and make sure your posts tie in to these five themes. This will give you an online voice, and your crowd—if you have targeted well—will begin to respond."

Photos work well, as do teasers and other free content, social media marketers say. Fans want an exclusive look into artists' lives. They also want posts, pictures, video, and other content that makes musicians seem like real people rather than marketing machines. Musician and Firefly Media founder Tiana Gustafson recommends looking at the leaders in your genre for ideas. What kind of content gets the most feedback from fans and what can you learn from their social media strategy overall?

She says it's also important to make every post professional and positive, and to save relationship drama for songwriting sessions rather than airing it through Facebook and Twitter.

A FEW TIPS AND TOOLS

SOCIAL MEDIA SCHEDULING PROGRAMS (INCLUDING LATERGRAM.ME, HOOTSUITE, AND THE TOOLS AVAILABLE WITHIN PLATFORMS LIKE FACEBOOK): These tools allow songwriters to time posts for when their audiences are most active and schedule content to appear at regular intervals even when tied up on tour or in a studio session. "If you don't, it will get away from you because we are all human," says Barker. "It's just treating it like a job."

PROFESSIONAL PHOTOS: "Number one is having professional photographs taken. And it's not just for famous people," says Gustafson. For musicians without a marketing budget, she suggests bartering with a photographer. Offer to sing at a party in exchange for a portfolio of professional pics.

CREATIVE APPS: Once you have professional photos and are also taking your own pictures with Instagram, Gustafson recommends the app Rhonna Designs, which allows you to pair words and images. "That's so effective. And you can do that for a gig, an album release, or just everyday life. But you can make all these images your own and really create your own brand for free."

"I always try to think *If my favorite songwriter was posting, what would I want from that?* I'd love to hear what songs inspire them, for example," she says. "So if you are thinking about what you'd like to hear from your favorite people, you can just provide that content to your followers."

Rather than looking at social media strategizing as time away from her music, Gustafson approaches it as another opportunity to have fun, be creative, and interact with fans.

"I could spend all day writing songs, but nobody's going to know who wrote them or who I am unless I get out there and engage," she says.

Wells also spends a lot of time following musician friends and observing what works for the artists she enjoys. She finds herself following the Twitter feeds of artists whose pithy posts keep her entertained and engaged. And her favorites on social media do it all in a way that seems authentic and unforced.

"Some use a combo of personal pages and music pages. Some really draw you in with unique photos. And some—the ones that really grab my attention—are doing what we're trying to do," says Wells. "They are sponsoring particular Facebook posts that really get their message out in a simple, clear, and concise way. The others that really grab my attention are ones where the personality of the band or one of the band members really shines through."

To maintain that authenticity, it's important to post content that entertains, informs, or inspires your followers. Sharing interesting links can be a great way to draw people. And sometimes the most compelling content shines a light on others, either through recognizing other artists or giving fans a face and voice on their favorite singer's social media channels.

"We get so overwhelmed by what we are trying to promote and sell that we forget that social media is 'social.' No one likes the person at the party who cannot take any social cues and keeps taking about himself, or they go on and on when people are not in-

....

... sometimes the most compelling content shines a light on others, either through recognizing other artists or giving fans a face and voice on their favorite singer's social media channels.

....

terested and they are not engaged," says Hyatt. "Don't be that person on social media."

Indeed, Saxe makes a point of responding to each comment or Tweet. She knows she's much more likely to stay engaged in a crowdfunding campaign if the artist sends her a personal message thanking her for a contribution, for example, so she tries to provide the same level of feedback for her own fans.

"Obviously, for a highly successful musician, that's just not possible. But for an independent artist who is growing their fan base, I think that is so important," she says. "And that's what works for me."

Spending just an hour a day planning posts, commenting on content, and responding to messages from fans can go a long way toward achieving your social media marketing goals, says Barker, who recommends scheduling fifteen-minute intervals throughout the day, just as you would plan meals and snacks. He also emphasizes approaching social media not as a chore that steals from your creative time, but as just another way to meaningfully connect with fans—which is the reason many became musicians in the first place.

"If you do it right, you are giving them access into your world," he says. "You are letting them know you know who they are and you are giving them a voice."

SONGWRITING CALENDAR

The best way for songwriters to achieve success is by setting concrete goals and meeting them. Goals are usually met by songwriters who give themselves, or are given, deadlines. Something about having an actual date to hit helps create a sense of urgency for most writers. This songwriting calendar is a great place to keep your important deadlines.

Also, this calendar is a good tool for recording upcoming events you'd like to attend or contests you'd like to enter. Or use this calendar to block out time for yourself—to just create.

Of course, you can use this calendar to record other special events, especially if you have a habit of remembering to write but of forgetting birthdays or anniversaries. After all, this calendar is now yours. Do with it what you will.

OCTOBER 2015

SUN	MON	TUE	WED	THURS	FRI	SAT
				1	2	3
4	5	6	7	8	9	10
11	12	13	14	15	16	17
18	19	20	21	22	23	24
25	26	27	28	29	30	31

Start a songwriting blog and make at least one post per week.

_____

_____

_____

_____

SUN	MON	TUE	WED	THU	FRI	SAT
1	2	3	4	5	6	7
8	9	10	11	12	13	14
15	16	17	18	19	20	21
22	23	24	25	26	27	28
29	30					

Try sending out one targeted demo per day.

DECEMBER 2015

SUN	MON	TUE	WED	THU	FRI	SAT
		1	2	3	4	5
6	7	8	9	10	11	12
13	14	15	16	17	18	19
20	21	22	23	24	25	26
27	28	29	30	31		

Evaluate your 2015 accomplishments and make 2016 goals.

_____

_____

_____

_____

SUN	MON	TUE	WED	THU	FRI	SAT
					1	2
3	4	5	6	7	8	9
10	11	12	13	14	15	16
17	18	19	20	21	22	23
24	25	26	27	28	29	30
31						

Make 2016 your best songwriting year yet!

FEBRUARY 2016

SUN	MON	TUE	WED	THU	FRI	SAT
	1	2	3	4	5	6
7	8	9	10	11	12	13
14	15	16	17	18	19	20
21	22	23	24	25	26	27
28	29					

Don't wait until April to file your 2015 taxes.

SUN	MON	TUE	WED	THU	FRI	SAT
		1	2	3	4	5
6	7	8	9	10	11	12
13	14	15	16	17	18	19
20	21	22	23	24	25	26
27	28	29	30	31		

Are you on Twitter? Try sending one promotional or meaningful tweet daily.

APRIL 2016

SUN	MON	TUE	WED	THU	FRI	SAT
					1	2
3	4	5	6	7	8	9
10	11	12	13	14	15	16
17	18	19	20	21	22	23
24	25	26	27	28	29	30

Sign up for a songwriting workshop.

SUN	MON	TUE	WED	THU	FRI	SAT
1	2	3	4	5	6	7
8	9	10	11	12	13	14
15	16	17	18	19	20	21
22	23	24	25	26	27	28
29	30	31				

Develop one song idea each week.

JUNE 2016

SUN	MON	TUE	WED	THU	FRI	SAT
			1	2	3	4
5	6	7	8	9	10	11
12	13	14	15	16	17	18
19	20	21	22	23	24	25
26	27	28	29	30		

Create a social network platform for your songs.

SUN	MON	TUE	WED	THU	FRI	SAT
					1	2
3	4	5	6	7	8	9
10	11	12	13	14	15	16
17	18	19	20	21	22	23
24	25	26	27	28	29	30
31						

Find a potential co-writer to work with.

AUGUST 2016

SUN	MON	TUE	WED	THU	FRI	SAT
	1	2	3	4	5	6
7	8	9	10	11	12	13
14	15	16	17	18	19	20
21	22	23	24	25	26	27
28	29	30	31			

Find a songwriting conference to attend.

_____

_____

_____

_____

SUN	MON	TUE	WED	THU	FRI	SAT
				1	2	3
4	5	6	7	8	9	10
11	12	13	14	15	16	17
18	19	20	21	22	23	24
25	26	27	28	29	30	

Look for a songwriting organization to join, if you haven't already.

OCTOBER 2016

SUN	MON	TUE	WED	THU	FRI	SAT
						1
2	3	4	5	6	7	8
9	10	11	12	13	14	15
16	17	18	19	20	21	22
23	24	25	26	27	28	29
30	31					

If you don't have it yet, find a copy of *2017 Songwriter's Market*.

SUN	MON	TUE	WED	THU	FRI	SAT
		1	2	3	4	5
6	7	8	9	10	11	12
13	14	15	16	17	18	19
20	21	22	23	24	25	26
27	28	29	30			

Try an unfamiliar writing style to help you grow as a writer.

MUSIC PUBLISHERS

///

Music publishers work with songwriters the same way literary agents work with authors: they find and review songs, represent artists, and find ways for artists to make money from their songs by plugging the songs to recording artists and entertainment firms. In return for a share of the money made from your songs, they take care of paperwork and accounting, help you vet new songs, seek out foreign licensing deals, set you up with co-writers (recording artists or other songwriters), fund demo productions, give advances against future royalties, and so on.

HOW DO MUSIC PUBLISHERS MAKE MONEY FROM SONGS?

Music publishers make money by getting songs recorded onto albums, film and TV soundtracks, commercials, etc. and other areas. While this is their primary function, music publishers also handle administrative tasks such as copyrighting songs; collecting royalties for the songwriter; negotiating and issuing synchronization licenses for use of music in films, television programs and commercials; arranging and administering foreign rights; auditing record companies and other music users; suing infringers; and producing new demos of new songs. In a small, independent publishing company, one or two people may handle all these jobs. Larger publishing companies are more likely to be divided into the following departments: creative (or professional), copyright, licensing, legal affairs, business affairs, royalty, accounting, and foreign.

HOW DO MUSIC PUBLISHERS FIND SONGS?

The *creative department* is responsible for finding talented writers and signing them to the company. Once a writer is signed, it is up to the creative department to develop and nurture the writer so he will write songs that create income for the company. Staff members often put writers together to form collaborative teams. And, perhaps most important, the creative department is responsible for securing commercial recordings of songs and pitching them for use in film and other media. The head of the creative department—usually called the "professional manager"—is charged with locating talented writers for the company.

HOW DO MUSIC PUBLISHERS GET SONGS RECORDED?

Once a writer is signed, the professional manager arranges for a demo to be made of the writer's songs. Even though a writer may already have recorded his own demo, the publisher will often re-demo the songs using established studio musicians in an effort to produce the highest-quality demo possible.

Once a demo is produced, the professional manager begins shopping the song to various outlets. He may try to get the song recorded by a top artist on his or her next album or get the song used in an upcoming film. The professional manager uses all the contacts and leads he has to get the writer's songs recorded by as many artists as possible. Therefore, he must be able to deal efficiently and effectively with people in other segments of the music industry, including A&R (artists and repertoire) personnel, recording artists, producers, distributors, managers and lawyers. Through these contacts, he can find out what artists are looking for new material, and who may be interested in recording one of the writer's songs.

HOW IS A PUBLISHING COMPANY ORGANIZED?

After a writer's songs are recorded, the other departments at the publishing company come into play.

- The **LICENSING AND COPYRIGHT DEPARTMENTS** are responsible for issuing any licenses for use of the writer's songs in film or TV and for filing various forms with the copyright office.
- The **LEGAL AFFAIRS DEPARTMENT** and **BUSINESS AFFAIRS DEPARTMENT** work with the professional department in negotiating contracts with writers.
- The **ROYALTY AND ACCOUNTING DEPARTMENTS** are responsible for making sure that users of music are paying correct royalties to the publisher and ensuring the writer is receiving the proper royalty rate as specified in the contract and that statements are mailed to the writer promptly.
- Finally, the **FOREIGN DEPARTMENT**'s role is to oversee any publishing activities outside of the U.S., to notify sub-publishers of the proper writer and ownership information of songs in the catalog and update all activity and new releases, and to make sure a writer is being paid for any uses of his material in foreign countries.

FINDING THE RIGHT MUSIC PUBLISHER FOR YOU

How do you go about finding a music publisher that will work well for you? First, you must find a publisher suited to the type of music you write. If a particular publisher works mostly with alternative music and you're a country songwriter, the contacts he has within the industry will hardly be beneficial to you.

Each listing in this section details, in order of importance, the type of music that publisher is most interested in; the music types appear in **boldface** to make them easier to locate. It's also very important to submit only to companies interested in your level of experience (refer to "A Sample Listing Decoded" in the article "Where Should I Send My Songs?"). You will also want to refer to the Category Indexes, which list companies by the type of music they work with. Publishers placing music in film or TV will be preceded by a ⊛ (see the Film & TV Index for a complete list of these companies).

Do Your Research!

It's important to study the market and do research to identify which companies to submit to.

- Many record producers have publishing companies or have joint ventures with major publishers who fund the signing of songwriters and who provide administration services. Since producers have an influence over what is recorded in a session, targeting the producer/publisher can be a useful avenue.
- Since most publishers don't open unsolicited material, try to meet the publishing representative in person (at conferences, speaking engagements, etc.) or try to have an intermediary intercede on your behalf (for example, an entertainment attorney, a manager, an agent, etc.).
- As to demos, submit no more than three songs unless that publisher makes it clear they want more songs.
- As to publishing deals, co-publishing deals (where a writer owns part of the publishing share through his or her own company) are relatively common if the writer has a well-established track record.
- Are you targeting a specific artist to sing your songs? If so, find out if that artist even considers outside material. Get a copy of the artist's latest album, and see who wrote most of the songs. If the artist wrote them all, he's probably not interested in hearing material from outside writers. If the songs were written by a variety of different writers, however, he may be open to hearing new songs.
- Check the album liner notes, which will list the names of the publishers of each writer. These publishers obviously have had luck pitching songs to the artist, and they may be able to get your songs to that artist, as well.
- If the artist you're interested in has a recent hit on the *Billboard* charts, the publisher of that song will be listed in the "Hot 100 A-Z" index. Carefully choosing which publishers will work best for the material you write may take time, but it will only increase your chances of getting your songs heard. "Shotgunning" your demo

packages (sending out many packages without regard for music preference or submission policy) is a waste of time and money and will hurt, rather than help, your songwriting career.

Once you've found some companies that may be interested in your work, learn what songs those publishers have handled successfully. Most publishers are happy to provide you with this information in order to attract high-quality material. As you're researching music publishers, keep in mind how you get along with them personally. If you can't work with a publisher on a personal level, chances are your material won't be represented as you would like it to be. A publisher can become your most valuable connection to all other segments of the music industry, so it's important to find someone you can trust and feel comfortable with.

Independent or Major Company?

Also consider the size of the publishing company. The publishing affiliates of the major music conglomerates are huge, handling catalogs of thousands of songs by hundreds of songwriters. Unless you are an established songwriter, your songs probably won't receive enough attention from such large companies. Smaller, independent publishers offer several advantages. First, independent music publishers are located all over the country, making it easier for you to work face-to-face rather than by mail or phone. Smaller companies usually aren't affiliated with a particular record company and are, therefore, able to pitch your songs to different labels and acts. Independent

music publishers are usually interested in a smaller range of music, allowing you to target your submissions more accurately. The most obvious advantage to working with a smaller publisher is the personal attention they can bring to you and your songs. With a smaller roster of artists to work with, the independent music publisher is able to concentrate more time and effort on each particular project.

SUBMITTING MATERIAL TO PUBLISHERS

When submitting material to a publisher, always keep in mind that a professional, courteous manner goes a long way in making a good impression. When you submit a demo through the mail, make sure your package is neat and meets the particular needs of the publisher. Review each publisher's submission policy carefully, and follow it to the letter. Disregarding this information will only make you look like an amateur in the eyes of the company you're submitting to.

Listings of companies in Canada are preceded by a ☺, and international markets are designated with a ☺. You will find an alphabetical list of these companies at the back of the book, along with an index of publishers by state in the Geographic Index.

PUBLISHING CONTRACTS

Once you've located a publisher you like and he's interested in shopping your work, it's time to consider the publishing contract—an agreement in which a songwriter grants certain rights to a publisher for one or more songs. The contract specifies any advances offered to the writer, the rights that will be transferred to the publisher, the royalties a songwriter is to receive, and the length of time the contract is valid.

- When a contract is signed, a publisher will ask for a 50-50 split with the writer. *This is standard industry practice*; the publisher is taking that 50 percent to cover the overhead costs of running his business and for the work he's doing to get your songs recorded.
- It is always a good idea to have a publishing contract (or any music business contract) reviewed by a competent entertainment lawyer.
- There is no "standard" publishing contract, and each company offers different provisions for its writers.

Make sure you ask questions about anything you don't understand, especially if you're new in the business. Songwriter organizations such as the Songwriters Guild of America (SGA) provide contract review services, and can help you learn about music business language and what constitutes a fair music publishing contract. See the Organizations section for more information on the SGA and other songwriting groups.

When signing a contract, it's important to be aware of the music industry's unethical practitioners. The "song shark," as he's called, makes his living by asking a songwriter to pay to have a song published. The shark will ask for money to demo a song and promote it to radio stations; he also may ask for more than the standard 50 percent publisher's share or ask you to give up all rights to a song in order to have it published. Although none of these practices is illegal, it's certainly not ethical, and no successful publisher uses these methods. *Songwriter's Market* works to list only honest companies interested in hearing new material.

Please read the article "Avoiding the Rip-Offs" for more information.

ADDITIONAL PUBLISHERS

There are **more publishers** located in other sections of the book! Use the Index to find listings within other sections who are also music publishers.

Icons

For more instructional information on the listings in this book, including explanations of symbols that coincide with certain listings, read the article "How To Use *Songwriter's Market*."

●○ ALL ROCK MUSIC

Netherlands. **E-mail:** info@collectorrecords.nl. **Website:** www.collectorrecords.nl. **Contact:** Cees Klop, president. Music publisher, record company (Collector Records) and record producer. Publishes 40 songs/year; publishes several new songwriters/year. Staff size: 3. Pays standard royalty.

○ Also see the listings for Collector Records in the Record Companies and Record Producers sections of this book.

AFFILIATES All Rock Music (United Kingdom).

HOW TO CONTACT Submit demo package by mail. Unsolicited submissions are OK. Prefers cassette. SAE and IRC. Responds in 2 months.

MUSIC Mostly **1950s rock**, **rockabilly** and **country rock**; also **piano boogie woogie**. Published *Rock Crazy Baby* (album), written and recorded by Art Adams (1950s rockabilly), released 2004; *Marvin Jackson* (album), by Marvin Jackson (1950s rockers), released 2005; *Western Australian Snake Pit R&R* (album), recorded by various (1950s rockers), released 2005, all on Collector Records.

TIPS "Send only the kind of material we issue/produce as listed."

○✪ ALPHA MUSIC, INC.

106 Apple St., Suite 302, Tinton Falls NJ 07724 United States. **E-mail:** info@trfmusic.com. **Website:** www.trfmusic.com. **Contact:** Michael Nurko, music publisher. Pays standard royalty.

○ Also see listing for TRF Production Music Libraries in the Advertising, Audiovisual & Commercial Music Firms section of this book.

AFFILIATES Dorian Music Publishers, Inc. (BMI) and TRF Music Inc.

HOW TO CONTACT "We accept submissions of new compositions. Submissions are not returnable."

MUSIC **All categories**, mainly **instrumental** and **acoustic** suitable for use as **production music**, including **theme and background music for TV and film**. "Have published more than 50,000 titles since 1931."

○ A NEW RAP JAM PUBLISHING

1017 Myrtle St., Marks MS 38646. **E-mail:** newexperiencerecords@yahoo.com. **Contact:** A&R Department. Professional Managers: William Roach (rap, clean); James Milligan (country, 1970s music, pop). Music publisher and record company (New Experience/Faze 4 Records, Pump It Up Records, and Rough Edge Records). Publishes 50-100 songs/year; Grind Blocc Records and Touch Tone Digital International Records publishes 5-10 new songwriters/year. Hires staff songwriters. Pays standard royalty.

AFFILIATES Songwriters Party House Publishing (BMI), Creative Star Management, and Rough Edge Records. Distribution through KVZ Distribution and States 51 Distribution.

HOW TO CONTACT *Write first to arrange personal interview or submit demo CD by mail.* Unsolicited submissions are OK. Prefers CD with 3-5 songs and lyric or lead sheet. Include SASE. Responds in 8 weeks. "Visit www.myspace.com/newexperiencerecords2 for more information."

MUSIC Mostly **R&B**, **pop**, **blues**, and **rock/rap** (clean); also **contemporary**, **gospel**, **country** and **soul**. Published "Lets Go Dancing" (single by Dion Mikel), recorded and released 2006 on Faze 4 Records/New Experience Records; "The Broken Hearted" (single) from *The Final Chapter* (album), recorded by T.M.C. the milligan connection (R&B/gospel); James, Jr.; Girl Like You feat. Terry Zapp Troutman, additional appearances by Kurtis Blow, King MC, Sugarfoot Lead Singer (Ohio Players) Lavel Jackson 2009/10 on New Experience/Pump It Up Records. Other artists include singer-songwriter James, Jr. on Faze 4 Records/Rough Edge Records Grind Blocc Records.

TIPS "We are seeking hit artists from the 1970s, 1980s, and 1990s who would like to be signed, as well as new talent and female solo artists. Send any available information supporting the group or act. We are a label that does not promote violence, drugs, or anything that we feel is a bad example for our youth. Establish music industry contacts, write and keep writing, and most of all believe in yourself. Use a good recording studio but be very professional. Just take your time and produce the best music possible. Sometimes you only get one chance. Make sure you place your best song on your demo first. This will increase your chances greatly. If you're the owner of your own small label and have a finished product, please send it. And if there is interest we will contact you. Also be, on the lookout for new artists on Rough Edge Records and Touch Tone Records. Now reviewing blues and soul music. If you have a developing record label and would like distribution, send us your artist listing record label information to be considered and thank you for considering us for your next project."

🐻 BEARSONGS

Box 944, Edgbaston, Birmingham B16 8UTT United Kingdom. +(44)0121-454-7020. **Website:** www.bigbearmusic.com. **Contact:** Jim Simpson, managing director; Russell Fletcher, professional manager. Music publisher and record company (Big Bear Records). Member PRS, MCPS. Publishes 25 songs/year; publishes 15-20 new songwriters/year. Pays standard royalty.

Also see the listings for Big Bear Records in the Record Companies section and Big Bear in the Record Producers section of this book.

HOW TO CONTACT Submit demo by mail. Unsolicited submissions are OK. Prefers CD. Does not return material. Responds in 3 months.

MUSIC Mostly **blues**, **swing** and **jazz**. Published *Blowing With Bruce* and *Cool Heights* (by Alan Barnes), recorded by Bruce Adams/Alan Barnes Quintet; and *Blues For My Baby* (by Charles Brown), recorded by King Pleasure & The Biscuit Boys, all on Big Bear Records.

TIPS "Have a real interest in jazz, blues, swing."

⊘ THE BICYCLE MUSIC CO.

Concord Bicycle Music, 100 N. Crescent Dr., Suite 323, Beverly Hills CA 90210. (310)286-6600. **Fax:** (310)286-6622. **E-mail:** info@bicyclemusic.com. **Website:** www.bicyclemusic.com. The Bicycle Music Co. is a globally influential independent music publisher, record label, and rights manager. "We are committed to innovative marketing, creative and administrative practices, promoting exceptional growth on behalf of our songwriters, recording artists, and investor partners."

HOW TO CONTACT The Bicycle Music Co. does not accept unsolicited material.

MUSIC Has published music by AFI, Alanis Morissette, Cyndi Lauper, Dave Matthews Band, Johnny Cash, Michael Jackson, Nine Inch Nails, Survivor, Willie Nelson, and more.

BIG FISH MUSIC PUBLISHING GROUP

12720 Burbank Blvd., Suite 124, Valley Village CA 91607. (818)508-9777. **E-mail:** clisag21@yahoo.com. **Website:** www.facebook.com/bigfishmusicbuilding; www.nimbitmusic.com/bigfishmusic. **Contact:** Chuck Tennin. Producer: Gary Black (country, pop, adult contemporary, rock, crossover songs, other styles). Professional Music Manager: Lora Sprague (jazz, New Age, instrumental, pop rock, R&B). Professional Music Manager: B.J. (pop, TV, film, and special projects). Professional Music and Vocal Consultant:

Zell Black (country, pop, gospel, rock, blues). Market Research Specialist: Georgia Paris. Producer, Independent Artists: Darryl Harrelson, Major Label Entertainment (country, pop and other genres). Nashville Music Associate: Ron Hebert (Abear/Songtown Publishing). Songwriter/Consultant: Jerry Zanandrea (Z Best Muzic). Staff Songwriters: BillyO'Hara, Joe Rull, Claire Applewhite. Music Publisher, record company (California Sun Records) and production company. Publishes 30-40 songs/year; publishes 30-40 new songwriters/year. Staff size: 10. Pays standard royalty. "We also license songs and music copyrights to users of music, especially TV and film, commercials, and recording projects." Member: BMI, ASCAP, CMA and ACM.

AFFILIATE(S) Big Fish Music (BMI) and California Sun Music (ASCAP).

HOW TO CONTACT *Write first and obtain permission to submit.* Include SASE for reply. "*Please do not call* or e-mail submissions. After permission to submit is confirmed, we will assign and forward to you a submission code number allowing you to submit up to 4 songs maximum, preferably on CD. Include a properly addressed cover letter, signed and dated, with your source of referral (*Songwriter's Market*) with your assigned submission code number and a SASE for reply and/or return of material. Include lyrics. *Unsolicited material will not be accepted.* This is our submission policy to review outside and new material." Responds in 2 weeks.

FILM & TV Places 6 songs in TV/year. Recently published "Even the Angels Knew" (by Cathy Carlson/Craig Lackey/MartyAxelrod); "Stop Before We Start" (by J.D. Grieco); "Oh Santa" (by Christine Bridges/John Deaver), all recorded by The Black River Girls in *Passions* (NBC); licensed "A Christmas Wish" (by Ed Fry/Eddie Max), used in *Passions* (NBC); "Girls Will Be Girls" (by Cathy Carlson/John LeGrande), recorded by The Black River Girls, used in *All My Children* (ABC); "The Way You're Drivin' Me" and "Ain't No Love 'Round Here" (by Jerry Zanandrea), both recorded by The Black River Girls, used in *Passions* (NBC); "Since You Stole My Heart"(by Rick Colmbra/Jamey Whiting), used in *Passions* (NBC); "Good Time To Fly", "All I Need Is A Highway", and "Eyes Of The Children" (by Wendy Martin), used in *Passions* (NBC); "It's An Almost Perfect Christmas" (by Michael Martin), used in *Passions* (NBC).

MUSIC Country, including **country pop**, **country A/C** and **country crossover** with "a cutting edge"; also **pop**, **rock**, **pop ballads**, **adult contemporary**, **uplift-**

ing, **praise**, **worship**, **spiritual**, and **inspirational adult contemporary gospel** "with a powerful message," **instrumental background and theme music** for TV, film, and commercials, **New Age/instrumental jazz** and **novelty**, **orchestral classical**, **R&B** and **children's music**, for all kinds of commercial use. Published "If Wishes Were Horses" (single by Billy O'Hara); "Purple Bunny Honey" (single by Robert Lloyd/Jim Love); "Leavin' You For Me" (single by J.D. Grieco).

TIPS "Demo should be professional, high quality, clean, simple, dynamic, and must get the song across on the first listen. Good clear vocals, a nice melody, a good musical feel, good musical arrangement, strong lyrics and chorus—a unique, catchy, clever song that sticks with you. Looking for unique country and pop songs with a different edge that can crossover to the mainstream market for ongoing Nashville music projects for hot female country acts that can crossover to adult contemporary and pop with great lush harmonies. Also, catchy, up-tempo songs with an attitude and a groove, preferably rock, that can be marketed to today's youth."

⊘ BIG LOUD SHIRT

1111 16th Ave. S., Suite 201, Nashville TN 37212. (615)329-1929. **Fax:** (615)329-1930. **E-mail:** info@bigloudshirt.com. **Website:** www.bigloudshirt.com. Big Loud Shirt is an independently owned and operated music publishing company that was established by multiple award-winning songwriter and producer Craig Wiseman. Boasts 36 No. 1 hits, over 60 singles, and countless awards. (ASCAP, BMI)

HOW TO CONTACT Big Loud Shirt does not accept unsolicited material.

MUSIC Country. Published "Live Like You Were Dying" (Tim McGraw), "Before He Cheats" and "Blown Away" (Carrie Underwood), "I Saw God Today" (George Strait), "Cruise" (Florida Georgia Line), and more.

⊘◐⊛ BIG YELLOW DOG

1313 16th St. S., Nashville TN 37212. **E-mail:** info@bigyellowdogmusic.com. **Website:** www.bigyellowdogmusic.com. Big Yellow Dog Music is an independent music publishing company based in Nashville, Tennessee, recognized with such accolades as 5 Grammys (including Song of the Year "Need You Now"), 20 Number Ones, 4 Song of the Year awards (ACM, BMI and two ASCAPs), an ASCAP Global Award, an ASCAP Pop Award, and many more.

HOW TO CONTACT Does not accept outside submissions.

MUSIC Catalog includes songs performed by Lady Antebellum, Adele, Sheryl Crow, Meghan Trainor, Demi Lovato, Carrie Underwood, Luke Bryan, Cole Swindell, Trent Dabbs, Jessie James Decker, Tim McGraw, Lee Brice, Blake Shelton, Fifth Harmony, Rascall Flatts, The Mavericks, Eli Young Band, Toby Keith, George Strait, Darius Rucker, Willie Nelson, Alison Krauss, Guy Clark, Jimmy Buffett, Dierks Bentley, and many more.

⊘⊛ BIXIO MUSIC GROUP & ASSOCIATES/ IDM MUSIC

111 E. 14th St., Suite 140, New York NY 10003. (212)695-3911. **E-mail:** info@bixio.com. **Website:** www.bixio.com. (ASCAP) Music publisher, record company and rights clearances. Estab. 1985. Publishes a few hundred songs/year; publishes 2 new songwriters/year. Staff size: 6. Pays standard royalty.

HOW TO CONTACT Does not accept unsolicited material.

MUSIC Mostly **soundtracks**. Published "La Strada Nel Bosco," included in the TV show *Ed* (NBC); "La Beguine Du Mac," included in the TV show *The Chris Isaac Show* (Showtime); and "Alfonsina Delle Camelie," included in the TV show *UC: Undercover* (NBC).

⊘ BLUEWATER MUSIC

P.O. Box 120904, Nashville TN 37212. (615)327-0808. **Fax:** (615)327-0809. **E-mail:** info@bluewatermusic.com. **Website:** www.bluewatermusic.com. **Contact:** Bennet Davidson, assistant, creative department. Now approaching its 30th year, Bluewater is embarking on a new venture—Artist Management. With its extensive contacts in the music industry and creative promotional ideas, Bluewater is set to increase the fan base of bands and musical acts of all genres. Kink Ador is the company's first signing and the band's new album, *Free World*, was released in early 2014.

⊘ Bluewater is not currently accepting unsolicited submissions.

⊘ BMG CHRYSALIS US

BMG Chrysalis US, 1745 Broadway, 19th Floor, New York NY 10019. **Website:** www.bmgchrysalis.com. BMG offers a new digital-age service alternative to songwriters, artists, and rights owners in the music industry. It is a rights management company equally representing music publishing and recording rights. (ASCAP, BMI) 8447 Wilshire Blvd., Suite 400, Beverly

Hills CA 90211. (323)658-9125. **Fax:** (323)658-8019. **Website:** chrysalismusicusa.com. **Contact:** David Stamm, vice president of A&R. Music publisher. Estab. 1968.

HOW TO CONTACT Chrysalis Music does not accept any unsolicited submissions.

MUSIC Published "Sum 41" (single), written and recorded by OutKast; "Light Ladder" (single), written and recorded by David Gray. Administer: David Lee Roth, Andrea Boccelli, Velvet Revolver, and Johnta Austin.

⊘ BOURNE CO. MUSIC PUBLISHERS

5 W. 37th St., New York NY 10018. (212)391-4300. **Fax:** (212)391-4306. **E-mail:** bourne@bournemusic.com; info@bournemusic.com. **Website:** www.bournemusic.com. Publishes educational material and popular music.

AFFILIATES ABC Music, Ben Bloom, Better Half, Bogat, Burke & Van Heusen, Goldmine, Harborn, Lady Mac and Murbo Music.

HOW TO CONTACT Does not accept unsolicited submissions.

MUSIC Piano/vocal, **band pieces** and **choral pieces**. Published "Amen" and "Mary's Little Boy Child" (singles by Hairston); "When You Wish Upon a Star" (single by Washington/Harline); and "San Antonio Rose" (single by Bob Willis, arranged John Cacavas).

○ BRANDON HILLS MUSIC, LLC (BMI)

N. 3425 Searle County Line Rd., Brandon WI 53919. (920)570-1076 or (920)398-3729. **E-mail:** martab@centurytel.net. **Website:** www.brandonhillsmusic.com. **Contact:** Marsha L. Brown. Publishes 4 new songwriters/year. Staff size: 2. Pays standard royalty of 50%.

HOW TO CONTACT Submit demo package by mail. Unsolicited submissions are OK. Prefers CD with 1-4 songs and cover letter. Does not return submissions. Responds only if interested.

MUSIC Mostly **country** (**traditional**, **modern**, **country rock**), **contemporary Christian**, **blues**; also **children's** and **bluegrass** and **rap**. Published "Let It Rain," recorded by Steff Nevers, written by Larry Migliore and Kevin Gallarello (Universal Records, Norway); "Do You Like My Body," recorded by Ginger-Ly, written by Nisa McCall (SEI Corp and Big Daddy G Music, CA); "Did I Ever Thank You Lord," recorded by Jacob Garcia, written by Eletta Sias (TRW Records); "Honky Tonk In Heaven," recorded by Buddy Lewis, written by Mike Heath and Bob Alexander (Ozark Records).

TIPS "We prefer studio-produced CDs. The lyrics and the CD must match. Cover letter, lyrics, and CD should have a professional look. Demos should have vocals up front and every word should be distinguishable. Please make sure your lyrics match your song. Submit only your best. The better the demo, the better the chance of getting your music published and recorded."

○ CALIFORNIA COUNTRY MUSIC

112 Widmar Place, Clayton CA 94517. **Contact:** Edgar J. Brincat, owner. (BMI) Publisher and record company (Roll On Records). Pays standard royalty.

AFFILIATES Sweet Inspirations Music (ASCAP).

◯ Also see the listing for Roll On Records in the Record Companies.

HOW TO CONTACT Submit demo by mail. Unsolicited submissions are OK. "Do not call or write. Any calls will be returned collect to caller." Send CD with 3 songs and lyric sheet. Include SASE. Responds in 6 weeks.

MUSIC Mostly MOR, contemporary country and pop. Does not want rap, metal or rock. Published *For Realities Sake* (album by F.L. Pittman/R. Barretta) and *Maddy* (album by F.L. Pittman/M. Weeks), both recorded by Ron Banks & L.J. Reynolds on Life & Bellmark Records; and *Quarter Past Love* (album by Irwin Rubinsky/Janet Fisher), recorded by Darcy Dawson on NNP Records.

⊘ CAPITOL CHRISTIAN MUSIC GROUP

101 Winners Circle, Brentwood TN 37027. (615)371-4300. **Website:** www.capitolchristianmusicgroup.com. (ASCAP, BMI, SESAC) Music publisher. Publishes more than 100 songs/year. Represents more than 35,000 songs and over 300 writers. Hires staff songwriters. Pays standard royalty.

AFFILIATES Birdwing Music (ASCAP), Sparrow Song (BMI), His Eye Music (SESAC), Ariose Music (ASCAP), Straightway Music (ASCAP), Shepherd's Fold Music (BMI), Songs of Promise (SESAC), Dawn Treader Music (SESAC), Meadowgreen Music Co. (ASCAP), River Oaks Music Co. (BMI), Stonebrook Music Co. (SESAC), Bud John Songs, Inc. (ASCAP), Bud John Music, Inc. (BMI), Bud John Tunes, Inc. (SESAC), WorshipTogether Songs, ThankYou Music, Thirst Moon River.

HOW TO CONTACT Does not accept unsolicited submissions.

MUSIC Published Chris Tomlin, Toby Mac, David Crowder, Jeremy Camp, Stephen Curtis Chapman, Delirious, Tim Hughes, Matt Redman, Demon Hunter, Underoath, Switchfoot, Third Day, Casting Crowns, and many others.

TIPS "Do what you do with passion and excellence and success will follow; just be open to new and potentially more satisfying definitions of what 'success' means."

⊘ CARLIN AMERICA

126 E. 38th St., New York NY 10016. (212)779-7977. **Website:** www.carlinamerica.com. Carlin America is among the largest of the few remaining independent music publishers in the US, and is still owned by the family of its founder, music industry icon Freddy Bienstock. Carlin's catalog spans 100 years of popular and classical music history. Vintage ballads, No. 1 hits from the rock 'n' roll years, numerous rock and pop bestsellers, great song standards, Broadway show tunes and significant classical works are among the vast range of Carlin titles that have been recorded by virtually every major recording artist.

AFFILIATES Alley Music Corp.; Bienstock Publishing Co.; Bro 'n Sis Music, Inc.; Carbert Music, Inc.; Carlin America, Inc.; Elvis Music, Inc.; Family Style Publishing, Inc.; Fort Knox Music, Inc.; Frank & Nancy Music, Inc.; Freddy Bienstock Music Co.; Herald Square Music Inc.; Johnny Bienstock Music, Inc.; Mandy Music; Edward B. Marks Music, Co.; Piedmont Music Co.; Range Road Music, Inc.; Sis 'n Bro Music, Inc.; White Haven Music, Inc.

HOW TO CONTACT Carlin America does not accept unsolicited material.

MUSIC Every conceivable genre: **jazz**, **country**, **R&B**, **soul**, **pop**, **rock**, **the great American songbook**, **classic music**, etc. Published "Back in Black" (AC/DC), "I Got You (I Feel Good)" (by James Brown), "Owner of a Lonely Heart" (by Yes), "Total Eclipse of the Heart" (by James Steinman), "Sky Pilot" (by the Animals), and more.

○ CARNIVAL MUSIC

Carnival Music, 24 Music Square W., Nashville TN 37203. (615)259-0841. **Fax:** (615)259-0843 **Website:** www.carnivalmusic.net. Carnival Music isn't a publishing company, or a record label, though it does the work of both. It's a music company, front to back, founded by industry veterans Frank Liddell and Travis Hill in 1997, not with the intent of using music to prop up a business, but to build a business that could find and nurture compelling, lasting music, and set the stage for compelling, lasting careers.

MUSIC Carnival's current roster includes country voices David Nail, Brent Cobb and Hailey Whitters, roots-rooted talents Stoney LaRue, Rob Baird, and Mando Saenz and the style-blending Logan Brill and Derik Hultquist. Each Carnival writer puts forth his or her own stylistic stamp; all possess that undeniable talent.

☼ CASABLANCA MEDIA PUBLISHING

249 Lawrence Ave. E., Toronto, ON M4N 1T5 Canada. (416)921-9214. **E-mail:** info@casablancamediapublishing.com. **E-mail:** agilbert@casaent.com. **Website:** www.casablancamediapublishing.com. **Contact:** Jennifer Mitchell, president; Jana Cleland, vice president. Casablanca is the largest independent music publisher in Canada. Provides domestic and foreign music publishing administration services to copyright owners around the globe.

HOW TO CONTACT E-mail a SoundCloud or Bandcamp streaming link for review. Do not send any attachments or CDs.

⊘ CHERRY HEART MUSIC

1510 16th Ave. S., Nashville TN 37212-2906. (615)468-3335. **Fax:** (615)298-3899. **Website:** www.cherryheart.com. Cherry Heart Music and Entertainment is a multi-faceted management and marketing company, which specializes in catering to the unique qualities of each client and building upon the foundation of what makes each project distinctive and exclusive for the marketplace. Cherry Heart Music, LLC (BMI), Red Cherry Heart Music (ASCAP), Big Cherry Heart Music (SESAC).

HOW TO CONTACT Cherry Heart does not accept unsolicited material.

MUSIC Country.

◐⊛ CHRISTMAS & HOLIDAY MUSIC

26642 Via Noveno, Mission Viejo CA 92691. (949)859-1615. **E-mail:** justinwilde@christmassongs.com. **Website:** www.christmassongs.com. **Contact:** Justin Wilde. Publishes 8-12 songs/year; publishes 8-12 new songwriters/year. Staff size: 1. "All submissions must be complete songs (i.e., music and lyrics)." Pays standard royalty.

AFFILIATES Songcastle Music (ASCAP).

HOW TO CONTACT Submit demo CD by mail. Unsolicited submissions are OK. *Do not call. Do not send unsolicited MP3s or links to websites.* See website for submission guidelines. "First-Class Mail only. Registered or certified mail not accepted." Prefers CD with no more than 3 songs with lyric sheets. Do not send lead sheets or promotional material, bios, etc." Include SASE but does not return material out of the US. Responds only if interested.

FILM & TV Places 10-15 songs in TV/year. Published Barbra Streisand's "It Must Have Been the Mistletoe."

MUSIC Strictly **Christmas, Halloween, Hanukkah, Mother's Day, Thanksgiving, Father's Day** and **New Year's Eve music** in every style imaginable: **easy listening, rock, pop, blues, jazz, country, reggae, rap, children's secular** or **religious**. *Please do not send anything that isn't a holiday song.* Published "It Must Have Been the Mistletoe" (single by Justin Wilde/Doug Konecky) from *Christmas Memories* (album), recorded by Barbra Streisand (pop Christmas), by Columbia; "What Made the Baby Cry?" (single by Toby Keith) and "Mr. Santa Claus" (single by James Golseth) from *Casper's Haunted Christmas* soundtrack (album), recorded by Scotty Blevins (Christmas) on Koch International.

TIPS "We only sign one out of every 200 submissions. Please be selective. If a stranger can hum your melody back to you after hearing it twice, it has 'standard' potential. Couple that with a lyric filled with unique, inventive imagery, that stands on its own, even without music. Combine the two elements, and workshop the finished result thoroughly to identify weak points. Submit to us only when the song is polished to perfection. Submit positive lyrics only. Avoid negative themes like 'Blue Christmas'."

COMBUSTION MUSIC

1004 18th Ave. S., Nashville TN 37212. (615)515-5490. **Website:** www.combustionmusic.com. Since opening, Combustion Music has become one of Nashville's most successful independent publishing companies, earning a multitude of platinum LPs and No. 1 singles, both domestically and internationally, and across several genres. Partnered with Atlas Music Publishing.

HOW TO CONTACT Combustion Music does not accept unsolicited material.

MUSIC All genres. Published "Jesus, Take the Wheel," "Use Somebody," "You're Gonna Miss This," and more.

COPPERFIELD MUSIC GROUP/PENNY ANNIE MUSIC (BMI)/TOP BRASS MUSIC (ASCAP)/BIDDY BABY MUSIC (SESAC)

1400 South St., Nashville TN 37212. **E-mail:** hkenbiddy@comcast.net. **Website:** www.copperfieldmusic.com. **Contact:** Ken Biddy.

HOW TO CONTACT Contact hkenbiddy@comcast.net first and obtain permission to submit a demo by

e-mail. Company does not return submissions or accept phone calls. Responds only if interested.

MUSIC Country only. Does not want rap or heavy/metal/rock. Recently published "Daddy Won't Sell the Farm" from *Tattoos and Scars* (album), recorded by Montgomery Gentry (country).

O CORELLI MUSIC GROUP

P.O. Box 2314, Tacoma WA 98401-2314. (253)735-3228. **E-mail:** JerryCorelli@yahoo.com; corellismusicgroup@yahoo.com. **Website:** www.corellimusicgroup.blogspot.com. **Contact:** Jerry Corelli. (BMI/ASCAP) Music publisher, record company (Omega III Records), record producer (Jerry Corelli/Angels Dance Recording Studio) and booking agency (Tone Deaf Booking). Publishes 12 songs/year; publishes 6 new songwriters/year. Staff size: 3. Pays standard royalty.

AFFILIATES My Angel's Songs (ASCAP); Corelli's Music Box (BMI).

HOW TO CONTACT Submit demo by mail. Unsolicited submissions are OK. "No phone calls, e-mails, or letters asking to submit." CD only with no more than 3 songs, lyric sheet and cover letter. "*We do not accept mp3s vie e-mail.* We want love songs with a message and overtly Christian songs. Make sure all material is copyrighted. *You must include SASE or we do not respond!*" Responds in 2 months.

MUSIC Mostly **contemporary Christian, Christian soft rock** and **Christmas**; also **love songs, ballads** and **new country.** Does not want songs without lyrics or lyrics without music. Published "I'm Not Dead Yet" (by Jerry Corelli), "Fried Bologna" (by Jerry Corelli), and "His Name is Jesus" (by Jerry Corelli), all from *I'm Not Dead Yet* (album), released 2010 on Omega III Records.

TIPS "Success is obtained when opportunity meets preparation! If a SASE is not sent with demo, we don't even listen to the demo. Be willing to do a rewrite. Don't send material expecting us to place it with a Top Ten artist. Be practical. Do your songs say what's always been said, except differently? Don't take rejection personally. Always send a #10 self-adhesive envelope for your SASE."

THE CORNELIUS COMPANIES/ GATEWAY ENTERTAINMENT, INC.

Dept. SM, 9 Music Square S., Suite 92, Nashville TN 37203. (615)256-9253. **E-mail:** corneliuscompanies@bellsouth.net; terry@gatewayentertainment.com. **Website:** www.corneliuscompanies.com. (BMI,

ASCAP, SESAC) Music publisher and record producer (Ron Cornelius). Publishes 60-80 songs/year; publishes 2-3 new songwriters/year. Occasionally hires staff writers. Pays standard royalty.

AFFILIATES RobinSparrow Music (BMI), Strummin' Bird Music (ASCAP) and Bridgeway Music (SESAC).

HOW TO CONTACT *Contact by e-mail or call for permission to submit material.* Submit demo package by mail. Unsolicited submissions are OK. "Send demo on CD format only with 2-3 songs." Include SASE. Responds in 2 months.

MUSIC Mostly **country** and **pop**; also **positive country**, **gospel** and **alternative**. Published songs by Confederate Railroad, Faith Hill, David Allen Coe, Alabama and over 50 radio singles in the positive Christian/country format.

TIPS "Looking for material suitable for film."

🌑 CRINGE MUSIC (PRS, MCPS)

The Cedars, Elvington Lane, Hawkinge, Kent CT18 7AD United Kingdom. (01)(303)893-472. **E-mail:** info@cringemusic.co.uk. **Website:** www.cringemusic.co.uk. **Contact:** Christopher Ashman. Music publisher and record company (Red Admiral Records). Estab. 1979. Staff size: 2.

HOW TO CONTACT Submit demo package by e-mail. Unsolicited submissions are OK. Submission materials are not returned. Responds if interested.

MUSIC All styles.

⊘ CURB MUSIC

48 Music Square E., Nashville TN 37203. (615)321-5080. **Website:** www.curb.com. (ASCAP, BMI, SESAC)

⬤ *Curb Music only accepts submissions through reputable industry sources and does not accept unsolicited demos.*

AFFILIATES Mike Curb Music (BMI); Curb Songs (ASCAP); and Curb Congregation Songs (SESAC).

◑ DAYWIND MUSIC PUBLISHING

114A Commerce Ave., Hendersonville TN 37075. (615)826-8101. **E-mail:** info@daywindpublishing. com. **Website:** www.daywindpublishing.com. **Contact:** Rick Shelton, vice president. Since its inception in 1995, Daywind Music Publishing has emerged as the premier source of new songs for the Southern Gospel and Church Print/Choral markets. In early 2012, Daywind expanded publishing to include Christian Contemporary staff and writers and has already made an impressive start to its year including cuts by Hawk Nelson, Hyland, Jamie Slocum and Nate Sallie. DMP boasts of an exclusive staff of 13 prestigious songwriters. Daywind Music Publishing has been blessed with more than 75 Singing News Song of the Year and Gospel Music Association (Dove) nominations, as well as 37 radio singles hitting the top position on the charts. BMI awarded DMP's Christian Taylor Music, Christian Music Publisher of the Year in both 2002 and 2004.

MUSIC Daywind Music Publishing remains committed to the exhortation and encouragement of the church through the advancement of quality Christian music.

DEFINE SOMETHING IN NOTHING MUSIC

11213 W. Baden St., Avondale AZ 85323. (360)421-9225. **E-mail:** definesinm@gmail.com. **Website:** dsinm.weebly.com. **Contact:** Jaime Reynolds. Music agency. Staff Size: 5. Pays 75% of gross revenue.

HOW TO CONTACT Prefers MP3s sent to e-mail only. "Please do not contact for permission, just send your music." Does not return submissions. Responds in 2 weeks if interested.

MUSIC Interested in all styles. "We welcome everything all over the world."

TIPS "Please e-mail a zip file via yousendit.com. No phone calls or mail, no CDs or cassettes."

⊘ DELEV MUSIC CO.

7231 Mansfield Ave., Philadelphia PA 19138-1620. (215)780-0183. **E-mail:** delevmusic@msn.com. **Contact:** William Lucas, president/CEO; Darryl Lucas, A&R. (ASCAP, BMI) Music publisher. Publishes 6-10 songs/year; publishes 6-10 new songwriters/year. Pays standard royalty.

AFFILIATES Sign of the Ram Music (ASCAP) and Delev Music (BMI).

HOW TO CONTACT *Does not accept unsolicited material. Write or call first to obtain permission to submit.* Prefers CDs with 1-4 songs and lyric sheet. "We will not accept certified mail or SASE." Does not return material. Responds in 1-2 months.

MUSIC Mostly **R&B ballads** and **dance-oriented**; also **pop ballads**, **christian/gospel**, **crossover** and **country/western**. We do not accept rap song material. Published "Angel Love" (single by Barbara Heston/Geraldine Fernandez) from *The Silky Sounds of Debbie G* (album), recorded by Debbie G (light R&B/easy listening), released 2000 on Blizzard Records; *Vari-*

ety (album), produced by Barbara Heston, released on Luvya Records; and "Ever Again" by Bernie Williams, released 2003 on SunDazed Records. (Original version of "Ever Again" by Gene Woodbury has been re-released by several record companies, with last cover in Latter 2013.)

TIPS "Persevere regardless if it is sent to our company or any other company. Most of all, no matter what happens, believe in yourself."

DELLA MUSIC PUBLISHING

Della Music Publishing LLC, 509 Mandeville St., New Orleans LA 70117. (917)517-0357. **Fax:** (504)304-4754. **E-mail:** deborahevansmusic@gmail.com. **Website:** https://sites.google.com/site/dellamusicpublishingllc/. **Contact:** Deborah Evans. Deborah Evans started Della Music Publishing in August 2007, and represents both domestic and foreign catalogs. Maintains and promotes the catalogs of many rap and hip hop artists such as Reggie Noble (pka Redman) and Erick Sermon, the Keep On Kicking Music classic reggae catalogue, Sweet River Music, and professional artists and songwriters such as Randy Klein and Anya Singleton. She represents several overseas publishers such as Cee Dee Music from the UK and Editions Ozella from Germany. She is a member of the Association of Independent Music Publishers (AIMP), the Copyright Society of the USA (CSUSA), and the National Music Publishers' Association (NMPA).

DISNEY MUSIC PUBLISHING

500 S. Buena Vista St., Burbank CA 91521. (818)569-3241. **Fax:** (818)845-9705. **Website:** music.disney.com. (ASCAP, BMI)

Part of the Buena Vista Music Group.

AFFILIATES Seven Peaks Music and Seven Summits Music.

HOW TO CONTACT "We cannot accept any unsolicited material."

DOWNTOWN MUSIC PUBLISHING

485 Broadway, 3rd Floor, New York NY 10013. **Website:** www.dmpgroup.com. Established in 2007, Downtown Music Publishing is a leading independent music publisher. Over the past six years, Downtown's catalog has grown to include over 60,000 copyrights, including the works of John Lennon and Yoko Ono, hard rock legends Mötley Crüe, renowned film composer Hans Zimmer, influential punk rockers Social Distortion, pop songstress Ellie Goulding and the

critically acclaimed artist and actor Mos Def. Downtown writers have penned hit singles for artists such as Beyonce, Bruno Mars, Carrie Underwood, Katy Perry, Keith Urban, and Rihanna. Managed by a team of executives with backgrounds in music supervision, advertising, and licensing, Downtown works to match its clients' interests with a broad range of media. In addition to traditional placement in film, TV, advertising, and video games, Downtown excels in digital and mobile licensing, product placement, merchandising, and integrated brand partnerships. Affiliates include Songtrust and MAS: Music and Strategy.

EARTHSCREAM MUSIC PUBLISHING CO.

8375 Westview Dr., Houston TX 77055. **Website:** www.soundartsrecording.com. Music publisher, record company and record producer. Publishes 12 songs/year; publishes 4 new songwriters/year. Pays standard royalty.

Also see the listing for Sound Arts Recording Studio in the Record Producers section of this book.

AFFILIATES Reach For The Sky Music Publishing (ASCAP).

HOW TO CONTACT Submit demo by mail. Unsolicited submissions are OK. Prefers CD with 2-5 songs and lyric sheet. Does not return material. Responds in 6 weeks.

MUSIC Mostly **new rock**, **country**, **blues**. Published "Baby Never Cries" (single by Carlos DeLeon), recorded by Jinkies on Surface Records (pop); "Telephone Road" (single), written and recorded by Mark May (blues) on Icehouse Records; "Do You Remember" (single by Barbara Pennington), recorded by Perfect Strangers on Earth Records (rock), and "Sheryl Crow" (single), recorded by Dr. Jeff and the Painkillers (pop); "Going Backwards" (single), written and recorded by Tony Vega (Gulf swamp blues), released on Red Onion Records.

ELECTRIC MULE PUBLISHING COMPANY (BMI)/NEON MULE MUSIC (ASCAP)

1019 17th Ave. S., Nashville TN 37212. (615)321-4455. **E-mail:** emuleme@aol.com.
MUSIC Country, pop.

EMF PRODUCTIONS

1000 E. Prien Lake Rd., Suite D, Lake Charles LA 70601. (337)474-0435. **Website:** www.emfproductions.com. **Contact:** Ed Fruge, president. (ASCAP) Music publisher and record producer. Pays standard royalty.

HOW TO CONTACT Submit demo package by mail. Unsolicited submissions are OK. Prefers CD or DVDs with 3 of your best songs and lyric sheets. Does not return material. Responds in 6 weeks.

MUSIC Mostly **R&B**, **pop** and **rock**; also **country** and **gospel**.

⊘ EMI MUSIC PUBLISHING

75 Ninth Ave., 4th Floor, New York NY 10011. (212)492-1200. **Fax:** (212)492-1865. Website: www. emimusicpub.com. See website for other offices.

HOW TO CONTACT Does not accept unsolicited material. Only accepts material referred by an attorney, manager, and/or the recommendation of an existing artist. In consortium with Sony/ATV.

MUSIC Published "All I Need" (single) by F. Evans/R. Lawrence/S. Combs), recorded by Faith Evans featuring Puff Daddy on Bad Boy; "You" (by C. Roland/J. Powell), recorded by Jesse Powell on Silas and "I Was" (by C. Black/P. Vassar), recorded by Neal McCoy on Atlantic.

TIPS "Don't bury your songs. Less is more—we will ask for more if we need it. Put your strongest songs first."

ⓞ EMSTONE MUSIC PUBLISHING

P.O. Box 398, Hallandale FL 33008. **E-mail:** webmaster@emstonemusicpublishing.com. **Website:** www. emstonemusicpublishing.com. **Contact:** Mitchell Stone; Madeline Stone. (BMI)

HOW TO CONTACT Submit demo CD by mail with any number of songs. Include a lyrics sheet for each song. Unsolicited submissions are OK. Does not return material. Responds only if interested. "Also check out our sister company at SongwritersBestSong. com." Also accepts demos via e-mail.

MUSIC All types. Published *Greetings from Texas* (2009) (album), by Greetings From Texas; "Gonna Recall My Heart" (written by Dan Jury) from *No Tears* (album), recorded by Cole Seaver and Tammie Darlene, released on CountryStock Records; and "I Love What I've Got" (single by Heather and Paul Turner) from *The Best of Talented Kids* (compilation album) recorded by Gypsy; "My Christmas Card to You" (words and music by Madeline and Mitchell Stone); and "Your Turn to Shine" (words and music by Mitchell Stone).

TIPS "Keep the materials inside your demo package as simple as possible. Just include a brief cover letter (with your contact information) and lyric sheets.

Avoid written explanations of the songs; if your music is great, it'll speak for itself. We only offer publishing contracts to writers whose songs exhibit a spark of genius. Anything less can't compete in the music industry."

◗◖⊛ FIRST TIME MUSIC (PUBLISHING) U.K.

Ebrel House, 2a Penlee Close, Praa Sands, Penzance, Cornwall TR20 9SR, United Kingdom. +44(01736)762826. **E-mail:** panamus@aol.com. **Website:** www.panamamusic.co.uk. Music publisher, record company (Digimix Records Ltd, Rainy Day Records, Mohock Records, Pure Gold Records). Estab. 1986. Publishes 50 songs/year; 20-50 new songwriters/year. Staff size: 5. Hires staff writers. Pays standard royalty of 50%. "We consider established and up-and-coming writers with the right attitude."

AFFILIATES Scamp Music Publishing, Panama Music Library, Musik Image Library, Caribbean Music Library, PSI Music Library, ADN Creation Music Library, Promo Sonor International, Eventide Music, Melody First Music Library, Piano Bar Music Library, Corelia Music Library, Panama Music Ltd, Panama Music Productions, Digimix Worldwide Digital Publishing.

HOW TO CONTACT Submit demo package by mail. Unsolicited submissions are OK. Submit on CD only, "of broadcast transmission quality," with unlimited number of songs/instrumentals and lyric or lead sheets. Responds in 1 month. SAE and IRC required for reply.

FILM & TV Places 200 songs in film and TV/year. "Copyrights and phonographic rights of Panama Music Ltd. and its associated catalog idents have been used and subsist in many productions broadcasts and adverts produced by major and independent production companies, TV, film/video companies, radio broadcasters (not just in the UK, but in various countries worldwide) and by commercial record companies for general release and sale. In the UK and Republic of Ireland they include the BBC networks of national/regional TV and radio, ITV network programs and promotions (Channel 4, Border TV, Granada TV, Tyne Tees TV, Scottish TV, Yorkshire TV, HTV, Central TV, Channel TV, LWT, Meridian TV, Grampian TV, GMTV, Ulster TV, Westcountry TV, Channel TV, Carlton TV, Anglia TV, TV3, RTE (Ireland), Planet TV, Rapido TV, VT4 TV, BBC Worldwide, etc.), independent radio stations, satellite Sky Television

(BskyB), Discovery Channel, Learning Channel, National Geographic, Living Channel, Sony, Trouble TV, UK Style Channel, Hon Cyf, CSI, etc., and cable companies, GWR Creative, Premier, Spectrum FM, Local Radio Partnership, Fox, Manx, Swansea Sound, Mercury, 2CRFM, Broadland, BBC Radio Collection, etc. Some credits include copyrights in programs, films/videos, broadcasts, trailers and promotions such as *Desmond's*, *One Foot in the Grave*, *EastEnders*, *Hale and Pace*, *Holidays from Hell*, *A Touch of Frost*, *999 International*, and *Get Away*."

MUSIC **All styles**. Published "I Get Stoned" (hardcore dance), recorded by AudioJunkie & Stylus, released by EMI records (2009) on *Hardcore Nation 2009*; "Long Way to Go" (country/MOR) on *Under Blue Skies*, recorded by Charlie Landsborough, released on Rosette Records (2008); "Mr Wilson" (folk) from *Only the Willows are Weeping*, released on Digimix Records (2014); "Born to be Free" (progressive rock/goth rock), recorded by Bram Stoker on *Heavy Rock Spectacular*, released by Belle–Marquee Inc., Japan, and many more.

TIPS "Have a professional approach—present well-produced demos. First impressions are important and may be the only chance you get. Writers are advised to join the Guild of International Songwriters and Composers in England (www.songwriters-guild.co.uk and www.myspace.com/guildofsongwriters)."

⊘ FOX MUSIC

Website: www.foxmusic.com. The contributions of Fox Music over the last 70 years transcend the field of film and TV music. Introduced by this department are such monuments of modern culture as "Love is a Many Splendored Thing," "On the Good Ship Lollipop," the score from *Laura* and the theme from *M*A*S*H*.

MUSIC Fox Music does not accept unsolicited materials.

◑ FRICON MUSIC CO.

11 Music Square E., Nashville TN 37203. (615)826-2288. **Fax:** (615)826-0500. **E-mail:** fricon@comcast. net. **Contact:** Terri Fricon, president; Madge Benson, professional manager. Publishes 25 songs/year; publishes 1-2 new songwriters/year. Staff size: 6. Pays standard royalty.

AFFILIATES Fricout Music Co. (ASCAP) and Now and Forever Songs (SESAC).

HOW TO CONTACT *Contact first and obtain permission to submit.* Prefers CD with 3-4 songs and lyric or lead sheet. "Prior permission must be obtained or packages will be returned." Include SASE. Responds in 2 months.

MUSIC Mostly **country**.

○ GLAD MUSIC CO.

14340 Torrey Chase, Suite 380, Houston TX 77014. (281)397-7300. **E-mail:** hwesdaily@gladmusicco.com. **Website:** www.gladmusicco.com. **Contact:** Wes Daily. Music publisher, record company and record producer. Publishes 3 songs/year; publishes 2 new songwriters/year. Staff size: 2. Pays standard royalty.

AFFILIATES Bud-Don (ASCAP), Rayde (SESAC), and Glad Music (BMI).

HOW TO CONTACT Submit via CD or mp3 with 3 songs maximum, lyric sheet and cover letter. Lyric sheet should be folded around CD and submitted in a rigid case and secured with rubber band. Does not return material. Responds in 6 weeks. SASE or e-mail address for reply.

MUSIC Mostly **country**. Does not want weak songs. Published *Love Bug* (album by C. Wayne/W. Kemp), recorded by George Strait, released 1995 on MCA and again in 2014 on his live CD, DVD, and CMT; *Walk Through This World With Me* (album), recorded by George Jones; *Race Is On* (album by D. Rollins), recorded by George Jones, both released 1999 on Asylum; "The Party's Over," "What A Way To Live," and "Night Life" by Willie Nelson.

◐ G MAJOR PUBLISHING

P.O. Box 3331, Fort Smith AR 72913. **E-mail:** Alex@ Gmajor.org. **Website:** https://sites.google.com/a/gmajor.org/www/. **Contact:** Alex Hoover.

HOW TO CONTACT *No unsolicited submissions.* Submit inquiry by mail with SASE. Prefers CD or MP3. Submit up to 3 songs with lyrics. Include SASE. Responds in 4-6 weeks.

MUSIC Mostly **country** and **contemporary Christian**. Published *Set The Captives Free* (album by Chad Little/Jeff Pitzer/Ben Storie), recorded by Sweeter Rain (contemporary Christian), for Cornerstone Television; "Hopes and Dreams" (single by Jerry Glidewell), recorded by Carrie Underwood (country), released on Star Rise; and "Be Still" (single by Chad Little/Dave Romero/Bryan Morse/Jerry Glidewell), recorded CO3 (contemporary Christian), released on Flagship Records.

TIPS "We are looking for 'smash hits' to pitch to the country and Christian markets."

◐⊛ GOODNIGHT KISS MUSIC

10153 1/2 Riverside Dr. #239, Toluca Lake CA 91602. (831)479-9993; (808)331-0707. **Website:** www.goodnightkiss.com; www.smalluses.com. **Contact:** Janet Fisher. (BMI, ASCAP) Publishes 6-8 songs/year; publishes 4-5 new songwriters/year. Pays standard royalty.

○ Goodnight Kiss Music specializes in placing music in movies and TV.

AFFILIATES Scene Stealer Music (ASCAP).

HOW TO CONTACT "Check our website or subscribe to newsletter (www.goodnightkiss.com) to see what we are looking for and to obtain codes. Packages must have proper submission codes or they are discarded." Only accepts material that is requested on the website. Does not return material. Responds in 6 months.

FILM & TV Places 3-5 songs in film/year. Published "I Do, I Do, Love You" (by Joe David Curtis), recorded by Ricky Kershaw in Road Ends; "Bee Charmer's Charmer" (by Marc Tilson) for the MTV movie *Love Song*; "Right When I Left" (by B. Turner/J. Fisher) in the movie *Knight Club*.

MUSIC All modern styles. Published and produced *Addiction: Highs & Lows* (CD), written and recorded by various artists (all styles), released 2004; *Tall Tales of Osama Bin Laden* (CD), written and recorded by various artists (all styles parody), released 2004; and *Rythm of Honor* (CD), written and recorded by various artists (all styles), slated release 2005, all on Goodnight Kiss Records.

TIPS "The absolute best way to keep apprised of the company's needs is to subscribe to the online newsletter. Only specifically requested material is accepted, as listed in the newsletter (what the industry calls us for is what we request from writers). We basically use an SGA contract, and there are never fees to be considered for specific projects or albums. However, we are a real music company, and the competition is just as fierce as with the majors."

⊘ GREEN HILLS MUSIC GROUP

P.O. Box 159298, Nashville TN 37215. **Website:** www.greenhillsmusicgroup.com. Green Hills Music Group, a boutique-style home for exceptional songwriters, represents the music of such hit makers as Bob Regan, Bonnie Baker, Georgia Middleman, Rick Giles, Steve Williams, and Paul Duncan. Green Hills has had songs recorded by numerous artists, including Rascal Flatts, George Strait, Bomshel, Hunter Hayes, Bucky Covington, Luke Bryan, Jake Owen, Jimmy Wayne, Claire Lynch, Edens Edge, Mark Chesnutt and The Derailers.

HOW TO CONTACT Green Hills Music Group is not currently accepting unsolicited material.

MUSIC Country.

⊘ R L HAMMEL ASSOCIATES, INC.

P.O. Box 531, Alexandria IN 46001. **Website:** www.rl-hammel.com. **E-mail:** rlh@rlhammel.com. **Contact:** A&R Department. President: Randal L. Hammel. Music publisher, record producer and consultant. Estab. 1974. Staff size: 3-5. Pays standard royalty. "Consultants to the Music, Recording & Entertainment Industries."

AFFILIATES LADNAR Music (ASCAP) and LEMMAH Music (BMI).

HOW TO CONTACT Not accepting unsolicited submissions at this time.

MUSIC Mostly **pop, R&B** and **Christian**; also **MOR, light rock, pop country** and **feature film title cuts**. Produced/arranged *The Wedding Collection Series* for WORD Records. Published *Lessons For Life* (album by Kelly Hubbell/Jim Boedicker) and *I Just Want Jesus* (album by Mark Condon), both recorded by Kelly Connor, released on iMPACT Records. Produced major oratorio "Testament" written by David Featherstone.

◖◐⊛ HEUPFERD MUSIKVERLAG GMBH

Ringwaldstr. 18, Dreieich 63303 Germany. **E-mail:** heupferd@t-online.de. **Website:** www.heupferd-musik.de. **Contact:** Christian Winkelmann, general manager. Music publisher and record company (Viva La Difference). GEMA. Publishes 30 songs/year. Staff size: 3. Pays "royalties after GEMA distribution plan."

AFFILIATES *Song Bücherei* (book series). "Vive La Difference!" (label).

HOW TO CONTACT Does not accept unsolicited submissions.

FILM & TV Places 1 song in film/year. Published "El Grito Y El Silencio" (by Thomas Hickstein), recorded by Tierra in *Frauen sind was Wunderbares*.

MUSIC Mostly **folk, jazz** and **fusion**; also **New Age, rock** and **ethnic music**. Published "Mi Mundo" (single by Denise M'Baye/Matthias Furstenberg) from *Havana—Vamos A Ver* (album), recorded by Havana (Latin), released 2003 on Vive La Difference; printed *Andy Irvine: Aiming For the Heart—Irish Song Affairs*, released in 2007; Jake Walton: *Sunlight and Shade—Celtic Song Affairs*, released in 2014.

◎⊘ HICKORY LANE PUBLISHING AND RECORDING

19854 Butternut Lane, Pitt Meadows BC V3Y 2S7 Canada. (604)465-1258. **E-mail:** hickorylanerecords@shaw.ca. **Website:** chrisurbanski.weebly.com. **Contact:** Chris Urbanski. (ASCAP, SOCAN) Music publisher, record company and record producer. Estab. 1988. Hires staff writers. Publishes 30 songs/year; publishes 5 new songwriters/year. Pays standard royalty.

HOW TO CONTACT Does not accept unsolicited submissions.

MUSIC Mostly **country** and **country rock**. Published "Just Living For Today" (single by Chris Urbanski), recorded by Chris Michaels (country), released 2005 on Hickory Lane Records; "This is My Sons" (single by Tyson Avery/Chris Urbanski/Alex Bradshaw), recorded by Chris Michaels (country), released 2005 on Hickory Lane Records; "Stubborn Love" (single by Owen Davies/Chris Urbanski/John Middleton), recorded by Chris Michaels (country), released 2005 on Hickory Lane Records.

TIPS "Send us a professional-quality demo with the vocals upfront. We are looking for hits, and so are the major record labels we deal with. Be original in your approach; don't send us a cover tune."

◎⊛ HIP SON MUSIC

Boston MA. **E-mail:** info@hipsonmusic.com. **Website:** www.hipsonmusic.com. Hip Son Music is a music publishing, music production and record company based in Boston. "Both Hip Son Music and Hip Son Publishing (BMI) work with talented music artists, producers, songwriters and performers involved in electronic, world, alternative and pop music. Our vocal and instrumental music catalog has been licensed for various movies, documentaries and TV shows on the networks including MTV, VH1, Fox TV, BBC, and ITV UK."

MUSIC Hip Son Music offers instrumental and vocal electronic and pop music for use in TV, film, TV commercials, Flash presentations, ring tones and other digital media. Our vocal and instrumental music catalog has been licensed for various movies and TV shows including: independent movies *Exploring Love, Road To Victory, Ghost In Cabin*, MTV shows (*The Real World, Road Rules, MADE, RR/RW Challenge, Pimp My Ride, Making the Band, Undressed*), VH1

(*Band Reunited, Born To Diva*), Fox TV (*Girl Next Door*—Playboy special), BBC (*The World*), featured in the documentary *Picture Me Enemy* (the winner of Philadelphia's Film Festival), on Flash movies. DVD products and promo campaigns produced by Berkleemusic.

◎ HITSBURGH MUSIC CO.

P.O. Box 1431, 233 N. Electra, Gallatin TN 37066. (615)452-0324. **Contact:** Harold Gilbert. Publishes 12 songs/year. Staff size: 4. Pays standard royalty.

AFFILIATES 7th Day Music (BMI).

HOW TO CONTACT Submit demo by mail. Unsolicited submissions are OK. Prefers cassette or quality videocassette with 2-4 songs and lead sheet. Prefers studio produced demos. Include SASE. Responds in 6 weeks.

MUSIC Mostly **country gospel** and **MOR**. Published "That Kind'a Love" (single by Kimolin Crutchet and Dan Serafini), from *Here's Cissy* (album), recorded by Cissy Crutcher (MOR), released 2005 on Vivaton; "Disorder at the Border" (single), written and recorded by Donald Layne, released 2001 on Southern City; and "Blue Tears" (single by Harold Gilbert/Elaine Harmon), recorded by Hal, released 2006 (reissue) on Southern City.

◉⊘ HORIPRO ENTERTAINMENT GROUP

Nashville TN. **Website:** www.horipro.com. HoriPro Entertainment Group, Inc. (H.E.G.) is a full-service, independent music publisher. Offering songwriter development, song pitching/plugging, music licensing, record production and first-class administration services, HoriPro Entertainment Group provides a total publishing solution for its valued clients.

HOW TO CONTACT HoriPro does not accept unsolicited material.

MUSIC Primarily a foreign music publisher, but has worked with artists such as KISS, Marilyn Manson, REO Speedwagon, George Strait, and more.

IDOL PUBLISHING

P.O. Box 140344, Dallas TX 75214. (214)321-8890. **E-mail:** info@idolrecords.com. **Website:** www.IdolRecords.com. **Contact:** Erv Karwelis, president. Record publisher. Releases 30 singles, 80 LPs, 20 EPs and 10-15 CDs/year. Pays negotiable royalty to artists on contract; negotiable rate to publisher per song on record.

HOW TO CONTACT See website for submission policy. No phone calls or e-mail follow-ups.

MUSIC Mostly **rock**, **pop**, and **alternative**. Released *The Boys Named Sue—The Hits Vol. Sue!* (album), The O's—*We are the Os* (album), Little Black Dress—*Snow in June* (album), *The Man* recorded by Sponge (alternative); *Movements* (album), recorded by Black Tie Dynasty (alternative); *In Between Days* (album), recorded by Glen Reynolds (rock), all released 2006/2006 on Idol Records. Other artists include Flickerstick, DARYL, Centro-matic, The Deathray Davies, GBH, PPT, The Crash that Took Me, Shibboleth, Trey Johnson.

⊘ IMAGEM MUSIC

229 W. 28th St., Floor 11, New York NY 10001. (212)699-6588. **Fax:** (212)358-5309. **E-mail:** us@imagem.com. **Website:** us.imagemmusic.com. "In a publishing world where quantity seems to trump quality, where rollups, mergers and cost cutting dominate headlines, Imagem Music stands alone as a true independent publishing home for great talent. We are a place where creativity meets proactivity, where works of art meet worth ethic."

HOW TO CONTACT Imagem Music does not accept unsolicited material.

MUSIC Any genre. Has worked with artists such as Phil Collins, Genesis, M.I.A., Pink Floyd, Vampire Weekend, Daft Punk, and more.

⊘ INGROOVES

55 Francisco St., #710, San Francisco CA 94113. (415)489-7000. **E-mail:** info@ingrooves.com. **Website:** www.ingrooves.com. "INgrooves Music Group is committed to powering creativity in today's dynamic music marketplace by providing the best distribution, marketing and rights management tools and services to content creators and owners. We develop state-of-the-art, cost-efficient and scalable technology platforms, and our partners benefit from our experienced, knowledgeable people, our unparalleled commitment to customer service and our thoughtful marketing solutions that drive results. We aspire to be the most transparent and solution-driven partner for all of the labels and artists we work with. We believe this approach helps us and our partners succeed today and for years to come."

HOW TO CONTACT "If you are interested in partnering with INgrooves, fill out the online form at www.ingrooves.com. A representative will get back to you ASAP."

◐◑ INSIDE RECORDS/OK SONGS

St.-Jacobsmarkt 76 (B1), 2000, Antwerp, Belgium. 32+(0)3-226-77-19. **Fax:** 32+(0)3-226-78-05. **E-mail:** info@inside-records.be. **Website:** www.inside-records.be. Music publisher and record company. Publishes 50 songs/year; publishes 30-40 new songwriters/year. Hires staff writers. Royalty varies "depending on teamwork."

HOW TO CONTACT Submit demo by mail. Unsolicited submissions are OK. Prefers CD copy with complete name, address, telephone and fax number. SAE and IRC. Responds in 2 months.

MUSIC Mostly **dance**, **pop** and **MOR contemporary**; also **country**, **reggae** and **Latin**. Published *Fiesta De Bautiza* (album by Andres Manzana); *I'm Freaky* (album by Maes-Predu'homme-Robinson); and *Heaven* (album by KC One-King Naomi), all on Inside Records.

◐⊘✦ INTOXYGENE SARL

27 rue Eugène carrière, Paris, France. **E-mail:** infos@intoxygene.com. **Website:** www.intoxygene.com; www.theyounggods.com. **Contact:** Patrick Jammes. Music publisher and record company. Staff size: 1. Publishes 30 songs/year. Pays 50% royalty.

HOW TO CONTACT Does not accept unsolicited submissions.

FILM & TV Places 3–5 songs in film and in TV/year.

MUSIC Mostly **new industrial** and **metal**, **lounge**, **electronic**, and **ambient**. Publisher for Peepingtom (trip-hop), Djaimin (house), Missa Furiosa by Thierry Zaboitzeff (progressive), The Young Gods (alternative), Alex Carter, Love Motel, Steve Tallis, and lo'n, amongst others.

◐◑ ISLAND CULTURE MUSIC PUBLISHERS

7005 Bordeaux, St. John 00830-9510, U.S. Virgin Islands. **E-mail:** islandking@islandkingrecords.com. **Website:** www.islandkingrecords.com. (BMI) Music publisher and record company (Island King Records). Estab. 1996. Publishes 10 songs/year; publishes 3 new songwriters/year. Hires staff songwriters. Staff size: 3. Pays standard royalty.

HOW TO CONTACT Submit demo package by mail. Unsolicited submissions are OK. Prefers CD with 8 songs and lyric sheet. Send bio and 8"×10" glossy. Does not return material. Responds in 1 month.

MUSIC Mostly **reggae**, **calypso**, and **zouk**; also **house**. Published *De Paris a Bohicon* (album), recorded by

Rasbawa (reggae), released 2006 on Island King Records; "Jah Give Me Life" (single by Chubby) from *Best of Island King* (album), recorded by Chubby (reggae), released 2003 on Island King Records; "When People Mix Up" (single by Lady Lex/L. Monsanto/Chubby) and "I Am Real" (single by L. Monsanto) from *Best of Island King* (album), recorded by Lady Lex (reggae), released 2003 on Island King Records.

○ IVORY PEN ENTERTAINMENT

P.O. Box 1097, Laurel MD 20725. **E-mail:** ivorypen@comcast.net. (ASCAP) Professional Managers: Steven Lewis (R&B, pop/rock, inspirational); Sonya Lewis (AC, dance) Wandaliz Colon (Latin, Ethnic); Cornelius Roundtree (gospel/inspirational). Music publisher. Publishes 10 songs/year. Staff size: 4. Pays standard royalty.

HOW TO CONTACT E-mail electronic press kit or MP3 no less than 128k. Unsolicited submissions are OK. Prefers CD with 3-5 songs and cover letter. Does not return material. Responds in 4 months. "Don't forget contact info with e-mail address for faster response! Always be professional when you submit your work to any company. Quality counts."

MUSIC Mostly **R&B**, **dance**, **pop/rock**, **Latin**, **adult contemporary**, and **inspirational**. Published Ryan Vetter (single), writer recorded by Alan Johnson (pop/rock), released on Ivory Pen Entertainment; and "Mirror" (single), by Angel Demone, on Vox Angel Inc./Ivory Pen Entertainment.

TIPS "Learn your craft. Always deliver high-quality demos. Remember, if you don't invest in yourself, don't expect others to invest in you. Ivory Pen Entertainment is a music publishing company that caters to the new songwriter, producer, and aspiring artist. We also place music tracks (no vocals) with artists for release."

① JANA JAE MUSIC

P.O. Box 35726, Tulsa OK 74153. (918)786-8896. **E-mail:** janajae@janajae.com. **Website:** www.janajae.com. **Contact:** Kathleen Pixley, secretary. Music publisher, record company (Lark Record Productions, Inc.) and record producer (Lark Talent and Advertising). Publishes 5-10 songs/year; publishes 1-2 new songwriters/year. Staff size: 8. Pays standard royalty.

HOW TO CONTACT Submit demo by mail. Unsolicited submissions are OK. Prefers CD or DVD with 3-4 songs and typed lyric and lead sheet if possible. Does not return material. Responds only if accepted for use.

MUSIC Mostly **country**, **bluegrass**, **jazz** and **instrumentals** (**classical** or **country**). Published *Mayonnaise* (album by Steve Upfold), recorded by Jana Jae; and *Let the Bible Be Your Roadmap* (album by Irene Elliot), recorded by Jana Jae, both on Lark Records.

JEROME PRODUCTIONS

5300 Peachtree Rd., Suite 1306, Atlanta GA 30341-2434. (770)982-7055. **Website:** www.jeromepromotions.com. **Contact:** Bill Jerome, president. (BMI) Staff size: 3. Pays standard royalty of 50%.

HOW TO CONTACT Contact first and obtain permission to submit a demo. Include CD or MP3 and cover letter. Does not return submissions. Responds in 1 week.

MUSIC Top 40, alt country. Also **alternative**, **crossover R&B** and **hip-hop**. Does not want rap, gospel, country. Published "She's My Girl," written by Lefkowith/Rogers, recorded by Hifi on Red/Generic (2009).

◯ QUINCY JONES MUSIC

6671 Sunset Blvd., #1574A, Los Angeles CA 90028. (323)957-6601. **Fax:** (323)962-5231. **E-mail:** info@quincyjonesmusic.com. **Website:** www.quincyjonesmusic.com. (ASCAP)

HOW TO CONTACT Quincy Jones Music does not accept unsolicited submissions.

MUSIC The Quincy Jones Music Publishing catalogue is home to over 1,600 titles spanning five decades of music covering numerous musical genres including jazz, R&B, pop, rock 'n' roll, Brazilian, alternative and hip-hop. Over the years, such legendary performers as Frank Sinatra, Count Basie, Sarah Vaughan, Louis Jordan, Lesley Gore, Barbra Streisand, Billy Eckstine and Tony Bennett have recorded our songs. We remain a presence in today's market by way of such artists as Michael Jackson, 98°, Tevin Campbell, K-Ci & Jo Jo, George Benson, Ivan Lins, S.W.V., Vanessa Williams, Patti Austin, The Manhattan Transfer, James Ingram, Barry White and Ray Charles. Our current roster of talent includes lyricists, composers, musicians, performers and producers.

○ PATRICK JOSEPH MUSIC

1012 18th Ave. S., Nashville TN 37125. **E-mail:** pat@pjmsongs.com. **Website:** www.songspub.com/PJM. **Contact:** Pat Higdon. In August of 2012, music publishing veteran, Pat Higdon relaunched his Patrick Joseph Music brand in the Nashville marketplace. The renewal of this successful publishing company marks a new partnership with New York and Los Angeles-based SONGS Music Publishing. Patrick Joseph Music will be dedicated to writer service, actively signing new writers, as well as developing the reach for existing catalogs and songs.

KAUPPS & ROBERT PUBLISHING CO.

P.O. Box 5474, Stockton CA 95205. (209)948-8186. **E-mail:** kauppsrobertbmi@yahoo.com. (BMI) Melissa Glenn, A&R coordinator (all styles). Production Manager (country, pop, rock): Rick Webb. Professional Manager (country, pop, rock): Bruce Bolin. President: Nancy L. Merrihew. Music publisher, record company (Kaupp Records), manager and booking agent (Merri-Webb Productions and Most Wanted Bookings). Estab. 1990. Publishes 15-20 songs/year; publishes 5 new songwriters/year. Pays standard royalty.

HOW TO CONTACT *Write first and obtain permission to submit.* Prefers cassette or VHS videocassette (if available) with 3 songs maximum and lyric sheet. "If artist, send PR package." Include SASE. Responds in 6 months.

MUSIC Mostly **country**, **R&B** and **A/C rock**; also **pop**, **rock** and **gospel**. Published "Rushin' In" (singles by N. Merrihew/B. Bolin), recorded by Valerie; "Goin Postal" (singles by N. Merrihew/B. Bolin), recorded by Bruce Bolin (country/rock/pop); and "I Gotta Know" (single by N. Merrihew/B. Bolin), recorded by Cheryl (country/rock/pop), all released on Kaupp Records.

TIPS "Know what you want, set a goal, focus in on your goals, be open to constructive criticism, polish tunes and keep polishing."

LAUREN KEISER MUSIC PUBLISHING

St. Louis MO (203)560-9436. **E-mail:** info@laurenkeisermusic.com. **Website:** www.laurenkeisermusic.com. **Contact:** Lauren Keiser. Veteran music publisher Lauren Keiser started Lauren Keiser Music Publishing (ASCAP) and Keiser Classical (BMI) from the purchase of MMB Music's assets of St. Louis and is joining it with new deals and editions he is creating and developing. His almost 40 years of being involved with Alfred, Cherry Lane and Carl Fischer Music publishing companies has provided a basis and foundation for a new music publishing company based on his experience. The firm publishes performance and music copyrights of gifted concert and symphonic composers in addition to producing publications of talented writers and artists.

MUSIC Classical composers represented include Claude Baker, David Baker, Daniel Dorff, Peng-Peng Gong, Sheila Silver, David Schiff, David Stock, George Walker, and many more.

KINGSPIRIT MUSIC

(615)712-7870. **E-mail:** kingspiritmusic@gmail.com. **Website:** www.kingspiritmusic.com. **Contact:** Todd Wilkes, president. Nearly 30 years after achieving over 400 cuts leading to more than 100 million album sales to date, owner and founder Todd Wilkes combined his vast knowledge of publishing and strong industry relationships in 2012 to create KingSpirit Music. "KingSpirit Music is a dynamic independent music publishing company, consulting company, artist development and independent song-pitching company that focuses on the representation of songwriters, artists and other publishing affiliations to secure the correct placement of their music. KingSpirit Music is known for delivering only the highest quality of songs to artists, labels, managers and producers. Upon the company's commencement, KingSpirit partnered with Nashville's Universal Music Publishing Group, and jointly signed Kalisa Ewing to an exclusive worldwide publishing deal."

TIPS "Be a sponge. Listen. I have learned more by listening than talking. The music business is fundamentally no different really from any other business… you have to show up and be ready to answer the door when opportunity knocks. Know your weaknesses and strengthen them."

KOBALT

8201 Beverly Blvd., 4th Floor, Suite 400, Los Angeles CA 90048. (310)967-3087. **Fax:** (310)967-3089. **E-mail:** info@kobaltmusic.com. **Website:** www.kobaltmusic.com. "Kobalt Music Publishing, Kobalt Label Services and Kobalt Neighbouring Rights divisions each offer a modern alternative to the traditional music business model, empowering creators with flexible contracts, ownership, control, and total transparency. We represent over 8,000 artists and songwriters, 600,000 songs and 500 publishing companies, servicing our clients with global licensing management, works and rights distribution, royalty collection and processing, online data and royalty statements, creative services, synch and brand partnerships, record release management and marketing."

HOW TO CONTACT Kobalt does not accept unsolicited material.

MUSIC All genres. Published music by Big and Rich, Busta Rhymes, Eddie Vedder, Gotye, Kelly Clarkson, Kid Cudi, LMFAO, Maroon 5, Paul McCartney, and more.

LAKE TRANSFER PRODUCTIONS & MUSIC

11300 Hartland St., North Hollywood CA 91605. (818)508-7158. **E-mail:** info@laketransfer.com. **Website:** www.laketransfer.com. **Contact:** Jim Holvay, professional manager (pop, R&B, soul); Tina Antoine (hip-hop, rap); Steve Barri Cohen (alternative rock, R&B). Music publisher and record producer (Steve Barri Cohen). Estab. 1989. Publishes 11 songs/year; publishes 3 new songwriters/year. Staff size: 6. Pay "depends on agreement, usually 50% split."

AFFILIATES Lake Transfer Music (ASCAP) and Transfer Lake Music (BMI).

MUSIC Mostly **alternative pop**, **R&B/hip-hop** and **dance**. Does not want country and western, classical, New Age, jazz or swing. Published "Tu Sabes Que Te Amo (Will You Still Be There)" (single by Steve Barri Cohen/Rico) from *Rico: The Movement II* (album), recorded by Rico (rap/hip-hop), released 2004 on Lost Empire/Epic-Sony; "When Water Flows" (single by Steve Barri Cohen/Sheree Brown/Terry Dennis) from *Sheree Brown "83"* (album), recorded by Sheree Brown (urban pop), released 2004 on BBEG Records (a division of Saravels, LLC); and "Fair Game" (single by LaTocha Scott/Steve Barri Cohen) *Soundtrack from the movie Fair Game* (album), recorded by LaTocha Scott (R&B/hip-hop), released 2004 on Raw Deal Records, College Park, Georgia. "All our staff are songwriters/producers. Jim Holvay has written hits like 'Kind of a Drag' and 'Hey Baby They're Playin our Song' for the Buckinghams. Steve Barri Cohen has worked with every one from Evelyn 'Champagne' King (RCA), Phantom Planets (Epic), Meredith Brooks (Capitol) and Dre (Aftermath/Interscope).

TIPS "Trends change, but it's still about the song. Make sure your music and lyrics have a strong (POV) point of view."

LEVY MUSIC PUBLISHING

22509 Carbon Mesa Road, Malibu CA 90265. (310)571-5389. **E-mail:** info@levymusic.tv. **Website:** levymusic.tv. Levy Music Publishing, LLC. is a companion entity to the Levy Entertainment Group. With over 400 artists and composers our clients are given the option to easily license all types of music from our exclusive publishing catalog. Longstanding relationships with major and indie record labels and music publishers, ensuring the most excellent and affordable results.

HOW TO CONTACT Submit songs online through 1-800-PLAY.com.

MUSIC "Levy Entertainment Group & Levy Music Publishing are based from The Studio Malibu Estate. Many of the biggest names in entertainment have recently utilized our studio & other services provided. Including James Cameron, Ron Howard, Nicki Minaj, Britney Spears & Sean Combs just to name a few."

LITA MUSIC

P.O. Box 40251, Nashville TN 37204. (615)269-8682. **Fax:** (615)269-8929. **E-mail:** justinpeters@songsfortheplanet.com; songsfortheplanet@songsfortheplanet.com; newwritersubmission@songsfortheplanet.com. **Website:** songsfortheplanet.com. **Contact:** Justin Peters. (ASCAP)

AFFILIATES Justin Peters Music, Platinum Planet Music and Tourmaline (BMI).

HOW TO CONTACT Contact via e-mail, and a detailed submission policy will be sent.

MUSIC Mostly **country**, **classic rock**, **Southern rock**, **inspirational AC Pop**, **Southern gospel/Christian** and **worship songs**. Published "The Bottom Line" recorded by Charley Pride on Music City Records (written by Art Craig, Drew Bourke, and Justin Peters); "No Less Than Faithful" (single by Don Pardoe/Joel Lyndsey), recorded by Ann Downing on Daywind Records, Jim Bullard on Genesis Records and Melody Beizer (#1 song) on Covenant Records; "No Other Like You" (single by Mark Comden/Paula Carpenter), recorded by Twila Paris and Tony Melendez (#5 song) on Starsong Records; "Making A New Start" and "Invincible Faith" (singles by Gayle Cox), recorded by Kingdom Heirs on Sonlite Records; "I Don't Want To Go Back" (single by Gayle Cox), recorded by Greater Vision on Benson Records; and "HE HAD MERCY ON ME" (by Constance and Justin Peters) recorded by Shining Grace.

LYRIC HOUSE PUBLISHING

6266 Sunset Blvd., Suite B, Hollywood CA 90028. (323)505-6339. **Website:** www.lyrichouseco.com. Lyric House is a full-service music publishing and licensing company. Offers creative and administrative publishing services for bands, artists, and songwriters, both nationally and internationally.

HOW TO CONTACT Submit through online contact form. Listens to every submission, but unable to respond to everyone due to the volume of submissions. Include links to recorded music. Accepts lyric-only submissions.

MUSIC All genres. Catalog available online.

○ M & T WALDOCH PUBLISHING, INC.

4803 S. Seventh St., Milwaukee WI 53221. **Contact:** Timothy J. Waldoch, creative management (rockabilly, pop, country), vice president; Mark T. Waldoch, professional manager (country, top 40). (BMI) Publishes 2-3 songs/year; publishes 2-3 new songwriters/year. Staff size: 2. Pays standard royalty.

HOW TO CONTACT Submit demo package by mail. Unsolicited submissions are OK. Prefers CD with 3-6 songs and lyric or lead sheet. Include SASE. Responds in 3 months.

MUSIC Mostly **country/pop**, **rock**, **top 40 pop**; also **melodic metal, dance, R&B**. Does not want rap. Published "It's Only Me" and "Let Peace Rule the World" (by Kenny LePrix), recorded by Brigade on SBD Records (rock).

TIPS "Study the classic pop songs from the 1950s through the present time. There is a reason why good songs stand the test of time. Today's hits will be tomorrow's classics. Send your best well-crafted, polished song material."

⊘ ♥ MAJOR BOB MUSIC

(615)329-4150. **Fax:** (615)329-1021. **Website:** www.majorbob.com. **Contact:** Tina Crawford, director of A&R. "Bob Doyle began his music publishing company with a firm belief in his heart that the American dream could still be realized. So he left a safe, comfortable job as director of member relations at ASCAP where he had 7 years tenure and mortgaged his home for the start-up funds to pursue his dream. Armed with a deep conviction in a then-unknown songwriter named Garth Brooks, Doyle began to build a collection of musical copyrights that he believed in. Today those copyrights have been recorded by country, R&B, soul and pop artists and heard in movies, TV and videos throughout the world. Systematically, Doyle chose songwriters he could nurture and teach the intricacies of the craft of songwriting. Instead of joining the wave of today's corporate consolidation mentality, Doyle has chosen not to sell his independent publishing group. He continues to carefully build his publishing interests and partner with both new and seasoned songwriters. The publishing group has accumulated over 50 awards from performing rights organizations including Song of the Year for 'The Fool,' a song penned by 3 struggling songwriters who had never had a hit previously. Doyle's songs have been on over 30 platinum and gold certified albums in the U.S., representing units sold of over 130 million records."

MUSIC Kenny Chesney's "There Goes My Life," Rascal Flatts' "I Melt," "Take Me There," and "Fast Cars & Freedom," and cuts ranging from The Plain White T's to Carrie Underwood. Garth Brooks has written 14 of his 25 No. 1 singles for Doyle's publishing company.

◐ MANY LIVES MUSIC PUBLISHERS (SOCAN)

RR #1, Kensington PE C0B 1M0 Canada. (902)432-0006. **E-mail:** musicpublisher@amajorsound.com; paul@amajorsound.com. **Website:** www.amajorsound.com/manylivespublishers.html. **Contact:** Paul C. Milner, publisher; Don Coleman, A&R. "Owners of Shell Lane Studio (www.shelllanestudio.com), complete in-house production facility." Pays standard royalty.

HOW TO CONTACT Submit demo by mail, myspace, or SonicBids. Unsolicited submissions are OK. Prefers CD and lyric sheet (lead sheet if available). Does not return material. Responds in 3 months if interested.

MUSIC All styles. *Six Pack EP* and *Colour* (album), written and recorded by Chucky Danger (Pop/Rock), released 2005 on Landwash Entertainment. Chucky Danger's *Colour* album was named Winner Best Pop Recording at the East Coast Music Awards 2006, "Sweet Symphony" was nominated for Single of the Year, and Chucky Danger was nominated for Best New Group. Released *Temptation* (album by various writers), arrangement by Paul Milner, Patrizia, Dan Cutrona (rock/opera), released 2003 on United One Records; *The Edge Of Emotion* (album by various writers), arrangement by Paul Milner, Patrizia, Dan Cutrona (rock/opera), released 2006 on Nuff entertainment /United One Records. The single "Temptation" won a SOCAN #1 award. *Saddle River Stringband* (album) written and recorded by The Saddle River Stringband (Bluegrass) released on Panda Digital/Save As Music 2007. Winners of best Bluegrass recording East Coast Music Awards 2007. *Pat Deighan and the Orb Weavers* (album) "In A Fever In A Dream" (Alternative Rock) written by Pat Deighan, released on Sandbar Music April 2008.

MATERIAL WORTH PUBLISHING

46 First St., Walden NY 12586. (845)778-7768. **E-mail:** materialworthpub@aol.com. **Website:** www.material-worth.com. **Contact:** Frank Sardella, owner. (ASCAP) Music publisher. Staff size: 3. Pays standard royalty of 50%.

HOW TO CONTACT *E-mail or visit website for how to obtain permission to submit. Must have permission before sending. Do not call first.* "If your material is on the web, please provide a link so we may check it directly." Prefers MP3 or online player. CD, lyric sheet, and cover letter also are accepted; "no cassette tapes please." Does not return submissions. Responds in 6–8 weeks.

MUSIC Mostly **female pop** or **pop/country crossover**, **singer-songwriter**, **male pop alternative rock**.

MAUI ARTS & MUSIC ASSOCIATION/ SURVIVOR RECORDS/TEN OF DIAMONDS MUSIC

P.O. Box 344, Wailuku, Maui HI 96793. **Website:** www.dreammaui.org. Music publisher and record producer. Estab. 1974. Publishes 1-2 artists/year. Staff size: 2. Pays standard royalty.

HOW TO CONTACT Send e-mail with a little about yourself or your group (pictures or a video of you performing, your music genre, a brief bio) and your best contact information. Subject line: Musician.

MUSIC Mostly **pop**, **country**, **R&B**, and **New Age**. Does not want rock. Published "In the Morning Light" (by Jack Warren), recorded by Jason (pop ballad); "Before the Rain" (by Giles Feldscher), recorded by Jason (pop ballad), both on *Survivor*; and "Then I Do" (single), written and recorded by Lono, released on Ono Music.

TIPS "Looking for a great single only! Surprise us!"

MCCLURE & TROWBRIDGE PUBLISHING, LTD. (ASCAP, BMI)

P.O. Box 148548, Nashville TN 37214. (615)504-8435. **E-mail:** manager@trowbridgeplanetearth.com. **Website:** trowbridgeplanetearth.com. Music publisher, record label (JIP Records), and production company (George McClure, producer). Publishes 35 songs/year. Publishes 5 new songwriters/year. Staff size: 8. Pays standard royalty of 50%.

HOW TO CONTACT *Follow directions ONLINE ONLY—obtain Control Number to submit a demo via U.S. mail.* Requires CD with 1-5 songs, lyric sheet, and

cover letter. Does not return submissions. Responds in 3 weeks if interested.

MUSIC Country, gospel, roots and swing. Publisher of "Women in Country and Band of Writers" (BOW) series. Published "Experience (Should Have Taught Me)" album 2010 on JIP Records; *The Lights Of Christmas* album; "Playboy Swing," released 2008 on JIP Records; "Miles Away" (single) on Discovery Channel's "The Deadliest Catch"; and "Playboy Swing," released 2008 on JIP Records.

JIM MCCOY MUSIC

25 Troubadour Lane, Berkeley Springs WV 25411. **Website:** www.troubadourlounge.com. **Contact:** Bertha and Jim McCoy, owners. Music publisher, record company (Winchester Records) and record producer (Jim McCoy Productions). Publishes 20 songs/year; publishes 3-5 new songwriters/year. Pays standard royalty.

AFFILIATES New Edition Music (BMI).

HOW TO CONTACT Submit demo by mail with lyric sheet. Unsolicited submissions are OK. Prefers cassette or CD with 6 songs. Include SASE. Responds in 1 month.

MUSIC Mostly **country**, **country/rock** and **rock**; also **bluegrass** and **gospel**. Published *Jim McCoy and Friends Remember Ernest Tubb*; "She's the Best" recorded by Matt Hahn on Troubadour Records (written by Jim McCoy); "Shadows on My Mind" recorded by Sandy Utley (written by Jim McCoy), "Rock and Roll Hillbilly Redneck Girl" recorded by Elaine Arthur (written by Jim McCoy), released in 2007.

MCJAMES MUSIC, INC.

1724 Stanford St., Suite B, Santa Monica CA 90404. (310)712-1916. **Fax:** (419)781-6644. **E-mail:** tim@mcjamesmusic.com; steven@mcjamesmusic.com. **Website:** www.mcjamesmusic.com. **Contact:** Tim Jame; Steven McClintock. (BMI) Writers include: Kevin Fisher, Franki Love, Pamela Phillips Oland, Stephen Petree, Jeremy Dawson, Chad Petree, Brian Stoner, Cathy-Anne McClintock, Tim James, Steven McClintock, Ryan Lawhon. Publishes 50 songs/year. Staff size: 4. Pays standard royalty. Does administration and collection for all foreign markets for publishers and writers.

AFFILIATES 37 Songs (ASCAP) and McJames Music, Inc. (BMI) (Sequence 37 SESAC)

HOW TO CONTACT *Only accepts material referred by a reputable industry source.* Prefers CD with 2 songs and cover letter. Does not return material. Responds in 6 months.

FILM & TV Places 2 songs in film and 3 songs in TV/year. Music supervisor: Tim James/Steven McClintock. *Blood and Chocolate, 3 Day Weekend, Dirty Sexy Money, Brothers and Sisters, Dancing with the Stars, Dexter, Always Sunny in Philadelphia, America's Top Model.* Commercials include Honda Australia, Scion California, Motorola Razr 2 worldwide.

MUSIC Mostly **modern rock, country, pop, jazz** and **euro dance**; also **bluegrass** and **alternative**. Will accept some mainstream rap but no classical. Published "Le Disko"; "You are the One"; "Rainy Monday" (singles from Shiny Toy Guns on Universal), "Be Sure"; "What It Is" (singles from Cris Barber), "Keeps Bringing Me Back" (from Victoria Shaw on Taffita), "Christmas Needs Love to be Christmas" (single by Andy Williams on Delta), recent cover by ATC on BMG/Universal with "If Love is Blind"; single by new Warner Bros. act Sixwire called "Look at me Now."

TIPS "Write a song we don't have in our catalog or write an undeniable hit. We will know it when we hear it."

⊘⊛ MIDI TRACK PUBLISHING (BMI)

P.O. Box B, Milford PA 18337. (718)767-8995. **E-mail:** info@allrsmusic.com. **Website:** www.allrsmusic.com. **Contact:** Renee Silvestri-Bushey, president; F. John Silvestri, founder, vice president, A&R; Leslie Migliorelli, director of operations. Music publisher, record company (MIDI Track Records), music consultant, artist management, record producer. Voting member of NARAS/National Academy of Recording Arts and Sciences (The Grammy Awards), voting member of the Country Music Association (CMA Awards); SGMA/Southern Gospel Music Association, SGA/Songwriters Guild of America (Diamond Member). Staff size: 6. Publishes 3 songs/year; publishes 2 new songwriters/year. Pays standard royalty.

AFFILIATES ALLRS Music Publishing Co. (ASCAP).

HOW TO CONTACT "Write or e-mail first to obtain permission to submit. We do not accept unsolicited submissions." Prefers CD with 3 songs, lyric sheet and cover letter. Does not return material. Responds in 6 months only if interested.

FILM & TV Places 1 song in film/year. Published "Why Can't You Hear My Prayer" (single by F. John Silvestri/Leslie Silvestri), recorded by Iliana Medina in a documentary by Silvermine Films.

MUSIC Mostly **country, gospel, top 40, R&B, MOR** and **pop**. Does not want showtunes, jazz, classical or rap. Published "Why Can't You Hear My Prayer" (single by F. John Silvestri/Leslie Silvestri), recorded by eight-time Grammy nominee Huey Dunbar of the group DLG (Dark Latin Groove), released on MIDI Track Records (including other multiple releases); "Chasing Rainbows" (single by F. John Silvestri/Leslie Silvestri/Darin Kelly), recorded by Tommy Cash (country), released on MMT Records (including other multiple releases); "Because of You" (single by F. John Silvestri/Leslie Silvestri), recorded by Iliana Medina, released 2002 on MIDI Track Records (including other multiple releases also recorded by Grammy nominee Terri Williams, of Always, Patsy Cline, Grand Ole Opry member Ernie Ashworth), released on KMA Records and including other multiple releases; "My Coney Island" (single by F. John Silvestri/Leslie Silvestri), recorded by eight-time Grammy nominee Huey Dunbar, released 2005-2009 on MIDI Track Records.

TIPS "Attend workshops, seminars, and visit our blog on our website for advice, tips, and info on the music industry."

⊘ MOONJUNE

E-mail: noanoamusic@moonjune.com. **Website:** www.moonjune.com. The ongoing goal of MoonJune is to support music that transcends stylistic pigeonholing, but operates within an evolutionary progressive musical continuum that places jazz at one end and rock at the other. The ever-expanding boundaries of these two musical categories have since come to include everything from progressive rock to ethnojazz, from experimental avante-garde to jazz-rock, and anything in between.

⊘ MORAINE MUSIC GROUP

500 E. Iris, Nashville TN 37204. (615)383-0400. **Website:** www.morainemusic.com. "Moraine Music Group is one of Nashville's leading independent publishing and production companies with decades of hits spanning various genres. Over the years, Moraine has gained a reputation for representing unique songwriters, delivering breakthrough singles and songs that have been included on numerous Grammy-winning records."

HOW TO CONTACT Moraine Music Group does not accept unsolicited material.

MUSIC Published music by Kelly Clarkson, Taylor Swift, The Dixie Chicks, Garth Brooks, Kenny Wayne Shepherd, Kenny Chesney, Tim McGraw, Lee Brice, Justin Moore, Alan Jackson, Lee Ann Womack, The Judds, Trisha Yearwood, Tina Turner and more.

MPL MUSIC PUBLISHING

41 W. 54th St., New York NY 10019. (212)246-5881. **Fax:** (212)246-7852. **E-mail:** contact@mplcommunications.com. **Website:** www.mplcommunications. com. Founded by Paul McCartney, MPL's music publishing business has been marked by considered acquisitions and sensitive, honest handling of copyrights.

HOW TO CONTACT E-mail a link to your song. "Don't call us. If we like what we hear, we'll be in touch."

MUSIC Published classics such as "Ac-Cent-Tchu-Ate The Positive," "Autumn Leaves," "Baby, It's Cold Outside," "Big Girls Don't Cry," "The Christmas Song," "One for My Baby," "It's So Easy," "Blue Suede Shoes," "Sentimental Journey," "Tenderly," and more.

⊘ THE MUSIC ROOM PUBLISHING GROUP

525 S. Francisca Ave., Redondo Beach CA 90277. (310)316-4551. **E-mail:** mrp@aol.com. **Website:** musicroomonline.com; www.musicroom.us. **Contact:** John Reed. (ASCAP)/MRP MUSIC (BMI) Music publisher and record producer. Pays standard royalty.

AFFILIATES MRP Music (BMI).

HOW TO CONTACT Not accepting unsolicited material.

MUSIC Mostly **pop/rock/R&B** and **crossover**. Published "That Little Tattoo," "Mona Lisa" and "Sleepin' with an Angel" (singles by John E. Reed) from *Rock With An Attitude* (album), recorded by Rawk Dawg (rock), released 2002; "Over the Rainbow" and "Are You Still My Lover" (singles) from *We Only Came to Rock* (album), recorded by Rawk Dawg, released 2004 on Music Room Productions.

◐ MUST HAVE MUSIC

P.O. Box 801181, Santa Clarita CA 91380. (323)932-9524. **E-mail:** info@musthavemusic.com. **Website:** www.musthavemusic.com. (ASCAP, BMI) Music publisher and music library. Estab. 1990. Pays standard royalty.

AFFILIATES Must Have More Music (ASCAP); Must Have Music (BMI).

HOW TO CONTACT Obtain permission via e-mail before submitting a demo. Submit demo by mail with

a personal e-mail address included for directors response. Prefers CD with lyric sheet and cover letter. Does not return submissions. Responds in 2 months.

FILM & TV Music supervisor: Ken Klar, managing director.

MUSIC Mostly **pop/ R& B**, **pop/country** and **rock**; also **AAA**, **adult contemporary**, and **contemporary Christian/gospel**. Does not want instrumental music. "We only work with completed songs with lyric and vocal."

TIPS "Write what you know and what you believe. Then rewrite it!"

◑ ◯ NERVOUS PUBLISHING

5 Sussex Crescent, Northolt, Middlesex UB5 4DL United Kingdom. +44(20) 8423 7373. **Fax:** +44(20) 8423 7773. **E-mail:** info@nervous.co.uk. **Website:** www.nervous.co.uk. **Contact:** Roy Williams, owner. Music publisher, record company (Nervous Records) and record producer. MCPS, PRS and Phonographic Performance Ltd. Publishes 100 songs/year; publishes 25 new songwriters/year. Pays standard royalty; royalties paid directly to US songwriters.

◯   Nervous Publishing's record label, Nervous Records, is listed in the Record Companies section.

HOW TO CONTACT Submit demo by mail. Unsolicited submissions are OK. Prefers CD with 3-10 songs and lyric sheet. "Include letter giving your age and mentioning any previously published material." SAE and IRC. Responds in 3 weeks.

MUSIC Mostly **psychobilly**, **rockabilly** and **rock** (impossibly fast music—e.g., Stray Cats but twice as fast); also **blues**, **country**, **R&B** and **rock** (1950s style). Published *Trouble* (album), recorded by Dido Bonneville (rockabilly); *Rockabilly Comp* (album), recorded by various artists; and *Nervous Singles Collection* (album), recorded by various artists, all on Nervous Records.

TIPS "Submit *no* rap, soul, funk—we want *rockabilly*."

◑ NEWBRAUGH BROTHERS MUSIC

228 Morgan Lane, Berkeley Springs WV 25411-3475. (304)258-3656. **E-mail:** Nbtoys@verizon.net. **Contact:** John S. Newbraugh. (ASCAP, BMI) Music publisher, record company (NBT Records, BMI/ASCAP). Publishes 124 songs/year. Publishes 14 new songwriters/year. Staff size: 1. Pays standard royalty.

AFFILIATES NBT Music (ASCAP) and Newbraugh Brothers Music (BMI).

HOW TO CONTACT Submit demo by mail. Unsolicited submissions are OK. Prefers cassette or CD with any amount of songs, a lyric sheet and a cover letter. Include SASE. Responds in 6 weeks. "Please don't call for permission to submit. Your materials are welcomed."

MUSIC Mostly **rockabilly**, **hillbilly**, **folk** and **bluegrass**; also **rock**, **country**, and **gospel**. "We will accept all genres of music except songs with vulgar language." Published released *Ride the Train Series Vol. 25; Layin' It On the Line* by Night Drive (2009); "Love Notes" by The Sisters Two; "The Country Cowboy" by Jack Long; "Original Praise Songs" by Russ and Donna Miller.

TIPS "Find out if a publisher/record company has any special interest. NBT, for instance, is always hunting 'original' train songs. Our 'registered' trademark is a train and from time to time we release a compilation album of all train songs. We welcome all genres of music for this project."

⊘ NEWCREATURE MUSIC

P.O. Box 1444, Hendersonville TN 37077. (615)585-9301. **E-mail:** ba@landmarkcommunicationsgroup.com. **Website:** www.landmarkcommunicationsgroup.com. **Contact:** Bill Anderson, Jr., president. Music publisher, record company, record producer (Landmark Communications Group) and radio and TV syndicator. Publishes 25 songs/year; publishes 2 new songwriters/year. Pays standard royalty.

AFFILIATES Mary Megan Music (ASCAP).

HOW TO CONTACT *Contact first and obtain permission to submit.* Prefers CD or videocassette with 4-10 songs and lyric sheet. Include SASE. Responds in 6 weeks.

MUSIC Mostly **country**, **gospel**, **jazz**, **R&B**, **rock** and **top 40/pop**. Published *Let This Be the Day* by C.J. Hall; *When a Good Love Comes Along* by Gail Score; *The Wonder of Christmas* by Jack Mosley.

◑ NEXT DECADE ENTERTAINMENT

65 W. 55th St., Suite 4F, New York NY 10019. (212)583-1887, ext. 10. **Fax:** (212)813-9788. **E-mail:** info@nextdecade-ent.com. **Website:** www.nextdecade-ent.com. **Contact:** Stu Cantor, president. "Next Decade is more than just a music publisher. We're experts with years of experience and knowledge about music and licensing. Our approach is hands-on and service-oriented. We work with clients closely to make sure their copyrights are not only protected and properly exploited, but that

opportunities for growth and development are identified and that we are involved with the newest companies and people for licensing opportunities."

MUSIC Represents such artists as Boston, Harry Belafonte, Millie Jackson, Ray Griff, Eric Lindell, Vic Mizzy, and more.

⊘ NOTTING HILL MUSIC

8961 Sunset Blvd., Suite 2E, West Hollywood CA 90069. (310)273-4230. **Fax:** (310)273-4237. **Website:** www.nottinghillmusic.com. "The Notting Hill Music Group Ltd. is a truly international music publishing operation, based in London and Los Angeles, with first-class representation in every corner of the globe."

HOW TO CONTACT Notting Hill Music does not accept unsolicited material.

MUSIC Any genre. Published music by 50 Cent, Aretha Franklin, Black Eyed Peas, Bob Dylan, Calvin Harris, Elton John, Jay Z, Lionel Richie, Madonna, and more.

⊘⊛ OLD SLOWPOKE MUSIC

P.O. Box 52626, Utica Square Station, Tulsa OK 74152. (918)742-8087. **Fax:** (888)878-0817. **E-mail:** ryoung@oldslowpokemusic.com. **Website:** www.oldslowpokemusic.com. **Contact:** Rodney Young, president. (BMI) Music publisher and record producer. Publishes 10-20 songs/year; publishes 2 new songwriters/year. Staff size: 2. Pays standard royalty.

HOW TO CONTACT CDs only, no cassettes.

FILM & TV 1 song in film/year. Recently published "Samantha," written and recorded by George W. Carroll in *Samantha*. Placed two songs for Tim Drummond in movies: "Hound Dog Man" in *Loving Lu Lu* and "Fur Slippers" in the CBS movie *Shake, Rattle & Roll*.

MUSIC Mostly **rock**, **country** and **R&B**; also **jazz**. Published *Promise Land* (album), written and recorded by Richard Neville on Cherry Street Records (rock).

TIPS "Write great songs. We sign only artists who play an instrument, sing and write songs."

⊘⊛ OLE

266 King St. W., Suite 500, Toronto, Ontario M5V 1H8 Canada. **E-mail:** majorlyindie@olemm.com. **Website:** www.majorlyindie.com. Ole is the world's fastest-growing rights management company. Founded in 2004, and with offices in Toronto, Nashville, New York, and Los Angeles, Ole boasts a team of 45 experienced industry professionals focused on acquisitions, creative development and worldwide copyright administration. Ole has recently entered the produc-

tion music space with the acquisition of MusicBox and Auracle, which have operations in New York, Toronto and Los Angeles. Ole is committed to the creative development of its 60-plus staff songwriters, legacy writers and composers, and the cultivation of its catalogs and client catalogs. Ole has ongoing co-ventures with Last Gang Publishing (Alt Rock), Roots Three Music (Country), and tanjola (Pop/Rock/Urban).

HOW TO CONTACT Does not accept unsolicited submissions.

MUSIC Notable copyrights with Ole include those by Taylor Swift, Rascal Flatts, Justin Timberlake, Jay-Z, Eric Church, Kelly Clarkson, Pink, Aerosmith, Tim McGraw, and many more.

⊘ PEERMUSIC

2397 Shattuck Ave., Suite 202, Berkeley CA 94704. (510)848-7337. **Fax:** (510)848-7355. **E-mail:** sfcorp@peermusic.com. **Website:** www.peermusic.com. Music publisher and artist development promotional label. Hires staff songwriters. "All deals negotiable."

AFFILIATES Songs of Peer Ltd. (ASCAP) and Peermusic III Ltd. (BMI).

HOW TO CONTACT "We do NOT accept unsolicited submissions. We only accept material through agents, attorneys and managers." Prefers CD and lyric sheet. Does not return material.

MUSIC Mostly **pop**, **rock** and **R&B**. Published music by David Foster (writer/producer, pop); Andrew Williams (writer/producer, pop); Christopher "Tricky" Stewart (R&B, writer/producer).

⊘ PERLA MUSIC

134 Parker Ave., Easton PA 18042. (212)957-9509. **Fax:** (917)338-7596. **E-mail:** PM@PMRecords.org. **Website:** www.pmrecords.org. **Contact:** Gene Perla. (ASCAP) Music publisher, record company (PMRecords.org), record producer (Perla.org), studio production (TheSystemMSP.com) and Internet Design (CCINYC.com). Publishes 5 songs/year. Staff size: 5.

HOW TO CONTACT E-mail first and obtain permission to submit.

MUSIC Mostly **jazz** and **rock**.

○ JUSTIN PETERS MUSIC

P.O. Box 40251, Nashville TN 37227. (615)269-8682. **Fax:** (615)269-8929. **E-mail:** justinpeters@songsfortheplanet.com; songsfortheplanet@songsfortheplanet.com. **Website:** songsfortheplanet.com. **Contact:** Justin Peters. (BMI) Music publisher.

AFFILIATES Platinum Planet Music (BMI), Tourmaline (BMI) and LITA Music (ASCAP).

HOW TO CONTACT Submit demo package by mail. Unsolicited submissions are OK. Prefers CD with 5 songs and lyric sheet. Does not return material. "Place code '2015' on each envelope submission."

MUSIC Mostly **pop**, **reggae**, **country** and **comedy**. Published "Saved By Love" (single), recorded by Amy Grant on A&M Records; "From the Center of my Heart," by Shey Baby on JAM Records; "A Gift That She Don't Want" (single), recorded by Bill Engvall on Warner Brother Records; "The Bottom Line," recorded by Charley Pride on Music City Records, cowritten by Justin Peters; "Heaven's Got to Help Me Shake These Blues" (single), written by Vickie Shaub and Justin Peters, recorded by B.J. Thomas; "Virginia Dreams" and "Closer to You" (Jimmy Fortune/Justin Peters), recorded by Jimmy Fortune.

○ PLATINUM PLANET MUSIC, INC.

P.O. Box 40251, Nashville TN 37204. (615)269-8682. **Fax:** (615)269-8929. **E-mail:** justinpeters@songsfortheplanet.com. **Website:** songsfortheplanet.com. **Contact:** Justin Peters. (BMI) Music publisher.

AFFILIATES Justin Peters Music (BMI), Tourmaline (BMI) and LITA Music (ASCAP). Sonwriters: Lee Anna Culp, Rich Fehle, Bill McCorvey, Tommy Stillwell, Dez Dickerson.

HOW TO CONTACT Submit demo package by mail. Unsolicited submissions are OK. Prefers CD with 5 songs and lyricsheet. Does not return material. "Place code '2015' on each envelope submission."

MUSIC Mostly film/TV, **Americana/Alternative**, **R&B**, **reggae**, **sports themes**, **educational themes**, **dance** and **country**; also represents many **Christian** artists/writers. Published "Happy Face" (single by Dez Dickerson/Jordan Dickerson), recorded by Squirt on Absolute Records; "Carry Me Away" and "I DO" (Lee Anna Culp), recorded by Lee Anna Culp on Platinum Planet Records; "Love's Not A Game" (single), written by Art Craig and J. Peters and recorded by Kashief Lindo on Heavybeat Records; "Merry Christmas, Merry Christmas" (single) "What Makes You Good Enough" (single) written by Lee Anna Culp & Justin Peters recorded by Lee Anna Culp on Platinum Planet Records. and "Loud" (single), written and recorded by These Five Down on Absolute Records.

🌑 POLLYBYRD PUBLICATIONS, LTD.

(ASCAP, BMI, SESAC), 468 N. Camden Dr., Suite 200, Beverly Hills CA 90210. (818)506-8533. **Fax:** (310)860-7400. **E-mail:** pplzmi@aol.com. **Website:** www.pplzmi.com. **Contact:** Dakota Hawk, vice president. Professional managers: Cisco Blue (country, pop, rock); Tedford Steele (hip-hop, R&B). Music publisher, record company (PPL Entertainment) and management firm (Sa'mall Management). Publishes 100 songs/year; publishes 25-40 new songwriters/year. Hires staff writers. Pays standard royalty.

AFFILIATES Kellijai Music (ASCAP), Pollyann Music (ASCAP), Ja'Nikki Songs (BMI), Velma Songs International (BMI), Lonnvanness Songs (SESAC), PPL Music (ASCAP), Zettitalia Music, Butternut Music (BMI), Zett Two Music (ASCAP), Plus Publishing and Zett One Songs (BMI).

HOW TO CONTACT *Write first and obtain permission to submit.* No phone calls. Prefers CD with 4 songs and lyric and lead sheet. Include SASE. Responds in 2 months.

MUSIC Published *Return of the Players* (album) by Juz-Cuz 2004 on PPL; "Believe" (single by J. Jarrett/S. Cuseo) from *Time* (album), recorded by Lejenz (pop), released 2001 on PRL/Credence; *Rainbow Gypsy Child* (album), written and recorded by Riki Hendrix (rock), released 2001 on PRL/Sony; and "What's Up With That" (single by Brandon James/Patrick Bouvier) from *Outcast* (album), recorded by Condottieré; (hip-hop), released 2001 on Bouvier.

TIPS "Make those decisions—are you really a songwriter? Are you prepared to starve for your craft? Do you believe in delayed gratification? Are you commercial or do you write only for yourself? Can you take rejection? Do you want to be the best? If so, contact us."

🌑🌑🌑 RANCO MUSIC PUBLISHING

(formerly Lilly Music Publishing), 61 Euphrasia Dr., Toronto, Ontario M6B 3V8 Canada. **E-mail:** panfilo@sympatico.ca; obbiemusic@sympatico.ca. **Website:** www.myspace.com/rancorecords. **Contact:** Panfilo Di Matteo, president. Music publisher and record company (P. & N. Records). Publishes 20 songs/year; publishes 8 new songwriters/year. Staff size: 3. Pays standard royalty.

AFFILIATES San Martino Music Publishing and Paglieta Music Publishing (CMRRA).

HOW TO CONTACT Submit demo by mail. Unsolicited submissions are OK. Prefers CD (or videocassette if available) with 3 songs and lyric and lead sheets. "We will contact you only if we are interested in the material." Responds in 1 month.

FILM & TV Places 12 songs in film/year.

MUSIC Mostly **dance**, **ballads**, and **rock**; also **country**. Published "I'd Give It All" (single by Glenna J. Sparkes), recorded by Suzanne Michelle (country crossover), released on Lilly Records.

RAZOR & TIE ENTERTAINMENT

214 Sullivan St., Suite 5, New York NY 10012. (212)598-2259. **Fax:** (212)473-9173. **E-mail:** bprimont@razorandtie.com. **Website:** www.razorandtiemusicpublishing.com. **Contact:** Brooke Primont, senior vice president, music placement, and licensing.

HOW TO CONTACT Does not accept unsolicited material.

MUSIC Songwriters and groups represented include Dar Williams, Bad Books, David Ford, Finch, Brand New, Emerson Lake & Palmer, BeBe Winans, Joe Jackson, Joan Baez, Nonpoint, Yellowcard, Foreigner, HIM, Saves the Day, Suzanne Vega, and many more.

🌑 RED SUNDOWN RECORDS

1920 Errel Dowlen Rd., Pleasant View TN 37146. (615)746-0844. **E-mail:** rsdr@bellsouth.net. (BMI)

HOW TO CONTACT *Does not accept unsolicited submissions.* Submit CD and cover letter. Does not return submissions.

MUSIC **Country**, **rock**, and **pop**. Does not want rap or hip-hop. Published "Take A Heart" (single by Kyle Pierce) from *Take Me With You* (album), recorded by Tammy Lee (country) released in 1998 on Red Sundown Records.

🌑🌑 ROCHAMBEAU MUSIC

228 Dexter Ave. N., Seattle WA 98119. **E-mail:** info@rochambeaumusic.com. **Website:** www.rochambeaumusic.com. **Contact:** Glenn Lorbecki, CEO. Rochambeau Music represents songwriters, composers, and artists in the areas of music publishing, licensing, placement and production. "In conjunction with our full-service recording studio, Glenn Sound/Seattle, we offer services from artist development to full-scale album production and strive to work with the best new and established talent in taking their creativity to the next level. Capitalizing on our industry-wide contacts, we are opening new opportunities for master placement in film/TV/game soundtracks, forging new relationships for song placement with global art-

ists, and seeking to introduce the music of our partners to the international marketplace."

MUSIC Represents such artists as Emi Meyer (jazz), Tim Huling (composer), Mycle Wastman (R&B), Jeffrey Alan (pop/rock), and more.

⊘ RONDOR MUSIC INTERNATIONAL/ ALMO/IRVING MUSIC, A UNIVERSAL MUSIC GROUP CO.

Part of Universal Music Publishing Group, 2440 Sepulveda Blvd., Suite 119, Los Angeles CA 90064. (310)235-4800. **Fax:** (310)235-4801. **E-mail:** rondor-la@umusic.com. **Website:** www.universalmusicpublishing.com. The Rondor catalog embodies the works of such important songwriters as The Beach Boys, Al Green, Otis Redding, Peter Frampton, Isaac Hayes, Supertramp, Tom Petty and Leon Russell. Rondor also represents many significant songwriters and artists including Rod Temperton, Mark Knopfler, Emmylou Harris, William Orbit, Saliva, Will Jennings, Garbage, Jurassic 5, Shep Crawford, and Steven Van Zandt. (ASCAP, BMI)

AFFILIATES Almo Music Corp. (ASCAP) and Irving Music, Inc. (BMI).

HOW TO CONTACT Does not accept unsolicited submissions.

⊘ ROUND HILL MUSIC

400 Madison Ave., 18th Floor, New York NY 10017. (212)380-0080. **E-mail:** info@roundhillmusic.com. **Website:** www.roundhillmusic.com. Round Hill Music is a full-service, creative music company with a core focus on music publishing. "We take a thoughtful, long-term approach to building both a stellar song catalog and a roster of talented active writers that our team is proud to work so closely with on a daily basis. Our ultimate goal is to deliver value from every single song in our catalog, while simultaneously providing all of our writers with the individualized attention they need to succeed. The Round Hill team achieves this goal through everything from synch licensing and song placements to setting up co-writes and performing international song registration, all while maintaining one of the most transparent and accurate royalty accounting systems in the music publishing marketplace. We're on a mission to bring back the kind of personalized creative attention that was so inherent to the initial heyday of music publishing, and our boutique size gives us the agility we need to realize that mission. From the iconic hits of yesterday

to the future chart toppers of tomorrow, our love for our music is at the center of everything we do."

🌑O R.T.L. MUSIC

Perthy Farm, The Perthy, Shropshire SY12 9HR United Kingdom. **E-mail:** info@rtlmusic.co.uk. **Website:** www.rtlmusic.co.uk. **Contact:** Tanya Woof, international A&R manager. Music publisher, record company (Le Matt Music) and record producer. Publishes approximately 30 songs/year. Pays standard royalty.

AFFILIATES Lee Music (publishing), Swoop Records, Grenouille Records, Check Records, Zarg Records, Pogo Records, R.T.F.M. (all independent companies).

HOW TO CONTACT Submit demo by mail. Unsolicited submissions are OK. Prefers CD, cassette, MDisc or DVD (also VHS 625/PAL system videocassette) with 1-3 songs and lyric and lead sheets; include still photos and bios. "Make sure name and address are on CD or cassette." Send IRC. Responds in 6 weeks.

MUSIC All types. Published "The Old Days" (single by Ron Dickson) from *Groucho* (album), recorded by Groucho (pop); "Orphan in the Storm" (single by M.J. Lawson) from *Emmit Till* (album), recorded by Emmit Till (blues); "Donna" (single by Mike Sheriden) from *Donna* (album), recorded by Mike Sheriden (pop), all released 2006 on Swoop.

O RUSTIC RECORDS, INC. PUBLISHING

6337 Murray Lane, Brentwood TN 37027. (615)371-0646. **E-mail:** rusticrecordsam@aol.com. **Website:** www.rusticrecordsinc.com. **Contact:** Jack Schneider, president; Nell Schneider, executive vice president, office manager. (ASCAP, BMI, SESAC) Music publisher, record company (Rustic Records, Inc.) and record producer. Publishes 20 songs/year. Pays standard royalty.

AFFILIATES Covered Bridge Music (BMI), Town Square Music (SESAC), Iron Skillet Music (ASCAP).

HOW TO CONTACT Submit demo by mail. Unsolicited submissions are OK. Prefers CD with 3-4 songs and lyric sheet. Include SASE. Responds in 3 months.

MUSIC Mostly **country.** Published "In Their Eyes" (single by Jamie Champa); "Take Me As I Am" (single by Bambi Barrett/Paul Huffman); and "Yesterday's Memories" (single by Jack Schneider), recorded by Colte Bradley (country), released 2003.

TIPS "Send 3 or 4 traditional country songs, novelty songs, 'foot-tapping, hand-clapping' gospel songs with strong hook for male or female artist of duet. Enclose SASE (manila envelope)."

SALT WORKS MUSIC

80 Highland Dr., Jackson OH 45640-2074. (740)286-1514. **Fax:** (740)286-6561. **Contact:** Professional managers: Jeff Elliott (country/gospel); Mike Morgan (country). Music publisher and record producer (Mike Morgan). Staff size: 2. Pays standard royalty.

AFFILIATES Salt Creek Music (ASCAP) and Sojourner Music (BMI).

HOW TO CONTACT Submit demo package by mail. Unsolicited submissions are OK. Prefers CD. Include SASE. Responds in 2 weeks.

MUSIC Mostly **country**, **gospel** and **pop**. Does not want rock, jazz or classical. Published "The Tracks You Left On Me" (single by Ed Bruce/Jeff Elliott/Mike Morgan) and "Truth Is I'm A Liar" (single by Jeff Elliott/Mike Morgan) from *This Old Hat* (album), recorded by Ed Bruce (country), released 2002 on Sony/Music Row Talent.

SANDALPHON MUSIC PUBLISHING

P.O. Box 18197, Panama City Beach FL 32417. **E-mail:** sandalphonmusic@yahoo.com. **Contact:** Ruth Otey. Music publisher, record company (Sandalphon Records), and management agency (Sandalphon Management). Staff size: 2. Pays standard royalty of 50%.

HOW TO CONTACT Submit demo by mail. Unsolicited submissions are fine. Prefers CD with 1-5 songs, lyric sheet, and cover letter. Include SASE or SAE and IRC for outside U.S. Responds in 6-8 weeks.

MUSIC Mostly **rock**, **country**, and **alternative**; also **pop**, **blues**, and **gospel**.

SAVANNAH MUSIC GROUP

(615)504-7732. **Fax:** (615)383-8117. **E-mail:** info@savannahmusicgroup.com. **Website:** www.savannahmusicgroup.com. **Contact:** Daisy Dern, creative director. Savannah Music Group is a grassroots music publishing company located in the heart of Nashville's Music Row.

MUSIC The current songwriting roster includes Kevin "Swine" Grantt, Jack Williams, and Dave Gibson. The company has had releases by Montgomery Gentry, The Blind Boys of Alabama, Brad Paisley, The Randy Rogers Band, Tommy Steele, The Mulch Brothers, Kristina Cornell, and The Dirt Drifters, and has songs in the motion picture releases *Country Strong*, *Sucker*, and TV series *Good Christian Belles*. Savannah Music Group is positioned to be competitive at the highest level in the publishing community with its current roster of writers and executive team.

SB21 MUSIC PUBLISHING

1610 16th Ave. S., 2nd Floor, Nashville TN 37212. (615)775-0254. **E-mail:** info@sb21music.com. **Website:** www.sb21music.com. SB21 Music is an independent music publishing company started by Steve Pasch. Writers with SB21 have had country cuts with major artists, such as Tim McGraw, Wynonna, John Michael Montgomery, and Clay Walker, including 2006 Billboard Country's "Most Played Song of the Year" Rodney Adkins' "Watching You."

SHAWNEE PRESS, INC.

1221 17th Ave. S., Nashville TN 37212. **E-mail:** info@shawneepress.com. **Website:** www.ShawneePress.com. **Contact:** Joseph M. Martin, director of church music publications (sacred choral music); Greg Gilpin, director of school music publications (secular choral music). Music publisher. Publishes 150 songs/year. Staff size: 12. Pays negotiable royalty.

AFFILIATES GlorySound, Harold Flammer Music, Mark Foster Music, Wide World Music, Concert Works.

HOW TO CONTACT Submit ms. Unsolicited submissions are OK. See website for guidelines. Prefers ms; recording required for instrumental submissions. Include SASE. Responds in 4 months. "No unsolicited musicals or cantatas."

MUSIC Mostly **church/liturgical**, **educational choral** and **instrumental**.

TIPS "Submission guidelines appear on our website."

SILICON MUSIC PUBLISHING CO.

222 Tulane St., Garland TX 75043. **E-mail:** support@siliconmusic.us. **Website:** siliconmusic.us. **Contact:** Steve Summers, public relations. Music publisher and record company (Front Row Records). Publishes 10-20 songs/year; publishes 2-3 new songwriters/year. Pays standard royalty.

Also see the listing for Front Row Records in the Record Companies section of this book.

HOW TO CONTACT Submit demo package by mail. Unsolicited submissions are OK. Prefers CD with 1-2 songs. Does not return material. Responds ASAP.

MUSIC Mostly **rockabilly** and **1950s material**; also **old-time blues/country** and **MOR**. Published "Rockaboogie Shake" (single by James McClung) from *Rebels and More* (album), recorded by Lennerockers (rockabilly), released 2002 on Lenne (Germany); "Be-Bop City" (single by Dan Edwards), "So" (single by Dea Summers/Gene Summers), and "Little Lu Ann" (single by James McClung) from *Do Right Daddy* (album), recorded by Gene Summers (rockabilly/1950s rock 'n' roll), released 2004 on Enviken (Sweden).

TIPS "We are very interested in 1950s rock and rockabilly original masters for release through overseas affiliates. If you are the owner of any 1950s masters, contact us first! We have releases in Holland, Switzerland, United Kingdom, Belgium, France, Sweden, Norway and Australia. We have the market if you have the tapes! Our staff writers include James McClung, Gary Mears (original Casuals), Robert Clark, Dea Summers, Shawn Summers, Joe Hardin Brown, Bill Becker and Dan Edwards."

⊘⊛ SILVER BLUE MUSIC/OCEANS BLUE MUSIC

3940 Laurel Canyon Blvd., Suite 441, Studio City CA 91604. (818)980-9588. **E-mail:** jdiamond20@aol.com. **Website:** www.joeldiamond.com. **Contact:** Joel Diamond. (ASCAP, BMI) Music publisher and record producer (Joel Diamond Entertainment). Publishes 50 songs/year. Pays standard royalty.

HOW TO CONTACT *Does not accept unsolicited material.* "No CDs returned."

FILM & TV Places 4 songs in film and 6 songs in TV/year.

MUSIC Mostly **pop** and **R&B**; also **rap** and **classical.** Produced and managed The 5 Browns-3 #1 CDs on Sony. Published "After the Lovin" (by Bernstein/Adams), recorded by Engelbert Humperdinck; "This Moment in Time" (by Alan Bernstein/Ritchie Adams), recorded by Engelbert Humperdinck. Other artists include David Hasselhoff, Kaci (Curb Records), Ike Turner, Andrew Dice Clay, Gloria Gaynor, Tony Orlando, Katie Cassidy, and Vaneza.

●● SINUS MUSIK PRODUKTION, ULLI WEIGEL

Geitnerweg 30a, D-12209, Berlin, Germany. **Website:** www.ulli-weigel.de. **Contact:** Ulli Weigel, owner. Music publisher, record producer and screenwriter. Wrote German lyrics for more than 500 records. Member: GEMA, GVL. Publishes 20 songs/year; publishes 6 new songwriters/year. Staff size: 3. Pays standard royalty.

AFFILIATES Sinus Musikverlag H.U. Weigel GmbH.

HOW TO CONTACT Submit demo package by mail. Prefers CD or cassette with up to 10 songs and lyric sheets. If you want to send MP3 attachments, you should contact me before. Attachments from unknown senders will not be opened. Responds in 2 months by e-mail. "If material should be returned, please send 2 International Reply Coupons (IRC) for cassettes and 3 for a CD. No stamps."

MUSIC Mostly **rock, pop** and **New Age**; also **background music for movies and audio books**. Published "Simple Story" (single), recorded by MAANAM on RCA (Polish rock); *Die Musik Maschine* (album by Klaus Lage), recorded by CWN Productions on Hansa Records (pop/German), "Villa Woodstock" (film music/comedy) Gebrueder Blattschuss, Juergen Von Der Lippe, Hans Werner Olm (2005).

TIPS "Take more time working on the melody than on the instrumentation. I also am looking for master-quality recordings for non-exclusive release on my label (and to use them as soundtracks for multimedia projects, TV and movie scripts I am working on)."

⊘ SONY/ATV MUSIC PUBLISHING

8 Music Square W., Nashville TN 37203. (615)726-8300. **Fax:** (615)726-8329. **E-mail:** info@sonyatv.com. **Website:** www.sonyatv.com. ASCAP, BMI, SESAC.

HOW TO CONTACT Sony/ATV Music does not accept unsolicited submissions.

⊘⊛ STILL WORKING MUSIC GROUP

1625 Broadway, Suite 200, Nashville TN 37203. (615)242-4201. **Website:** stillworkingmusicgroup. com. (ASCAP, BMI, SESAC) Music publisher and record company (Orby Records, Inc.).

AFFILIATES Still Working for the Woman Music (ASCAP), Still Working for the Man Music (BMI) and Still Working for All Music (SESAC).

HOW TO CONTACT Does not accept unsolicited submissions.

FILM & TV Published "First Noel," recorded by The Kelions in Felicity.

MUSIC Mostly **rock, country** and **pop**; also **dance** and **R&B**. Published "If You See Him/If You See Her" (by Tommy Lee James), recorded by Reba McIntire/Brooks & Dunn; "Round About Way" (by Wil Nance), recorded by George Strait on MCA; and "Wrong Again" (by Tommy Lee James), recorded by Martina McBride on RCA (country).

TIPS "If you want to be a country songwriter you need to be in Nashville where the business is. Write what is in your heart."

● SUPREME ENTERPRISES INT'L CORP.

P.O. Box 1373, Agoura Hills CA 91376. (818)707-3481. **E-mail:** seicorp@earthlink.net. **Website:** www.

seicorp.net. (ASCAP, BMI) Music publisher, record company and record producer. Publishes 20-30 songs/year; publishes 2-6 new songwriters/year. Pays standard royalty.

AFFILIATES Fuerte Suerte Music (BMI), Big Daddy G. Music (ASCAP).

HOW TO CONTACT *No phone calls.* Submit demo by mail. Unsolicited submissions are OK. Prefers CD. Does not return material and you must include an e-mail address for a response. "Please copyright material before submitting and include e-mail." Responds in 12-16 weeks if interested.

MUSIC Mostly **reggae**, **rap**, and **dance**. Published "Paso La Vida Pensando," recorded by Jose Feliciano on Universal Records; "Cucu Bam Bam" (single by David Choy), recorded by Kathy on Polydor Records (reggae/pop); "Volvere Alguna Vez" recorded by Matt Monro on EMI Records and "Meneaito" (single), recorded by Gaby on SEI Records.

TIPS "A good melody is a hit in any language."

● T.C. PRODUCTIONS/ETUDE PUBLISHING CO.

121 Meadowbrook Dr., Hillsborough NJ 08844. (908)359-5110. **Fax:** (908)359-1962. **E-mail:** tonycamillo@gmail.com. **Website:** www.tonycamillo.com. (BMI) Music publisher and record producer. Publishes 25-50 songs/year; publishes 3-6 new songwriters/year. Pays negotiable royalty.

AFFILIATES We Iz It Music Publishing (ASCAP), Etude Publishing (BMI), and We B Records (BMI).

HOW TO CONTACT *Write or call first and obtain permission to submit.* Prefers CD or cassette with 3-4 songs and lyric sheet. Include SASE. Responds in 1 month.

MUSIC Mostly **R&B** and **dance**; also **country** and **outstanding pop ballads**. Published "I Just Want To Be Your Everything" (single) from *A Breath of Fresh Air* (album), recorded by Michelle Parto (spiritual), released 2006 on Chancellor Records; and *New Jersey Jazz* (album).

TIPS "Michelle Parto will soon be appearing in the film musical *Sing Out*, directed by Nick Castle and written by Kent Berhard."

⊘ TEN TEN MUSIC GROUP

33 Music Square W., Suite 110, Nashville TN 37203. (615)255-9955. **Fax:** (615)255-1209. **E-mail:** info@tentenmusic.com. **Website:** www.tentenmusicgroup.com. **Contact:** Barry Coburn, president; Nathan Nicholson, vice president and creative director. "Ten Ten Music Group, Inc. has established itself as one of the most successful independent music publishing companies in Nashville. Appearing on Billboard's list of Top Song Publishers from 2004 to 2006, Ten Ten Music continues to expand its footprint across multiple genres. With cuts by major rock groups like Papa Roach, Shinedown, Halestorm, and Cavo, as well as other superstars, including One Direction, Bonnie Raitt and Selena Gomez, the diverse talent of Ten Ten Music's writing staff has ventured far beyond Nashville."

MUSIC "The writing staff at Ten Ten has also enjoyed recent success with cuts by country artists such as Tim McGraw, Miranda Lambert, Pistol Annie's, Reba McEntire, David Nail and many others. Continuing a tradition of developing and nurturing the careers of such superstars as Alan Jackson and Keith Urban, Ten Ten has also been working to shape the careers of up-and-coming artists Clare Dunn and Femke Weidema."

○ TINDERBOX MUSIC

3148 Bryant Ave. S., Minneapolis MN 55408. (612)375-1113. **Fax:** (612)341-3330. **E-mail:** brady@tinderboxmusic.com; patrick@tinderboxmusic.com; staff@tinderboxmusic.com. **Website:** www.tinderboxmusic.com. Tinderbox is a music promotions and distribution company. "We work with unsigned, indie label, and major label artists across the country by obtaining press and radio airplay in appropriate markets and formats. We specialize in college radio and the artists that fit the CMJ (*College Music Journal*) and secondary FM and community formats. We also provide local and national distribution for artists, as well as publishing and music licensing opportunities."

HOW TO CONTACT "There are two ways to submit: physically or digitally. As we live in a digital age, it is probably easier for you to submit your music to us via Bandcamp, Facebook, Reverbnation, Soundcloud, or Sonicbids. Got links? We'll take them! Just e-mail them to us. If you are a hip-hop or electronic artist, please submit your music to jordan@tinderboxmusic.com." Do not send songs as an attachment. Links only. Include a short bio. "If you have a one sheet that is less than 7MB in size, you may attach that. If you like to do things old school, you also can send us physical submissions. Your CD must be radio ready. By this, we mean that it should have been professionally recorded, mixed, and mastered. Watch out for profanity.

145

When sending a physical submission, please send us 2 or 3 copies of your CD (depending on which departments you're interested in). More than one person will probably want to review your CD. We do promise that we will get back to everyone who submits material via phone, e-mail, or snail mail regarding your submission and you can typically expect to hear from us within 48 hours." More details available at the website.

MUSIC "We specialize in **indie**, **pop/alternative**, **modern rock**, **triple-A**, **rock**, and **acoustic-based rock**, **hip-hop** and **electronic music**. Although we love jazz, we don't regularly promote jazz, sorry. Featured artists include Imagine Dragons, Gentleman Hall, Twenty One Pilots, Stars Go Dim, others."

◐ TOURMALINE MUSIC, INC.

P.O. Box 40251, Nashville TN 37204. (615)269-8682. **Fax:** (615)269-8929. **E-mail:** justinpeters@songsfortheplanet.com. **Website:** songsfortheplanet.com. **Contact:** Justin Peters. (BMI) Music publisher.

AFFILIATES Justin Peters Music (BMI), LITA Music (ASCAP) and Platinum Planet Music (BMI). Songwriters: Ben Peters, George Searcy, Mike Hunter, Art Craig, J. Craig Dunnagan, and many others.

HOW TO CONTACT Submit demo package by mail. Unsolicited submissions are OK. Prefers CD with 5 songs and lyric sheet. Does not return material. "Place code '2014' on each envelope submission."

MUSIC Mostly **rock 'n' roll**, **classy alternative**, **adult contemporary**, **classic rock**, **country**, **Spanish gospel**, and some **Christmas** music. Published "Making War In The Heavenlies," written by George Searcy, recorded by Ron Kenoly (Integrity); "The Hurt is Worth TheChance," by Justin Peters/Billy Simon, recorded by Gary Chapman on RCA/BMG Records, and "The Bottom Line," by Art Craig, Drew Bourke, and Justin Peters, recorded by Charley Pride (Music City Records).

◐✪ TOWER MUSIC GROUP

P.O. Box 2435, Hendersonville TN 37077. (615)447-3319. **E-mail:** castlerecords@castlerecords.com. **Website:** www.castlerecords.com. **Contact:** Dave Sullivan, Ed Russell, Eddie Bishop. (ASCAP, BMI) Music publisher, record company (Castle Records) and record producer. Publishes 50 songs/year; publishes 10 new songwriters/year. Staff size: 15. Pays standard royalty.

AFFILIATES Cat's Alley Music (ASCAP) and Alley Roads Music (BMI).

HOW TO CONTACT See submission policy on website. Prefers CD with 3 songs and lyric sheet. Does

not return material. "You may follow up via e-mail." Responds in 3 months only if interested.

FILM & TV Places 2 songs in film and 26 songs in TV/year. Published "Run Little Girl" (by J.R. Jones/Eddie Ray), recorded by J.R. Jones in Roadside Prey.

MUSIC Mostly **country** and **R&B**; also **blues**, **pop** and **gospel**. Published "If You Broke My Heart" (single by Condrone) from *If You Broke My Heart* (album), recorded by Kimberly Simon (country); "I Wonder Who's Holding My Angel Tonight" (single) from *Up Above* (album), recorded by Carl Butler (country); and "Psychedelic Fantasy" (single by Paul Sullivan/Priege) from *The Hip Hoods* (album), recorded by The Hip Hoods (power/metal/y2k), all released 2001 on Castle Records. "Visit our website for an up-to-date listing of published songs."

TIPS "Please follow our submission policy at our web site, www.CastleRecords.com."

○ TRANSITION MUSIC CORP.

P.O. Box 2586, Toluca Lake CA 91610. (323)860-7074. **E-mail:** submissions@transitionmusic.com; info@transitionmusic.com. **Website:** www.transitionmusic.com. Publishes 250 songs/year; publishes 50 new songwriters/year. Variable royalty based on song placement and writer.

AFFILIATES Pushy Publishing (ASCAP), Creative Entertainment Music (BMI) and One Stop Shop Music (SESAC).

HOW TO CONTACT Submit one song (make it your best) online only to submissions@transitionmusic. com. We accept all genres and unsolicited music. *Responses will not be given due to the high volume of submissions daily. Please do not call/e-mail to inquire about us receiving your submission. TMC will only contact who they intend on signing.*

FILM & TV "TMC provides music for all forms of visual media. Mainly Television."

MUSIC All styles. TMC is a music library and publishing company generating over 95,000 performances in film, TV, commercials, games, Internet, and webisodes over the past year. In the last few months, TMC launched its newest division, Ultimate Exposure, exposing new independent artists to the world of visual media.

TIPS "Supply master-quality material with great songs."

∅ TRIO PRODUCTIONS, INC./ SONGSCAPE MUSIC, LLC

1026 15th Ave. S., Nashville TN 37212. (615)726-5810. **E-mail:** info@trioproductions.com; robyn@triopro-

ductions.com. **Website:** www.trioproductions.com. **Contact:** Robyn Taylor-Drake.
AFFILIATES ASCAP, BMI, SESAC, Harry Fox Agency, CMA, WMBA, IPA
HOW TO CONTACT Contact first by e-mail to obtain permission to submit demo. *Unsolicited material will not be listened to or returned.* Submit CD with 3-4 songs and lyric sheet. Submit via MP3 once permission to send has been received. Include a lyric sheet.
MUSIC Country, pop, and **Americana.**

⊘ UNIVERSAL MUSIC PUBLISHING
2100 Colorado Ave., Santa Monica CA 90404 United States. (310)235-4700. **Fax:** (310)235-4900. **Website:** www.umusicpub.com. (ASCAP, BMI,SESAC)
HOW TO CONTACT Does not accept unsolicited submissions.

◐ UNKNOWN SOURCE MUSIC (ASCAP)
120-4d Carver Loop, Bronx NY 10475. **E-mail:** unknownsourcemusic@hotmail.com. **Website:** www.unknownsourcemusic.com. Music publisher, record company (Smokin Ya Productions) and record producer. Publishes 5-10 songs/year; publishes 5-10 new songwriters/year. Pays standard royalty.
AFFILIATES Songwriters: Unks (ASCAP), Critique Records, WMI Records.
HOW TO CONTACT *Send e-mail first, then mail.* Unsolicited submissions are OK. Prefers MP3s. Responds within 6 weeks.
MUSIC Mostly **rap/hip-hop, R&B,** and **alternative.** Published "LAH" recorded by Daforce; "Nothing Better" recorded by Curtis Dayne.
TIPS "Keep working with us, be patient, be willing to work hard. Send your very best work."

◐ VAAM MUSIC GROUP
P.O. Box 29550, Hollywood CA 90029. **E-mail:** request@vaammusic.com. **Website:** www.vaammusic.com. **Contact:** Pete Martin, president. (BMI) Music publisher and record producer (Pete Martin/Vaam Productions). Estab. 1967. Publishes 9-24 new songs/year. Pays standard royalty.
AFFILIATES Pete Martin Music (ASCAP).
MUSIC "Please visit the website for up-to-date, current 'song requests.' We mostly work with country, Top 40, and R&B. Submitted material must have potential of reaching top 5 on charts."
TIPS "Study the top 10 charts in the style you write. Stay current and up-to-date with today's market."

◐ VINE CREEK MUSIC
P.O. Box 171143, Nashville TN 37217. **E-mail:** vinecreek1@aol.com. **Website:** www.myspace.com/vinecreekmusic; www.darleneaustin.com. **Contact:** Louise Cook. (ASCAP) Administration: Jayne Negri. Creative director: Brenda Madden.
HOW TO CONTACT *Vine Creek Music does not accept unsolicited submissions.* "Only send material of good competitive quality. We do not return CDs unless SASE is enclosed."

◐ WALKERBOUT MUSIC GROUP
P.O. Box 24454, Nashville TN 37202. (615)269-7074. **Fax:** (888)894-4934. **E-mail:** matt@walkerboutmusic.com; info@aristomedia.com. **Website:** www.walkerboutmusic.com. **Contact:** Matt Watkins, director of operations. (ASCAP, BMI, SESAC) Publishes 50 songs/year; 5-10 new songwriters/year. Pays standard royalty.
AFFILIATES Goodland Publishing Co. (ASCAP), Marc Isle Music (BMI), Gulf Bay Publishing (SESAC), Con Brio Music (BMI), Wiljex Publishing (ASCAP), Concorde Publishing (SESAC).
HOW TO CONTACT "Please see website for submission information."
MUSIC Mostly **country/Christian** and **adult contemporary.**

⊕⊘ WARNER/CHAPPELL MUSIC, INC.
10585 Santa Monica Blvd., Los Angeles CA 90025. (310)441-8600. **Fax:** (310)470-8780. **Website:** www.warnerchappell.com.
HOW TO CONTACT Warner/Chappell does not accept unsolicited material.

◐ WEAVER OF WORDS MUSIC
2239 Bank St., Baltimore MD 21231. (276)970-1583. **E-mail:** weaverofwordsmusic@gmail.com. **Website:** www.weaverofwordsmusic.com. **Contact:** H.R. Cook, president. (BMI) Music publisher and record company (Fireball Records). Publishes 12 songs/year. Pays standard royalty.
AFFILIATES Weaver of Melodies Music (ASCAP).
HOW TO CONTACT Submit demo by mail. Unsolicited submissions are OK. Prefers CD with 3 songs and lyric or lead sheets. "We prefer CD submissions but will accept MP3s—limit 2." Include SASE. Responds in 3 weeks.
MUSIC Mostly **country, pop, bluegrass, R&B, film and TV** and **rock.** Published "Zero To Love" (single by H. Cook/Brian James Deskins/Rick Tiger) from

It's Just The Night (album), recorded by Del McCoury Band (bluegrass), released 2003 on McCoury Music; "Muddy Water" (Alan Johnston) from *The Midnight Call* (album), recorded by Don Rigsby (bluegrass), released 2003 on Sugar Hill; "Ol Brown Suitcase" (H.R. Cook) from *Lonesome Highway* (album), recorded by Josh Williams (bluegrass), released 2004 on Pinecastle; and "Mansions of Kings" from *Cherry Holmes II* (album), recorded by IBMA 2005 Entertainer of the Year Cherry Holmes (bluegrass), released 2007 on Skaggs Family Records.

◐○ BERTHOLD WENGERT (MUSIKVERLAG)

Hauptstrasse 36, Pfinztal-Sollingen D-76327 Germany. **Contact:** Berthold Wengert. Music publisher. Pays standard GEMA royalty.

HOW TO CONTACT Prefers cassette and complete score for piano. SAE and IRC. Responds in 1 month. "No cassette returns!"

MUSIC Mostly **light music** and **pop**.

⊘ WRENSONG/REYNSONG

1229 17th Ave. S., Nashville TN 37212. (615)321-4487. **Fax:** (615)327-7917. **E-mail:** christina.wrensong@gmail.com. **Website:** www.reynsong.com. **Contact:** Christina Mitchell. Wrensong/Reynson is an independent music publishing company with offices in Nashville and Minneapolis. Conceived by father/daughter team Reyn Guyer and Ree Guyer Buchan-an, the company began with only 20 songs and is now home to over 3,000. "Our current writer roster consists of Jon Randall, Ashely Monroe, John Wiggins, Clint & Bob Moffatt (Like Strangers), Trevor Rosen, Jacob Davis amd Shelley Skidmore." "Wrensong/Reynsong offers full in-house administration services for our writers and the catalogs we represent, as well as outside writers and catalogs."

HOW TO CONTACT Does not accept unsolicited material.

◑ YOUR BEST SONGS PUBLISHING

1402 Auburn Way N., Suite 396, Auburn WA 98002. **Contact:** John Markovich, general manager. Music publisher. Publishes 1-5 songs/year; publishes 1-3 new songwriters/year. Query for royalty terms.

HOW TO CONTACT *Write first and obtain permission to submit.* Prefers CD with 1-3 songs and lyric sheet. "Submit your 1-3 best songs per type of music. Use separate CDs per music type and indicate music type on each CD." Include SASE. Responds in 3 months.

MUSIC Mostly **country**, **rock/blues**, and **pop/rock**; also **progressive**, **A/C**, some **heavy metal** and **New Age**.

TIPS "We just require good lyrics, good melodies and good rhythm in a song. We absolutely do not want music without a decent melodic structure. We do not want lyrics with foul language or lyrics that do not inspire some form of imaginative thought."

RECORD COMPANIES

Record companies release and distribute records, cassettes and CDs—the tangible products of the music industry. They sign artists to recording contracts, decide what songs those artists will record, and determine which songs to release. They also are responsible for providing recording facilities, securing producers and musicians, and overseeing the manufacture, distribution and promotion of new releases.

MAJOR LABELS & INDEPENDENT LABELS

Major labels and independent labels—what's the difference between the two?

The Majors

As of this writing, there are three major record labels, commonly referred to as the "Big 3":

- **SONY BMG** (Columbia Records, Epic Records, RCA Records, Arista Records, J Records, Provident Label Group, etc.)
- **UNIVERSAL MUSIC GROUP** (Universal Records, Interscope/Geffen/A&M, Island/Def Jam, Dreamworks Records, MCA Nashville Records, Verve Music Group, etc.)
- **WARNER MUSIC GROUP** (Atlantic Records, Bad Boy, Asylum Records, Warner Bros. Records, Maverick Records, Sub Pop, etc.)

Each of the "Big 3" is a large, publicly traded corporation beholden to shareholders and quarterly profit expectations. This means the major labels have greater financial resources and promotional muscle than a smaller "indie" label, but it's also harder to get signed to a major. A big major label may also expect more contractual control over an artist's or band's sound and image.

As shown in the above list, they also each act as umbrella organizations for numerous other well-known labels—former major labels in their own right, well-respected former independent/boutique labels, as well as subsidiary "vanity" labels fronted by successful major label recording artists. Each major label also has its own related worldwide product distribution system, and many independent labels will contract with the majors for distribution into stores.

If a label is distributed by one of these major companies, you can be assured any release coming out on that label has a large distribution network behind it. It will most likely be sent to most major retail stores in the United States.

The Independents

Independent labels go through smaller distribution companies to distribute their product. They usually don't have the ability to deliver records in massive quantities as the major distributors do. However, that doesn't mean independent labels aren't able to have hit records just like their major counterparts. A record label's distributors are found in the listings after the **Distributed by** heading.

Which Do I Submit To?

Many of the companies listed in this section are independent labels. They usually are the most receptive to receiving material from new artists. Major labels spend more money than most other segments of the music industry; the music publisher, for instance, pays only for items such as salaries and the costs of making demos. Record companies, at great financial risk, pay for many more services, including production, manufacturing and promotion. Therefore, they must

be very selective when signing new talent. Also, the continuing fear of copyright infringement suits has closed avenues to getting new material heard by the majors. Most don't listen to unsolicited submissions, period. Only songs recommended by attorneys, managers, and producers who record company employees trust and respect are being heard by A&R people at major labels (companies with a referral policy have a ⊘ preceding their listing). But that doesn't mean all major labels are closed to new artists. With a combination of a strong local following, success on an independent label (or strong sales of an independently produced and released album) and the right connections, you could conceivably get an attentive audience at a major label.

But the competition is fierce at the majors, so you shouldn't overlook independent labels. Since they're located all over the country, indie labels are easier to contact and can be important in building a local base of support for your music (consult the Geographic Index at the back of the book to find out which companies are located near you). Independent labels usually concentrate on a specific type of music, which will help you target those companies your submissions should be sent to. And since the staff at an indie label is smaller, there are fewer channels to go through to get your music heard by the decision makers in the company.

HOW RECORD COMPANIES WORK

Independent record labels can run on a small staff, with only a handful of people running the day-to-day business. Major record labels are more likely to be divided into the following departments: A&R, sales, marketing, promotion, product management, artist development, production, finance, business/legal and international.

- The **A&R DEPARTMENT** is staffed with A&R representatives who search out new talent. They go out and see new bands, listen to demo tapes, and decide which artists to sign. They also look for new material for already-signed acts, match producers with artists and oversee recording projects. Once an artist is signed by an A&R rep and a record is recorded, the rest of the departments at the company come into play.
- The **SALES DEPARTMENT** is responsible for getting a record into stores. They make sure record stores and other outlets receive enough copies of a record to meet consumer demand.
- The **MARKETING DEPARTMENT** is in charge of publicity, advertising in magazines and other media, promotional videos, album cover artwork, in-store displays, and any other means of getting the name and image of an artist to the public.
- The **PROMOTION DEPARTMENT**'s main objective is to get songs from a new album played on the radio. They work with radio programmers to make sure a product gets airplay.
- The **PRODUCT MANAGEMENT DEPARTMENT** is the ringmaster of the sales, marketing and promotion departments, assuring that they're all going in the same direction when promoting a new release.
- The **ARTIST DEVELOPMENT DEPARTMENT** is responsible for taking care of things while an artist is on tour, such as setting up promotional opportunities in cities where an act is performing.
- The **PRODUCTION DEPARTMENT** handles the actual manufacturing and pressing of the record and makes sure it gets shipped to distributors in a timely manner.
- People in the **FINANCE DEPARTMENT** compute and distribute royalties, as well as keep track of expenses and income at the company.
- The **BUSINESS/LEGAL DEPARTMENT** handles and oversees any and all contracts for the company, not only between the record company and artists but with foreign distributors, record clubs, etc.
- And finally, the **INTERNATIONAL DEPARTMENT** is responsible for working with international companies for the release of records in other countries.

LOCATING A RECORD LABEL

With the abundance of record labels out there, how do you go about finding one that's right for the music you create? First, it helps to know exactly what kind of music a record label releases. Become familiar with the records a company has released, and see if they fit in with what you're doing. Each listing in this section details the type of music a particular record company is interested in releasing. You will want to refer to the Category Index to help you find those companies most receptive to the type of music you write. You should only approach companies open to your level of experience (see "A Sample Listing Decoded" in the article "How to Use *Songwriter's Market*"). Visiting a company's website also can provide valuable information about a company's philosophy, the artists on the label and the music they work with.

NETWORKING

Recommendations by key music industry people are an important part of making contacts with record companies. Songwriters must remember that talent alone does not guarantee success in the music business. You must be recognized through contacts, and the only way to make contacts is through networking. Networking is the process of building an interconnecting web of acquaintances within the music business. The more industry people you meet, the larger your contact base becomes, and the better your chances are of meeting someone with the clout to get your demo into the hands of the right people. If you want to get your music heard by key A&R representatives, networking is imperative.

Networking opportunities can be found anywhere industry people gather. A good place to meet key industry people is at regional and national music conferences and workshops. There are many held all over the country for all types of music (see the Workshops and Conferences section for more information). You should try to attend at least one or two of these events each year; it's a great way to increase the number and quality of your music industry contacts.

Creating a Buzz

Another good way to attract A&R people is to make a name for yourself as an artist. By starting your career on a local level and building it from there, you can start to cultivate a following and prove to labels that you can be a success. A&R people figure if an act can be successful locally, there's a good chance they could be successful nationally. Start getting booked at local clubs, and start a mailing list of fans and local media. Once you gain some success on a local level, branch out. All this attention you're slowly gathering, this "buzz" you're generating, will not only get to your fans but to influential people in the music industry, as well.

SUBMITTING TO RECORD COMPANIES

When submitting to a record company, major or independent, a professional attitude is imperative. Be specific about what you are submitting and what your goals are. If you are strictly a songwriter and the label carries a band you believe would properly present your song, state that in your cover letter. If you are an artist looking for a contract, showcase your strong points as a performer. Whatever your goals are, follow submission guidelines closely, be as neat as possible and include a top-notch demo. If you need more information concerning a company's requirements, write or call for more details. (For more information on submitting your material, see the articles "Where Should I Send My Songs?" and "Demo Recordings.")

RECORD COMPANY CONTRACTS

Once you've found a record company that is interested in your work, the next step is signing a contract. Independent label contracts are usually not as long and complicated as major label ones, but they are still binding, legal contracts. Make sure the terms are in the best interest of both you and the label. Avoid anything in your contract that you feel is too restrictive. It's important to have your contract reviewed by a competent entertainment lawyer. A basic recording contract can run from 40-100 pages, and you need a lawyer to help you understand it. A lawyer also will be essential in helping you negotiate a deal that is in your best interest.

Recording contracts cover many areas, and just a few of the things you will be asked to consider are: What royalty rate is the record label willing to pay? What kind of advance are they offering? How many records will the company commit to? Will they offer tour support? Will they provide a budget for video? What sort of a recording budget are they offering? Are they asking you to give up any publishing rights? Are they offering you a publishing advance? These are only a few of the complex issues raised by a recording contract, so it's vital to have an entertainment lawyer at your side as you negotiate. For more information on contracts, lawyers, and payment, please see the interview with entertainment lawyer Barry Shrum—"For the Love of the Money."

ADDITIONAL RECORD COMPANIES

There are **more record companies** located in other sections of the book! Use the Index to find additional record companies within other sections.

The Case for Independents

If you're interested in getting a major label deal, it makes sense to look to independent record labels to get your start. Independent labels are seen by many as a stepping stone to a major recording contract. Very few artists are signed to a major label at the start of their careers; usually, they've had a few independent releases that helped build their reputation in the industry. Major labels watch independent labels closely to locate up-and-coming bands and new trends. In the current economic atmosphere at major labels—with extremely high overhead costs for developing new bands and the fact that only 10 percent of acts on major labels actually make any profit—they're not willing to risk everything on an unknown act. Most major labels won't even consider signing a new act that hasn't had some indie success.

But independents aren't just farming grounds for future major label acts; many bands have long-term relationships with indies and prefer it that way. While they may not be able to provide the extensive distribution and promotion that a major label can (though there are exceptions), indie labels can help an artist become a regional success, and may even help the performer to see a profit, as well. With the lower overhead and smaller production costs an independent label operates on, it's much easier to "succeed" on an indie label than on a major.

Icons

For more instructional information on the listings in this book, including explanations of symbols, read the article "How To Use *Songwriter's Market*."

4AD

17-19 Alma Rd., London SW18 1AA United Kingdom. **E-mail:** 4AD@4AD.com. **Website:** www.4ad.com. **HOW TO CONTACT** Submit demo (CD or vinyl only) by mail, attention A&R, 4AD. "Sadly, there just aren't enough hours in the day to respond to everything that comes in. We'll only get in touch if we really like something."

MUSIC Mostly **rock, indie/alternative**. Current artists include Blonde Redhead, Bon Iver, Camera Obscura, The Breeders, The National, TV On The Radio, and more.

ALBANY RECORDS

915 Broadway, Albany NY 12207. **E-mail:** infoalbany@aol.com. **Website:** www.albanyrecords.com. Do you enjoy classical music that is off the beaten path? Are you frustrated by the lack of imaginative releases by the major classical labels? Albany Records is where you should look. Albany Records is devoted to music by American composers (with a few notable exceptions) performed by the best of America's artists. From premiere recordings of orchestral music by Roy Harris, Morton Gould and Don Gillis to music by George Lloyd and Andrei Eshpai, there is something for everyone on Albany Records—provided your interests are just a bit out of the ordinary."

MUSIC Choral, **chamber, opera, instrumental**, organ, **wind** and **brass, percussion, classical, world**, etc.

ARIANA RECORDS

1312 S. Avenida Polar, #A-8, Tucson AZ 85710. (520)790-7324. **E-mail:** jtiom@aol.com. **Website:** www.arianarecords.net. **Contact:** James M. Gasper, president; Tom Dukes, vice president (pop, rock); Tom Privett (funk, experimental, rock) and Scott Smith (pop, rock, AOR), partners. Record company, music publisher (Myko Music/BMI) and record producer. Estab. 1980. Releases 5 CDs a year and 1 compilation/year. Pays negotiable rates.

DISTRIBUTED BY LoneBoy Records London, The Yellow Record Co. in Germany, and Groovetune Music distributors in Alberta, Canada. Started talks with RCD Records for German distribution in early 2012.

HOW TO CONTACT "Send finished masters only. No demos! Unsolicited material OK."

MUSIC Mostly **rock, funk, jazz**, anything weird, strange, or lo-fi (must be mastered to CD). Released *Rustling Silk* (electronic) by BuddyLoveBand; *Porn-Muzik 2* (ambient); *T.G.I.F4* (electronica); *UnderCov-*

er Band; *2010* (pop rock and funk); *Catch the Ghost* (hard rock). New releases *Musika* 2011 CD compilation, *Fun and Games* EP by Alien Workshop, and the single, "Hey Mr. President" by the Bailout Boys. Recently signed Perfect Paris (an electronic duo) and A Thousand Poets (an industrial/electronic duo).

TIPS "Keep on trying."

ARKADIA ENTERTAINMENT CORP.

P.O. Box 77, Saugerties NY 12477. (845)246-9955. **Fax:** (845)246-9966. **E-mail:** info@view.com. **E-mail:** acquisitions@view.com. **Website:** www.view.com/arkadia.aspx. Labels include Arkadia Jazz and Arkadia Chansons. Record company, music publisher (Arkadia Music), record producer (Arkadia Productions), and Arkadia Video. Estab. 1995.

HOW TO CONTACT Write or call first and obtain permission to submit.

MUSIC Mostly **jazz, classical**, and **pop/R&B**; also **world**.

ASTRALWERKS

101 Avenue of the Americas, 10th Floor, New York NY 10013. **E-mail:** astralwerks.astralwerks@gmail.com. **Website:** www.astralwerks.com.

Astralwerks is a subsidiary of the EMI Group, one of the "Big 4" major labels. EMI is a British-based company.

HOW TO CONTACT Does not accept unsolicited submissions.

MUSIC Mostly **alternative/indie/electronic**. Artists include VHS or BETA, Badly Drawn Boy, The Beta Band, Chemical Brothers, Turin Breaks, and Fatboy Slim.

ATLAN-DEC/GROOVELINE RECORDS

2529 Green Forest Court, Snellville GA 30078-4183. (877)751-5169. **E-mail:** atlandec@prodigy.net. **Website:** www.atlan-dec.com. **Contact:** Wileta J. Hatcher, art director. This company has grown to boast a roster of artists representing different genres of music. "Our artists' diversity brings a unique quality of musicianship to our CDs and tapes. This uniqueness excites our listeners and has gained us the reputation of releasing only the very best in recorded music." Atlan-Dec/Grooveline Records CDs and tapes are distributed worldwide through traditional and virtual online retail stores. Record company, music publisher and record producer. Staff size: 2. Releases 3-4 singles, 3-4 LPs and 3-4 CDs/year. Pays 10-25% royalty to artists on contract; statutory rate to publisher per song on record.

DISTRIBUTED BY C.E.D. Entertainment Dist.

HOW TO CONTACT Submit demo package by mail. Unsolicited submissions are OK. Prefers CD with lyric sheet. Does not return material. Responds in 3 months.

MUSIC Mostly **R&B/urban**, **hip-hop/rap**, and **contemporary jazz**; also **soft rock**, **gospel**, **dance**, and **new country**. Released "Temptation" by Shawree, released 2004 on Atlan-Dec/Grooveline Records; *Enemy of the State* (album), recorded by Lowlife (rap/hip-hop); *I'm The Definition* (album), recorded by L.S. (rap/hip-hop), released 2007; "AHHW" (single), recorded by LeTebony Simmons (R&B), released 2007. Other artists include Furious D (rap/hip-hop), Mark Cocker (new country), and Looka, "From the Top" (rap/hip-hop) recorded in 2008.

ATLANTIC RECORDS

1290 Avenue of the Americas, New York NY 10104. (212)707-2000. **Fax:** (212)581-6414. **E-mail:** contact@atlanticrecords.com. **Website:** www.atlanticrecords.com. Labels include Big Beat Records, LAVA, Nonesuch Records, Atlantic Classics, and Rhino Records. Record company. Pays negotiable royalty to artists on contract; negotiable rate to publisher per song on record.

Atlantic Records is a subsidiary of Warner Music Group, one of the "Big 3" major labels.

DISTRIBUTED BY WEA.

HOW TO CONTACT Does not accept unsolicited material. "No phone calls, please."

MUSIC Artists include Missy Elliott, Simple Plan, Lupe Fiasco, Phil Collins, B.O.B., Jason Mraz, and Death Cab For Cutie.

AWAL UK LTD.

Sheffield Technology Park, Arundel St., Sheffield S1 2NS United Kingdom. **E-mail:** info@awal.com. **Website:** www.awal.com.

DISTRIBUTED BY Primarily distributes via digital downloads but physical distribution available.

HOW TO CONTACT Submit demo by mail. Unsolicited submissions are OK. Prefers CD with 5 songs, lyric sheet, cover letter and press clippings. Does not return materials.

MUSIC Mostly **pop**, **world**, and **jazz**; also **techno**, **teen**, and **children's**. Released *Go Cat Go* (album by various), recorded by Carl Perkins on ArtistOne.com;

Bliss (album), written and recorded by Donna Delory (pop); and *Shake A Little* (album), written and recorded by Michael Ruff, both on Awal Records.

AWARE RECORDS

800 18th Ave., Suite C, Nashville TN 37203. (615)864-8043. **E-mail:** awareinfo@awaremusic.com. **Website:** www.awaremusic.com.

HOW TO CONTACT Does not accept unsolicited submissions.

MUSIC Mostly **rock/pop**. Artists include Mat Kearney and Guster.

BAD TASTE RECORDS

P.O. Box 1243, S - 221 05 Lund, Sweden. **E-mail:** info@badtasterecords.se. **Website:** www.badtasterecords.se.

HOW TO CONTACT "We listen to everything we receive. It usually takes a while because we receive a lot of demos, but eventually we always listen to it. Send CDs to the address above. Do not e-mail MP3s. With the amount of demo tapes we receive there is rarely time to write back, unless, of course, we're interested in releasing your band or including a song on one of our compilations. Please don't be too disappointed by this. We would love to be able to write back to everyone, but we are already working days, nights and weekends to try and get things done. Just in case, though, please include your e-mail address." More details are posted on the website.

MUSIC Works with bands such as Danko Jones, Logh, Quit Your Dayjob, Embee, Lemonheads, Langhorns, and more.

BIG COFFEE RECORDS

4867 Ashford Dunwoody Rd. #6202, Atlanta GA 30338. **E-mail:** info@bigcoffeerecords.com. **Website:** www.bigcoffeerecords.com. Big Coffee Records is an independent record label located in Atlanta, Georgia, dedicated to releasing like-minded, quality local music in many genres, including: rock, Southern rock, blues, rhythm and blues, Americana, contemporary jazz, smooth jazz, groove, club, as well as New Age, stress relief, meditation, healing, with music for film, TV, and advertising placement.

MUSIC Artists include Mose Jones, Steve McRay, Java Monkey, Cole/Taylor, Francine Reed, etc.

BIG FACE ENTERTAINMENT

100 State St., Suite 360, Albany NY 12207. **E-mail:** info@bigfaceonline.com. **Website:** www.bigfaceonline.com. Big Face Entertainment, your hybrid record

label that offers multi-dimensional services that cater to the artists. "In other words, we are the house that creates the product and puts it out there! We focus on what is truly important at our company opposed to others: investing in the music and talented artists that create the content. We believe in creating a collaborative and innovative environment where our artists can thrive and reach their full capacity in a stress-free atmosphere."

MUSIC Artists include Legend, Island Boy, Daytona, and more. **Rap**, **hip-hop**, **pop**, etc.

BIG HEAVY WORLD

P.O. Box 428, Burlington VT 05402-0428. **E-mail:** info@bigheavyworld.com. **Website:** www.bigheavy-world.com. Big Heavy World has been pulling together compilations of Vermont artists since 1996 with the release of Sonic Tonic, the indie-alt-core battle cry of our veteran scene-pimping phalanx. We've plowed lovingly through more than 15 titles and continue to unite regional musicians within projects that ultimately, we hope, bring recognition to Vermont's deserving music community and maybe make the world a better place in the process. Most Big Heavy World compilations and their release parties have created exposure and fiscal support for worthy humanitarian organizations like Spectrum Youth and Family Services, the Make-A-Wish Foundation, the Women's Rape Crisis Center, 242 Main, and Vietnam Assistance for the Handicapped.

BLACKHEART RECORDS

636 Broadway, New York NY 10012. (212)353-9600. **Fax:** (212)353-8300. **E-mail:** blackheart@blackheart. com. **Website:** www.blackheart.com.
HOW TO CONTACT Unsolicited submissions are OK. Prefers CD with 1-3 songs and lyric sheets. Include SASE. Responds only if interested.
MUSIC Mostly **rock**. Artists include Joan Jett & the Blackhearts, The Dollyrots, The Vacancies, Girl In A Coma, and The Eyeliners.

BLANK TAPE RECORDS

E-mail: blanktaperecords@gmail.com. **Website:** www.blanktaperecords.org. Blank Tape Records is a collectively owned and operated independent record label based in southern Colorado dedicated to creating and sharing music. "Our artists make up songs, wander and sing cross-country, conjure spirits and invent albums, so that we might do the impossible and make a living out of our curiosities." Since 2008, Blank Tape has released over 20 albums, the majority featuring the diverse and talented music scene of the front range.

MUSIC Roster includes The Changing Colors, The Haunted Windchimes, Mike Clark & The Sugar Sounds, Grant Sabin, Desirae Garcia, and more.
TIPS "We are friends helping friends put out records, working through an organic process. We don't make our artists sign contracts, so our relationships are based on friendship, a good work ethic and trust. We all contribute to the Blank Tape Family in some way, shape or form; we are artists, designers, social media managers, photographers, envelope stuffers, web designers, audio engineers and videographers dedicated to each other's vision and dream. New bands and artists come into the fold when they have made a mark within our community and there is a mutual agreement that we can benefit from one another."

CAMBRIA RECORDS & PUBLISHING

P.O. Box 374, Lomita CA 90717. (310)831-1322. **Fax:** (310)833-7442. **E-mail:** cambriamus@aol.com. **Website:** cambriamus.com.
DISTRIBUTED BY Albany Distribution.
HOW TO CONTACT *Write first and obtain permission to submit.* Accepts CD and cassette. Include SASE. Responds in 1 month.
MUSIC Mostly **classical**. Released *Songs of Elinor Remick Warren* (album) on Cambria Records. Other artists include Marie Gibson (soprano), Leonard Pennario (piano), Thomas Hampson (voice), Mischa Lefkowitz (violin), Leigh Kaplan (piano), North Wind Quintet, and Sierra Wind Quintet.

CAPITOL RECORDS

1750 N. Vine St., Hollywood CA 90028. (323)462-6252. **Fax:** (323)469-4542. **Website:** www.capitolrecords.com. Labels include Blue Note Records, Grand Royal Records, Pangaea Records, The Right Stuff Records and Capitol Nashville Records.

Capitol Records is a subsidiary of the EMI Group, one of the "Big 3" major labels.
DISTRIBUTED BY EMD.
HOW TO CONTACT Capitol Records does not accept unsolicited submissions.
MUSIC Artists include Coldplay, The Decemberists, Beastie Boys, Katy Perry, Interpol, Lily Allen, and Depeche Mode.

⊘⊛ CAPP RECORDS

P.O. Box 150871, San Rafael CA 94915-0871. (415)457-8617. **E-mail:** tim@capprecords.com. **Website:** www.capprecords.com. **Contact:** Tim Davis.

HOW TO CONTACT Submit 1-3 best songs by e-mail only to Tim Davis / A&R. Unsolicited submissions are OK. Prefers MP3 (320k) files or direct streaming links for listening. Only responds if interested.

FILM & TV Places 100-plus songs in TV, film, and advertising per year. Currently doing music placements: NBC/Universal, Arnold Advertising, *Keeping Up With the Kardashians*, MTV, VH1, A&E Network, Discovery Channel, and more.

MUSIC Represents all styles of premium-quality recordings only.

⊘ COLUMBIA RECORDS

550 Madison Ave., 23rd Floor, New York NY 10022. (212)833-4000. **Fax:** (212)833-4389. **Website:** www.columbiarecords.com. Record company.

◖   Columbia Records is a subsidiary of Sony BMG, one of the "Big 3" major labels.

DISTRIBUTED BY Sony.

HOW TO CONTACT Columbia Records does not accept unsolicited submissions.

MUSIC Artists include Aerosmith, Marc Anthony, Beyonce, Bob Dylan, and Patti Smith.

⊘ COSMOTONE RECORDS

2951 Marina Bay Dr., Suite 130, PMB 501, League City TX 77573-2733. **E-mail:** marianland@earthlink.net. **Website:** www.marianland.com/music.html; www.cosmotonerecords.com. Record company, music publisher (Cosmotone Music, ASCAP), and record producer (Rafael Brom).

DISTRIBUTED BY www.marianland.com

HOW TO CONTACT "Sorry, we do not accept material at this time." Does not return materials.

MUSIC Mostly **Christian pop/rock**. Released *Rafael Brom I*, *Padre Pio* by Lord Hamilton, *Dance for Padre Pio*, *Peace of Heart*, *Music for Peace of Mind*, *The Sounds of Heaven*, *The Christmas Songs*, *Angelophany*, *The True Measure of Love*, *All My Love to You Jesus* (albums), and *Rafael Brom Unplugged* (live concert DVD), *Life is Good, Enjoy it While You Can, Change*, by Rafael Brom, *Refugee from Socialism* by Rafael Brom, and *Move Your Ass* by Rafael Brom, *Peanut Regatta* by Rafael Brom, and *Best of Rafael Brom*, Volume I, II, III and IV.

CULT RECORDS

New York NY **E-mail:** info@cultrecords.com. **Website:** www.cultrecords.com. Founded and run by Julian Casablancas, Cult Records is an indie record label. Focused on quality over quantity, Cult is pledged to the highest standard for every song on each record it puts out.

MUSIC "Our current roster includes Julian Casablancas + The Voidz, Karen O, Har Mar Superstar, Nelson London (C O L O R), Rey Pila, Cerebral Ballzy and Albert Hammond, Jr." Previous releases include The Virgins, Exclamation Pony, and Reputante.

⊘ CURB RECORDS

48 Music Square E., Nashville TN 37203. (615)321-5080. **Fax:** (615)327-1964. **Website:** www.curb.com.

HOW TO CONTACT Curb Records does not accept unsolicited submissions; accepts previously published material only. Do not submit without permission.

MUSIC Released *Everywhere* (album), recorded by Tim McGraw; *Sittin' On Top of the World* (album), recorded by LeAnn Rimes; and *I'm Alright* (album), recorded by Jo Dee Messina, all on Curb Records. Other artists include Mary Black, Merle Haggard, David Kersh, Lyle Lovett, Tim McGraw, Wynonna, and Sawyer Brown.

◯ DENTAL RECORDS

P.O. Box 20058, New York NY 10017. (212) 486-4513. **Website:** www.dentalrecords.com.

HOW TO CONTACT "Check website to see if your material is appropriate." *Not currently accepting unsolicited submissions.*

MUSIC **Pop-derived structures**, **jazz-derived harmonies**, and **neo-classic-wannabe-pretenses**. Claims no expertise, nor interest, in urban, heavy metal, or hard core. Released *Perspectivism* (album), written and recorded by Rick Sanford (instrumental), released 2003 on Dental Records. Other artists include Les Izmor.

DIM MAK

Los Angeles CA **E-mail:** demos@dimmak.com. **Website:** www.dimmak.com. Dim Mak is an independent record label, events company, and lifestyle brand founded by Steve Aoki. The label has released music in punk, indie rock, hardcore, and electronic dance.

DIZZYBIRD RECORDS

Grand Rapids MI **Website:** dizzybirdrecords.com. Dizzybird Records was established "by a couple of kids who decided to ignore various reports claiming the music industry was unfit for dreamers. After years of putting a magnifying glass up to liner notes, giving into the addiction that compels one to not miss a show, swimming laps in an ocean of beer, programming community radio shows, curating jukebox playlists, and staring at the moon with a glorious mixture of confusion and excitement ... this bird has landed."

HOW TO CONTACT Contact via online form.

TIPS "There are two of us here. At any given moment, we are either texting each other about how we disagree on promo artwork or sharing dreamy-fuzzed-out songs we just discovered. It's like living in a snow globe. That said, feel free to reach out using those Internet windows over there. Maybe we can dream together?!!? Chirp."

DOMINO RECORDING CO.

P.O. Box 47029, London SW18 1EG United Kingdom. **Website:** www.dominorecordco.us. The Domino Record Co. was founded by Laurence Bell, and its first release was Sebadoh's "Soul and Fire." Since then, the label has developed a mix of lo-fi and experimental acts.

HOW TO CONTACT Domino is no longer accepting postal submissions of demos. "If you truly believe your music belongs on Domino, you can submit your recordings via a message through our environmentally friendly Soundcloud. Log in to your Soundcloud account and then click on the Send a Message icon below our logo."

DOUBLE DOUBLE WHAMMY

338 W. Ridgewood Ave., Ridgewood NJ **E-mail:** hello@dbldblwhmmy.com. **Website:** dbldblwhmmy.com. Double Double Whammy aims to produce and distribute quality cassettes, phonograph records and compact discs in the physical realm.

HOW TO CONTACT Send e-mail clearly marked "DEMO" in the subject line. Streaming only! No attachments! No physical submissions, please. "We listen, but cannot respond to everything."

MUSIC Currently releasing records and tapes from LVL UP, Crying, Frankie Cosmos, Free Cake For Every Creature, QUARTERBACKS, Radiator Hospital, Flashlight O, Mitski, and Liam Betson.

EARACHE RECORDS

4402 11th St., #400A, Long Island City NY 11101. (347)507-1402. **Website:** www.earache.com.

MUSIC **Rock, industrial, heavy metal techno, death metal, grindcore**. Artists include Municipal Waste,

Dillinger Escape Plan, Bring Me the Horizon, Deicide, Oceano, and more.

◎ ELEKTRA RECORDS

75 Rockefeller Plaza, 17th Floor, New York NY 10019. **Website:** www.elektra.com.

◐ Elektra Records is a subsidiary of Warner Music Group, one of the "Big 4" major labels.

DISTRIBUTED BY WEA.

HOW TO CONTACT *Elektra does not accept unsolicited submissions.*

MUSIC Mostly alternative/modern rock. Artists include Bruno Mars, Cee Lo, Justice, Little Boots, and *True Blood*.

◎ EPIC RECORDS

550 Madison Ave., 23rd Floor, New York NY 10022. (212)833-8000. **Fax:** (212)833-4054. **Website:** www.epicrecords.com. Labels include Beluga Heights, Daylight Records and E1 Music. Record company.

◐ Epic Records is a subsidiary of Sony BMG, one of the "Big 4" major labels.

DISTRIBUTED BY Sony Music Distribution.

HOW TO CONTACT *Write or call first and obtain permission to submit* (New York office only). Does not return material. Responds only if interested. *Santa Monica and Nashville offices do not accept unsolicited submissions.*

MUSIC Artists include Sade, Shakira, Modest Mouse, The Fray, Natasha Bedingfield, Sean Kingston, Incubus, The Script.

TIPS "Do an internship if you don't have experience or work as someone's assistant. Learn the business and work hard while you figure out what your talents are and where you fit in. Once you figure out which area of the record company you're suited for, focus on that, work hard at it, and it shall be yours."

◎ EPITAPH RECORDS

2798 Sunset Blvd., Los Angeles CA 90026. (213)355-5000. **E-mail:** publicity@epitaph.com. **Website:** www.epitaph.com. Record company. Contains imprints Hellcat Records and Anti. "Epitaph Records was founded by Bad Religion guitarist Brett Gurewitz with the aim of starting an artist-friendly label from a musicians' point of view. Perhaps most well known for being the little indie from L.A. that spawned the 1990s' punk explosion."

HOW TO CONTACT "Post your demos online at one of the many free music portals, then simply fill out the Demo submission form" on website.

MUSIC Artists include Social Distortion, Alkaline Trio, Rancid, The Weakerthans, Weezer, Bad Religion, Every Time I Die.

◯ EQUAL VISION RECORDS

P.O. Box 38202, Albany NY 12203-8202. (518)458-8250. **E-mail:** info@equalvision.com. **E-mail:** music@equalvision.com. **Website:** equalvision.com. "We're an independent record label entirely owned and operated with no outside financial support. We are, however, distributed by the Alternative Distribution Alliance (ADA Music), which is a subsidiary of Warner Music Group. ADA also distributes some of our favorite independent labels like Sub Pop, Epitaph, Saddle Creek, Atlantic, Doghouse, Fearless, Hopeless, Matador, Merge, Polyvinyl, and more."

HOW TO CONTACT In an effort to become more environmentally friendly, Equal Vision Records no longer accepts unsolicited physical demos. Instead, please e-mail music@equalvision.com with a link to where we can check out songs on the web. It's much faster, cheaper, and easier for us to listen to music online. If we like your tunes, we'll request a CD or demo package.

TIPS "We love talking about music, but, unfortunately, we can't respond or give tips to every band that sends in a submission ... there just aren't enough hours in the day, and we need to devote our time to our current artists. Instead, spend your time writing the best music you can. Travel, tour, flier, and build your band on your own. The harder you work, the more likely we are to notice."

◖ ETERNAL OTTER RECORDS

8 Mayo St. #2, Portland ME 04101. **Website:** www.eternalotterrecords.com. Eternal Otter Records is an online music label devoted to limited-edition recordings of exceptional musical talents, drawn primarily from the Portland, Maine, area. The criterion for all Eternal Otter releases is not simply the talent of the individual artist. It is, to a larger extent, defined by the enduring, timeless nature of the music itself.

HOW TO CONTACT Contact via online form.

MUSIC Artists include Cerebus Soul, Lady Lamb and Beekeeper, The Milkman's Union, Jesse Pilgrim & the Bonfire, Panda Bandits, and more.

FATHER/DAUGHTER RECORDS

San Francisco CA **E-mail:** daughter@fatherdaughterrecords.com. **Website:** www.fatherdaughterrecords.com. Father/Daughter are 2 folks, bound by blood but years apart. Run out of 2 homes in San Francisco and Miami, the love of music brings this long-distance family just that much closer.

HOW TO CONTACT "Got some tunes to send our way or just want to say, 'Hi?' E-mail us at daughter@fatherdaughterrecords.com."

⊘ FAT POSSUM RECORDS

Oxford MS **Website:** www.fatpossum.com. Fat Possum Records is an independent record label that was originally focused on recording previously unknown Mississippi blues artists but has recently signed some younger acts to its roster.

⊘ FAT WRECK CHORDS

2196 Palon Ave., San Francisco CA 94124. **E-mail:** mailbag@fatwreck.com. **Website:** www.fatwreck.com.

MUSIC **Punk**, **rock**, **alternative**. Artists include NOFX, Rise Against, The Lawrence Arms, Anti-Flag, Me First and the Gimme Gimmes, Propagandhi, Dillinger Four, Against Me!, and more.

FEARLESS RECORDS

13772 Goldenwest St. #545, Westminster CA 92683. **E-mail:** demos@fearlessrecords.com. **Website:** www.fearlessrecords.com.

HOW TO CONTACT Send all demos to mailing address. "Do not e-mail us about demos or with links to MP3s."

MUSIC **Alternative, pop, indie, rock, metal**. Artists include Plain White T's, Mayday Parade, Blessthefall, Breathe Carolina, The Summer Set, Forever The Sickest Kids, The Downtown Fiction, Real Friends, Jason Lancaster (Go Radio), Motionless In White, and more.

◯ FIREANT

2009 Ashland Ave., Charlotte NC 28205. (704)335-1400. **E-mail:** lewh@fireantmusic.com. **Website:** www.fireantmusic.com.

DISTRIBUTED BY The Orchard, City Hall Records, and eMusic.com.

HOW TO CONTACT Submit demo by mail. Unsolicited submissions are OK. Does not return material.

MUSIC Mostly **progressive, traditional**, and **musical hybrids**. "Anything except New Age and MOR." Released *Loving the Alien: Athens Georgia Salutes David Bowie* (album), recorded by various artists (rock/alternative/electronic); and *Good Enough* (album), recorded by Zen Frisbee. Other artists include Mr. Peters' Belizean Boom and Chime Band.

FLYING HEART RECORDS

4015 NE 12th Ave., Portland OR 97212. **E-mail:** flyheart@teleport.com. **Website:** home.teleport.com/~flyheart.

DISTRIBUTED BY Burnside Distribution Co.

HOW TO CONTACT Submit demo by mail. Unsolicited submissions are OK. Prefers CD with 1-10 songs and lyric sheets. Does not return material. "SASE required for *any* response." Responds in 3 months.

MUSIC Mostly **R&B**, **blues**, and **jazz**; also **rock**. Released *Vexatious Progr.* (album), written and recorded by Eddie Harris (jazz); *Juke Music* (album), written and recorded by Thara Memory (jazz); and *Lookie Tookie* (album), written and recorded by Jan Celt (blues), all on Flying Heart Records. Other artists include Janice Scroggins, Tom McFarland, Thara Memory, and Snow Bud & The Flower People.

FOOL'S GOLD

536 Metropolitan Ave., Brooklyn NY 11211. **E-mail:** info@foolsgoldrecs.com. **E-mail:** demos@foolsgoldrecs.com. **Website:** www.foolsgoldrecs.com. Fool's Gold was founded by DJs A-Trak and Nick Catchdubs and quickly established itself with a non-stop series of releases bridging the worlds of hip-hop and electronic music.

FORGED ARTIFACTS

5000 Lyndale Ave. S., Unit 1, Minneapolis MN 55419. **E-mail:** forgedartifacts@gmail.com. **Website:** www.forgedartifacts.com. **Contact:** Matt Linden. An indie record company based in Minneapolis, Minnesota.

HOW TO CONTACT Feel free to send demos/sounds to forgedartifacts@gmail.com. Streamable links please. If you have physical demos, send them to the address above.

MUSIC Artists include Some Pulp, Baked, Gloss, France Camp, Nice Purse, and more.

FRENCHKISS RECORDS

111 E. 14th St., Suite 229, New York NY 10003. **E-mail:** info@frenchkissrecords.com. **Website:** www.frenchkissrecords.com. Frenchkiss Records was founded by Syd Butler.

HOW TO CONTACT Does not accept demo submissions via mail. "Submit your 2 best songs (no downloads; e-mails with downloads get deleted) via e-mail with 'DEMO' in the subject line."

TIPS "We listen to everything we get; if we like what we hear, we will contact you."

FUELED BY RAMEN

1633 Broadway, 10th Floor, New York NY 10019. **Website:** www.fueledbyramen.com.

HOW TO CONTACT Send demos by mail to address above. Do not e-mail about demos. Make sure there's a bio, contact information, touring information, and more. "Your music will speak for itself, but the packaging is our first impression of your band. There is no bigger frustration than opening a package and seeing a demo that looks like it was sent without even trying."

MUSIC Alternative, **Rock**, **Indie**. Artists include The Academy Is..., Cobra Starship, Gym Class Heroes, Panic! at the Disco, Paramore, Sublime with Rome, This Providence, and more.

TIPS "To be honest, each one of our bands has been signed for different reasons, and there are numerous things that we always look for—from your music, to your work ethic, to your personalities, to everything in between. The most important thing you can do is to work hard and accomplish as much as you can for your band before trying to get signed to a label. Develop a local following, tour the country, record an EP, start a street team, get interviewed by your local publications, etc.—we look for bands that are creating their own buzz and aren't depending on somebody else to do it for them. Putting all you can into your band will attract labels wishing to do the same."

MARTY GARRETT ENTERTAINMENT

320 W. Utica Place, Broken Arrow OK 74011. (918)451-6780. **E-mail:** martygarrett@earthlink.net. **Website:** martygarrettentertainment.com; www.musicbusinessmoney.com. **Contact:** Marty R. Garrett, president. Labels include MGE Records and Lonesome Wind Records. Record company, record producer, music publisher, and entertainment consultant. Authorized agent for Christian music artist David Ingles. Releases 1 CD/year. Pays negotiable royalty to artists on contract; statutory rate to publisher per song on record.

HOW TO CONTACT Call or check website first to review submission instructions and if submissions are currently being accepted. Prefers CD only with maximum 10 songs and lyric or lead sheets with chord progressions listed. Does not return material. Do not send press packs or bios unless specifically instructed to do so. Responds in 4-6 weeks.

MUSIC Mostly scripture-based **Christian** and **gospel**, **honky tonk**, and **traditional country**. Co-produced and released The Very Best Of David Ingles on DIP Records.

TIPS "We help artists record and release major label quality CD products to the public for sale through any number of methods, including radio and 1-800 Television. Although we do submit finished products to major record companies for review, our main focus is to establish and surround each artist with his or her own long-term production, promotion and distribution organization. Professional studio demos are not required, but make sure vocals are distinct, up-front, and up-to-date. I personally listen to each submission received, so call or check website FIRST to see if I am conducting reviews."

GLASSNOTE RECORDS

770 Lexington Ave., 16th Floor, New York NY 10065. (646)214-6000. **Fax:** (646)237-2711. **E-mail:** demos@ glassnotemusic.com. **Website:** www.glassnotemusic. com. Glassnote Entertainment Group is a full-service independent music company founded by Daniel Glass, one of the most accomplished and respected music people in the industry. His devotion to music and the artists that create this magic is what drove him to create the new company.

HOW TO CONTACT Send submissions by post or e-mail. However, do not e-mail MP3s to all e-mail addresses—only to the demos e-mail address.

TIPS "We do receive a lot of submissions, but someone will listen to it. We understand you've worked hard on your music, and we think you've earned at least that. However, submissions that come from managers, lawyers, agents or other persons that we know or would like to know do receive priority."

○ GRAVEFACE

5 West 40th St., Savannah GA 31401. **E-mail:** mail@ graveface.com. **Website:** www.graveface.com. Graveface is an extremely small recording label. "We are constantly searching for brilliant music to release to the world. If you are a fan of the music we already release, feel free to send us samples of your brilliance. We might reply back to you and we might not. We are happy with our little roster but if you really impress us, you will certainly be getting an e-mail."

MUSIC Artists include The Appleseed Cast, Creepoid, Dosh, The Loose Salute, The Casket Girls, The Stargazer Lilies, Hospital Ships, Gramma's Boyfriend, Dreamend, and many more.

○ HACIENDA RECORDS & RECORDING STUDIO

1236 S. Staples St., Corpus Christi TX 78404. (361)882-7066. **Fax:** (361)882-3943. **E-mail:** sales@ haciendarecords.com. **Website:** hacienda-records. myshopify.com.

HOW TO CONTACT Submit demo package by mail. Unsolicited submissions are OK. Prefers CD with cover letter. Does not return material. Responds in 6 weeks.

MUSIC Mostly **tejano**, **regional Mexican**, **country** (Spanish or English), and **pop**. Released "Chica Bonita" (single), recorded by Albert Zamora and D.J. Cubanito; "Si Quieres Verme Llorar" (single) from *Lisa Lopez con Mariachi* (album), recorded by Lisa Lopez (mariachi); "Tartamudo" (single) from *Una Vez Mas* (album), recorded by Peligro (norteno); and "Miento" (single) from *Si Tu Te Vas* (album), recorded by Traizion (tejano). Other artists include Gary Hobbs, Steve Jordan, Grammy Award nominees Mingo Saldivar and David Lee Garza, Michelle, Victoria Y Sus Chikos, La Traizion.

◐ HARDROC RECORDS

Website: www.hardrocrecords.com. HardRoc Records is an independent record label based out of Newark, New Jersey. With its deep connection to street music and support of mainstream flair, Hardroc has made itself the base for the most relevant and promising artists from New Jersey and the Tri-State area.

HOW TO CONTACT Use online form to contact.

MUSIC Artists include Nice and Ill, Roky Reign, Chad B., 22 McGraw, Aitch, and more. Hip-hop, rap, pop, trance, etc.

∅ HEADS UP INT., LTD.

Concord Music Group, 100 N. Crescent Dr., Garden Level, Beverly Hills CA 90210. **Website:** www.concordmusicgroup.com/labels/Heads-Up/.

MUSIC Mostly **jazz**, **R&B**, **pop** and **world**. Does not want anything else. Released *Long Walk to Freedom* (album), recorded by Ladysmith Black Mambazo (world); *Pilgrimage* (album), recorded by Michael Brecker (contemporary jazz); *Rizing Sun* (album), recorded by Najee (contemporary jazz). Other artists include Diane Schuur, Mateo Parker, Victor Wooten, Esperanza Spalding, Incognito, George Doke, Take 6, Fourplay.

⬤ HOPELESS RECORDS

P.O. Box 7495, Van Nuys CA 91409. **E-mail:** information@hopelessrecords.com. **E-mail:** ar@hopelessrecords.com. **Website:** www.hopelessrecords.com. Founded in 1993, Hopeless Records is a Southern California independent record label home to Yellowcard, All Time Low, Silverstein, Bayside, Enter Shikari, The Wonder Years, Taking Back Sunday, The Used, and many more. Throughout the 20-year history of Hopeless Records, the label has released over 100 albums and launched the careers of Avenged Sevenfold, Thrice, and Melee. In 1999, Hopeless Records formally started supporting nonprofit organizations under the Sub City name with charitable albums, tours, and events. Now itself a registered 501(c)(3) nonprofit organization, Sub City continues this mission of raising funds and awareness for worthy causes and, to date, has raised over $2 million dollars for over 50 nonprofit organizations.

HOW TO CONTACT E-mail ar@hopelessrecords.com with your band name in the subject. Send us your bio, MySpace, YouTube videos, EPKs, etc. If you attach MP3s, do not attach more than 1-2 of your best songs to the e-mail. We are no longer accepting physical submissions.

MUSIC Works with such artists as Divided by Friday, Bayside, Driver Friendly, New Found Glory, The Used, Taking Back Sunday, Neck Deep, and more.

⬤ IDOL RECORDS

P.O. Box 140344, Dallas TX 75214. (214)370-5417. **E-mail:** info@idolrecords.com. **Website:** www.idolrecords.com. **Contact:** Erv Karwelis, president. Releases 30 singles, 80 LPs, 20 EPs and 10-15 CDs/year. Pays negotiable royalty to artists on contract; negotiable rate to publisher per song on record.

DISTRIBUTED BY Super D (SDID).

HOW TO CONTACT See website at www.IdolRecords.com for submission policy. No phone calls or e-mail follow-ups.

MUSIC Mostly **rock**, **pop**, and **alternative**; also some **hip-hop**. *The O's - Between The Two* (album), *Here Holy Spain - Division* (album), *Calhoun - Heavy Sugar* (album), *Little Black Dress - Snow in June* (album), all released 2009-12 on Idol Records. Other artists include Flickerstick, DARYL, Centro-matic, The Deathray Davies, GBH, PPT, The Crash that Took Me, Shibboleth, Trey Johnson, Black Tie Dynasty, Old 97's.

⬤ IMAGEN RECORDS

3905 National Dr., Suite 440, Burtonsville MD 20866. **E-mail:** info@imagenrecords.com. **Website:** www.imagenrecords.com. Imagen Records is a full-service Indie label based in the Washington, D.C., area. Imagen artists represent the best in rock, pop, hip-hop and R&B. With a growing roster of innovative artists, Imagen Records has significant resources and experience that supports its artists to maximize success. Founded by a musician and business person, Imagen artists enjoy a fully collaborative artist development process with a 360-degree perspective. In the current market environment, Imagen has the ability to make significant investments in new talent that creates a strong competitive edge in the marketplace. As a label that was founded in 2007, Imagen employs the newest, most innovative methods to maximize the use of new media and technologies, including new fan base management and content delivery methods.

HOW TO CONTACT Contact via online form.

MUSIC Rock, pop, hip-hop, and R&B. Artists include Framing & Hanley, New Medicine, 3 Years Hollow, Separation, and Candlelight Red.

⊘ INTERSCOPE/GEFFEN/A&M RECORDS

2220 Colorado Ave., Santa Monica CA 90404. (310)865-1000. **Fax:** (310)865-7908. **Website:** www.interscope.com. Labels include Blackground Records, Cherrytree Records, will.i.am music group and Aftermath Records. Record company.

⬤ Interscope/Geffen/A&M is a subsidiary of Universal Music Group, one of the "Big 3" major labels.

HOW TO CONTACT Does not accept unsolicited submissions.

MUSIC Artists include Beck, U2, M.I.A, Keane, Lady Gaga, and ...And You Will Know Us By The Trail Of Dead.

⊘ ISLAND/DEF JAM MUSIC GROUP

1755 Broadway, New York NY 10019. (212)333-8000. **Fax:** (212)603-7654. **Website:** www.islanddefjam.com.

⬤ Island/Def Jam is a subsidiary of Universal Music Group, one of the "Big 3" major labels.

HOW TO CONTACT Island/Def Jam Music Group does not accept unsolicited submissions. Do not send material unless requested.

MUSIC Artists include Bon Jovi, Rick Ross, Fall Out Boy, The Gaslight Anthem, Kanye West, Rihanna, The Killers, Jay-Z, Babyface, Snow Patrol, and Ludacris.

JAGJAGUWAR

1499 W. Second St., Bloomington IN 47403. **E-mail:** info@jagjaguwar.com. **E-mail:** demos@jagjaguwar.com. **Website:** www.jagjaguwar.com. Jagjaguwar is an independent indie rock record label.

HOW TO CONTACT "We do accept links to properly labeled, high-quality MP3s or streams as demos; please direct these to demos@jagjaguwar.com. Please do not e-mail MP3s directly, as we will not accept them as such."

TIPS "Please include all your contact information along with your electronic demo submissions; we will contact you if we are interested in what you have sent."

◑ KILL ROCK STARS

107 SE Washington St. Suite 155, Portland OR 97214. **Website:** www.killrockstars.com.

DISTRIBUTED BY Redeye Distribution.

HOW TO CONTACT *Does not accept or listen to demos sent by mail.* Will listen to links online only if in a touring band coming through Portland. "If you are not touring through Portland, don't send us anything." Prefers link to web page or EPK. Does not return material.

MUSIC Mostly **punk rock**, **neo-folk**, or **anti-folk** and **spoken word**. Artists include Deerhoof, The Decemberists, Boats, Xiu Xiu, The Gossip, Horse Feathers, Erase Errata, The Thermals, Kinski, Marnie Stern, and Two Ton Boa.

TIPS "We will only work with touring acts, so let us know if you are playing Portland. Particularly interested in young artists with indie-rock background."

KORDA RECORDS

P.O. Box 2346, Minneapolis MN 55402. **E-mail:** info@kordarecords.com; allison@kordarecords.com. **Website:** www.kordarecords.com. **Contact:** Allison LaBonne. Korda Records is a Minneapolis-based record label cooperative launched by Allison LaBonne (Typsy Panthre, The Starfolk, The Owls), David Schelzel (The Ocean Blue), Brian Tighe (The Starfolk, The Hang Ups, The Owls) and the Legendary Jim Ruiz (Jim Ruiz Set).

MAD DECENT

Los Angeles CA **E-mail:** info@maddecent.com. **E-mail:** demos@maddecent.com. **Website:** www.maddecent.com. Mad Decent is the name of the Los Angeles-based record label spearheaded by Wesley Pentz, better known as Diplo. As an influential label, Mad Decent aims to bring new genres and cultures to light in the ever-diversifying music community. Aside from the music released, Mad Decent is also known for its annual Block Parties, a series of outdoor party/concerts in select cities across the U.S. and Canada.

◑ MAGNA CARTA RECORDS

A-1 Country Club Rd., East Rochester NY 14445. (585)381-5224. **E-mail:** info@magnacarta.net. **Website:** www.magnacarta.net.

HOW TO CONTACT Submit physical demo CD to the address above. Requirements: Artist must be touring. Artist must be established in his or her local scene. Artist must have a Web presence: Myspace, Facebook, Twitter, YouYube, etc. When sending a physical demo, please the take time and effort to package it properly. Include all relevant materials.

MUSIC Mostly **progressive metal**, **progressive rock**, and **progressive jazz**.

⊘ MATADOR RECORDS

304 Hudson St., 7th Floor, New York NY 10013. (212)995-5882. **Fax:** (212)995-5883. **E-mail:** info@matadorrecords.com. **Website:** www.matadorrecords.com.

HOW TO CONTACT "We are sorry to say that we no longer accept unsolicited demo submissions."

MUSIC Alternative rock. Artists include Lou Reed, Pavement, Belle and Sebastian, Cat Power, Jay Reatard, Sonic Youth, Yo La Tengo, Mogwai, The New Pornographers, and more.

◐⊘ MCA NASHVILLE

1904 Adelicia St., Nashville TN 37212. (615)340-5400. **Fax:** (615)340-5491. **Website:** www.umgnashville.com.

◖   MCA Nashville is a subsidiary of Universal Music Group, one of the "Big 4" major labels.

HOW TO CONTACT MCA Nashville cannot accept unsolicited submissions.

MUSIC Artists include Tracy Byrd, George Strait, Vince Gill, Sugarland, The Mavericks, and Shania Twain.

○ MEGAFORCE RECORDS

P.O. Box 63584, Philadelphia PA 19147. (215)922-4612. **Fax:** (509)757-8602. **Website:** www.megaforcerecords.com.

DISTRIBUTED BY Red/Sony Distribution.

HOW TO CONTACT Contact first and obtain permission to submit. Submissions go to the Philadelphia office.

MUSIC Mostly **rock**. Artists include Truth and Salvage, The Meat Puppets, and The Disco Biscuits.

MERGE RECORDS

Durham NC **E-mail:** merge@mergerecords.com. **Website:** www.mergerecords.com. Merge Records is an independent record label founded by Laura Ballance and Mac McCaughan. Started as a way to release music from its band, Superchunk, Merge Records now releases music by world-famous artists, including Arcade Fire and Robert Pollard.

◐ METAL BLADE RECORDS

5737 Kanan Rd. #143, Agoura Hills CA 91301. (805)522-9111. **Fax:** (805)522-9380. **E-mail:** metalblade@metalblade.com. **Website:** www.metalblade.com.

HOW TO CONTACT Submit demo through website form. Does not accept physical copies of demos. Unsolicited submissions are OK. Response time varies, but "be patient."

MUSIC Mostly **heavy metal** and **industrial**; also **hardcore**, **gothic** and **noise**. Released "Gallery of Suicide," recorded by Cannibal Corpse; "Voo Doo," recorded by King Diamond; and "A Pleasant Shade of Gray," recorded by Fates Warning, all on Metal Blade Records. Other artists include As I Lay Dying, The Red Chord, The Black Dahlia Murder, and Unearth.

TIPS "Metal Blade is known throughout the underground for quality, metal-oriented acts."

MEXICAN SUMMER

87 Guernsey St., Brooklyn NY 11222. **Website:** www.mexicansummer.com. Founded by Kemado Records, Mexican Summer is an independent record label that started out by releasing limited-edition, ornately packaged vinyl pieces. Mexican Summer has since expanded its catalog to more than 100 releases across multiple formats.

◐ MINT 400 RECORDS

E-mail: mint400recs@yahoo.com. **Website:** www.fairmontmusic.com/1/m4r.html. **Contact:** Neil Sabatino, owner. A northern New Jersey indie-rock record label focusing on the digital marketplace.

HOW TO CONTACT Send links to streaming music.

MUSIC Acts include Fairmont, Any Day Parade, The Trashpickers, Dave Charles, Jack Skuller, Ladybirds, Depression State Troopers, Sink Tapes, and many more.

TIPS "I like a lot of different kinds of music and on the label we have everything from old timey country to surf to indie rock to 1960s motown. What I am most interested in is great songwriting and an original singing voice. We do digital distro, recording, producing, engineering, mastering, video editing, Web design, art and graphic design, music licensing, radio promotion and a little PR. Some bands need all of our services and some do not, but we are more than willing to help with every aspect of your music career. We do not give cash advances or tour support. We, as well, deal only in digital records and do not press anything. However, for bands who foot the bill for pressings of vinyl we do have distro."

○ MODAL MUSIC, INC.

P.O. Box 6473, Evanston IL 60204-6473. (847)864-1022. **E-mail:** info@modalmusic.com. **E-mail:** modalmusic@juno.com. **Website:** www.modalmusic.com.

HOW TO CONTACT Submit demo package by mail. Unsolicited submissions are OK. Prefers CD with bio, PR, brochures, any info about artist and music. Does not return material. Responds in 4 months.

MUSIC Mostly **ethnic** and **world**. Released "St. James Vet Clinic" (single by T. Doehrer/Z. Doehrer) from *Wolfpak Den Recordings* (album), recorded by Wolfpak; "Dance The Night Away" (single by T. Doehrer) from *Dance The Night Away* (album), recorded by Balkan Rhythm Band™; "Sid Beckerman's Rumanian" (single by D. Jacobs) from *Meet Your Neighbor's Folk Music*™ (album), recorded by Jutta & The Hi-Dukes™; and *Hold Whatcha Got* (album), recorded by Razzemetazz™, all on Modal Music Records. Other artists include Ensemble M'chaiya™, Nordland Band™ and Terran's Greek Band™.

TIPS "Please note our focus is primarily traditional and traditionally based ethnic, which is a very limited, non-mainstream market niche. You waste your time and money by sending us any other type of music. If you are unsure of your music fitting our focus, please call us before sending anything. Put your name and contact info on every item you send!"

MOM + POP MUSIC

New York NY **Website:** www.momandpopmusic.com. Mom + Pop Music is an independent record label launched by Michael Goldstone.

MUSIC Indie and alternative music. Mom + Pop Music hosts a total of 22 active artists, including Andrew Bird, Metric, Ingrid Michaelson, and Flume.

MUTE RECORDS

E-mail: mute@mute.com. **E-mail:** demos@mute.com. **Website:** www.mute.com. Mute was founded by Daniel Miller and has since signed and developed some of the world's most influential recording artists, including Depeche Mode, Goldfrapp, and Erasure. The label has always been a champion of electronic music. **HOW TO CONTACT** "We love to receive your demos. Please don't send too much material to begin with—3 or 4 of your best tracks is a great start. We're not able to reply individually to everyone, but we can assure you that all demos are reviewed, and we'll be in touch if we like what we hear." Submit no more than 4 streaming links by e-mail.

TIPS "We no longer accept demos submitted by post."

NEON GOLD

New York NY **Website:** www.neongoldrecords.com. Neon Gold Records is a boutique record label founded by Derek Davies and Lizzy Plapinger. Initially operating as a vinyl-only singles label, Neon Gold has launched the debut releases of many acts, including Passion Pit, Ellie Goulding, Gotye, and Icona Pop. In 2014, Neon Gold teamed up with Atlantic Records to make Neon Gold an imprint under Atlantic.

NERVOUS RECORDS

5 Sussex Crescent, Northolt, Middx UB5 4DL United Kingdom. 44(020)8423 7373. **Fax:** 44(020)8423 7713. **E-mail:** info@nervous.co.uk. **Website:** www.nervous. co.uk. **Contact:** R. Williams. Record company (Nervous Records), record producer and music publisher (Nervous Publishing and Zorch Music). Member: MCPS, PRS, PPL, ASCAP, NCB. Releases 2 albums/year. Pays 8-12% royalty to artists on contract; statutory rate to publisher per song on records. Royalties paid directly to US songwriters and artists or through US publishing or recording affiliate.

Nervous Records' publishing company, Nervous Publishing, is listed in the Music Publishers section.

HOW TO CONTACT Unsolicited submissions are OK. Prefers CD with 4-15 songs and lyric sheet. SAE and IRC. Responds in 3 weeks.

MUSIC Mostly **psychobilly** and **rockabilly**. "No heavy rock, AOR, stadium rock, disco, soul, pop—only wild rockabilly and psychobilly." Released *Ex-*

tra Chrome, written and recorded by Johnny Black; *It's Still Rock 'N' Roll to Me*, written and recorded by The Jime. Other artists include Restless Wild and Taggy Tones.

NIGHT SLUGS

London United Kingdom. **Website:** www.nightslugs. net. Night Slugs is an electronic music label established by Alex Sushon (aka Bok Bok) and James Connolly (aka L-Vis 1990). It was started in response to artists featured at the founders' club nights being unsigned.

OGLIO RECORDS

3540 W. Sahara Ave. #308, Las Vegas NV 89102. (702)800-5500. **Website:** oglio.com.

HOW TO CONTACT No unsolicited demos. Use online form to contact.

MUSIC Mostly **alternative rock** and **comedy**. Released *Shine* (album), recorded by Cyndi Lauper (pop); *Live At The Roxy* (album), recorded by Brian Wilson (rock); *Team Leader* (album), recorded by George Lopez (comedy).

ORCHID TAPES

Brooklyn NY **E-mail:** orchidtapes@gmail.com. **Website:** orchidtapes.com. Orchid Tapes is a cassette, vinyl and free download-based record label run by Warren Hildebrand and Brian Vu, a couple with a shared interest in the creation and curation of music and artwork that breaks free of the established norm, disregards trends, reflects the dedication of its creator and provokes a strong emotional resonance with whomever experiences it. The overall goal of Orchid Tapes is to share and explore music that reflects these ideals with those who are willing and able to listen, and also to unite and expose like-minded artists from all over the world under a collective-style label.

HOW TO CONTACT "While we do accept demo e-mails from bands and musicians, we'd encourage you to read a link on our website that clarifies our position on demo submissions a bit."

THE PANAMA MUSIC GROUP OF COMPANIES

Ebrel House, 2a Penlee Close, Praa Sands, Penzance, Cornwall TR20 9ST England. +44 (0)1736 762826. **E-mail:** panamus@aol.com. **Website:** www.songwriters-guild.co.uk; www.panamamusic.co.uk. **Contact:** Roderick G. Jones, CEO; Jack Golding, A&R. Labels include Pure Gold Records, Panama Music Library,

Rainy Day Records, Panama Records, Mohock Records, Digimix Records Ltd. (www.digimixrecords.com and www.myspace.com/digimixrecords). Registered members of Phonographic Performance Ltd. (PPL). Record company, music publisher, production and development company (Panama Music Library, Melody First Music Library, Eventide Music Library, Musik Image Music Library, Promo Sonor International Music Library, Caribbean Music Library, ADN Creation Music Library, Piano Bar Music Library, Corelia Music Library, PSI Music Library, Scamp Music, First Time Music Publishing U.K.), Digimix Music Publishing, registered members of the Mechanical Copyright Protection Society (MCPS) and the Performing Right Society (PRS) (London, England UK), management firm and record producer (First Time Management & Production Co.). Staff size: 6. Pays variable royalty to artists on contract; statutory rate to publisher per song on record subject to deal.

DISTRIBUTED BY Media U.K. Distributors and Digimix Worldwide Digital Distribution.

HOW TO CONTACT Submit demo package by mail. Unsolicited submissions are OK. CD or MP3 only with unlimited number of songs/instrumentals and lyric or lead sheets where necessary. "We do not return material so there is no need to send return postage. We will, due to volume of material received, only respond to you if we have any interest. Please note: no MP3 submissions, attachments, downloads, or referrals to websites in the first instance via e-mail. Do not send anything by recorded delivery or courier as it will not be signed for. If we are interested, we will follow up for further requests and offers as necessary."

MUSIC All styles. Published by Scamp Music: "F*ck Me I'm Famous" written by Paul Clarke & Matthew Dick (film/DVD [Universal Films, Hollywood] and single and album track [Universal Records]), released worldwide in *Get Him to the Greek*, Universal films Hollywood, starring Russell Brand, recorded by Dougal & Gammer, "We Killed The Rave" (voted best hardcore track of 2013), recorded by Dougal & Gammer, released as an album track on Clubland Xtreme Hardcore 9 by Universal Records in 2013, published by Scamp Music. Also published "Get Your Lovekicks" (soul/R&B), recorded by Leonie Parker, released by Digimix Records Ltd.; "Country Blues" (country), recorded by The Glen Kirton Country Band on Digimix Records Ltd, published by Scamp Music; "Guitar Hero" (hardcore), recorded by Dougal & Gammer, re-

leased by Universal Records/All Around the World; published by Scamp Music: "I Get Stoned" (hardcore dance) recorded by AudioJunkie & Stylus, released by EMI records on *Hardcore Nation 2009*, published by Panama Music Library; "Everytime I Hear Your Name" (pop dance), recorded by Cascada, released by All Around The World/Universal Records, published by Scamp Music; "Illumination—Deep Skies 5" seven-track album (holistic, mind, body, and soul) by Kevin Kendle release 2015 by Eventide Music and Digimix Records Ltd., published by Panama Music Library; "Heavy Rock Spectacular" progressive rock, recorded by Bram Stoker released by Digimix Records Ltd. 2015, published by Scamp Music, and many more.

PAPER GARDEN RECORDS

170 Tillary St., Apt. 608, Brooklyn NY 11201. **E-mail:** info@papergardenrecords.com. **E-mail:** demos@papergardenrecords.com. **Website:** www.papergardenrecords.com. "Paper Garden Records is a boutique record label in Brooklyn run by 2 lovers, 2 cats, and their friends."

PAPER + PLASTICK

E-mail: e.customer@paperandplastick.com. **Website:** paperandplastick.com.

MUSIC Rock, punk, and more. Artists include: Dopamines, Andrew Dost, Coffee Project, Foundation, Gatorface, Blacklist Royals, Landmines, We are the Union, and more.

◉ PARLIAMENT RECORDS

357 S. Fairfax Ave. #430, Los Angeles CA 90036. (323)653-0693. **Fax:** (323)653-7670. **E-mail:** parlirec@aol.com. **Website:** www.parliamentrecords.com.

HOW TO CONTACT Submit demo package by mail. Unsolicited submissions are OK. Prefers CD with 3-10 songs and lyric sheet. Include SASE. "Mention *Songwriter's Market*. Please make return envelope the same size as the envelopes you send material in; otherwise we cannot send everything back." Responds in 6 weeks.

MUSIC Mostly **R&B, soul, dance,** and **top 40/pop;** also **gospel** and **blues.** Artists include Rapture 7 (male gospel group), Wisdom Gospel Singers (male gospel group), Chosen Gospel Recovery (female gospel group), Jewel With Love (female gospel group), Apostle J. Dancy (gospel), TooMiraqulas (rap), The Mighty Voices of Joy (male gospel group) L'Nee (hip-hop/soul).

TIPS "Parliament Records will listen to 'tracks' only. If you send tracks, please include a letter stating what equipment you record on—ADAT, Protools or Roland VS recorders."

ⓘ PARTISAN RECORDS

281 N. 7th St., #2, Brooklyn NY 11211. **E-mail:** info@partisanrecords.com. **Website:** www.partisanrecords.com. **Contact:** Tim Putnam and Ian Wheeler. Partisan Records is a Brooklyn-based artist-run independent label dedicated to the unique visions of those we are so privileged to represent. We believe that artistry in its many forms essentially has a singular purpose: to createa nd share the next new story. At Partisan, our artists create the stories that others will tell.

MUSIC Current artists include Callers, Ages of Ages, Deer Tick, Amy Wells, Dolorean, Middle Brother, Heartless Bastards, Lumerians, Phox, Mountain Man, and more.

PC MUSIC

London United Kingdom. **E-mail:** demos@pcmusic.info. **Website:** pcmusic.info. PC Music is a record label and music-making collective run by producer A.G. Cook. The label has an eccentric roster of artists who devise alternate personas often inspired by cyberculture. Its releases focus on dance music with pitch-shifted, feminine vocals.

PEAPOD RECORDINGS

P.O. BOX 2631, South Portland ME 04116. **E-mail:** info@peapodrecordings.com. **Website:** www.peapodrecordings.com. **Contact:** Ron Harrity. Peapod Recordings is a small label based out of Portland, Maine. **HOW TO CONTACT** "At this time we're not looking for new artists. However, we do love to hear new music, so if you just feel like sharing what you've been up to, please e-mail us with MP3 or .zip file links only. Please no attached MP3s. Also keep in mind that we can't always return e-mails regarding your music. Thanks!"

MUSIC Artists include Dead End Armory, Foam Castles, Brown Bird, If and It, Olas, Dan Blakeslee, Hearts by Darts, Honey Clouds, and many more.

ⓘ QUARK RECORDS

P.O. Box 452, Newtown CT 06470. (917)687-9988. **E-mail:** ar@quarkmusicgroup.com. **Website:** www.quarkrecordsusa.com. **Contact:** Curtis Urbina, CEO. Record company and music publisher (Quarkette Music/BMI and Freedurb Music/ASCAP). Releases 3 singles and 3 LPs/year. Pays negotiable royalty to artists on contract; 3/4 statutory rate to publisher per song on record.

HOW TO CONTACT Prefers CD with 2 songs (maximum). Include SASE. "Must be an absolute 'hit' song!" Responds in 6 weeks.

MUSIC Pop and electronica music only.

ⓘ RADICAL RECORDS

222 Dean St. #1, Brooklyn NY 11217. (212)475-1111. **Fax:** (212)475-3676. **E-mail:** info@radicalrecords.com; keith@radicalrecords.com. **Website:** www.radicalrecords.com. **Contact:** Keith Masco, president; Bryan Mechutan, general manager/sales and marketing. "We do accept unsolicited demos, however, please allow ample time for a response; also please note that we deal almost exclusively with punk rock. Feel free to send us your hip-hop/folk/jazz fusion, demo but don't be surprised when we don't show up at your door with a contract. Please make sure you have an e-mail address clearly printed on the disc or case. Most importantly: Don't call us, we'll call you."

DISTRIBUTED BY City Hall, Revelation, Select-O-Hits, Choke, Southern, Carrot Top, and other indie distributors.

HOW TO CONTACT *E-mail first for permission to submit demo.* Prefers CD. Does not return material. Responds in 1 month.

MUSIC Mostly **punk, hardcore, glam** and **rock.**

TIPS "Create the best possible demos you can and show a past of excellent self-promotion."

ⓘ RAVE RECORDS, INC.

Attn: Production Dept., 13400 W. Seven Mile Rd., Detroit MI 48235. **E-mail:** info@raverecords.com. **Website:** www.raverecords.com. **Contact:** Carolyn and Derrick, production managers. Record company and music publisher (Magic Brain Music/ASCAP).

DISTRIBUTED BY Action Music Sales.

HOW TO CONTACT "We do not accept unsolicited submissions."

MUSIC Mostly **alternative rock** and **dance.** Artists include Cyber Cryst, Dorothy, Nicole, and Bukimi 3.

ⓘⓘ RCA RECORDS

550 Madison Ave., New York NY 10022. **Website:** www.rcarecords.com. Labels include RCA Records Nashville and RCA Victor. Record company.

ⓘ   RCA Records is a subsidiary of Sony BMG, one of the "Big 3" major labels.

DISTRIBUTED BY BMG.

HOW TO CONTACT RCA Records does not accept unsolicited submissions.

MUSIC Artists include The Strokes, Dave Matthews Band, Christina Aguilera, and Foo Fighters.

⊘ REPRISE RECORDS

3300 Warner Blvd., 4th Floor, Burbank CA 91505. (818)846-9090. **Website:** www.warnerbrosrecords.com.

○ Reprise Records is a subsidiary of Warner Music Group, one of the "Big 3" major labels.

DISTRIBUTED BY WEA.

HOW TO CONTACT Reprise Records does not accept unsolicited submissions.

MUSIC Artists include Eric Clapton, My Chemical Romance, Michael Bublé, The Used, Green Day, Alanis Morissette, Fleetwood Mac, and Neil Young.

○ RHYMESAYERS ENTERTAINMENT

Minneapolis MN **Website:** www.rhymesayers.com. Rhymesayers is an independent hip-hop record label. Years after it all began, Rhymesayers boasts one of independent hip-hop's strongest and most respected rosters.

RISE RECORDS

15455 NW Greenbrier Pkwy., Suite 115, Beaverton OR 97006. **E-mail:** matthew@riserecords.com. **Website:** www.riserecords.com. **Contact:** Matthew Gordner.

HOW TO CONTACT E-mail a link to your music (Facebook, Bandcamp, YouTube, Myspace or Purevolume) using the e-mail form on the website. "Please save your money and don't mail a press kit. Also, less is more. Just send the link to your music. If we need more information, we'll let you know."

MUSIC Rock, metal, alternative. Artists include Bouncing Souls, Memphis May Fire, Of Mice & Men, Secrets, Poison The Well, Transit, Hot Water Music, and more.

◐ ROADRUNNER RECORDS

1290 Avenue of the Americas, 28th Floor, New York NY 10104. **E-mail:** publicity@roadrunnerrecords.com. **Website:** www.roadrunnerrecords.com.

HOW TO CONTACT Submit demo by e-mail at signmeto@roadrunnerrecords.com. Submissions are currently open.

MUSIC Rock, metal, alternative. Artists include Korn, Killswitch Engage, Opeth, Nickelback, Lenny Kravitz, Lynyrd Skynyrd, Megadeth, Slipknot, and more.

○ ROBBINS ENTERTAINMENT LLC

35 Worth St., 4th Floor, New York NY 10013. (212)675-4321. **Fax:** (212)675-4441. **E-mail:** info@robbinsent.com. **Website:** www.robbinsent.com.

DISTRIBUTED BY Sony/BMG.

HOW TO CONTACT "If you're interested in submitting a demo to Robbins Entertainment, please follow these instructions: 1) Make sure that everything is labeled properly, from artist and title to your contact information; 2) Please send us no more than 3 tracks, and make sure they are representative of your very best; 3) Radio edits preferred. If you'd like to send a digital demo, please use download links only (YouSendit, SoundCloud, or FTP, etc.) and write to info@robbinsent.com. Do not send MP3s attached to an e-mail. These will automatically be discarded. We do listen to everything that comes through, but please keep in mind that we get a lot of submissions every week. If we like what we hear, we will contact you."

MUSIC Commercial dance only. Released top 10 pop smashes, "Heaven" (single), recorded by DJ Sammy; "Everytime We Touch" (single), recorded by Cascada; "Listen To Your Heart" (single), recored by DHT; as well as Hot 100 records from Rockell, Lasgo, Reina and K5. Other artists include September, Andain, Judy Torres, Jenna Drey, Marly, Dee Dee, Milky, Kreo and many others.

TIPS "Do not send your package 'Supreme-Overnight-Before-You-Wake-Up' delivery. Save yourself some money. Do not send material if you are going to state in your letter that, 'If I had more (fill in the blank) it would sound better.' We are interested in hearing your best and only your best. Do not call us and ask if you can send your package. The answer is yes. We are looking for dance music with crossover potential."

◑ ROLL CALL RECORDS

Los Angeles CA **E-mail:** info@rollcallrecords.com. **Website:** www.rollcallrecords.com. Come download some music for free at our website.

MUSIC Released albums by such artists as Army Navy, Isbells, Royal Canoe, Typhoon, WinHeadhaclal, and more.

○ ROLL ON RECORDS

112 Widmar Place, Clayton CA 94517. **E-mail:** rollon-records@aol.com. **Contact:** Edgar J. Brincat. Record company and music publisher (California Country Music). Pays 10% royalty to artists on contract; statutory rate to publisher per song on record. Member of Harry Fox Agency.

DISTRIBUTED BY Tower.

HOW TO CONTACT Submit demo package by mail. Unsolicited submissions are OK. "Do not call or write for permission to submit. If you do you will be rejected." Prefers CD with 3 songs and lyric sheet. Include SASE and phone number. Responds in 6 weeks.

MUSIC Mostly **contemporary/country** and **modern gospel**. Released "Broken Record" (single by Horace Linsley/Dianne Baumgartner), recorded by Edee Gordon on Roll On Records; *Maddy* and *For Realities Sake* (albums both by F.L. Pittman/Madonna Weeks), recorded by Ron Banks/L.J. Reynolds on Life Records/Bellmark Records.

TIPS "Be patient and prepare to be in it for the long haul. A successful songwriter does not happen overnight. It's rare to write a song today and have a hit tomorrow. If you give us your song and want it back, then don't give it to us to begin with."

ROTTEN RECORDS

P.O. Box 56, Upland CA 91786. (909)920-4567. **Fax:** (909)920-4577. **E-mail:** rotten@rottenrecords.com. **Website:** www.rottenrecords.com. **Contact:** Ron Peterson, president.

DISTRIBUTED BY RIOT (Australia), Sonic Rendezvous (NL), RED (US) and PHD (Canada).

HOW TO CONTACT Submit demo package by mail. Unsolicited submissions are OK. Prefers CD or Myspace link. Does not return material.

MUSIC Mostly **rock**, **alternative** and **commercial**; also **punk** and **heavy metal**. Released *Paegan Terrorism* (album), written and recorded by Acid Bath; *Kiss the Clown* (album by K. Donivon), recorded by Kiss the Clown; and *Full Speed Ahead* (album by Cassidy/Brecht), recorded by D.R.T., all on Rotten Records.

TIPS "Be patient."

◑ ROUGH TRADE RECORDS

66 Golborne Rd., London W10 5PS United Kingdom. **E-mail:** demos@roughtraderecords.com. **Website:** www.roughtraderecords.com.

HOW TO CONTACT Demo submissions are welcome, however, we are not entitled to return any ma-terials submitted to us. Please make sure you keep copies for yourself. Demos should be marked for attention of Paul Jones. "Due to the postal delays, you're advised to send MP3 demos online using our Soundcloud page (info on website)." To e-mail, use online form on the website.

MUSIC Alternative. Artists include Super Furry Animals, Jarvis Cocker, The Hold Steady, Emiliana Torrini, British Sea Power, The Libertines, My Morning Jacket, Jenny Lewis, The Strokes, The Mystery Jets, The Decemberists, and more.

◐ RUSTIC RECORDS

6337 Murray Lane, Brentwood TN 37027. (615)371-0646. **E-mail:** zach@rusticrecordsinc.com. **Website:** rusticrecordsinc.com. **Contact:** Jack Schneider, president and founder; Nell Schneider; Brien Fisher.

DISTRIBUTED BY CDBaby.com and available on iTunes, MSN Music, Rhapsody, and more.

HOW TO CONTACT Submit professional demo package by mail. Unsolicited submissions are OK. CD only; no MP3s or e-mails. Include no more than 4 songs with corresponding lyric sheets and cover letter. Include appropriately sized SASE. Responds in 4 weeks.

MUSIC Good combination of traditional and modern **country**. Releases: *Ready to Ride* - debut album from Nikki Britt, featuring "C-O-W-B-O-Y," "Do I Look Like Him," "Star in My Car," and "You Happened"; *Hank Stuff* from DeAnna Cox - featuring "I'm a Long Gone Mama," and "I'm so Lonesome I Could Cry."

TIPS "Professional demo preferred."

SADDLE CREEK

P.O. Box 8554, Omaha NE 68108. **Website:** www.saddle-creek.com. Saddle Creek is an independent record label that supports musicians it believes have the authenticity and talent to captivate and transform culture at-large. "We pride ourselves on creating an independent, artist-friendly environment by championing creative control and acting in the best interests of our partners."

HOW TO CONTACT "We don't listen to demos every day, but check them out periodically. If we're interested, we'll get back to you." Submit through online demo submission page.

TIPS "Please note, though, we have never signed a band based on a demo."

SECRET STASH RECORDS

1621 Hennepin Ave., #150A, Minneapolis MN 55403. **E-mail:** info@secretstashrecords.com. **Website:** www. secretstashrecords.com. Secret Stash Records is an independent record label owned and operated in Minneapolis, Minnesota. "We are dedicated to one thing: releasing great music in great collectible LP packages. Whether you are a DJ looking for rare grooves to sample, or just an average Joe looking for great music, we've got you covered."

HOW TO CONTACT Use online form to contact.
MUSIC Funk, soul, blues.

SILVER WAVE RECORDS

P.O. Box 7943, Boulder CO 80306. (303)443-5617. **Fax:** (303)443-0877. **E-mail:** info@silverwave.com. **Website:** www.silverwave.com. **Contact:** Valerie Sanford, art director.

MUSIC Mostly **Native American** and **world**.

SIMPLY GRAND MUSIC INC.

P.O. Box 770208, Memphis TN 38177-0208. (901)763-4787 or (615)515-7772. **E-mail:** info@simplygrandmusic.com. **Website:** www.simplygrandmusic.com. **Contact:** Linda Lucchesi, president. Record company (Simply Grand Music) and music publisher (Beckie Publishing Co.). Staff size: 5. Released 5 CDs last year. Royalties are negotiable. Distributed by The Orchard, Ace Records and various others.

HOW TO CONTACT Contact first and obtain permission to submit a demo. E-mail links to download MP3 with lyrics, preferred. If sending physical mail, include CD and limit 3 songs per submission. Please give 2-4 weeks for a response. Please include lyrics and a SASE if you want any materials returned.

MUSIC Mostly interested in **country**, **soul/R&B**, **pop**; also interested in **top 40**, **soft rock**. Recent placements include the TV series *Sleepy Hollow*, *Forever*, *Public Morals*, *Graceland*, *Rookie Blues*, and films *The Diary of a Teenage Girl* and *Criminal Activity*. Recent releases include "More Lost Soul Gems From Sounds of Memphis" on Ace Records, "Sweet Talk" by Ciera Ouellette, and the Ciera Ouellette Collection.

SMALL STONE RECORDS

P.O. Box 02007, Detroit MI 48202. (248)219-2613. **Fax:** (248)541-6536. **E-mail:** sstone@smallstone.com. **Website:** www.smallstone.com.

DISTRIBUTED BY ADA, Bertus, Cargo Records GmbH.

HOW TO CONTACT Submit CD/CD Rom by mail. Unsolicited submissions are OK. Does not return material. Responds in 2 months.

MUSIC Mostly **alternative**, **rock** and **blues**; also **funk (not R&B)**. Released *Fat Black Pussy Cat*, written and recorded by Five Horse Johnson (rock/blues); *Wrecked & Remixed*, written and recorded by Morsel (indie rock, electronica); and *Only One Division*, written and recorded by Soul Clique (electronica), all on Small Stone Records. Other artists include Acid King, Perplexa, and Novadriver.

TIPS "Looking for esoteric music along the lines of Bill Laswell to Touch & Go/Thrill Jockey records material. Only send along material if it makes sense with what we do. Perhaps owning some of our records would help."

SMOG VEIL RECORDS

1093 A1A Beach Blvd. #343, St. Augustine Beach FL 32080. (904)547-1393. **E-mail:** franklisa@aol.com. **Website:** svrshop.myshopify.com. Smog Veil Records has been releasing records since 1991, most geared to the post-young, most of which are ridiculous, bombastic, and otherwise under-appreciated rock 'n' roll from northeastern Ohio. "You may have bought one."

HOW TO CONTACT Submit CD or CD-R to Frank Mauceri by mail. Does not accept submissions by e-mail or links to website. Submissions must inlcude a contact, press kit, and plans for touring. Response time is slow. Demo submissions cannot be returned to the submitter.

MUSIC Artists include Batusis, David Thomas, Thor, This Moment in Black History, Butcher Boys, and Prisoners.

SONY BMG

550 Madison Ave., New York NY 10022. **Website:** www.sonymusic.com.

Sony BMG is one of the primary "Big 3" major labels.

HOW TO CONTACT For specific contact information, see the listings in this section for Sony subsidiaries Columbia Records, Epic Records, Sony Nashville, RCA Records, J Records, Arista, and American Recordings.

SONY MUSIC NASHVILLE

1400 18th Ave. S., Nashville TN 37212-2809. Labels include Columbia Nashville, Arista Nashville, RCA, BNA, and Provident Music Group.

Sony Music Nashville is a subsidiary of Sony BMG, one of the "Big 3" major labels.

HOW TO CONTACT Sony Music Nashville does not accept unsolicited submissions.

STAX RECORDS

Stax Records / Concord Music Group, 100 N. Crescent Dr., Beverly Hills CA 90210. **E-mail:** publicity@ concordmusicgroup.com. **Website:** www.staxrecords. com. Stax Records is critical in American music history as it's one of the most popular soul music record labels of all time—second only to Motown in sales and influence, but first in gritty, raw, stripped-down soul music. In 15 years, Stax placed more than 167 hit songs in the Top 100 on the pop charts, and a staggering 243 hits in the Top 100 R&B charts. It launched the careers of such legendary artists as Otis Redding, Sam & Dave, Rufus & Carla Thomas, Booker T, & the MGs, and numerous others. Among the many artists who recorded on the various Stax Records labels were the Staple Singers, Luther Ingram, Wilson Pickett, Albert King, Big Star, Jesse Jackson, Bill Cosby, Richard Pryor, the Rance Allen Group, and Moms Mabley.

MUSIC Current Stax recording artists include Ben Harper, Booker T. Jones, and others.

STONES THROW RECORDS

2658 Griffith Park Blvd. #504, Los Angeles CA 90039. **E-mail:** losangeles@stonesthrow.com. **Website:** www. stonesthrow.com.

HOW TO CONTACT "Stones Throw recieves a lot of unsolicited demos that we don't always have time to listen to, but don't let that discourage you from sending us your music. Please take the time to check the following points before sending anything. Acceptable formats are vinyl, CD, even cassette. No MP3 files via e-mail. They will be blocked and unheard. We get a lot of Bandcamp, Soundcloud, Myspace and other links with music—too many to listen to, but we hear them, too. We receive hundreds of demos every year, so put your best track first.We cannot acknowledge receipt of your submission. Calling or e-mailing to make sure the package has been received will not improve your chances of it being heard."

MUSIC One of the leading names in underground hip-hop. Artists include 7 Days of Funk, Anika, J Rocc, The Stepkids, James Pants, Madvillain, Arabian Prince, Jonwayne, more.

SUB POP RECORDS

2013 Fourth Ave., 3rd Floor, Seattle WA 98121. (206)441-8441. **Fax:** (206)441-8245. **E-mail:** info@ subpop.com. **Website:** www.subpop.com. Sub Pop Records is a medium-sized independent record label that has released music by several well-known artists, including Nirvana, Soundgarden, Sebadoh, Hot Hot Heat, The Shins, Iron and Wine, Flight of the Conchords, Beach House, and others.

TIPS "It is our intent to market and sell the recorded music (and related merchandise) of artists whose music some shifting definition of 'we' really and truly love. We mean to represent these artists as faithfully and diligently as possible and hold out hope that this is enough for us to remain solvent in the face of the well-documented collapse of the music industry at large."

SUGAR HILL RECORDS

E-mail: info@sugarhillrecords.com. **Website:** www. sugarhillrecords.com.

Welk Music Group acquired Sugar Hill Records in 1998.

HOW TO CONTACT No unsolicited submissions. "If you are interested in having your music heard by Sugar Hill Records or the Welk Music Group, we suggest you establish a relationship with a manager, publisher, or attorney who has an ongoing relationship with our company. We do not have a list of such entities."

MUSIC Mostly **Americana**, **bluegrass**, and **country**. Artists include Nitty Gritty Dirt Band, Sarah Jarosz, Donna the Buffalo, The Infamous Stringdusters, Joey + Rory, and Sam Bush.

TEXAS ROSE RECORDS

2002 Platinum St., Garland TX 75042. (972)898-2032. **E-mail:** txrr1@aol.com. **Website:** www.texasroserecords.com. **Contact:** Nancy Baxendale, president. Record company, music publisher (Yellow Rose of Texas Publishing) and record producer (Nancy Baxendale). Staff size: 1. Releases 3 CDs/year. Pays negotiable royalty to artists on contract; statutory rate to publisher per song on record.

DISTRIBUTED BY Self distribution.

HOW TO CONTACT E-mail first for permission to submit. Submit maximum of 2 songs via MP3 file with copy of lyrics in Word format. Does not return material. Responds only if interested.

MUSIC Mostly **country**, **soft rock**, **pop**, and **R&B**. Does not want hip-hop, rap, heavy metal. Released *Fl-*

yin' High Over Texas (album), recorded by Dusty Martin (country); *High On The Hog* (album), recorded by Steve Harr (country); *Time For Time to Pay* (album), recorded by Jeff Elliot (country); *Double XXposure* (album), recorded by Jeff Elliott and Kim Neeley (country), *Pendulum Dream* (album) recorded by Maureen Kelly (Americana) and "Cowboy Super Hero" (single) written and recorded by Robert Mauldin.

TIPS "We are interested in songs written for today's market with a strong musical hook and a great chorus. No home recordings, please."

TINY ENGINES

Charlotte NC **E-mail:** info@tinyengines.net. **E-mail:** submissions@tinyengines.net. **Website:** www.tinyengines.net. Tiny Engines is an indie record label based in the Carolinas. The label is an evolution of ideas and a gathering of like-minded people who dig inspiring music, a tight-knit community of friends and strong, independent DIY ethics.

HOW TO CONTACT "We do not accept physical submissions. But, you can e-mail submissions to submissions@tinyengines.net. Do not send submissions to any other e-mail address. Please include a streaming link and a download link if possible. Do not attach MP3 or zip files. Also, please do not follow up with us. We do our best to listen to everything and if we like it we will definitely be in touch."

⊘ TOMMY BOY ENTERTAINMENT LLC

120 Fifth Ave., 7th Floor, New York NY 10011. **E-mail:** info@tommyboy.com. **Website:** www.tommyboy.com.

DISTRIBUTED BY WEA, Subway Records.

HOW TO CONTACT E-mail to obtain current demo submission policy.

MUSIC Artists include Chavela Vargas, Afrika Bambaataa, Biz Markie, Kool Keith, and INXS.

◐ TOPCAT RECORDS

P.O. Box 670234, Dallas TX 75367. (972)484-4141. **E-mail:** info@topcatrecords.com. **Website:** www.topcatrecords.com.

DISTRIBUTED BY City Hall.

HOW TO CONTACT *Call first and obtain permission to submit.* Prefers CD. Does not return material. Responds in 1 month.

MUSIC Mostly **blues**, **swing**, **rockabilly**, **Americana**, **Texana** and **R&B**. Released *If You Need Me* (album), written and recorded by Robert Ealey (blues); *Texas Blueswomen* (album by 3 Female Singers), recorded by

various (blues/R&B); and *Jungle Jane* (album), written and recorded by Holland K. Smith (blues/swing), all on Topcat. Released CDs: *Jim Suhler & Alan Haynes—Live*; Bob Kirkpatrick *Drive Across Texas*; *Rock My Blues to Sleep* by Johnny Nicholas; *Walking Heart Attack* by Holland K. Smith; *Dirt Road* (album), recorded by Jim Suhler; *Josh Alan Band* (album), recorded by Josh Alan; *Bust Out* (album), recorded by Robin Sylar. Other artists include Grant Cook, Muddy Waters, Big Mama Thornton, Big Joe Turner, Geo. "Harmonica" Smith, J.B. Hutto and Bee Houston. "View our website for an up-to-date listing of releases."

TIPS "Send me blues (fast, slow, happy, sad, etc.) or good blues-oriented R&B. No pop, hip-hop, or rap."

TOUCH AND GO/QUARTERSTICK RECORDS

P.O. Box 25520, Chicago IL 60625. (773)388-8888. **Fax:** (773)388-3888. **E-mail:** info@tgrec.com. **Website:** www.tgrec.com.

HOW TO CONTACT Mail to one or the other (staffed by same people, no need to send to both labels). "Demos are listened to by any and all staffers who want to or have time to listen to them. Do not call or e-mail us about your demo." Do not e-mail MP3s or Web URLs.

MUSIC All Styles. Artists include Therapy?, TV on the Radio, Pinback, Naked Raygun, Blonde Redhead, Henry Rollins, Yeah Yeah Yeahs, Girls Against Boys, and more.

◐ TRANSDREAMER RECORDS

P.O. Box 1955, New York NY 10113. **Website:** www.transdreamer.com. Transdreamer Records started as a small alternative label with a vision to develop extremely high quality artists. The name, Transdreamer, symbolizes artists and projects that attempt to transcend normal genre conventions. The Transdreamer logo does not subscribe to the typical "steady product flow, cram-as-many-releases-into-the-market-as-possible, hopefully-one-will-hit" mentality. Fewer releases hopefully means focus, a high level of excellence and great music.

DISTRIBUTED BY Red/Sony.

HOW TO CONTACT Feel free to send in your demo to the above address, but please don't call us asking if it's any good. If we are interested, we will harass you. Thanks.

MUSIC Mostly **alternative/rock**. Artists include The Delgados, Arab Strap, Dressy Bessy, The Dig, and Holly Golightly.

⊘ UNIVERSAL MOTWON RECORDS

1755 Broadway, #6, New York NY 10019. (212)373-0600. **Fax:** (212)373-0726. **Website:** www.universalmotown.com.

○ Universal Motown Records is a subsidiary of Universal Music Group, one of the "Big 4" major labels.

HOW TO CONTACT Does not accept unsolicited submissions.

MUSIC Artists include Lil' Wayne, Erykah Badu, Days Difference, Kem, Paper Route, and Kelly Rowland.

⊘ VAGRANT RECORDS

6351 Wilshire Blvd., Los Angeles CA 90048. **E-mail:** info@vagrant.com. **Website:** www.vagrant.com.

HOW TO CONTACT "We do not accept unsolicited demos."

MUSIC Rock, alternative. Artists include PJ Harvey, The 1975, Active Child, Bad Suns, Blitzen Trapper, California Wives, Eels, James Vincent McMorrow, Wake Owl, Bombay Bicycle Club, Benjamin Francis Leftwich, AlunaGeorge, Edward Sharpe and the Magnetic Zeros, Black Joe Lewis, Reptar, and more.

⊘ THE VERVE MUSIC GROUP

1755 Broadway, 3rd Floor, New York NY 10019. (212)331-2000. **E-mail:** contact@vervemusicgroup.com. **Website:** www.vervemusicgroup.com. Record company. Labels include Verve, GRP, and Impulse! Records.

○ Verve Music Group is a subsidiary of Universal Music Group, one of the "Big 3" major labels.

HOW TO CONTACT The Verve Music Group does not accept unsolicited submissions.

MUSIC Artists include Boney James, Diana Krall, Ledisi, Herbie Hancock, Queen Latifah, and Bruce Hornsby & The Noisemakers.

VICTORY RECORDS

346 N. Justine St., Suite #504, Chicago IL 60607. **E-mail:** contact@victoryrecords.com. **Website:** www.victoryrecords.com.

HOW TO CONTACT Submit demo using online submission manager.

MUSIC Alternative, metal, rock. Artists include The Audition, Bayside, Catch 22, Funeral For A Friend, Otep, Hawthorne Heights, Ringworm, Secret Lives of the Freemasons, Silverstein, The Tossers, Voodoo Glow Skulls, William Control, Streetlight Manifesto, and more.

⊘ VIRGIN MUSIC GROUP

5750 Wilshire Blvd., Los Angeles CA 90036. (323)462-6252. **Fax:** (310)278-6231. **Website:** www.virginrecords.com.

○ Virgin Records is a subsidiary of the EMI Group, one of the "Big 3" major labels.

DISTRIBUTED BY EMD.

HOW TO CONTACT *Virgin Music Group does not accept recorded material or lyrics unless submitted by a reputable industry source.* "If your act has received positive press or airplay on prior independent releases, we welcome your written query. Send a letter of introduction accompanied by all pertinent artist information. Do not send a tape until requested. All unsolicited materials will be returned unopened."

MUSIC Mostly **rock** and **pop**. Artists include Lenny Kravitz, Placebo, Joss Stone, Ben Harper, Iggy Pop, and Gorillaz.

WARNER BROS. RECORDS

3300 Warner Blvd., Burbank CA 91505. (818)953-3361; (818)846-9090. **Fax:** (818)953-3232. **Website:** www.wbr.com.

DISTRIBUTED BY WEA.

HOW TO CONTACT *Warner Bros. Records does not accept unsolicited material.* "All unsolicited material will be returned unopened. Those interested in having their tapes heard should establish a relationship with a manager, publisher or attorney that has an ongoing relationship with Warner Bros. Records."

MUSIC Released *Van Halen 3* (album), recorded by Van Halen; *Evita* (soundtrack); and *Dizzy Up the Girl* (album), recorded by Goo Goo Dolls, both on Warner Bros. Records. Other artists include Faith Hill, Tom Petty & The Heartbreakers, Jeff Foxworthy, Porno For Pyros, Travis Tritt, Yellowjackets, Bela Fleck and the Flecktones, Al Jarreau, Joshua Redmond, Little Texas, and Curtis Mayfield.

◐ WARP RECORDS

London United Kingdom. **Website:** www.warp.net. Warp was founded by Steve Beckett and the late Rob Mitchell and soon became home to artists who would be influential in electronic music. In 2013, Warp won Independent Label of the Year at the AIM Awards.

⊘ WIND-UP ENTERTAINMENT

72 Madison Ave., 7th Floor, New York NY 10016. **Website:** www.winduprecords.com. Wind-up Records is a privately owned, full-service music entertainment firm founded in 1997. The company has successfully launched numerous multi-platinum artists, including Evanescence, Creed, Seether, and Finger Eleven, and has further built on the successes of Five for Fighting and O.A.R. In addition to these marquee acts, Wind-up has scouted and developed several award-winning, newer artists, such as Civil Twilight, Company of Thieves, and Thriving Ivory. Since its inception nearly 15 years ago, the company has shipped over 60 million units worldwide, generating over $700 million in gross revenue. Wind-up has garnered 7 multi-platinum albums (including 1 diamond—sales over 10 million) and 7 gold albums. The company has licensed music to high-profile TV shows and motion pictures and has released several motion picture soundtracks, most notably the platinum-selling, "Walk the Line" and "Daredevil," which went on to sell over 700,000 copies. Combining a team of creative A&R scouts, in-house writers, and engineers with its own recording studio and housing in New York, Wind-up cultivates a fluid and collaborative recording process with its artists, independent of points in their career.

DISTRIBUTED BY BMG.

HOW TO CONTACT *Write first and obtain permission to submit.* Use online form. Prefers CD or DVD. Does not return material or respond to submissions.

MUSIC Mostly **rock**, **folk** and **hard rock**. Artists include Seether, Evanescence, Finger Eleven, Creed, and People In Planes.

TIPS "We rarely look for songwriters as opposed to bands, so writing a big hit single would be the rule of the day."

◐ XEMU RECORDS

2 E. Broadway, Suite 901, New York NY 10038. (212)807-0290. **E-mail:** xemurecord@aol.com. **Website:** www.xemu.com. **Contact:** Cevin Solling. Xemu Records is an independent record label, founded in 1990 in New York by writer, filmmaker, philosopher, musician, music producer and artist Cevin Soling as a vehicle for his music and music production endeavors. Originally conceived as a "record label" nod to underground cult movements of the 1960s and 1970s, the label has since grown to be a home to burgeoning young bands in the psychedelic music and independent music scenes.

DISTRIBUTED BY Redeye Distribution.

HOW TO CONTACT *Write first and obtain permission to submit.* Prefers CD with 3 songs. Does not return material. Responds in 2 months.

MUSIC Mostly **alternative**. Released *Happy Suicide, Jim!* (album) by The Love Kills Theory (alternative rock); *Howls From The Hills* (album) by Dead Meadow; *The Fall* (album), recorded by Mikki James (alternative rock); *A is for Alpha* (album), recorded by Alpha Bitch (alternative rock); *Hold the Mayo* (album), recorded by Death Sandwich (alternative rock); *Stockholm Syndrome* (album), recorded by Trigger Happy (alternative rock) all released on Xemu Records. Other artists include Morning After Girls, Spindrift, and Rumpleville.

◓ XL RECORDINGS

One Codrington Mews, London W11 2EH United Kingdom. **Website:** www.xlrecordings.com.

HOW TO CONTACT Contact via online form.

MUSIC **Alternative rock**. Artists include Adele, Basement Jaxx, Radiohead, Beck, M.I.A, Peaches, Radiohead, Sigur Ros, The Horrors, The Raconteurs, The White Stripes, Thom Yorke, Vampire Weekend, and more.

RECORD PRODUCERS

The independent producer can best be described as a creative coordinator. He's often the one with the most creative control over a recording project and is ultimately responsible for the finished product. Some record companies have in-house producers who work with the acts on that label (although, in more recent years, such producer-label relationships are often non-exclusive). Today, most record companies contract out-of-house, independent record producers on a project-by-project basis.

WHAT RECORD PRODUCERS DO

Producers play a large role in deciding what songs will be recorded for a particular project and are always on the lookout for new songs for their clients. They can be valuable contacts for songwriters because they work so closely with the artists whose records they produce. They usually have a lot more freedom than others in executive positions and

are known for having a good ear for potential hit songs. Many producers are songwriters and musicians themselves. Since they wield a great deal of influence, a good song in the hands of the right producer at the right time stands a good chance of being cut. And even if a producer is not working on a specific project, he is well acquainted with record company executives and artists and often can get material through doors not open to you.

SUBMITTING MATERIAL TO PRODUCERS

It can be difficult to get your tapes to the right producer at the right time. Many producers write their own songs and even if they don't write, they may be involved in their own publishing companies so they have instant access to all the songs in their catalogs. Also, some genres are more dependent on finding outside songs than others. A producer working with a rock group or a singer-songwriter will rarely take outside songs.

It's important to understand the intricacies of the producer/publisher situation. If you pitch your song directly to a producer first, before another publishing company publishes the song, the producer may ask you for the publishing rights (or a percentage thereof) to your song. You must decide whether the producer is really an active publisher who will try to get the song recorded again and again or whether he merely wants the publishing because it means extra income for him from the current recording project. You may be able to work out a co-publishing deal, where you and the producer split the publishing of the song. That means he will still receive his percentage of the publishing income, even if you secure a cover recording of the song by other artists in the future. Even though you would be giving up a little bit initially, you may benefit in the future.

Some producers will offer to sign artists and songwriters to "development deals." These can range from a situation where a producer auditions singers and musicians with the intention of building a group from the ground up, to development deals where a producer signs a band or singer-songwriter to his production company with the intention of developing the act and producing an album to shop to labels (sometimes referred to as a "baby record deal").

You must carefully consider whether such a deal is right for you. In some cases, such a deal can open doors and propel an act to the next level. In other worst-case scenarios, such a deal can result in loss of artistic and career control, with some acts held in contractual bondage for years at a time. Before you consider any such deal, be clear about your goals, the producer's reputation, and the sort of compromises you are willing to make to reach those goals. If you have any reservations whatsoever, don't do it.

The listings that follow outline which aspects of the music industry each producer is involved in, what type of music he is looking for, and what records and artists he's recently produced. Study the listings carefully, noting the artists each producer works with, and consider if any of your songs might fit a particular artist's or producer's style. Then determine whether they are open to your level of experience (see "A Sample Listing Decoded" in the article "How to Use Songwriter's Market").

Consult the Category Index to find producers who work with the type of music you write, and the Geographic Index at the back of the book to locate producers in your area.

ADDITIONAL RECORD PRODUCERS

There are **more record producers** located in other sections of the book! Use the Index to find listings within other sections that are also record producers.

Icons

For more instructional information on the listings in this book, including explanations of symbols, read the article "How To Use Songwriter's Market."

WILLIAM ACKERMAN

P.O. Box 419, Bar Mills ME 04004. **E-mail:** will@williamackerman.com. **Website:** www.williamackerman.com.

MUSIC Has worked with George Winston, Michael Hedges, Heidi Anne Breyer, Fiona Joy Hawkins, Devon Rice, Erin Aas. Music: **acoustic**, **alternative**, **instrumental**.

⊘ ADR STUDIOS

250 Taxter Rd., Irvington NY 10533. (914)591-5616. **Fax:** (914)591-5617. **E-mail:** adrstudios@adrinc.org. **Website:** www.adrinc.org. **Contact:** Stuart J. Allyn. Produces 6 singles and 3-6 CDs/year. Fee derived from sales royalty and outright fee from recording artist and record company.

◯ *Does not accept unsolicited submissions.*

MUSIC Mostly **pop**, **rock**, **jazz**, and **theatrical**; also **R&B** and **country**. Produced *Thad Jones Legacy* (album), recorded by Vanquard Jazz Orchestra (jazz), released on New World Records. Other artists include Billy Joel, Aerosmith, Carole Demas, Michael Garin, The Magic Garden, Bob Stewart, The Dixie Peppers, Nora York, Buddy Barnes and various video and film scores.

ALLRS MUSIC PUBLISHING CO. (ASCAP)

P.O. Box B, Milford PA 18337. (718)767-8995. **E-mail:** info@allrsmusic.com. **Website:** www.allrsmusic.com. **Contact:** Renee Silvestri-Bushey, president. Music publisher, record company (MIDI Track Records), music consultant, artist management, record producer. Voting member of: NARAS (The Grammy Awards); the Country Music Association (The CMA Awards); SGMA; and Songwriters Guild of America (Diamond member). Staff size: 5. Publishes 3 songs/year; publishes 2 new songwriters/year. Pays standard royalty.

AFFILIATES Midi-Track Publishing Co. (BMI).

HOW TO CONTACT "Write/e-mail to obtain permission to submit. *We do not accept unsolicited submissions.*" Prefers CD with 3 songs, lyric sheet and cover letter. Responds via e-mail in 6 months only if interested.

MUSIC Mostly **country**, **gospel**, **top 40**, **R&B**, **MOR**, and **pop**. Does not want show tunes, jazz, classical or rap. Published "Why Can't You Hear My Prayer" (single by F. John Silvestri/Leslie Silvestri), recorded by 10-time Grammy nominee Huey Dunbar of the group DLG (Dark Latin Groove) released on Midi

Track Records including other multiple releases); "Chasing Rainbows" (single by F. John Silvestri/Leslie Silvestri), recorded by Tommy Cash (country), released on MMT Records (including other multiple releases); "Because of You" (single by F. John Silvestri/Leslie Silvestri), recorded by Iliana Medina, released on MIDI Track Records, also recorded by Grammy nominee Terri Williams of Always ... Patsy Cline, released on MIDI Track Records; also recorded by Grand Ole Opry member Ernie Ashworth, and other multiple releases.

TIPS "Attend workshops, seminars, and visit our blog on our website for advice and info on the music industry."

◐◑ A MAJOR SOUND CORP.

RR # 1, Kensington PE COB 1MO Canada. **E-mail:** info@amajorsound.com; musicpublisher@amajorsound.com. **Website:** www.amajorsound.com. **Contact:** Paul Milner, producer/engineer/mixer. Record producer and music publisher. Produces 8 CDs/year. Fee derived in part from sales royalty when song or artist is recorded, and/or outright fee from recording artist or record company, or investors. Submit demo package by mail. Unsolicited submissions are OK. Prefers CD with 5 songs and lyric sheet (lead sheet if available). Does not return material. Responds only if interested in 3 months.

MUSIC Mostly **rock**, **A/C**, **alternative** and **pop**; also **Christian** and **R&B**. Produced *COLOUR* (album written by J. MacPhee/R. MacPhee/C. Buchanan/D. MacDonald), recorded by The Chucky Danger Band (pop/rock); winner of ECMA award; *Something In Between* (album, written by Matt Andersen), recorded by Matt Andersen and Friends (blues), released on Weatherbox / Andersen; *In A Fever In A Dream* (album, written by Pat Deighan), recorded by Pat Deighan and The Orb Weavers (rock), released on Sandbar Music; *Saddle River String Band* (album, written by Saddle River Stringband), recorded by Saddle River Stringband (bluegrass) released on Save As Music; winner of ECMA award.

AMERICANA PRODUCTION

6566 Rolling Fork Dr., Nashville TN 37205. (615)974-5836. **E-mail:** tim@timlorsch.com. **Website:** www.timlorsch.com. **Contact:** Tim Lorsch. Tim Lorsch is a Nashville-based producer, session player, arranger and songwriter. He has produced critically acclaimed records and played on thousands of recordings covering a wide spectrum of musical styles. He has made contributions to Grammy and Emmy Award-winning projects, performed on TV and scored for the theater. Artists he has performed and/or recorded with include Kris Kristofferson, Kenny Chesney, Keith Urban, Pat Green, Ray Price, Percy Sledge, Lorrie Morgan, Andrew Gold, Joy Lynn White, Goose Creek Symphony, Mel McDaniel, Mary Gauthier, Hank Thompson, Jo-El Sonnier, Allison Moorer, Danni Leigh, Townes Van Zandt, The Kinleys, Keith Gaddis, Lucinda Williams, Rodney Crowell, Kevin Welch and Sam Baker.

MUSIC **Americana**. Has worked with Amanda Pearcy, Sam Baker, and more.

TIM ANDERSEN

(651)271-0515. **E-mail:** tandersen2005@yahoo.com. **Website:** www.timandersenrecordingengineer.com. "Can offer all those techniques to make your project rise above 'the usual' to something extraordinary, the way real records are made."

MUSIC Has worked with House of Pain, Shaq, Judgement Night, SDTRK, De Jef, Patti LaBelle, Temptations, Hiroshima, Krazy Bone, Snoop Dogg. Music: **rock**, **R&B**, **hip-hop**, **rap**, **acoustic**.

○✪ ANDREW LANE

Atlanta GA (213)400-4007. **E-mail:** andrewlanester@gmail.com. **Website:** www.drewrightmusic.com. **Contact:** Andrew Lane, Queen Throngkompol (executive assistant).

HOW TO CONTACT E-mail Andrew Lane or call his Executive Assistant Queen Throngkompol.

MUSIC Has produced such artists as The Backstreet Boys, Irene Cara, Keith Sweat, Kelly Rowland, Keana, The Clique Girls, and more. TV and film clients include Disney, Nickelodeon, MTV, BET, Country Music Network, HBO, ESPN, ABC Family, etc.

○ AUDIO 911

P.O. Box 212, Haddam CT 06438. (860)916-9947. **E-mail:** request@audio911.com. **Website:** www.audio911.com. Produces 4-8 singles, 3 LPs, 3 EPs and 4 CDs/year. Fee derived from outright fee from recording artist or record company. Submit demo by mail. Unsolicited submissions are OK. Prefers CD or DVDs with several songs and lyric or lead sheet. "Include live material if possible." Does not return material. Responds in 3 months.

MUSIC Mostly **rock**, **pop**, **top 40** and **country/acoustic**. Produced *Already Home* (album), recorded by

Hannah Cranna on Big Deal Records (rock); *Under the Rose* (album), recorded by Under the Rose on Utter Records (rock); and *Sickness & Health* (album), recorded by Legs Akimbo on Joyful Noise Records (rock). Other artists include King Hop!, The Shells, The Gravel Pit, G'nu Fuz, Tuesday Welders and Toxic Field Mice.

WILLIE BASSE

Los Angeles CA (818)731-9116. **E-mail:** williebasse@gmail.com. **Website:** www.williebasse.com. **Contact:** James Wright.

MUSIC Has worked with: Canned Heat, Finis Tasby, Frank Goldwasser, Paul Shortino, Jeff Nothrup, Black Sheep. Music: **rock**, **blues**, **heavy metal**.

EVAN BEIGEL

P.O. Box 801556, Santa Clarita CA 91380. (818)321-5472. **E-mail:** mail@evanjbeigel.com. **Website:** www.evanjbeigel.com. Evan J. Beigel is a composer, producer, and recording engineer who learned his craft through a traditional music education and mentorships with world-class producers and engineers, such as Keith Olsen (Fleetwood Mac), Taavi Mote (U2, Madonna), and Pat Regan (Rainbow, Deep Purple).

MUSIC Has worked with Troup, Badi Assad, Ray Kurzweil, Gilli Moon, Michelle Featherstone, Killer Tracks. Music: **rock**, **indie**, **alternative**, **folk**, **dance/electronica**.

◐ BIG BEAR

P.O. Box 944, Edgbaston, Birmingham, B16 8UT United Kingdom. (0)(121)454-7020. **Fax:** (0)(121)454-9996. **E-mail:** jim@bigbearmusic.com; admin@bigbearmusic.com. **Website:** www.bigbearmusic.com. **Contact:** Jim Simpson, managing director. Record producer, music publisher (Bearsongs) and record company (Big Bear Records). Produces 10 LPs/year. Fee derived from sales royalty. *Write first about your interest, then submit demo tape and lyric sheet.* Does not return material. Responds in 2 weeks.

○ Also see the listings for Bearsongs in the Music Publishers section of this book and Big Bear Records in the Record Companies section of this book.

MUSIC **Blues**, **swing**, and **jazz**.

BLACK CROW MUSIC GROUP

1806 Division St., Nashville TN 37201. (615)586-0621. **E-mail:** jimhyatt.nashville@gmail.com. **Website:** www.blackcrowmusicgroup.com. **Contact:** Jim Hyatt. Offers options for recording an album or recording singles. Black Crow Music Group is a full-service music production and talent management company. **MUSIC** Any genre, but mostly **country**, **pop**, and **R&B**. Has worked with Colin Lockey, Brittni Renee, Colt Prather, Arianna Reiter, and more.

BLUES ALLEY RECORDS

Rt. 1, Box 288, Clarksburg WV 26301. (304)598-2583. **E-mail:** hswiger@bluesalleymusic.com. **Website:** www.bluesalleymusic.com. Record producer, record company and music publisher (Blues Alley Publishing/BMI). Produces 4-6 LPs and 2 EPs/year. Fee derived from sales royalty when song or artist is recorded. Submit demo package by mail. Unsolicited submissions are OK. Will only accept CDs with lead sheets and typed lyrics. Does not return material. Responds in 6 weeks.
MUSIC Mostly **country**, **pop**, **Christian**, and **rock**. Produced *Monongalia*, recorded by The New Relics (country), 2009; *Chasing Venus*, recorded by The New Relics (acoustic rock), 2006; *Sons of Sirens*, recorded by Amity (rock), 2004; and *It's No Secret*, recorded by Samantha Caley (pop country), 2004.

CLIFF BRODSKY

Beverly Hills CA **E-mail:** cliff@brodskyentertainment.com. **Website:** www.brodskyentertainment.com.
MUSIC Has worked with Rose Rossi, Daize Shayne, Jason Kirk, Burning Retna, Future Kings of Spain, Jordy Towers, Brentley Gore, Cat Switzer, Justin Lanning, Warner Brothers, Universal, Sony, MCA, Virgin, Interscope. Music: **indie**, **pop**, **rock**.

KIM COPELAND PRODUCTIONS

1216 17th Ave. S., Nashville TN 37212. (615)293-9545 or (615)429-5032. **E-mail:** info@kimcopelandproductions.com. **Website:** www.kimcopelandproductions.com. **Contact:** Kim Copeland, Susan Tucker. "At its core, Kim Copeland Productions is a full-service music production company in the heart of Music Row, perfect for everything from songwriter demos through label pitch packages to mastered albums."
MUSIC Mostly **country**. Has worked with Brenda Lee White, James Kevin O'Connor, Family Tree, Matt Strasner, Lisa Lambert, Maddie Deneault, Tim Sweeney, Sim Balkey, Chris Monaghan, and more.

ERIC CORNE

Los Angeles CA (310)500-8831. **E-mail:** eric@ericcornemusic.com. **Website:** www.ericcornemusic.com. **Contact:** Eric Corne, producer.
MUSIC Has worked with Glen Campbell, Lucinda Willaims, Joanna Wang, Michelle Shocked, DeVotchKa, Instant Karma. Music: **rock**, **indie**, **Americana**, **country**, **blues**, **jazz**, **folk**.

CREATIVE SOUL

Nashville TN 37179. (615)400-3910. **E-mail:** firstcontact@creativesoulrecords.com. **Website:** www.creativesoulonline.com. Record producer. Produces 10-25 singles and 10-15 albums/year. Fee derived from outright fee from recording artist or company. Other services include consulting/critique/review services. *Contact first by e-mail to obtain permission to submit demo.* Prefers 2-3 MP3s via e-mail. Responds only if interested.
MUSIC Mostly **contemporary Christian**, including **pop**, **rock**, **jazz**, **world**, and **ballads** in the **Christian** and **gospel** genre. No southern gospel, rap, or hip-hop, please. Produced Faithful, recorded by Count Laws (contemporary Christian); The Best is Yet to Be, recorded by Eternity Focus (contemporary Christian); In My Head, recorded by Skylar Kaylan (contemporary Christian), all released on Creative Soul Records. Other artists include Leslie McKee, Stephen Bautista, Stephanie Newton, Mike Westendorf, Frances Drost, and Jen Haugland.
TIPS "Contact us first by e-mail; we are here in Nashville for you. We offer weekly free online information and monthly consults in Nashville for Christian artists and songwriters. We want to meet you and talk with you about your dreams. E-mail us and let's start talking about your music and ministry!"

MARC DESISTO

Sherman Oaks CA (818)259-4235. **E-mail:** marcdmix@gmail.com. **Website:** www.marcdesisto.com.
MUSIC Has worked with Stevie Nicks, Michelle Branch, Unwritten Law, Melissa Ethridge, Rick Knowles, Don Henley, Patti Smith, Mark Opitz, Tom Petty, U2. Music: **rock**, **alternative**, **pop**, **indie**.

JEANNIE DEVA

P.O. Box 2847, Hollywood CA 90078. (323)536-9004. **E-mail:** sing@jeanniedeva.com. **Website:** www.jeanniedeva.com. **Contact:** Jeannie Deva.

MUSIC Has worked with Rounder Records, Charisse Arrington, MCA, Dar Williams, Razor and Tie Records, Alldaron West. Music: all **contemporary** styles.

⊘ JOEL DIAMOND ENTERTAINMENT

3940 Laurel Canyon Blvd., Suite 441, Studio City CA 91604. (818)980-9588. **E-mail:** jdiamond20@aol.com. **Website:** www.joeldiamond.com. **Contact:** Joel Diamond, president and CEO. Record producer, music publisher and manager. Fee derived from sales royalty when song is recorded or outright fee from recording artist or record company.

◖ Also see the listing for Silver Blue Music/Oceans Blue Music in the Music Publishers section of this book.

MUSIC Mostly **dance**, **R&B**, **soul** and **top 40/pop**. The 5 Browns—3 No. 1 CDs for Sony/BMG, David Hasselhoff; produced "One Night In Bangkok" (single by Robey); "I Think I Love You," recorded by Katie Cassidy (daughter of David Cassidy) on Artemis Records; "After the Loving" (single), recorded by E. Humperdinck; "Forever Friends," recorded by Vaneza (featured on Nickelodeon's *The Brothers Garcia*); and "Paradise" (single), recorded by Kaci.

LES DUDEK

EFLAT Productions, P.O. Box 726, Auburndale FL 33823-0726. **Website:** www.lesdudek.com. **MUSIC** Has worked with Stevie Nicks, Steve Miller Band, Cher, Dave Mason, The Allman Brothers, Mike Finnigan, Bobby Whitlock. Music: **southern rock**.

◐ FINAL MIX INC.

2219 W. Olive Ave., Suite 102, Burbank CA 91506. **E-mail:** rob@finalmix.com. **Website:** www.finalmix.com. Releases 70 singles and 5-7 LPs and CDs/year. Fee derived from sales royalty when song or artist is recorded.

◖ *Does not accept unsolicited submissions.*

MUSIC Primarily **pop**, **rock**, **dance**, **R&B**, and **rap**. Produced and/or mixer/remixer for Mary Mary, New Boyz, Kirk Franklin, Charlie Wilson, LeAnn Rimes, Charice, Train, Aaliyah, Hilary Duff, Jesse McCartney, Christina Aguilera, American Idol, Ray Charles, Quincy Jones, Michael Bolton, K-Ci and Jo Jo, Will Smith, and/or mixer/remixer for Janet Jackson, Ice Cube, Queen Latifah, Jennifer Paige, and The Corrs.

JUD FRIEDMAN STUDIO

Los Angeles CA **E-mail:** jud@judfriedmanmusic.com. **Website:** www.judfriedmanmusic.com. Jud Friedman is a Los Angeles-based songwriter and producer. He's worked with artists who have had 65 million records sold worldwide, been nominated for 2 Academy Awards, 2 Grammys, 2 Golden Globes, as well as nominations for 2 more Grammys and a Soul Train Award. **MUSIC** Any genre. Has worked with Whitney Houston, Kenny Loggins, Barbra Streisand, Ray Charles, Tina Turner, Rod Stewart, Leann Rimes, and more.

◑ CHRIS GAGE

Austin TX **Website:** www.chrisgage.biz.
MUSIC Artists produced include 8 1/2 Souvenirs (co-produced with Jack Hazzard for RCA Records) Bill Small, Jody Mills, Steve Brooks, Michael Austin, Cowboy Johnson, Albert and Gage, Christine Albert, Abi Tapia, Rio King, Sharon Bousquet, Lawrence J. Clark, Boyd Bristow, Jimmie Dale Gilmore (2 songs) and Willie Nelson (1 duet with Jimmie Dale Gilmore).

MAURICE GAINEN

4470 Sunset Blvd., Suite 177, Hollywood CA 90027. (323)662-3642. **E-mail:** mauricegainen@gmail.com; info@mauricegainen.com. **Website:** www.mauricegainen.com. "We provide complete start-to-finish CD production, including help in choosing songs and musicians through CD mastering. We also pride ourselves on setting a budget and keeping to it."
MUSIC Has worked with Stacy Golden, Yuka Takara, Donna Loren, James Webber, Andy McKee, Rafael Moreira, Alex Skolnick Trio, Metro, Mel Elias, Shelly Rudolph, Kenny Tex, Rachael Owens. Music: **R&B**, **jazz**, **alternative**, **rock**, **pop**.

BRIAN GARCIA

Los Angeles CA (626)487-0410. **E-mail:** brian@briangarcia.net; info@briangarcia.net. **Website:** www.briangarcia.net.
MUSIC "Producer-mixer-engineer Brian Garcia specializes in the genres of rock and pop. He has been part of 22 million records sold, debuts at No. 1 in 30 countries, a Grammy-winning album, and a No. 1 single on iTunes as a co-writer/producer/mixer. Brian has taken artists from development to securing record deals and producing albums for EMI and Sony/BMG." He has worked with Our Lady Peace, Earshot, Until June, Galactic Cowboys, Avril Lavigne, Kelly Clarkson, Michelle Branch, Dizmas, Chantal Kreviazuk, King's X, Diana Degarmo, The Library, Pushmonkey, The Daylights, Precious Death, Joy Drop. Music: **rock**, **pop**, **indie**.

MCKAY GARNER

1873 Eighth Ave. Suite A, San Francisco CA 94122. E-mail: info@mckaygarner.com. **Website:** www.mckaygarner.com.

MUSIC Producer, engineer for hire only that has worked with Red Hot Chili Peppers, Styles of Beyond, Flogging Molly, J Dilla doppio, Valencia, Mike Shinoda, Michael Bublé, Sara Melson.

CARMEN GRILLO

Big Surprise Music, 16161 Ventura Blvd., Suite C-522, Encino CA 91436. (818)905-7676. **E-mail:** info@carmengrillo.com. **Website:** www.carmengrillo.com.

MUSIC Has worked with Manhattan, Transfer, Chicago, Bill Champlin, Mike Finnigan, Tower of Power. Music: **R&B, pop, rock, jazz, blues.**

H2M SOUND

Nashville TN E-mail: howiemoscovitch@yahoo.ca. **Website:** www.howiemoscovitch.com. **Contact:** Howie Moscovitch. "Howie Moscovitch is a Canadian-born writer/producer/multi-instrumentalist working in Nashville. He is comfortable and experienced with all styles but specializes in pop and Top 10 of all charts including hip-hop, dance, and R&B. His productions have very current beats, sounds and arrangements. His influences come from all manner of music."

MUSIC Mostly **rap, hip-hop, R&B,** and **pop.**

◉ HEART CONSORT MUSIC

410 First St. SW, Mt. Vernon IA 52314. **E-mail:** mail@heartconsortmusic.com. **Website:** www.heartconsortmusic.com. **Contact:** James Kennedy. Produces 2-3 CDs/year. Fee derived from sales royalty when song or artist is recorded. Submit demo package by mail. Unsolicited submissions are OK. Prefers CD with 3 songs and 3 lyric sheets. Include SASE. Responds in 3 months.

MUSIC Mostly **jazz, New Age** and **contemporary.** Produced *New Faces* (album), written and recorded by James Kennedy on Heart Consort Music (world/jazz).

TIPS "We are interested in jazz/New Age artists with quality demos and original ideas. We aim for an international audience."

HEATHER HOLLEY

Los Angeles CA **E-mail:** info@heatherholley.com. **Website:** heatherholley.com. Heather Holley is a multi-platinum-selling pop music producer and songwriter based in Los Angeles and New York. She specializes in artist development and is known for her role in launching Christina Aguilera's career. Her songs have been featured in global ad campaigns for Pepsi, Mercedes; feature films and trailers *Pursuit of Happyness, Honey, Kiss of the Dragon*; TV series *Grey's Anatomy, The Office, 90210, Private Practice,* and many more. Her article about the craft of songwriting, "Soaring With Christina Aguilera," was published in The Wall Street Journal.

MUSIC Has worked with Christina Aguilera, Skylar Grey, Itaal Shur, Katie Costello, Nikki Williams. Music: **pop, dance, indie, R&B.**

JIMMY HUNTER

Hollywood CA (323)655-0615. **E-mail:** jimmy@jimmyhunter.com. **Website:** www.jimmyhunter.com. "When you work with Jimmy Hunter, you find a fellow artist who will help you to achieve and refine your vision. He has the experience and tools to get the ultimate sound for your music and bring out the very best in you."

MUSIC Has worked with Todd Standford, Dr. Alias, Savannah Phillips, Mr. Smoove, Mark R. Kent, Della Reese, Lisa Gold, Jamie Palumbo, The Ramblers. Music: **rock, pop, R&B.**

◉ SIMON ILLA

Atlanta GA **E-mail:** info@simonilla.com. **Website:** www.simonilla.com.

MUSIC Has worked with Onyx, Vivian Green, Floetry, Roscoe P. Coldchain, The Answer. Music: **hip-hop, R&B, pop, folk, rock, gospel, emo.**

◉ INTEGRATED ENTERTAINMENT

1815 JFK Blvd., #1612, Philadelphia PA 19103-1713. (267)408-0659. **E-mail:** lawrence@gelboni.com. **Website:** www.gelboni.com. Estab. 1991. Produces up to 6 projects/year. Compensation is derived from outright fee from recording artist or record company and sales royalties.

HOW TO CONTACT Submit demo package by mail. Solicited submissions only. CD only with 3 songs. "Draw a guitar on the outside of envelope so we'll know it's from a songwriter." Will respond if interested.

MUSIC Mostly **rock** and **pop.** Produced *Gold Record* (album), written and recorded by Dash Rip Rock (rock) on Ichiban Records and many others.

◉ KAREN KANE PRODUCER/ENGINEER

(910)681-0220. **E-mail:** karenkane@mixmama.com. **Website:** www.mixmama.com. **Contact:** Karen Kane.

Record producer and recording engineer. Produces 3-5 CDs/year. Fee derived from sales royalty when song or artist is recorded or outright fee from recording artist or record company. *E-mail first and obtain permission to submit. Unsolicited submissions are not OK.* "Please note: I am not a song publisher. My expertise is in album production." Does not return material. Responds in 1 week.

MUSIC Mostly **acoustic music of any kind**, **rock**, **blues**, **pop**, **alternative**, **R&B/reggae**, **country**, and **bluegrass**. Produced *Good to Me* (album), recorded by Nina Repeta; *Topless* (Juno-nominated album), recorded by Big Daddy G, released on Reggie's Records; *Mixed Wise and Otherwise* (Juno-nominated album), recorded by Harry Manx (blues). Other artists include Tracy Chapman (her first demo), Katarina Bourdeaux, Crys Matthews, Laura Bird, L Shape Lot, The Hip Hop Co-op, Barenaked Ladies (live recording for a TV special), and The Coolidge Band.

TIPS "Get proper funding to be able to make a competitive, marketable product."

TIM DAVID KELLY

Los Angeles CA (818)601-7047. **E-mail:** info@timdavidkelly.com. **Website:** www.timdavidkelly.com.
MUSIC Has worked with Kicking Harold, Shiny Toy Guns, Dokken. Music: **alternative**, **metal**, **Americana**, **rock**, **acoustic pop**.

○ L.A. ENTERTAINMENT, INC.

7095 Hollywood Blvd., #826, Hollywood CA 90028. **E-mail:** info@warriorrecords.com. **Website:** www.warriorrecords.com. Record producer, record company (Warrior Records [distributed via Universal Music Distribution]) and music publisher (New Entity Music/ASCAP, New Copyright Music/BMI, New Euphonic Music/SESAC). Fee derived from sales royalty when song or artist is recorded. Submit demo package by mail. Unsolicited submissions are OK. Prefers CD and/or DVD with original songs, lyric and lead sheet if available. "We do not review Internet sites. Do not send MP3s, unless requested. All written submitted materials (e.g., lyric sheets, letter, etc.) should be typed." Does not return material unless SASE is included. Responds in 2 months only via e-mail or SASE.
MUSIC All styles. "All genres are utilized with our music supervision company for film and TV, but our original focus is on **alternative rock** and **urban genres** (e.g., **R&B**, **rap**, **gospel**).

○ BEN LINDELL

EMW Music Group, 42 Broadway 22nd Floor, New York NY 10004. **E-mail:** ben@benlindell.com. **Website:** www.benlindell.com. **Contact:** Ben Lindell. Ben Lindell is a New York-based producer/mixer/engineer who has worked with hundreds of artists including MGMT, 50 Cent, Wale, Bebel Giberto and many more. "In addition to being a fantastic musician he is also a tremendous geek. It's his marriage of musical creativity and technical know-how that makes him an in-demand producer/mixer/engineer."

HOW TO CONTACT Use online form to contact.
MUSIC Select clients include: 50 Cent, Soulja Boy, Wale, Ryan Leslie, Genasis, Lloyd Banks, Tony Yayo, Roshon, Illmind, Red Cafe, J.Period, Olivia, Kelly Rowland, Locnville, Chromeo, MGMT, Bebel Giberto, Rufus Wainright, Edie Brickell, and more.

○ LINEAR CYCLE PRODUCTIONS

P.O. Box 2608, North Hills CA 91393. **E-mail:** accessiblyliveoffline@gmail.com. **Website:** www.linearcycleproductions.com. **Contact:** Mason "Manny" Pandancski, executive producer.
MUSIC Mostly **rock/pop**, **R&B/blues** and **country**; also **gospel** and **comedy**. Produced "Never Peal The Truth" (single by E. Link), recorded by NeverMynd (pop/dance), released on SideStep SoundsCollection, "We Are So Their" recorded By Olif Spear and released on "Fail" brand MP3s (alternative) and "Wee Bea Ever Wha..?" (single by Billy Wymp) recorded by Eye Cant, and offered by Giveaway Recordings (genre TBA).

TIPS "We only listen to songs and other material recorded on quality tapes and CDs. We will not accept any submissions via e-mail. If your demo is recorded on an MP3 or AIFF sound file, you must either burn the file onto a CD, or download the sound file into an MP3 player and send the player with the songs to our attention. Otherwise, anything sent via e-mail will be disposed of and will not be considered."

BOB LUNA

Los Angeles CA (310)202-8043 or (310)508-1356. **E-mail:** bobluna@earthlink.net. **Website:** boblunamusic.net.
MUSIC Live and **midi orchestration**. Live performance/arranging/recording credits include Paul McCartney, Dionne Warwick, Reba McEntire, Denice Williams, Randy Crawford, Alanis Morissette, Sister Sledge, others.

PETER MALICK

Los Angeles CA (866)884-9919, ext. 2. **E-mail:** peter-malick@gmail.com. **Website:** www.petermalick.com. **MUSIC** Has worked with Norah Jones, Jung Yong Hwa, CNBLUE, Daphne Willis, Ruby Friedman, Spencer Livingston/Livingmore, Mercy Malick, Kill My Coquette, Robert Tepper, Courtney Jones, Suzanne Santos/HoneyHoney, Chelsea Williams. Music: **pop**, **K-pop**, **roots**, **Americana**, **R&B**.

⊘ COOKIE MARENCO

P.O. Box 874, Belmont CA 94002. (650)595-8475. **E-mail:** bluecoastpress@gmail.com. **Website:** cookiemarenco.com.

HOW TO CONTACT "No speculative projects." Does not accept unsolicited material. Must have budget.

MUSIC Mostly acoustic, high-resolution, live performance-oriented **alternative modern rock**, **country**, **folk**, **rap**, **ethnic** and **avante-garde**; also **classical**, **pop** and **jazz**. Produced *Winter Solstice II* (album), written and recorded by various artists for Windham Hill Records (instrumental). Artists include Tony Furtado, Brain, Buckethead, Alex Degrassi, Turtle Island String Quartet, Praxis, Oregon, Mary Chapin Carpenter, Max Roach and Charle Haden & Quartet West.

TIPS "Specialist in high-quality ANALOG recording. Mixing to 1/2" or DSD digital. Full-service mastering and dynamic website development."

DENNY MARTIN MUSIC

1004 Regents Park Circle, Antioch TN 37013. (615)361-6073. **E-mail:** dennymartinmusic@comcast.net. **Website:** www.dennymartinmusic.com. **Contact:** Denny Martin. Offers full-service production from "a lifelong music pro," collaborative process with top musicians and singers; takes on all levels of projects from demos to indie projects, guitar/vocal to full band.

MUSIC Any genre. Has worked with Gerald Flemming, Infinitely More, Becca Richter, Don McNatt, Sue Lopez, Paul Hurtado, Todd Kramer, Haley Olivia, Dave Saunders, and more.

◑◯ SCOTT MATHEWS, D/B/A HIT OR MYTH PRODUCTIONS INC.

246 Almonte Blvd., Mill Valley CA 94941. **E-mail:** scott@scottmathews.com. **Website:** www.scottmathews.com. **Contact:** Scott Mathews, CEO and founder. Record producer, "song doctor," multi-instrumentalist, studio owner, music industry execu-

tive, and professional consultant. Produces 3-5 projects/year. Fee derived from recording artist or record company (with royalty points).

Scott Mathews has more than 20 gold and multi-platinum awards for sales of more than 30 million records. He has worked with more than 80 Rock and Roll Hall of Fame inductees and on a combination of nearly 30 Grammy- and Oscar-winning or nominated releases. He is currently working primarily with emerging artists while still making music with his legendary established artists such as Billie Joe Armstrong (Green Day), James Hatfield (Metallica), Pat Monohan (Train), Sammy Hagar, Ann Wilson, Joe Satriani, and Van Dyke Parks. His latest No. 1 Billboard hit came in 2012; his first was in 1976, and he has achieved No. 1s in every decade since he began.

HOW TO CONTACT "We are only seeking self-contained artists. We do not place songs with artists because we work with artists that write their own material." Submit artist demo for production consideration by e-mail. "Unsolicited submissions are often the best ones and readily accepted. All early-stage business is conducted via e-mail." Responds in 2 months.

MUSIC Mostly **rock/pop**, **alternative**, **country** and **singer/songwriters of all styles**. In 2014, he was awarded 7 more gold and multi-platinum records by Eric Clapton, Van Morrison, David Bowie, B.B. King, The Beach Boys, Bonnie Raitt, and Sammy Hagar. In 2004, Mathews earned a gold album for "Smile" by Brian Wilson. Has produced Elvis Costello, Roy Orbison, Rosanne Cash, Jerry Garcia, Huey Lewis, Sammy Hagar, Bob Weird, and many more iconic artists. Has worked with Barbra Streisand, John Lee Hooker, Keith Richards, George Harrison, Mick Jagger, Van Morrison, Bonnie Raitt, Ringo Starr, Brian Wilson, Zac Brown, Chris Isaak, Eric Clapton, and a long list of music's greatest.

TIPS "If you are not independent, you are dependent. The new artists that are coming up and achieving success in the music industry are the ones that prove they have a vision and can make incredible records without the huge financial commitment of a label. When an emerging artist makes great product for the genre they are in, they are in the driver's seat to be able to make a fair and equitable deal for distribution, be it with a major or independent label. My philosophy is to go where you are loved. The truth is, a smaller label that is completely dedicated to you and shares your vision may help your career far more than a huge label that will not keep you around if you don't sell millions of units. Perhaps no label is needed at all, if you are up for the challenge of wearing a lot of hats. I feel too much pressure is put on the emerging artist when they have to pay huge sums back to the label in order to see their first royalty check. We all know those records can be made for a fraction of that cost without compromising quality or commercial appeal, and I am proving that every day. I still believe in potential, and our company is in business to back up that belief. It is up to us as record makers/visionaries to take that potential into the studio and come out with music that can compete with anything else on the market. Discovering, developing and producing artists who can sustain long careers is our main focus at Hit or Myth Productions. We are proud to be associated with so many legendary and timeless artists and our track record speaks for itself. If you love making music, don't let anyone dim that light. We look forward to hearing from you if you are an emerging artist looking for production to kick your career into high gear. (Please check out www.scottmathews.com for more info, and also www.wikipedia.org, keyword: Scott Mathews.)"

BILL METOYER

16209 Victory Blvd., #132, Lake Balboa CA 91406. (818)780-5394. **E-mail:** bill@skullseven.com. **Website:** www.skullseven.com.

MUSIC Has worked with Slayer, W.A.S.P., Fates Warning, Six Feet Under, Armored Saint, DRI, COC, Tourniquet, Skrew, Rigor Mortis, Sacred Steel, Cement. Music: **hard rock, metal**.

BILLY MITCHELL

P.O. Box 284, S. Pasadena CA 91031. (626)574-5040. **Fax:** (626)446-2584. **E-mail:** billymitchell2k@aol.com. **Website:** www.billy-mitchell.com.

MUSIC Has worked with Chartmaker Records, Vista Records, PRC Records, USA Music Group. Music: **contemporary jazz, pop**.

ADAM MOSELEY

Los Angeles CA (323)316-4932. **E-mail:** adammoseley@mac.com. **Website:** www.adammoseley.net.

MUSIC Has worked with Claudio Valenzuela, Lisbeth Scott, Wolfmother, Nikka Costa, Abandoned Pools, John Cale, AJ Croce, Lucybell, The Cure, KISS, Rush, Roxette, Maxi Priest. Music: **rock, alternative, electronica, acoustic**.

⊙ MUSICJONES ENTERTAINMENT

250 Denver Way, Henderson NV 89015. (702)858-6427. **E-mail:** mike@musicjones.com. **Website:** www.musicjones.com.

MUSIC Mostly **country, folk** and **pop**; also **rock**. Recent album releases: *The Highway Revisited* featuring Mike Jones, *Live from the Bistro*, featuring Terry Alexander and Mike Jones. Also produced "Lonelyville," and "Alabama Slammer" (singles), both written and recorded by Wake Eastman; and "Good Looking Loser" (single), written and recorded by Renee Rubach, all on MusicJones Records (country). Other artists include Matt Dorman, Steve Gilmore, The Tackroom Boys, The Las Vegas Philharmonic, and J.C. Clark.

TIPS "Put your ego on hold. Don't take criticism personally. Advice is meant to help you grow and improve your skills as an artist/songwriter. Be professional and business-like in all your dealings."

ZAVE NATHAN

2 Village Lane, Bear Valley Springs CA 93561. (661)839-6370. **E-mail:** zave2004@yahoo.com; info@zavemusic.net. **Website:** zavemusic.net.

MUSIC Songwriter / Arranger / Producer. Has worked with Headsandwich, Sahaloop, The Joy House, Dan Bern, Indya, Edouardo Torres. Music: **rock, blues, R&B, funk, acoustic, hard rock**.

⊙ NEU ELECTRO PRODUCTIONS

P.O. Box 1582, Bridgeview IL 60455. (630)257-6289. **E-mail:** neuelectro@email.com. **Website:** www.neuelectro.com. **Contact:** Bob Neumann.

MUSIC Mostly **dance, house, techno, rap** and **rock**; also **experimental, New Age** and **top 40**. Produced "Juicy" (single), written and recorded by Juicy Black on Dark Planet International Records (house); "Make Me Smile" (single), written and recorded by Roz Baker (house); *Reactovate-6* (album by Bob Neumann), recorded by Beatbox-D on N.E.P. Records (dance); and *Sands of Time* (album), recorded by Bob Neumann (New Age). Other artists include Skid Marx and The Deviants.

⊙ NEW EXPERIENCE RECORDS/FAZE 4 RECORDS/PUMP IT UP RECORDS/TOUCH TONE RECORDS

1017 Myrtle St., Marks MS 38646. **E-mail:** newexperiencerecords@yahoo.com. **Contact:** James L. Milligan Jr., president, CEO, and music publisher. Record producer, music publisher (A New Rap Jam Publishing/ASCAP), management firm (Creative Star Management) and record company (New Experience Records, Rough Edge Records, Grand-Slam Records, and Pump It Up Records). Produces 15-30 12" singles, 3 EPs and 2-5 CDs/year. Fee derived from sales royalty when song or artist is recorded or outright fee from record company, "depending on services required." Distributed by KVZ Distribution and States 51 Distribution.

Also see the listings for A New Rap Jam Publishing (ASCAP) in the Music Publishers section of this book.

HOW TO CONTACT Contact A&R department or write first to arrange personal interview. Address material to A&R department or Talent Coordinator. Prefers CD with a minimum of 3 songs and lyric or lead sheet (if available). "If CDs are to be returned, proper postage should be enclosed and all CDs and letters should have SASE for faster reply." Responds in 6-8 weeks.

MUSIC Mostly **pop**, **R&B**, and **rap**; also **gospel**, **soul**, **contemporary gospel** and **rock**. Produced "The Son of God" (single by James Milligan/Anthony Milligan/Melvin Milligan) from *The Final Chapter* (album), recorded by T.M.C. Milligan Conection (R&B, Gospel), released 2002 on New Experience/Pump It Up Records. Other artists include Dion Mikel, Paulette Mikel, Melvin Milligan and Venesta Compton.

TIPS "Do your homework on the music business. Be aware of all the new sampling laws. There are too many sound-alikes. Be yourself. I look for what is different, vocal ability, voice range and sound stage presence, etc. Be on the lookout for our new blues label, Rough Edge Records/Rough Edge Entertainment. Blues material is now being reviewed. Send your best studio-recorded material. Also, be aware of the new digital downloading laws. People are being jailed and fined for recording music that has not been paid for. Do your homework. Labels: New Experience Records, Touch Tone Records, Grind Blocc Records, Pump It Up Records; now we can better serve our customers with great distribution. You can also e-mail us at newexperiencerecords@yahoo.com for further information on our services. We are reviewing hip-hop and rap material that is positive, clean, and commercial; please no gangsta rap if you want a deal with us, as well as airplay. Also reviewing gospel music, gospel rap and anything with commercial appeal."

◯ NICK EIPERS

E-mail: nick@nickeipers.com. **Website:** www.nickeipers.com. "I am a freelance recording engineer and producer, specializing in music. Currently based in the Chicago area, I am on staff at Tranquility One Studios, and am available to work freelance almost anywhere. I have worked at Chicago Recording Co., Studiomedia Recording Co., Hinge Studios, Rax Trax Recording, IV Lab Studios, Gallery of Carpet Recording, Shantyville Recording Studio, Gravity Studios, Studiochicago, Star Trax Recording and Chicago Trax, as well as various remote locations and private studios. We choose the recording space based on the aesthetic and practical needs of your music."

MUSIC Specializing in **jazz**, **fusion**, **world**, **indie**, **alternative**, **singer/songwriter**, **folk**, **classical**.

◯ NIGHTWORKS RECORDS

355 W. Potter Dr., Anchorage AK 99518. (907)562-3754. **E-mail:** surrealstudiosak@gmail.com. **Website:** www.surrealstudios.com. **Contact:** Kurt Riemann, owner/engineer.

HOW TO CONTACT Submit demo package by mail. Unsolicited submissions are OK. Prefers CD with 2-3 songs "produced as fully as possible. Send jingles and songs on separate CDs." Does not return material. Responds in 1 month.

MUSIC Produces a variety of music from **native Alaskan** to **techno** to **Christmas**.

CARLA OLSON

11684 Ventura Blvd., Suite 583, Studio City CA 91604. **E-mail:** carlawebsite@aol.com. **Website:** www.carlaolson.com.

MUSIC Has worked with Paul Jones, Jake Andrews, Davis Gaines, Joe Louis Walker, Astrella Celeste, Youngblood Hart, Billy Joe Royal, Kim Wilson.

⊘ PHIL EK

E-mail: info@philek.com. **Website:** www.philek.com. **Contact:** Steve Moir, Moir Entertainment, Inc.

MUSIC Worked with such acts as Fleet Foxes, Band of Horses, Boy & Bear, The Walkmen, The Cave Singers, Run River South, Father John Misty, Shout Out Louds, Modest Mouse, The Dodos, Sea Wolf, Animal Kingdom, Mudhoney, The Shins, Spanish for 100, David Cross, Jana McCall, Dinosaur Jr., Feed, Built to Spill, Sick Bees, Fumes, and others.

PLATINUM STUDIOS

Los Angeles CA (818)994-5368. **E-mail:** paulhilton123@sbcglobal.net. **Website:** www.paulhiltonmusic.com. "Platinum sound at affordable rates."

MUSIC Has worked with Janet Klein, Matt Zane & Society 1, Bon Jovi, Spencer Davis, Big Joe Turner, Billy Vera, Metallica, Ratt, Motley Crue, Morgana King, Jack Mack & the Heart Attack, Rodney O & Joe Cooley, WASP, Carlos Rico, Mera, Sam Glaser. Music: **Latin**, **rock**, **blues**.

WILL RAY

106 Sunset Hills CT., Asheville NC 28803. (828)299-1422. **E-mail:** will@willray.biz. **Website:** www.willray.biz.

MUSIC Has worked with The Hellecasters, Solomon Burke, Wylie & the Wild West Show, Candye Kane, Jeffrey Steele, Clay DuBose, The Buzzards, Carrie James. Music: **country**, **folk**, **blues**.

TODD ROSENBERG

Los Angeles CA (310)926-5059. **E-mail:** todd@toddrosenberg.net. **Website:** www.toddrosenberg.net.

MUSIC Has worked with Pressure 45, Devil Driver, Mad Caddies, Motograter, Honda, Mitsubishi, Panasonic, Grooveworks. Music: **indie**, **rock**, **Americana**, **country**, **ska**, **punk**.

○ STEVE SATKOWSKI RECORDINGS

P.O. Box 3403, Stuart FL 34995. (772)225-3128. **Website:** www.clearsoulproductions.com/SteveSatkowski.html.

HOW TO CONTACT Submit demo by mail. Unsolicited submissions are OK. Prefers CD or cassette. Does not return material. Responds in 2 weeks.

MUSIC Mostly **classical**, **jazz** and **big band**. Produced recordings for National Public Radio and affiliates. Engineered recordings for Steve Howe, Patrick Moraz, Kenny G, and Michael Bolton.

MARK SAUNDERS

Beat 360 Studios, 630 Ninth Ave., Suite 710, New York NY 10036. **E-mail:** ollie@spark-mgmt.com. **Website:** www.marksaunders.com. **Contact:** Ollie Hammett.

MUSIC Has worked with The Cure, Tricky, Depeche Mode, Marilyn Manson, David Byrne, Cyndi Lauper, Shiny Toy Guns, Yaz, The Mission, John Lydon, The Farm, The Sugarcubes, Gravity Kills, Neneh Cherry. Music: **electronic**, **rock**.

◑ SKYELAB MUSIC GROUP

247 W. 38th St., Suite 601, New York NY 10018. (212)789-8942. **E-mail:** info@skyelab.com. **Website:** www.skyelab.com. **Contact:** Arty Skye. Arty Skye has worked with major stars such as Will Smith, Madonna, Alicia Keys, Santana, 98 Degrees, Queen Latifah, Missy Elliot, Public Enemy, Wu-Tang Clan and many more. Arty opened Skyelab Sound Studios in 1994, and has hosted such stars as James Taylor, Tito Puente, Mya, Pink, Hayle Duff, 98 Degrees , Lil 'Mo and many more.

○ SLANG MEDIAGROUP

1915 W. Superior St., Chicago IL 60622. (312)482-9001. **Fax:** (312)482-9007. **Website:** www.slangmusicgroup.com. **Contact:** Vince Lawrence. Chicago-based music producers that specialize in creating remix and original music for TV commercials, artists, film, and gaming. "Noted for achievements in house music, owner/producer Vince Lawrence has created a destination for electronic music makers of every genre. The Slang MusicGroup has multiple producer/artists and we have recieved many RIAA gold and platinum awards. Along with music for commercials, members of The Slang MusicGroup also have been working with burgeoning new talent from all over the world."

HOW TO CONTACT Contact via online form.

TIPS "House music is the heartbeat of every dancer ... no fluff or glitter, just the beat of the drum and the true passionate voice of a life worth living. House music is a tale of distant lovers trying to get back together, broken hearts mending, people finding true joy while they are just getting by. House knows no race, religion or sexual preference. House music isn't just for the rich or the poor, dumb or intellectual ... house music is the backing track to life. It moves in all directions."

◐ SOUND ARTS RECORDING STUDIO

8377 Westview Dr., Houston TX 77055. (713)464-4653. **E-mail:** brianbaker@soundartsrecording.com. **Website:** www.soundartsrecording.com. **Contact:** Brian Baker.

MUSIC Mostly **pop/rock**, **country** and **blues**. Produced *Texas Johnny Brown* (album), written and recorded by Texas Johnny Brown on Quality (blues); and "Sheryl Crow" (single), recorded by Dr. Jeff and the Painkillers. Other artists include Tim Nichols, Perfect Strangers, B.B. Watson, Jinkies, Joe "King" Carasco (on Surface Records), Mark May (on Icehouse Records), The Barbara Pennington Band (on

Earth Records), Tempest, Atticus Finch, Tony Vega Band (on Red Onion Records), Saliva (Island Records), Earl Gillian, Blue October (Universal Records), and The Wiggles.

CHRIS STAMEY

Modern Recording, Chapel Hill NC (919)929-5008. **E-mail:** mrstamey@gmail.com. **Website:** www.christamey.com. "The central philosophy behind my production and mixing these days is that the best records combine the recording of transcendent musical moments with the structuring of the carefully considered arrangement details that frame those moments. And the point of recording is to add new entries to that select list of best records." See website for rates.

MUSIC Has worked with Alejandro Excovedo, Ryan Adams/Whiskeytown, Amy Ray, Yo La Tengo, Squirrel Nut Zippers, Patrick Park, Le Tigre, Jeremy Larson, Chatham Country Line. Music: **rock**, **indie**, **alternative**.

◑ STUART AUDIO SERVICES

Houndog Recording, 134 Mosher Rd., Gorham ME 04038. (207)892-0960. **E-mail:** js@stuartaudio.com. **Website:** stuartaudio.com.

HOW TO CONTACT *Write or call first and obtain permission to submit or to arrange a personal interview.* Prefers CD with 4 songs and lyric sheet. Include SASE. Responds in 2 months.

MUSIC Mostly **alternative folk-rock**, **rock** and **country**; also **contemporary Christian**, **children's** and **unusual**. Produced *One of a Kind* (by various artists), recorded by Elizabeth Boss on Bosco Records (folk); *Toad Motel*, written and recorded by Rick Charrette on Fine Point Records (children's); and *Holiday Portrait*, recorded by USM Chamber Singers on U.S.M. (chorale). Other artists include Noel Paul Stookey, Beavis and Butthead (Mike Judge), Don Campbell, Jim Newton, and John Angus.

◯ STUDIO SEVEN

417 N. Virginia, Oklahoma City OK 73106. (405)236-0643. **Website:** www.lunacyrecords.com.

HOW TO CONTACT *Contact first and obtain permission to submit.* Prefers CD with lyric sheet. Include SASE. Responds in 6 weeks.

MUSIC Mostly **rock**, **jazz-blues**, **country**, and **Native American**.

RANDALL MICHAEL TOBIN

2219 W. Olive Ave. Suite 226, Burbank CA 91506. (818)9-555-5888. **E-mail:** rmt@rmtobin.com. **Website:** www.rmtobin.com.

MUSIC Has worked with Mel Carter, Bettie Ross, Isla St. Clair, Margaret MacDonald, Katheryne Levin. Music: **pop**, **rock**, **R&B**, **jazz**, **alternative**, **country**.

DAVE TOUGH - PRODUCER SONGWRITER

5801 Tee Pee Dr., Nashville TN 37013. **Website:** www.davetough.com.

HOW TO CONTACT See website for rates.

MUSIC Dove Award nominee. Has worked with Come & Go, Cindy Alter, Matt Heinecke, Craig Winquist, Jeff Dane, Lost Trailers and 100-plus film and TV placements. Music: **country**, **pop**, **rock**, **hip-hop**.

TRACK STAR STUDIOS

San Diego CA (619)697-7827. **E-mail:** info@trackstarstudios.com. **Website:** www.trackstarstudios.com. **Contact:** Josquin des Pres. "Josquin des Pres is a lifelong music impresario. As a renowned producer, songwriter, musician, manager, studio owner and prolific author, Josquin has consistently maintained the respect of his peers throughout the music industry."

HOW TO CONTACT Any genre. Has worked with Jack Johnson, Bernie Taupin, Gipsy Kings, Tech N9ne, Peter Frampton, Robert Lamm, and more.

BIL VORNDICK

6090 Fire Tower Rd., Nashville TN 37221. (615)352-1227. **Fax:** (615)353-1235. **E-mail:** bilinstudio@comcast.net. **Website:** www.bilvorndick.com. "Helping artists realize their dreams."

MUSIC Has worked with Alison Krauss, Rhonda Vincent, Jerry Douglas, Bela Fleck, Jim Lauderdale, Ralph Stanley, Claire Lynch, Lynn Anderson, Bob Dylan, John Oates.

DAVE WATERBURY

Laurel Canyon and Magnolia, Valley Village CA 91607. **E-mail:** davewaterbury91607@yahoo.com. **Website:** www.davewaterbury.net.

MUSIC Has worked with The XOTX, Robbie Krieger, Pink, Mark Krendal, David Eagle, Irv Kramer. Music: **rock**, **dance**, **electronica**, **pop**.

◑ WESTWIRES RECORDING USA

1042 Club Ave., Allentown PA 18109. (610)435-1924. **E-mail:** info@westwires.com. **Website:** www.westwires.com.

MUSIC Mostly **rock**, **R&B**, **dance**, **alternative**, **folk** and **eclectic**. Produced Ye Ren (Dimala Records), Weston (Universal/Mojo), Zakk Wylde (Spitfire Records). Other artists include Ryan Asher, Paul Rogers, Anne Le Baron, and Gary Hassay

TIPS "We are interested in singer/songwriters and alternative artists living in the mid-Atlantic area. Must have steady gig schedule and established fan base."

WILLPLAY MUSIC AND MEDIA

Nashville TN. **E-mail:** dre@willplaymandm.com. **Website:** www.willplaymandm.com. "WillPlay Music and Media may be headquartered in the heart of Nashville, but there's a lot more than country music being made in its studios. From jazz to pop, R&B to gospel—and, yes, country—Dre Williams and company are the best of the best in both live instrumentation and programming. The full-service production company specializes in artist development, demo production, full album production, live show programming, and more."

HOW TO CONTACT E-mail Dre with a brief description of your project and what services you need, and he will respond with a quote within 48 hours.

MUSIC All genres. "Dre has served as a musical director for a nationally touring country artist, worked as an in-house producer at Nashville's revered Sound Kitchen Studios ,and worked with multi-platinum selling R&B and gospel artists. He's also produced numerous independent artists—including a singer/ songwriter male duo, an R&B girl group, a neo-soul male act, and many others—helping them to craft a sound unique to their musical visions while garnering local and national attention."

WLM MUSIC/RECORDING

2808 Cammie St., Durham NC 27705-2020. (919)471-3086. **Fax:** (919)471-4326. **E-mail:** wlm-musicrecording@nc.rr.com; wlm-band@nc.rr.com. **Contact:** Watts Lee Mangum, owner. Record producer. Fee derived from outright fee from recording artist. "In some cases, an advance payment requested for demo production."

HOW TO CONTACT Submit demo by mail. Unsolicited submissions are OK. Prefers CD with 2-4 songs and lyric or lead sheet (if possible). Include SASE. Responds in 6 months.

MUSIC Mostly **country**, **country/rock**, and **blues/ rock**; also **pop**, **rock**, **blues**, **gospel** and **bluegrass**. Produced "911," and "Petals of an Orchid" (singles), both written and recorded by Johnny Scoggins (country); and "Renew the Love" (single by Judy Evans), recorded by Bernie Evans (country), all on Independent. Other artists include Southern Breeze Band and Heart Breakers Band.

MICHAEL WOODRUM

(818)848-3393. **Website:** www.woodrumproductions. com. "Michael Woodrum is a producer who's also an accomplished engineer. He gets sounds faster than you can think them up. You won't sit around waiting for something to sound right."

MUSIC Has worked with 3LW, Juvenile, 2Pac, Linkin Park, MC Lyte, Mary J. Blige, Eric Clapton, Joss Stone, Snoop Dogg, Bobby Rydell, B2K, Rocio Banquells, Queen Latifah, JoJo, Dr. Dre, John Guess, Tiffany Evans, Samantha Jade. Music: **rock**, **pop**, **R&B**, **rap**, **hip-hop**, **alternative**, **acoustic**, **indie**, **Americana**, **country**, **soul**.

ZIG PRODUCTIONS

P.O. Box 120931, Arlington TX 76012. **E-mail:** billy-herzig@hotmail.com. **Website:** www.zigproductions. com. "Occasionally, I produce a single that is recorded separate from a full CD project." Produces 6-10 albums. Fee derived from sales royalty when song or artist is recorded and/or outright fee from recording artist. "Sometimes there are investors."

MUSIC Mostly **country**, **Americana**, and **rock**; also **pop**, **R&B**, and **alternative**. Produced "Ask Me to Stay" (single by King Cone/Josh McDaniel) from *Gallery*, recorded by King Cone (Texas country/Americana), released on King Cone; "A Cure for Awkward Silence" (single), recorded by Tyler Stock (acoustic rock), released on Payday Records; "Take Me Back" (single) from *Peace, Love & Crabs*, written and recorded by Deanna Dove (folk-rock), released on Island Girl. Also produced Robbins & Jones (country), Jordan Mycoskie (country), Carla Rhodes (comedy), Four Higher (alternative), Charis Thorsell (country), Shane Mallory (country), Rachel Rodriguez (blues-rock), Jessy Daumen (country), Frankie Moreno (rock/r&b), Shawna Russell (country), and many others.

MANAGERS &
BOOKING AGENTS

Before submitting to a manager or booking agent, be sure you know exactly what you need. If you're looking for someone to help you with performance opportunities, the booking agency is the one to contact. They can help you book shows either in your local area or throughout the country. If you're looking for someone to help guide your career, you need to contact a management firm. Some management firms also may handle booking; however, it may be in your best interest to look for a separate booking agency. A manager should be your manager—not your agent, publisher, lawyer or accountant.

MANAGERS

Of all the music industry players surrounding successful artists, managers usually are the people closest to the artists themselves. The artist manager can be a valuable contact, both for the songwriter trying to get songs to a particular artist and for the songwriter/performer. A manager and his connections can be invaluable in securing the right publishing deal or recording contract if the writer is also an artist. Getting songs to an artist's manager is yet another way to get your songs recorded, since the manager may play a large part in deciding what material his client uses. For the performer seeking management, a successful manager should be thought of as the foundation for a successful career.

The relationship between a manager and his client relies on mutual trust. A manager works as the liaison between you and the rest of the music industry, and he must know exactly what you want out of your career in order to help you achieve your goals. His handling of publicity, promotion and finances, as well as the contacts he has within the industry, can make or break your career. You should never be afraid to ask questions about any aspect of the relationship between you and a prospective manager.

Always remember that a manager works *for the artist*. A good manager is able to communicate his opinions to you without reservation, and should be willing to explain any confusing terminology or discuss plans with you before taking action. A manager needs to be able to communicate successfully with all segments of the music industry in order to get his client the best deals possible. He needs to be able to work with booking agents, publishers, lawyers and record companies.

Keep in mind that you are both working together toward a common goal: success for you and your songs. Talent, originality, professionalism and a drive to succeed are qualities that will attract a manager to an artist—and a songwriter.

BOOKING AGENTS

The function of the booking agent is to find performance venues for his clients. Booking agents usually represent many more acts than a manager does, and have less contact with their acts. A booking agent charges a commission for his services, as does a manager. Managers usually ask for a 15 to 20 percent commission on an act's earnings; booking agents usually charge around 10 percent. In the area of managers and booking agents, more successful acts can negotiate lower percentage deals than the ones set forth above.

SUBMITTING MATERIAL TO MANAGERS & BOOKING AGENTS

The firms listed in this section have provided information about the types of music they work with and the types of acts they represent. You'll want to refer to the Category Index to find out which companies deal with the type of music you write, and the Geographic Index at the back of the book to help you locate companies near where you live. Then determine whether they are open to your level of experience (see A Sample Listing Decoded in the article "How to Use *Songwriter's Market*"). Each listing also contains submission requirements and information about what items to include in a press kit and also will specify whether the company is a management firm or a booking agency. Remember that your submission represents you as an artist, and should be as organized and professional as possible.

ADDITIONAL MANAGERS & BOOKING AGENTS

There are **more managers & booking agents** located in other sections of the book! Consult the Index to find additional Managers & Booking Agents listings within other sections.

Icons

For more instructional information on the listings in this book, including explanations of symbols, read the article "How To Use *Songwriter's Market*."

AIR TIGHT MANAGEMENT

115 West Rd., P.O. Box 113, Winchester Center CT 06094. (860)738-9139. **Fax:** (860)738-9135. **E-mail:** mainoffice@airtightmanagement.com. **Website:** www.airtightmanagement.com. **Contact:** Jack Forchette, president. Represents individual artists, groups or songwriters from anywhere; currently represents 7 acts. Receives 15-20% commission. Reviews material for acts.

HOW TO CONTACT *Write e-mail first and obtain permission to submit.* Prefers CD or DVD. If seeking management, press kit should include photos, bio, and recorded material. "Follow up with a fax or e-mail, not a phone call." Does not return material. Responds in 1 month.

MUSIC Mostly **rock**, **country**, and **jazz**. Current acts include P.J. Loughran (singer/songwriter), Kal David (blues singer/songwriter/guitarist), Kaitlyn Lusk (singer/songwriter and featured vocalist for Howard Shore's orchestral presentation of *Lord of the Rings*), Warren Hill (jazz singer/songwriter/saxophonist), Harvey Mason (percussionist/composer), George Marinelli (Americana/rock singer/songwriter/guitarist), and Rocco Prestia (songwriter/bassist).

ALERT MUSIC INC.

305-41 Britain St., Suite 305, Toronto ON M5A 1R7 Canada. **E-mail:** contact@alertmusic.com; gabriella@alertmusic.com. **Website:** www.alertmusic.com. As of 2015, this management company did not accept unsolicited contacts. Management firm, record company and recording artist. Represents local and regional individual artists and groups.

MUSIC All types. Works primarily with bands and singer/songwriters. Current acts include Holly Cole (jazz vocalist) and Kim Mitchell (rock singer/songwriter). Also worked with Michael Kaeshammer (pianist/singer) and Rozanne Potvin.

MICHAEL ALLEN ENTERTAINMENT DEVELOPMENT

P.O. Box 111510, Nashville TN 37222. (615)754-0059. **E-mail:** gmichaelallen@comcast.net. **Website:** www.gmichaelallen.com. **Contact:** Michael Allen. Management firm and public relations. Represents individual artists, groups and songwriters. Receives 15-25% commission. Reviews material for acts.

HOW TO CONTACT Submit demo package by mail. Unsolicited submissions are OK. Prefers CD/DVD with 3 songs and lyric or lead sheets. If seeking management, press kit should include photo, bio, press clippings, letter and CD/DVD. Include SASE. Responds in 3 months.

MUSIC Mostly **country** and **pop**; also **rock** and **gospel**. Works primarily with vocalists and bands. Currently doing public relations for Brenda Lee, The Imperials, Ricky Lynn Gregg, Kyle Rainer, and Lee Greenwood.

AMERICAN BANDS MANAGEMENT

3300 S. Gessner, Suite 207, Houston TX 77063. **Website:** www.americanbandsmanagement.com. There is a contact form on the website. Represents groups from anywhere. Receives 15-25% commission. Reviews material for acts.

HOW TO CONTACT Submit demo package by mail prior to making phone contact. Unsolicited submissions are OK. Prefers live videos. If seeking management, press kit should include cover letter, bio, photo, demo CD, press clippings, video, résumé, and professional references with names and numbers. Does not return material. Responds in 1 month.

MUSIC Mostly **rock (all forms)** and **modern country**. Works primarily with bands. Current acts include The Scars Heal In Time, Trey Gadler & Dead Man's Hand, Kenny Cordrey & Love Street, The Standells, Paul Cotton (from Poco), and Pearl (Janis Joplin tribute).

BILL ANGELINI ENTERPRISES/BOOKYOUREVENT.COM

P.O. Box 132, Seguin TX 78155. (210)363-4978. **Fax:** (830)401-0069. **E-mail:** bill@bookyourevent.com; bookyourevent@att.net. **Website:** www.bookyourevent.com. **Contact:** Bill Angelini, owner. Management firm and booking agency. Represents individual artists and groups from anywhere. Receives 10-15% commission. Reviews material for acts.

HOW TO CONTACT Submit demo package by mail or EPK. Unsolicited submissions are OK. Press kit should include pictures, bio, and discography. Does not return material. Responds in 1 month.

MUSIC Mostly **Latin American**, **Tejano**, and **international**; also **Norteno** and **country**. Current acts include Jay Perez (Tejano), Ram Herrera (Tejano), Michael Salgado (Tejano), Electric Cowboys (Tex-Mex), Los Caporales (Tejano), Grupo Solido (Tejano), and Texmaniacs (Tex-Mex).

APODACA PROMOTIONS INC.

717 E. Tidwell Rd., Houston TX 77022. (713)691-6677. **Fax:** (713)692-9298. **E-mail:** houston@apoda-

capromotions.com. **Website:** www.apodacapromotions.com. **Contact:** Domingo A. Barrera, manager. Management firm, booking agency, music publisher (Huina Publishing Co. Inc.). Represents songwriters and groups from anywhere; currently handles 40 acts. Reviews material for acts.

HOW TO CONTACT Submit demo package by mail. Unsolicited submissions are OK. Prefers CD and lyric and lead sheet. Include SASE. Responds in 2 months.

MUSIC Mostly **international** and **Hispanic**; also **rock**. Works primarily with bands and songwriters. Current acts include Alicia Villarreal, Boby Pulldo, Fanny Lu, Elephant, Angel Y Khriz, Golden Horse, and Ninel Conde.

◑ ARTIST REPRESENTATION AND MANAGEMENT

1257 Arcade St., St. Paul MN 55106. (651)483-8754. **Fax:** (651)776-6338. **E-mail:** Molly@armentertainment.com; jdr@armentertainment.com. **Website:** www.armentertainment.com. **Contact:** Roger Anderson, agent/manager. There are different agents to contact depending on where in the country you live. Visit the website's "Contact Us" page for this info. Management firm and booking agency. Estab. 1983. Represents artists from U.S./Canada. Receives 15% commission. Reviews material for acts.

HOW TO CONTACT Submit CD and DVD by mail. Unsolicited submissions are OK. Please include minimum 3 songs. If seeking management, current schedule, bio, photo, press clippings also should be included. "Priority is placed on original artists with product who are currently touring." Does not return material. Responds only if interested within 30 days.

MUSIC Mostly **melodic rock**. Current acts include Bret Michaels, Warrant, Firehouse, Winger, Skid Row, Head East, Frank Hannon of Tesla, LA Guns featuring Phil Lewis, Dokken, Adler's Appetite, and Vince Neil.

⊘ BILL SILVA

Website: www.billsilvaentertainment.com. Bill Silva Management (BSM) was formed in 1993 and offers a full house of specialized services helping to guide the careers of an eclectic roster of music artists and producers. Our roster includes Grammy Award-winning artist Jason Mraz; RCA Records rapper Brooke Candy; Greyson Chance; Olivia Holt; and Atlantic Records band Night Terrors of 1927. For all of our musical clients we also offer music licensing services

by placing their music in TV programs, movies, video games and commercials.

HOW TO CONTACT Use online form to contact.

MUSIC Artists include Jason Mraz, Midlake, Annie Stela, Ryan Hewitt, Brooke Candy, Olivia Holt, M. Ward, and many more.

◐ BROTHERS MANAGEMENT ASSOCIATES

141 Dunbar Ave., Fords NJ 08863. (732)738-0880. **Fax:** (732)738-0970. **E-mail:** bmaent@yahoo.com. **Website:** www.bmaent.com. **Contact:** Allen A. Faucera, president. Management firm and booking agency. Represents artists, groups and songwriters; currently handles 25 acts. Receives 15-20% commission. Reviews material for acts.

HOW TO CONTACT *Write first and obtain permission to submit.* Prefers CD or DVD with 3-6 songs and lyric sheets. Include photographs and résumé. If seeking management, include photo, bio, tape, and return envelope in press kit. Include SASE. Responds in 2 months.

MUSIC Mostly **pop**, **rock**, **MOR**, and **R&B**. Works primarily with vocalists and established groups. Current acts include Nils Lofgren of the E Street Band, Cover Girls, Harold Melvin's Blue Notes, and Gloria Gaynor.

TIPS "Submit very commercial material—make demo of high quality."

◐ CLOUSHER PRODUCTIONS

P.O. Box 1191, Mechanicsburg PA 17055. (717)766-7644. **Fax:** (717)766-1490. **E-mail:** cpinfo@msn.com. **Website:** www.clousherentertainment.com. **Contact:** Fred Clousher, owner. Booking agency and production company. Represents groups from anywhere; currently handles more than 100 acts.

HOW TO CONTACT Submit demo package by mail. Please, no electronic press kits. Unsolicited submissions are OK. Prefers CDs or DVD. Press kit also should include bio, credits, pictures, song list, references, and your contact information. Does not return material. "Performer should check back with us!"

MUSIC Mostly **country**, **oldies rock 'n' roll** and **ethnic** (German, Hawaiian, etc.); also **dance bands** (regional), **Dixieland**, and **classical musicians**. "We work mostly with country, old time rock 'n' roll, regional variety dance bands, tribute acts, and all types of variety acts." Current acts include Stanky & the

Coal Miners (polka), Lee Alverson (tribute artist), and Orville Davis & The Wild Bunch (country/rockabilly). **TIPS** "The songwriters we work with are entertainers themselves, which is the aspect we deal with. They usually have bands or do some sort of show, either with tracks or live music. We engage them for stage shows, concerts, etc. We do not review songs you've written. We do not publish music, or submit performers to recording companies for contracts. We strictly set up live performances for them."

ⓘ CONCEPT 2000 INC.

P.O. Box 2950, Columbus OH 43216-2950. (614)276-2000. **Fax:** (614)275-0163. **E-mail:** info2k@concept2k.com. **Website:** www.concept2k.com. **Contact:** Brian Wallace, president. Management firm and booking agency. Represents international individual artists, groups and songwriters. Receives 20% commission. Reviews material for acts.
HOW TO CONTACT Submit demo by mail. Unsolicited submissions are OK. Prefers CD with 4 songs. If seeking management, include demo, press clips, photo and bio. Does not return material. Responds in 2 weeks.
MUSIC Mostly **rock, country, pop**, and **contemporary gospel**. Current acts include Satellites Down (rock); Gene Walker (jazz); Endless Summer (show group); Thomas Wynn and the Believers (country).
TIPS "Send quality songs with lyric sheets. Production quality is not necessary."

○ COUNTDOWN ENTERTAINMENT

110 W. 26th Street, New York NY 10001-6805. **E-mail:** lovie@countdownentertainment.com. **Website:** www.countdownentertainment.com. Founded by James Citkovic in 1983, Countdown Entertainment is a full-service artist management firm representing established musicians, bands, producers and songwriters. Countdown Entertainment also brokers intellectual properties such as publishing catalogs and music masters. Countdown Entertainment accepts all styles of music from singers, songwriters, musicians, unsigned bands, signed bands, independent record labels, producers, film composers and others.
HOW TO CONTACT All unsolicited materials are accepted as long as they arrive to us with fully completed submissions forms (available at website).
MUSIC Deals secured include those for The Ramones, Joe Strummer, Steve Ronsen, The Fixx, Wood Ready, etc.

⊘ DAS COMMUNICATIONS, LTD.

83 Riverside Dr., New York NY 10024. 83 Riverside Dr., New York, NY 10024. (212)877-0400. **Fax:** (212)595-0176. Management firm. Estab. 1975. Represents individual artists, groups and producers from anywhere; currently handles 25 acts. Receives 20% commission.
HOW TO CONTACT *Does not accept unsolicited submissions.*
MUSIC Mostly **rock**, **pop**, **R&B**, **alternative** and **hip-hop**. Current acts include Joan Osborne (rock), Wyclef Jean (hip-hop), Black Eyed Peas (hip-hop), John Legend (R&B), Spin Doctors (rock), The Bacon Brothers (rock).

ⓘ DCA PRODUCTIONS

676A 9th Ave., #252, New York NY 10036. (800)659-2063. **Fax:** (609)259-8260. **E-mail:** info@dcaproductions.com. **Website:** www.dcaproductions.com. Management firm. Represents individual artists, groups, and songwriters from anywhere.
HOW TO CONTACT If seeking management, press kit should include cover letter, bio, photo, demo CD, and video. Prefers CD or DVD with 2 songs. "All materials are reviewed and kept on file for future consideration. Does not return material. We respond only if interested."
MUSIC Mostly **acoustic**, **rock**, and **mainstream**; also **cabaret** and **theme**. Works primarily with acoustic singer/songwriters, top 40 or rock bands. Current acts include And Jam Band (soulful R&B), Lorna Bracewell (singer/songwriter), and Jimmy and The Parrots (Jimmy Buffett cover band). "Visit our website for a current roster of acts."
TIPS "Please do not call for a review of material."

◑ⓘ DIVINE INDUSTRIES

(formerly Gangland Artists), Unit 191, #101-1001 W. Broadway, Vancouver BC V6H 4E4 Canada. (604)737-0091. **Fax:** (604)737-3602. **E-mail:** allenm@divineindustries.com. **Website:** www.divineindustries.com. **Contact:** Allen Moy. Management firm, production house and music publisher. Represents artists and songwriters; currently handles 5 acts. Reviews material for acts.
HOW TO CONTACT *Write first and obtain permission to submit.* Prefers audio links. "Videos are not entirely necessary for our company. It is certainly a nice touch. If you feel your CD is strong—send the video upon later request." Does not return material. Responds in 2 months.

MUSIC Rock, pop, and **roots**. Works primarily with rock/left-of-center folk show bands. Current acts include 54-40 (rock/pop), Blackie & The Rodeo Kings (folk rock), Ridley Bent, John Mann (of Spirit of the West).

JOHN ECKERT ENTERTAINMENT CONSULTANTS

(formerly Pro Talent Consultants), 7723 Cora Dr., Lucerne CA 95458. (323)325-6662. **Contact:** John Eckert, coordinator. Management firm and talent coordination. Represents individual artists and groups; currently handles 12 acts. Receives 15% commission. Reviews material for acts.

HOW TO CONTACT Submit demo package by mail. Unsolicited submissions are OK. "We prefer CD (4 songs). Submit DVD with live performance only." If seeking management, press kit should include an 8x10 photo, a CD of at least 4-6 songs, a bio on group/artist, references, cover letter, press clippings, video, and business card, or a phone number with address. Does not return material. Responds in 5 weeks.

MUSIC Mostly **country**, **country/pop**, and **rock**. Works primarily with vocalists, show bands, dance bands, and bar bands. Current acts include The Rose Garden (pop/rock/country band); The Royal Guardsmen (pop/rock/top 40); Sam the Sham (vocalist); Russ Varnell (country); and Buddy Allan Owens (country).

◯ SCOTT EVANS PRODUCTIONS

P.O. Box 814028, Hollywood FL 33081-4028. (954)963-4449. **E-mail:** evansprod@hotmail.com; evansprod@aol.com. **Website:** www.facebook.com/pages/Scott-Evans-Productions/. **Contact:** Jeffrey Birnbaum, new artists; Jeanne K., Internet marketing and sales. Management firm and booking agency. Represents local, regional or international individual artists, groups, songwriters, comedians, novelty acts and dancers; currently handles over 200 acts. Receives 10-50% commission. Reviews material for acts.

HOW TO CONTACT New artists can make submissions through the "Auditions" link located on the website. Unsolicited submissions are OK. "Please be sure that all submissions are copyrighted and not your original copy as we do not return material."

MUSIC Mostly **pop**, **R&B**, and **broadway**. Deals with "all types of entertainers; no limitations." Current acts include Scott Evans and Company (variety song and dance), Dorit Zinger (female vocalist), Jeff Geist, Actors Repertory Theatre, Entertainment Express, Joy Deco (dance act), Flashback (musical song and dance revue), and Around the World (international song and dance revue).

TIPS "Submit a neat, well-put together, organized press kit."

◯◑ THE FELDMAN AGENCY & MACKLAM FELDMAN MANAGEMENT

200-1505 W. 2nd Ave., Vancouver BC V6H 3Y4 Canada. (604)734-5945. **Fax:** (604)732-0922. **E-mail:** info@mfmgt.com; feldman@slfa.com. **Website:** www.mfmgt.com; www.slfa.com. Booking agency and artist management firm. Agency represents mostly established Canadian recording artists and groups.

HOW TO CONTACT *Write or call first to obtain permission to submit a demo.* Prefers CD, photo and bio. If seeking management, contact Watchdog for consideration and include video in press kit. SAE and IRC. Responds in 2 months.

MUSIC Current Macklam Feldman Management acts include The Chieftains, Diana Krall, Elvis Costello, Better Midler, Sarah McLachlan, Ylvis, James Taylor, Colin James, Ry Cooder, Tommy LiPuma, and Melody Gardot.

◯◑ B.C. FIEDLER MANAGEMENT

53 Seton Park Rd., Toronto ON M3C 3Z8 Canada. (416)421-4421. **Fax:** (416)421-0442. **E-mail:** info@bcfiedler.com. **Website:** www.bcfiedler.com. **Contact:** B.C. Fiedler. Management firm, music publisher (B.C. Fiedler Publishing) and record company (Sleeping Giant Music Inc.). Represents individual artists, groups and songwriters from anywhere. Receives 20-25% or consultant fees. Reviews material for acts.

HOW TO CONTACT *Call first and obtain permission to submit.* Prefers CD or DVD with 3 songs and lyric sheet. If seeking management, press kit should include bio, list of concerts performed in past 2 years including name of venue, repertoire, reviews and photos. Does not return material. Responds in 2 months.

MUSIC Mostly **classical/crossover**, **voice** and **pop**. Works primarily with classical/crossover ensembles, instrumental soloists, operatic voice and pop singer/songwriters. Current acts include Gordon Lightfoot, Dan Hill, Quartetto Gelato, and Patricia O'Callaghan.

TIPS "Invest in demo production using best-quality voice and instrumentalists. If you write songs, hire the vocal talent to best represent your work. Submit CD and lyrics. Artists should follow up 6-8 weeks after submission."

◐◑ FIRST TIME MANAGEMENT

Ebrel House, 2a Penlee Close, Praa Sands, Penzance, Cornwall TR20 9SR England, United Kingdom. (01736)762826. **Fax:** (01736)763328. **Website:** www. songwriters-guild.co.uk. **Contact:** Roderick G. Jones, managing director. Management firm, record company (Digimix Records Ltd. www.digimixrecords.com, Rainy Day Records, Mohock Records, Pure Gold Records), and music publisher (Panama Music Library, Melody First Music Library, Eventide Music Library, Musik' Image Music Library, Promo Sonor International Music Library, Caribbean Music Library, ADN Creation Music Library, Piano Bar Music Library, Corelia Music Library, PSI Music Library, Scamp Music Publishing, First Time Music [Publishing] U.K. [www.panamamusic.co.uk and www.myspace. com/scampmusicpublishing]—registered members of the Mechanical Copyright Protection Society [MCPS] and the Performing Right Society [PRS]). Represents local, regional, and international individual artists, groups, composers, DJs, and songwriters. Receives 15-25% commission. Reviews material for acts.

○ Also see the listings for First Time Music (Publishing) in the Music Publishers section of this book.

HOW TO CONTACT Submit demo package by mail. Unsolicited submissions are OK. Prefers CD with 3 songs, lyric sheets and also complete album projects where writer/performer has finished masters. If seeking management, press kit should include cover letter, bio, photo, demo tape/CD, press clippings and anything relevant to make an impression. Does not return material. Responds in 1 month only if interested.

MUSIC All styles. Works primarily with songwriters, composers, DJs, rappers, vocalists, bands, groups and choirs. Current acts include Leonie Parker (soul), The Glen Kirton Country Band (country), Bram Stoker (prog rock/gothic rock group), Kevin Kendle (New Age, holistic) Peter Arnold (folk/roots), David Jones (urban/R&B), Shanelle (R&B/dance), AudioJunkie & Stylus (dance/hardcore/funky house/electro house) Ray Guntrip (jazz); DJ Gammer (hardcore/hardhouse/dance); Toots Earl & Clown.

TIPS "Become a member of the Guild of International Songwriters and Composers (www.songwriters-guild. co.uk). Keep everything as professional as possible. Be patient and dedicated to your aims and objectives."

⊘ FOUNDATIONS ARTIST MANAGEMENT

307 7th Ave. Suite 403, New York NY 10001. **E-mail:** info@foundationsmusic.com; submissions@foundationsmgmt.com. **Website:** www.foundationsmusic. com. Foundations Artist Management was launched in 2000 by Steve Bursky, and has since grown into a full-service artist representation company focusing on building artists' careers from the ground up. The New York-based company prides itself on its work with its acts from the very early stages of their careers, helping them lay the necessary groundwork for a successful future in the music industry. With the addition of Brian Winton in 2004 as partner, and Drew Simmons in 2011 as general manager, Foundations has continued to build on its original vision: providing uncompromising support to great artists, assisting them in growing their careers as we grow our own.

HOW TO CONTACT "We do not accept unsolicited submissions. If you would like to submit music for review and consideration, please e-mail us."

MUSIC Represents such acts as Pacific Air, White Rabbits, Foy Vance, Dr. Dog, Dispatch, Owl City, Young The Giant, The Colourist, others.

◐ BILL HALL ENTERTAINMENT & EVENTS

138 Frog Hollow Rd., Churchville PA 18966-1031. (215)357-5189. **Fax:** (215)357-0320. **E-mail:** billhallevents@verizon.net. **Contact:** William B. Hall III, owner/president. Booking agency and production company. Represents individuals and groups. Receives 15% commission. Reviews material for acts.

HOW TO CONTACT Submit demo package by mail. Unsolicited submissions are OK. Prefers CD with 2-3 songs and photos and promo material. "We need quality material, preferably before a 'live' audience." Does not return material. Responds only if interested.

MUSIC Marching band, circus, and novelty. Works primarily with "unusual or novelty attractions in musical line, preferably those that appeal to family groups." Current acts include Fralinger and Polish-American Philadelphia Championship Mummers String Bands (marching and concert group), "Mr. Polynesian" Show Band and Hawaiian Revue (ethnic group), the "Phillies Whiz Kids Band" of Philadelphia Phillies baseball team, Mummermania Musical Quartet, Philadelphia German Brass Band (concert band), Vogelgesang Circus Calliope, Kromer's Carousel Band Organ, Reilly Raiders Drum & Bugle Corps,

Hoebel Steam Calliope, Caesar Rodney Brass Band, Philadelphia Police & Fire Pipes Band, Tim Laushey Pep & Dance Band, Larry Stout (show organist/keyboard player), Jersey Surf Drum & Bugle Corp, Caesar Rodney Brass Marching Band, Corporales San Simon Bolivian Dancers, Robinson's Grandmaster Concert Band Organ, and Bobby Burnett, vocalist/comedian. **TIPS** "Please send whatever helps us to most effectively market the attraction and/or artist. Provide something that gives you a clear edge over others in your field!"

⭕ HARDISON INTERNATIONAL ENTERTAINMENT CORP.

P.O. Box 1732, Knoxville TN 37901-1732. (865)293-7062 (prefers e-mail contact). **E-mail:** dennishardison@bellsouth.net. **Website:** www.dynamoreckless.com. **Contact:** Dennis K. Hardison, CEO/founder; Dennis K. Hardison II, president; Travis J. Hardison, president, Denlatrin Record (a division of Hardison International Entertainment Corp.). Management firm, booking agency, music publisher (Denlatrin Music) BMI, record label (Denlatrin Records), and record producer. Represents individual artists from anywhere; currently handles 3 acts. Receives 20% commission. Reviews material for acts. "We are seeking level-minded and patient individuals. Our primary interests are established recording acts with prior major deals."

🎧 This company has promoted many major acts and unsigned acts for 40 years.

HOW TO CONTACT Submit demo package by mail. Unsolicited submissions are OK. Prefers CD with 3 songs only. If seeking management, press kit should include bio, promo picture, and CD. Does not return materials. Responds in 6 weeks to the "best material" submitted.

MUSIC Mostly **R&B**, **hip-hop**, and **rap**. Current acts include Dynamo (hip-hop), Triniti (record producer, Universal Music, Public Enemy, Dynamo, among others; current engineer for Chuck D), and RapStation artists.

TIPS "We respond to the hottest material, so make it hot!"

HUNT TALENT MANAGEMENT

Website: www.hunttalentmanagement.com. **Contact:** Tammy Hunt. Hunt Talent Management brings over 25 years of professional experience in the film and music industry. As a management firm dedicat-

ed to the business side of the entertainment industry, we are determined to assist our clients achieve their career goals. Hunt Talent Management understands how to create a profitable business while strategically marketing your individual talents. We represent talent from all areas of the entertainment industry. In addition, Hunt Talent Management is partners with Gandolfo-Helin Literary Management to help promote our talented authors.

HOW TO CONTACT Contact via online form. **MUSIC** Clients include Ray Brown, Jr. (jazz), Sonya Kahn (singer/songwriter), Aziza (singer) and more.

⊘ INTERNATIONAL ENTERTAINMENT BUREAU

3612 N. Washington Blvd., Indianapolis IN 46205-3592. (317)926-7566. **E-mail:** ieb@prodigy.net. **Website:** leonardscorp.com/. **Contact:** David Leonards. Booking agency. Represents individual artists and groups from anywhere; currently handles 145 acts. Receives 20% commission.

HOW TO CONTACT No unsolicited submissions. **MUSIC** Mostly **rock**, **country**, and **A/C**; also **jazz**, **nostalgia**, and **ethnic**. Works primarily with bands, comedians and speakers. Current acts include Five Easy Pieces (A/C), Scott Greeson (country), and Cool City Swing Band (variety).

◑ JANA JAE ENTERPRISES

P.O. Box 35726, Tulsa OK 74153. (918)786-8896. **Fax:** (918)786-8897. **E-mail:** janajae@janajae.com. **Website:** www.janajae.com. **Contact:** Kathleen Pixley, agent. Booking agency, music publisher (Jana Jae Publishing/BMI) and record company (Lark Record Productions, Inc.). Represents individual artists and songwriters; currently handles 12 acts. Receives 15% commission. Reviews material for acts.

🎧 Also see the listings for Jana Jae Music in the Music Publishers section, Lark Record Productions in the Record Companies section and Lark Talent & Advertising in the Record Producers section of this book.

HOW TO CONTACT Submit demo by mail. Unsolicited submissions are OK. Prefers CD or DVD of performance. If seeking management, press kit should include cover letter, bio, photo, demo tape/CD, lyric sheets and press clippings. Does not return material. **MUSIC** Mostly **country**, **classical**, and **jazz instrumentals**; also **pop**. Works with vocalists, show and concert bands, solo instrumentalists. Represents Jana

Jae (country singer/fiddle player), Matt Greif (classical guitarist), Sydni (solo singer) and Hotwire (country show band).

○ KUPER PERSONAL MANAGEMENT/ RECOVERY RECORDINGS

515 Bomar St., Houston TX 77006. (713)520-5791. E-mail: info@recoveryrecordings.com. **Website:** www. recoveryrecordings.com. **Contact:** Koop Kuper, owner. Management firm, music publisher (Kuper-Lam Music/BMI, Uvula Music/BMI, and Meauxtown Music/ASCAP), and record label (Recovery Recordings). Represents individual artists, groups, and songwriters from Texas. Receives 20% commission. Reviews material for acts.

HOW TO CONTACT Submit demo package by mail. Unsolicited submissions are OK. Prefers CD. If seeking management, press kit should include cover letter, press clippings, photo, bio (1 page) tearsheets (reviews, etc.) and demo CD. Does not return material. Responds in 2 months.

MUSIC Mostly **singer/songwriters**, **AAA**, **roots rock**, and **Americana**. Works primarily with self-contained and self-produced artists.

TIPS "Create a market value for yourself, produce your own master tapes, and create a cost-effective situation."

○ RICK LEVY MANAGEMENT

4250 A1AS, D-11, St. Augustine FL 32080. (904)806-0817. **Fax:** (904)460-1226. **E-mail:** rick@ricklevy. com. **Website:** www.ricklevy.com. **Contact:** Rick Levy, president. Management firm, music publisher (Flying Governor Music/BMI), and record company (Luxury Records). Voting member of the Grammys. Represents local, regional, or international individual artists and groups; currently handles 5 acts. Also provides worldwide music promotion services. Receives 15-20% commission. Reviews material for acts.

HOW TO CONTACT *Write or call first and obtain permission to submit.* Prefers CD or DVD with 3 songs and lyric sheet. If seeking management, press kit should include cover letter, bio, demo CD, DVD demo, photo and press clippings. Include SASE. Responds in 2 weeks.

MUSIC Mostly **R&B** (no rap), **pop**, **country**, and **oldies**. Current acts include Jay & the Techniques (1960s hit group), The Limits (pop), Freddy Cannon (1960s), The Fallin Bones (blues/rock), Tommy Roe (1960s), Wax (rock).

TIPS "If you don't have 200% passion and commitment, don't bother. Be sure to contact only companies that deal with your type of music."

○ LOGGINS PROMOTION

5018 Franklin Pike, Nashville TN 37220. (310)325-2800. **E-mail:** staff@LogginsPromotion.com; info@ logginspromotion.com. **Website:** www.logginspromotion.com. **Contact:** Paul Loggins, CEO. Management firm and radio promotion. Represents individual artists, groups and songwriters from anywhere; currently handles several acts. Receives 20% commission. Reviews material for acts.

HOW TO CONTACT If seeking management, press kit should include picture, short bio, cover letter, press clippings and CD (preferred). "Mark on CD which cut you, as the artist, feel is the strongest." Does not return material. Responds in 2 weeks.

MUSIC Mostly **adult**, **top 40** and **AAA**; also **urban**, **rap**, **alternative**, **college**, **smooth jazz** and **Americana**. Works primarily with bands and solo artists.

○ ● THE MANAGEMENT TRUST, LTD.

471 Queen St. E., Unit 01, Toronto ON M5A 1T9 Canada. (416)979-7070. **Fax:** (416)979-0505. **E-mail:** mail@ mgmtrust.ca. **Website:** www.mgmtrust.ca. **Contact:** Lisa Ioannou, Admin. Management firm. Represents individual artists and/or groups.

HOW TO CONTACT "If you wish to submit material, please e-mail us a link to your website, social sites, or online EPK. (Do not send MP3s or other large attachments.) While we try to respond to all submissions, we are not always able to. Please be patient, and we will do our best to get back to you. You can e-mail us the above info to mail@mgmtrust.ca."

MUSIC All types.

MARMOSET

2105 SE 7th Ave., Portland OR 97214. (971)260-0201. **E-mail:** compass@marmosetmusic.com. **Website:** www.marmosetmusic.com. Marmoset is an off-the-beaten path, boutique music agency born among the green, mountainous landscapes of the rain-soaked Pacific Northwest. While we enjoy working on all kinds of inspired and creative endeavors, we spend most of our time crafting original music for story-driven media in the public eye. We also curate a hand-picked roster of some of the most fascinating independent artists on the planet, whose recordings are made available for licensing. Marmoset is made of real people, living real lives, making a real living crafting music and sound. We're talking about hard-working, blue-collar artists, crafting music with their hands and hearts. While some of these are full-time musicians, many are baristas and bartenders, too. Programmers and farmers. Fathers and mothers. Sisters and brothers.

RICK MARTIN PRODUCTIONS

125 Fieldpoint Rd., Greenwich CT 06830. **Website:** www.facebook.com/pages/Rick-Martin-Productions/167961766639449. **Contact:** Rick Martin, president. Personal manager and independent producer. Held the office of secretary of the National Conference of Personal Managers for 22 years. Represents vocalists; currently produces pop and country-crossover music artists in private project studio and looking for a female vocalist in the general area of Greenwich, Connecticut, for production project. Receives 15% commission as a personal manager and/or customary production and publishing distributions.

HOW TO CONTACT "Please e-mail for initial contact with your Web link. Do not submit unless permission received to do so."

MUSIC Any genre but hip-hop or rap.

TIPS "Your demo does not have to be professionally produced to submit to producers, publishers, or managers. In other words, save your money. It's really not important what you've done. It's what you can do now that counts."

NOTEWORTHY PRODUCTIONS

124 1/2 Archwood Ave., Annapolis MD 21401. (410)268-8232. **Fax:** (410)268-2167. **E-mail:** mcshane@mcnote.com. **Website:** www.mcnote.com. **Contact:** McShane Glover, president. Management firm and booking agency. Represents individual artists, groups, and songwriters from everywhere. Receives 15-20% commission. Reviews material for acts.

HOW TO CONTACT *Write first and obtain permission to submit.* Prefers CD/CDR with lyric sheet. If seeking management, press kit should include CD, photo, bio, venues played and press clippings (preferably reviews). "Follow up with a phone call 3-5 weeks after submission." Does not return material. Responds in 2 months.

MUSIC Mostly **Americana**, **folk**, and **Celtic**. Works primarily with performing singer/songwriters. Current acts include Toby Walker (blues) and Vicki Genfan (folk/jazz/soul).

PARADIGM TALENT AGENCY

360 N. Crescent Dr., North Bldg., Beverly Hills CA 90210. (310)288-8000. **Fax:** (310)288-2000. **Website:** www.paradigmagency.com. **Nashville:** 124 12th Ave. S., Suite 410, Nashville TN 37203. (615)251-4400. **Fax:** (615)251-4401. **New York:** 260 Park Ave. S., 16th Floor, New York, NY 10010. (212)897-6400. **Fax:** (212)764-8941. **Monterey:** 404 W. Franklin St., Monterey, CA 93940. (831)375-4889. **Fax:** (831)375-2623. Booking agency. Represents individual artists, groups from anywhere. Receives 10% commission. Reviews material for acts.

HOW TO CONTACT *Does not take unsolicited submissions.*

MUSIC Current acts include Ricky Skaggs, Junior Brown, Toby Keith, Kasey Chambers, Umphrey's McGee, Black Eyed Peas, Kirk Franklin, Lily Allen, My Chemical Romance, and Lauryn Hill.

PRIMARY WAVE

116 E. 16th St., 9th Floor, New York NY 10003. (212)661-6990. **E-mail:** management@primarywave-music.com. **Website:** www.primarywavemusic.com. Primary Wave Talent Management passionately and meticulously guides the careers of its clients to enhance, shape, and extend their brand—providing a solid foundation for longevity in an ever-changing industry. From multi-platinum-selling recording artists to hit-making songwriters and producers, we represent some of the biggest and brightest brands in entertainment. We leverage the full strength of Primary Wave's internal resources to ensure our clients' creative and commercial success. Our talent management division is powered by all divisions of Primary Wave including our in-house press division, A&R/writer-producer relations team, our branding company Brand Synergy Group, digital marketing arm BrightShop, as well as our in-house film, TV, video game, commercial advertising and TV development team.

MUSIC Primary Wave's unique music repertoire includes an interest in the Beatles songs written by John Lennon, the catalogs of Kurt Cobain/Nirvana, Steven Tyler/Aerosmith, Daryl Hall & John Oates, Chicago, Maurice White (Earth, Wind & Fire), Def Leppard, Steve Earle, Daniel Johnston, Marvin Hamlisch, The Matrix, Lamont Dozier and Steven Curtis Chapman, as well as artists such as Airborne Toxic Event, Albert Hammond, Jr., John Forte, The Boxer Rebellion, New

Boyz, Taddy Porter, Anberlin, writers such as Gregg Alexander, Ryan & Smitty, LP, RoccStar, among others; as well as marketing and administration agreements with Jimmy Webb, Katrina and The Waves, Graham Parker, Evolution Entertainment/Twisted Pictures, Hammer Films, Matt Serletic and Emblem Music Group, and many others

ⓞ PRIME TIME ENTERTAINMENT
2430 Research Dr., Livermore CA 94550. (925)449-1724. **Fax:** (925)605-0379. **E-mail:** info@primetimeentertainment.com. **Website:** www.primetimeentertainment.com. Management firm and booking agency. Represents individual artists, groups and songwriters from anywhere. Receives 10-20% commission. Reviews material for acts. This market is based in San Francisco and handles many activities in the Bay area.
HOW TO CONTACT Submit demo package by mail. Unsolicited submissions are OK. Prefers CD with 3-5 songs. If seeking management, press kit should include 8x10 photo, reviews, and CDs/tapes. Include SASE. Responds in 1 month.
MUSIC Mostly **jazz**, **country**, and **alternative**; also **ethnic**.
TIPS "It's all about the song."

ⓞ RAINBOW TALENT AGENCY LLC
146 Round Pond Lane, Rochester NY 14626. (585)723-3334. **E-mail:** carl@rainbowtalentagency.com; info@rainbowtalentagency.com. **Website:** www.rainbowtalentagency.com. **Contact:** Carl Labate, president. Management firm and booking agency. Represents artists and groups. Receives 15-25% commission.
HOW TO CONTACT Submit demo package by mail. Unsolicited submissions are OK. Prefers CD with minimum 3 songs. May send DVD if available; "a still photo and bio of the act; if you are a performer, it would be advantageous to show yourself or the group performing live. Theme videos are not helpful." If seeking management, include photos, bio, markets established, CD/DVD. Does not return material. Responds in 1 month.
MUSIC Mostly **blues**, **rock**, and **R&B**. Works primarily with touring bands and recording artists. Current acts include Russell Thompkins, Jr. & The New Stylistics (R&B), Josie Waverly (country), and Spanky Haschmann Swing Orchestra (high-energy swing).
TIPS "My main interest is with groups or performers that are currently touring and have some prod-

uct. And are at least 50% original. Strictly songwriters should apply elsewhere."

ⓞ RIOHCAT MUSIC
P.O. Box 764, Hendersonville TN 37077-0764. (615)824-1435. **E-mail:** tachoir@bellsouth.net. **Website:** www.tachoir.com. **Contact:** Robert Kayne, manager. Management firm, booking agency, record company (Avita Records) and music publisher. Represents individual artists and groups. Receives 15-20% commission.
◯   Also see the listing for Avita Records in the Record Companies section of this book.
HOW TO CONTACT *Contact first and obtain permission to submit.* Prefers CD and lead sheet. If seeking management, press kit should include cover letter, bio, photo, demo CD, and press clippings. Does not return material. Responds in 6 weeks.
MUSIC Mostly **contemporary jazz** and **fusion**. Works primarily with jazz ensembles. Current acts include Group Tachoir (jazz), Tachoir/Manakas Duo (jazz) and Jerry Tachoir (jazz vibraphone artist).

ⓞⓞ ROBERTSON ENTERTAINMENT
106 Harding Road Kendenup 6323, Western Australia Australia. (618)9851-4311. **Fax:** (618)9851-4225. **E-mail:** info@robertsonentertainment.com. **Website:** www.robertsonentertainment.com. **Contact:** Eddie Robertson. Booking agency. Represents individual artists and/or groups; currently handles 50 acts. Receives 20% commission. Reviews material for acts.
HOW TO CONTACT *Write first and obtain permission to submit.* Unsolicited submissions are OK. If seeking management, press kit should include photos, bio, cover letter, press clippings, video, demo, lyric sheets and any other useful information. Does not return material. Responds in 1 month.
MUSIC Mostly **top 40/pop**, **jazz**, and **1960s-90s**; also **reggae** and **blues**. Works primarily with show bands and solo performers. Current acts include Faces (dance band), Heart & Soul (easy listening), and Ruby Tuesday (contemporary pop/rock/classics).
TIPS "Send as much information as possible. If you do not receive a call after 4-5 weeks, follow up with letter or phone call."

ⓞ SA'MALL MANAGEMENT
468 N. Camden Dr., Suite 200, Beverly Hills CA 90210. (818)506-8533. **Fax:** (310)860-7400. **E-mail:** pplzmi@aol.com. **Website:** www.pplentertainmentgroup.com. **Contact:** Ted Steele, vice president of talent. Manage-

ment firm, music publisher (Pollybyrd Publications) and record company (PPL Entertainment Group). Represents individual artists, groups and songwriters worldwide; currently handles 10 acts. Receives 10-25% commission. Reviews material for acts.

○ Also see the listing for Pollybyrd Publications Ltd. in the Music Publishers section of this book.

HOW TO CONTACT E-mail first and obtain permission to submit. "Only professional full-time artists who tour and have a fan base need apply. No weekend warriors, please." Prefers CD or cassette. If seeking management, press kit should include picture, bio and tape. Include SASE. Responds in 2 months.

MUSIC All types. Current acts include Riki Hendrix (rock), Buddy Wright (blues), Fhyne, Suzette Cuseo, The Band AKA, LeJenz, B.D. Fuoco, MoBeatz, and Kenyatta Jarrett (Prince Ken).

○ SANDALPHON MANAGEMENT

P.O. Box 18197, Panama City Beach FL 32417. **E-mail:** sandalphonmusic@yahoo.com. **Contact:** Ruth Otey. Management firm, music publisher (Sandalphon Music Publishing/BMI), and record company (Sandalphon Records). Represents individual artists, groups, songwriters; works with individual artists and groups from anywhere. Receives negotiable commission. Reviews material for acts.

HOW TO CONTACT Submit demo by mail. Unsolicited submissions are fine. Prefers CD with 1-5 songs and lyric sheet, cover letter. "Include name, address, and contact information." Include SASE or SAE and IRC for outside the U.S.. Responds in 6-8 weeks.

MUSIC Mostly **rock**, **country**, and **alternative**; also **pop**, **gospel**, and **blues**. "We are looking for singers, bands, and singer/songwriters who are original but would be current in today's music markets. We help singers, bands, and singer-songwriters achieve their personal career goals."

TIPS "Submit material you feel best represents you: your voice, your songs, or your band. Fresh and original songs and style are a plus. We are a West Coast management company looking for singers, bands, and singer-songwriters who are ready for the next level. We are looking for those with talent who are capable of being national and international contenders."

○✣ SERGE ENTERTAINMENT GROUP

P.O. Box 5147, Canton GA 30114. (678)880-8207. **Fax:** (678)494-9289. **E-mail:** sergeent@aol.com. **Website:**

www.sergeentertainmentgroup.com. **Contact:** Sandy Serge, president. Management and PR firm and song publishers. Represents individual artists, groups, songwriters from anywhere; currently handles 20 acts. Receives 20% commission for management. Monthly fee required for PR acts.

HOW TO CONTACT *E-mail first for permission to submit.* Submit demo package by mail. Unsolicited submissions are OK. Prefers CD with 4 songs and lyric sheet. If seeking management, press kit should include 8x10 photo, bio, cover letter, lyric sheets, max of 4 press clips, DVD, performance schedule and CD. "All information submitted must include name, address and phone number on each item." Does not return material. Responds in 6 weeks if interested.

MUSIC Mostly **rock**, **pop**, and **country**; also **New Age**. Works primarily with singer/songwriters and bands. Current acts include Julius Curcio (alt), Erik Norlander (prog rock), and Lana Lane (prog rock).

○○ SIEGEL ENTERTAINMENT LTD.

1736 W. 2nd Ave, Vancouver BC V6J 1H6 Canada. (604)736-3896. **Fax:** (604)736-3464. **E-mail:** siegelent@telus.net. **Website:** www.siegelent.com. **Contact:** Robert Siegel, president. There is also a contact form for this market on its website. Management firm and booking agency. Represents individual artists, groups and songwriters from anywhere; currently handles more than 100 acts (for bookings). Receives 15-20% commission. Reviews material for acts.

HOW TO CONTACT Does not accept unsolicited submissions. E-mail or write for permission to submit. Does not return material. Responds in 1 month.

MUSIC Mostly **rock**, **pop**, and **country**; also **specialty** and **children's**. Current acts include Johnny Ferreira & The Swing Machine, Lee Aaron, Kenny Blues Boss Wayne (boogie) and Tim Brecht (pop/children's).

○ GARY SMELTZER PRODUCTIONS

P.O. Box 201112, Austin TX 78720-11112. (512)478-6020. **Fax:** (512)478-8979. **E-mail:** info@garysmeltzerproductions.com. **Website:** www.garysmeltzerproductions.com. **Contact:** Gary Smeltzer, president. Management firm and booking agency. Represents individual artists and groups from anywhere. Currently handles 20 acts. "We book about 100 different bands each year—none are exclusive." Receives 20% commission. Reviews material for acts.

HOW TO CONTACT Submit demo package by mail. Unsolicited submissions are OK. Prefers CD or DVD.

If seeking management, press kit should include cover letter, résumé, CD/DVD, bio, picture, lyric sheets, press clippings, and video. Does not return material. Responds in 1 month.

MUSIC Mostly **alternative**, **R&B** and **country**. Current acts include Rotel & the Hot Tomatoes (nostalgic 1960s showband).

TIPS "We prefer performing songwriters who can gig their music as a solo or group."

SOUND ADVICE MANAGEMENT

538 Frenchman St., New Orleans LA 70116. (504)298-6652. **E-mail:** kp@soundadvicemanagement.com. **Website:** www.soundadvicemanagement.com. **Contact:** Kimball Packard. For artists just starting out or looking to take it to the next level, we have a variety of à la carte options available on a contract basis, including creating your website, press kit, bio, identity and more. We are available for consultation on an hourly basis, as well, to guide you through any number of projects: your first CD release (recording, packaging, duplication, promotion), online presence, publishing questions, touring, etc. Call or e-mail for more information.

◐ SOUTHEASTERN ATTRACTIONS

1025 23rd St. S., Suite 302, Birmingham AL 35205. (205)307-6790. **Fax:** (205)307-6798. **E-mail:** info@southeasternattractions.com. **Website:** southeasternattractions.com. **Contact:** Agent. Booking agency. Represents groups from anywhere. Receives 20% commission.

HOW TO CONTACT Submit demo package by mail. Unsolicited submissions are OK. Prefers CD or DVD. Does not return material. Responds in 2 months.

MUSIC Mostly **rock**, **alternative**, **oldies**, **country**, and **dance**. Works primarily with bands. Current acts include The Undergrounders (variety to contemporary), The Connection (Motown/dance), and Rollin' in the Hay (bluegrass).

◐ STARKRAVIN' MANAGEMENT

11135 Weddington St., Suite 424, North Hollywood CA 91601. **Website:** www.benmclane.com. 11135 Weddington St., Suite 424, North Hollywood, CA 91601. (818)587-6801. **Fax:** (818)587-6802. **E-mail:** bcmclane@aol.com. **Website:** www.benmclane.com. **Contact:** B.C. McLane, Esq. Management and law firm. Estab. 1994. Represents individual artists, groups and songwriters. Receives 20% commission (management); $300/hour as attorney.

HOW TO CONTACT Submit demo package by mail. Unsolicited submissions are OK. Prefers CDs. Does not return material. Responds in 1 month if interested.

MUSIC Mostly **rock**, **pop** and **R&B**. Works primarily with bands.

○ ST. JOHN ARTISTS

P.O. Box 619, Neenah WI 54957-0619. (920)722-2222. **Fax:** (920)725-2405. **E-mail:** jon@stjohn-artists.com; information@stjohn-artists.com. **Website:** www.st-john-artists.com. **Contact:** Jon St. John and Gary Coquoz, agents. Booking agency. Represents local and regional individual artists and groups; currently handles 20 acts. Receives 15-20% commission. Reviews material for acts.

HOW TO CONTACT *Call first and obtain permission to submit.* Prefers CD or DVD. If seeking management, press kit should include cover letter, bio, photo, demo CD, video and résumé. Include SASE.

MUSIC Mostly **rock** and **MOR**. Current acts include Boogie & the Yo-Yo's (1960s to 2000s), Vic Ferrari (Top 40 1980s-2000s), Little Vito & the Torpedoes (variety 1950s-2000s), and Da Yoopers (musical comedy/novelty).

◐ TAS MUSIC CO./DAVID TASSÉ ENTERTAINMENT

N2467 Knollwood Dr., Lake Geneva WI 53147. (888)554-9898; (262)245-1335. **E-mail:** info@baybreezerecords.com. **Website:** www.baybreezerecords.com. **Contact:** David Tassé. There is a contact form on the website. Booking agency, record company and music publisher. Represents artists, groups, and songwriters; currently handles 21 acts. Receives 10-20% commission. Reviews material for acts.

HOW TO CONTACT Submit demo by mail. Unsolicited submissions are OK. Prefers CD with 2-4 songs and lyric sheet. Include performance videocassette if available. If seeking management, press kit should include tape, bio and photo. Does not return material. Responds in 3 weeks.

MUSIC Mostly **pop** and **jazz**; also **dance, MOR, rock, soul**, and **top 40**. Works primarily with show and dance bands. Current acts include Maxx Kelly (pop/rock) and Glenn Davis (blues band).

WHITESMITH ENTERTAINMENT

E-mail: Info@WhitesmithEnt.com. **Website:** www.whitesmithentertainment.com. **Contact:** LA: Keri Smith Esguia (keri@whitesmithent.com); NY: Emily White (emily@whitesmithent.com). Whitesmith

Entertainment is a full-service talent management firm based in Los Angeles and New York, spanning the music, comedy, film, TV, literary, and sports industries. We take pride in working with artists who have a unique voice, style and meaning to their fans. Whitesmith balances a youthful edge while maintaining a deep knowledge within the fields of touring, merchandising, online marketing, social networking, branding, sponsorship, as well as physical and modern content releases. Whitesmith Entertainment is available for outside consulting services in all areas of artist development, content releases, touring services, online marketing, and beyond.

MUSIC Artists represented include Brandan Benson, The Big Sleep, Hockey, The Autumn Defense, GOLD MOTEL, Urge Overkill, Future Monarchs, and many more.

WORLDSOUND, LLC

17837 1st Ave. S., Suite 3, Seattle WA 98148. (206)444-0300. **Fax:** (206)244-0066. **E-mail:** a-r@worldsound.com. **Website:** www.worldsound.com. **Contact:** Warren Wyatt, A&R manager. Management firm. Represents individual artists, groups and songwriters from anywhere. Receives 20% commission. Reviews material for acts.

HOW TO CONTACT "Online, send us an e-mail containing a link to your website where your songs can be heard and the lyrics are available; **please do not e-mail song files!** By regular mail, unsolicited submissions are OK." Prefers CD with 2-10 songs and lyric sheet. "If seeking management, please send an e-mail with a link to your website—your site should contain song samples, band biography, photos, video (if available), press and demo reviews. By mail, please send the materials listed above and include SASE." Responds in 1 month.

MUSIC Mostly **rock**, **pop**, and **world**; also **heavy metal**, **hard rock**, and **top 40**. Works primarily with pop/rock/world artists.

TIPS "Always submit new songs/material, even if you have sent material that was previously rejected; the music biz is always changing."

ZANE MANAGEMENT, INC.

One Liberty Place, 1650 Market St., 56th Floor, Philadelphia PA 19103. (215)575-3803. **Fax:** (215)575-3801. **Website:** www.zanemanagement.com. **Contact:** Lloyd Z. Remick, Esq., president. Entertainment/sports consultants and managers. Represents artists, songwriters, producers and athletes; currently handles 7 acts. Receives 10-15% commission.

HOW TO CONTACT Submit demo tape by mail. Unsolicited submissions are OK. Prefers CD and lyric sheet. If seeking management, press kit should include cover letter, bio, photo, demo tape and video. Does not return material. Responds in 3 weeks.

MUSIC Mostly **dance**, **easy listening**, **folk**, **jazz (fusion)**, **MOR**, **rock (hard and country)**, **soul** and **top 40/pop**. Current acts include Bunny Sigler (disco/funk), Peter Nero and Philly Pops (conductor), Pieces of a Dream (jazz/crossover), Don't Look Down (rock/pop), Christian Josi (pop-swing), Bishop David Evans (gospel), Kevin Roth (children's music), and Rosie Carlino (standards/pop).

MUSIC FIRMS

Advertising, Audiovisual & Commercial

///

It's happened a million times—you hear a jingle on the radio or television and can't get it out of your head. That's the work of a successful jingle writer, writing songs to catch your attention and make you aware of the product being advertised. But the field of commercial music consists of more than just memorable jingles. It also includes background music that many companies use in videos for corporate and educational presentations, as well as films and TV shows.

SUBMITTING MATERIAL

More than any other market listed in this book, the commercial music market expects composers to have made an investment in the recording of their material before submitting. A sparse, piano/vocal demo won't work here; when dealing with commercial music firms, especially audiovisual firms and music libraries, high-quality production is important. Your demo may

be kept on file at one of these companies until a need for it arises, and it may be used or sold as you sent it. Therefore, your demo tape or reel must be as fully produced as possible.

The presentation package that goes along with your demo must be just as professional. A list of your credits should be a part of your submission, to give the company an idea of your experience in this field. If you have no experience, look to local television and radio stations to get your start. Don't expect to be paid for many of your first jobs in the commercial music field; it's more important to get the credits and exposure that can lead to higher-paying jobs.

Commercial music and jingle writing can be a lucrative field for the composer/songwriter with a gift for writing catchy melodies and the ability to write in many different music styles. It's a very competitive field, so it pays to have a professional presentation package that makes your work stand out.

Three different segments of the commercial music world are listed here: advertising agencies, audiovisual firms, and commercial music houses/music libraries. Each looks for a different type of music, so read these descriptions carefully to see where the music you write fits in.

ADVERTISING AGENCIES

Ad agencies work on assignment as their clients' needs arise. Through consultation and input from the creative staff, ad agencies seek jingles and music to stimulate the consumer to identify with a product or service.

When contacting ad agencies, keep in mind they are searching for music that can capture and then hold an audience's attention. Most jingles are short, with a strong, memorable hook. When an ad agency listens to a demo, it is not necessarily looking for a finished product so much as for an indication of creativity and diversity. Many composers put together a reel of excerpts of work from previous projects, or short pieces of music that show they can write in a variety of styles.

AUDIOVISUAL FIRMS

Audiovisual firms create a variety of products, from film and video shows for sales meetings, corporate gatherings and educational markets, to motion pictures and TV shows. With the increase of home video use, how-to videos are a big market for audiovisual firms, as are spoken word educational videos. All of these products need music to accompany them. For your quick reference, companies working to place music in movies and TV shows (excluding commercials) have an ✪ preceding their listing (also see the Film & TV Index for a complete list of these companies).

Like ad agencies, audiovisual firms look for versatile, well-rounded songwriters. When submitting demos to these firms, you need to demonstrate your versatility in writing specialized background music and themes. Listings for companies will tell what facet(s) of the audiovisual field they are involved in and what types of clients they serve. Your demo tape should also be as professional and fully produced as possible; audiovisual firms often seek demo tapes that can be put on file for future use when the need arises.

COMMERCIAL MUSIC HOUSES & MUSIC LIBRARIES

Commercial music houses are companies contracted (either by an ad agency or the advertiser) to compose custom jingles. Since they are neither an ad agency nor an audiovisual firm, their main concern is music. They use a lot of it, too—some composed by in-house songwriters and some contributed by outside, freelance writers.

Music libraries are different in that their music is not custom composed for a specific client. Their job is to provide a collection of instrumental music in many different styles that, for an annual fee or on a per-use basis, the customer can use however he chooses.

In the following listings, commercial music houses and music libraries, which are usually the most open to works by new composers, are identified as such by **bold** type.

The commercial music market is similar to most other businesses in one aspect: experience is important. Until you develop a list of credits, pay for your work may not be high. Don't pass up opportunities if a job is non- or low-paying. These assignments will add to your list of credits, make you contacts in the field, and improve your marketability.

Money & Rights

Many of the companies listed in this section pay by the job, but there may be some situations where the company asks you to sign a contract that will specify royalty payments. If this happens, research the contract thoroughly, and know exactly what is expected of you and how much you'll be paid.

Depending on the particular job and the company, you may be asked to sell one-time rights or all rights. One-time rights involve using your material for one presentation only. All rights means the buyer can use your work any way he chooses, as many times as he likes. Be sure you know exactly what you're giving up, and how the company may use your music in the future.

In the commercial world, many of the big advertising agencies have their own publishing companies where writers assign their compositions. In these situations, writers sign contracts whereby they do receive performance and mechanical royalties when applicable.

ADDITIONAL LISTINGS

For additional names and addresses of ad agencies that may use jingles and/or commercial music, refer to the *Standard Directory of Advertising Agencies* (National Register Publishing). For a list of audiovisual firms, check out the latest edition of *AV Marketplace* (R.R. Bowker). Both these books may be found at your local library. To contact companies in your area, see the Geographic Index at the back of this book.

ADVERTEL, INC.

P.O. Box 18053, Pittsburgh PA 15236-0053. (412)714-4421. **E-mail:** info@advertel.com. **Website:** www.advertel.com. Submit demo of previous work. Prefers CD. "Most compositions are 2 minutes strung together in 6, 12, 18 minute length productions." Does not return material; prefers to keep on file. Responds "right away if submission fills an immediate need."

TIPS "Go for volume. We have continuous need for all varieties of music in 2-minute lengths. Advertel produces a religious radio program called 'Prayer-in-the-Air.' Feel free to submit songs with lyrics taken from scripture. We also look for catchy, memorable melodies. For those pro bono submissions, no compensation is offered—only national recognition."

COMMUNICATIONS FOR LEARNING

395 Massachusetts Ave., Arlington MA 02474. (781)641-2350. **E-mail:** comlearn395@gmail.com. **Website:** www.communicationsforlearning.com. **Contact:** Jonathan L. Barkan, executive producer/director. Video, multimedia, exhibit and graphic design firm. Clients include multi-nationals, industry, government, institutions, local, national and international nonprofits. Uses services of music houses and independent songwriters/composers as theme and background music for videos and multimedia. Commissions 1-2 composers/year. Pays $2,000-5,000/job and one-time use fees. Rights purchased vary. Submit demo and work available for library use. Prefers CD to Web links. Does not return material; prefers to keep on file. "For each job we consider our entire collection." Responds in 3 months.

TIPS "Please don't call. Just send your best material available for library use on CD. We'll be in touch if a piece works and negotiate a price. Make certain your name and contact information are on the CD itself, not only on the cover letter."

DBF A MEDIA COMPANY

9683 Charles St., La Plata MD 20646. (301)645-6110. **E-mail:** service@dbfmedia.com. **Website:** www.dbfmedia.com. Video production. Uses the services of music houses for background music for industrial, training, educational, and promo videos, jingles and commercials for radio and TV. Buys all rights. "All genre for MOH, industrial, training, video/photo montages and commercials."

HOW TO CONTACT Submit demo CD of previous work. Prefers CD or DVD with 5-8 songs and lead sheet. Include SASE, but prefers to keep material on file. Responds in 6 months.

K&R ALL MEDIA PRODUCTIONS LLC

28533 Greenfield Rd., Southfield MI 48076. (248)557-8276. **Website:** www.knr.net. Scoring service and **jingle/commercial music production house**. Clients include commercial and industrial firms. Services include sound for pictures (Foley, music, dialogue). Uses the services of independent songwriters/composers and lyricists for scoring of film and video, commercials and industrials and jingles and commercials for radio and TV. Commissions 1 composer/month. Pays by the job. Buys all rights.

HOW TO CONTACT Submit demo tape of previous work. Prefers CD or VHS videocassette with 5-7 short pieces. "We rack your tape for client to judge." Does not return material.

TIPS "Keep samples short. Show me what you can do in 5 minutes. Go to knr.net 'free samples' and listen to the sensitivity expressed in emotional music."

KEN-DEL PRODUCTIONS INC.

1500 First State Blvd., First State Industrial Park, Wilmington DE 19804-3596. (302)999-1111. **E-mail:** info@ken-del.com. **Website:** www.ken-del.com. Clients include publishers, industrial firms and advertising agencies, how-tos and radio/TV. Uses services of songwriters for radio/TV commercials, jingles and multimedia. Pays by the job. Buys all rights.

HOW TO CONTACT Submit all inquiries and demos in any format to general manager." Does not return material. Will keep on file for 3 years. Generally responds in 1 month or less.

◐✹ NOVUS VISUAL COMMUNICATIONS

59 Page Ave., Suite 300, Tower One, Yonkers NY 10704. (212)473-1377. **E-mail:** novuscom@aol.com. **Website:** www.novuscommunications.com. **Contact:** Robert Antonik, managing director. Integrated marketing company. Clients include Fortune 500 companies and nonprofits. Uses the services of music houses, independent songwriters/composers and lyricists for scoring, background music for documentaries, commercials, multimedia applications, website, film shorts, and commercials for radio and TV. Commissions 2 composers and 4 lyricists/year. Pay varies per job. Buys one-time rights.

HOW TO CONTACT *Request a submission of demo.* Query with a brief of sample and songs. Prefers CD with 2-3 songs or link to website. "We prefer to keep submitted material on file, but will return material if SASE is enclosed. Responds in 6 weeks.

MUSIC Uses all styles for a variety of different assignments.

TIPS "Always present your best and don't add quantity to your demo. Novus is a creative marketing and integrated communications company. We also work with special events companies, PR firms, artists' management and media companies."

OMNI COMMUNICATIONS

P.O. Box 302, Carmel IN 46082-0302. (317)846-2345. **Fax:** (317)846-6664. **E-mail:** omni@omniproductions. com. **Website:** www.omniproductions.com. OMNI Productions is an experienced interactive, digital media solutions provider offering the complete infrastructure for production and delivery of digital media services including interactive multipoint Internet training; live event and archived Web casting; video, DVD and CD-ROM production; and encoding, hosting and distribution of streaming video content. OMNI is recognized by Microsoft as a Windows Media Service Provider. This partnership with Microsoft was obtained through vigorous training, testing and experience to ensure that those we serve receive the highest-quality service from OMNI's experienced professionals. OMNI's staff includes technology experts certified by Microsoft and other industry vendors.

TIPS "Submit good demo tape with examples of your range to command the attention of our producers."

UTOPIAN EMPIRE CREATIVEWORKS

P.O. Box 9, Traverse City MI 49865. (231)715-1614. **E-mail:** traverse_city@utopianempire.com. **Website:** www.utopianempire.com. Web design, multimedia firm, and motion picture/video production company. Primarily serves commercial, industrial and nonprofit clients. "We provide the following services: advertising, marketing, design/packaging, distribution and booking. Uses services of music houses, independent songwriters/composers for jingles and scoring of and background music for multi-image/multimedia, film and video." Negotiates pay. Buys all or one-time rights.

HOW TO CONTACT Submit CD of previous work, demonstrating composition skills or query with resume of credits. Prefers CD. Does not return material; prefers to keep on file. Responds only if interested.

MUSIC Uses mostly industrial/commercial themes.

✪ VIDEO I-D, TELEPRODUCTIONS

105 Muller Rd., Washington IL 61571. (309)444-4323. **E-mail:** videoid@videoid.com. **Website:** www.videoid.com. **Contact:** Sam B. Wagner, president. Post production/teleproductions. Clients include law enforcement, industrial and business. Uses the services of music houses and independent songwriters/composers for background music for video productions. Pays per job. Buys one-time rights.

HOW TO CONTACT Submit demo of previous work. Prefers CD with 5 songs and lyric sheet. Does not return material. Responds in 1 month.

PLAY PRODUCERS
& PUBLISHERS

///

Finding a theater company willing to invest in a new production can be frustrating for an unknown playwright. But whether you write the plays, compose the music or pen the lyrics, it is important to remember not only where to start but how to start. Theater in the U.S. is a hierarchy, with Broadway, Off-Broadway, and Off-Off-Broadway being pretty much off limits to all but the Stephen Sondheims of the world.

Aspiring theater writers would do best to train their sights on nonprofit regional and community theaters to get started. The encouraging news is there are a great number of local theater companies throughout the U.S. with experimental artistic directors who are looking for new works to produce, and many are included in this section. This section covers two segments of the industry: theater companies and dinner theaters are listed under Play Producers, and publishers of musical theater works are listed under the Play Publishers heading. These

markets are actively seeking new works of all types for their stages or publications.

BREAKING IN

Starting locally will allow you to research each company carefully and learn about their past performances, the type of musicals they present, and the kinds of material they're looking for. When you find theaters you think may be interested in your work, attend as many performances as possible, so you know exactly what type of material each theater presents. Or volunteer to work at a theater, whether it be moving sets or selling tickets. This will give you valuable insight into the day-to-day workings of a theater and the creation of a new show. On a national level, you will find prestigious organizations offering workshops and apprenticeships covering every subject from arts administration to directing to costuming. But it could be more helpful to look into professional internships at theaters and attend theater workshops in your area. The more knowledgeable you are about the workings of a particular company or theater, the easier it will be to tailor your work to fit its style and the more responsive they will be to you and your work. (See the Workshops & Conferences section for more information.) As a composer for the stage, you need to know as much as possible about a theater and how it works, its history and the different roles played by the people involved in it. Flexibility is the key to successful productions, and knowing how a theater works will only help you in cooperating and collaborating with the director, producer, technical people and actors.

If you're a playwright looking to have his play published in book form or in theater publications, see the listings under the Play Publishers section. To find play producers and publishers in your area, consult the Geographic Index at the back of this book.

PLAY PRODUCERS

ARKANSAS REPERTORY THEATRE

601 Main St., P.O. Box 110, Little Rock AR 72201. (501)378-0445. **Website:** www.therep.org. Produces 6-10 plays and musicals/year. "We perform in a 354-seat house and also have a 99-seat second stage." Pays 5-10% royalty or $75-150 per performance.

HOW TO CONTACT Query with synopsis, character breakdown and set description. Include SASE. Responds in 6 months.

MUSICAL THEATER "Small casts, comedy or drama, and shows running 1:45 to 2 hours maximum are preferred. Simple is better; small is better, but we do produce complex shows. We aren't interested in children's pieces, puppet shows or mime. We always like to receive a tape of the music with the book."

PRODUCTIONS *Disney's Beauty & the Beast*, by Woolverton/Ashman/Rice/Menken (musical retelling of the myth); *Crowns*, by Taylor/Cunningham/Marberry (on the significance of African-American women's hats); and *A Chorus Line*, by Kirkwood/Hamlisch/Kleban (auditions).

TIPS "Include a good CD of your music, sung well, with the script."

CIRCA '21 DINNER PLAYHOUSE

1828 Third Ave., Rock Island IL 61201. (309)786-7733. **Website:** www.circa21.com. Plays produced for a general audience. Three children's works/year, concurrent with major productions. Payment is negotiable.

HOW TO CONTACT Query with synopsis, character breakdown and set description or submit complete ms, score and tape of songs. Include SASE. Responds in 3 months.

MUSICAL THEATER "We produce both full-length and one-act children's musicals. Folk or fairy tale themes. Works that do not condescend to a young audience yet are appropriate for entire family. We're also seeking full-length, small-cast musicals suitable for a broad audience." Would also consider original music for use in a play being developed.

PRODUCTIONS *A Closer Walk with Patsy Cline*, *Swingtime Canteen*, *Forever Plaid* and *Lost Highway*.

TIPS "Small, upbeat, tourable musicals (like *Pump Boys*) and bright musically sharp children's productions (like those produced by Prince Street Players) work best. Keep an open mind. Stretch to encompass a musical variety—different keys, rhythms, musical ideas and textures."

LA JOLLA PLAYHOUSE

P.O. Box 12039, La Jolla CA 92039. (858)550-1070. **Fax:** (858)550-1075. **E-mail:** information@ljp.org. **Website:** www.lajollaplayhouse.org. Produces 6-show season including 1-2 new musicals/year. Audience is University of California students to senior citizens. Performance spaces include a large proscenium theater with 492 seats, a 3/4 thrust (384 seats), and a black box with up to 400 seats.

HOW TO CONTACT Query with synopsis, character breakdown, 10-page dialogue sample, demo CD. Include SASE. Responds in 1-2 months.

MUSICAL THEATER "We prefer contemporary music but not necessarily a story set in contemporary times. Retellings of classic stories can enlighten us about the times we live in. For budgetary reasons, we'd prefer a smaller cast size."

PRODUCTIONS *Cry-Baby*, book and lyrics by Thomas Meehan and Mark O'Donnell, music by David Javerbaum and Adam Schlesinger; *Dracula, The Musical*, book and lyrics by Don Black and Christopher Hampton, music by Frank Wildhorn (adaptation of Bram Stoker's novel); *Thoroughly Modern Millie*, book by Richard Morris and Dick Scanlan, new music by Jeanine Tesori, new lyrics by Dick Scanlan (based on the 1967 movie); and *Jane Eyre*, book and additional lyrics by John Cairo, music and lyrics by Paul Gordon (adaptation of Charlotte Bronte's novel).

NORTH SHORE MUSIC THEATRE

62 Dunham Rd., Beverly MA 01915. (978)232-7200. **Fax:** (978)921-9999. **E-mail:** northshoremusictheatre@nsmt.org. **Website:** www.nsmt.org.

HOW TO CONTACT Submit synopsis and CD of songs. Include SASE. Responds within 6 months.

MUSICAL THEATER Prefers full-length adult pieces not necessarily arena-theater oriented. Cast sizes from 1-30; orchestra's from 1-16.

PRODUCTIONS *Tom Jones*, by Paul Leigh, George Stiles; *I Sent A Letter to My Love*, by Melissa Manchester and Jeffrey Sweet; *Just So*, by Anthony Drewe & George Stiles (musical based on Rudyard Kipling's fables); *Letters from 'Nam*, by Paris Barclay (Vietnam War experience as told through letters from GI's); and *Friendship of the Sea*, by Michael Wartofsky & Kathleen Cahill (New England maritime adventure musical).

TIPS "Keep at it!"

PRIMARY STAGES

307 W. 38th St., Suite 1510, New York NY 10018. (212)840-9705. **E-mail:** info@primarystages.org.

Website: www.primarystages.org. New York theater-going audience representing a broad cross-section, in terms of age, ethnicity, and economic backgrounds. 199-seat, Off-Broadway theater.

HOW TO CONTACT No unsolicited scripts accepted. Submissions by agents only. Include SASE. Responds in up to 8 months.

MUSICAL THEATER "We are looking for work of heightened theatricality, that challenges realism—musical plays that go beyond film and TV's standard fare. We are looking for small-cast shows with fewer than 6 characters total, with limited sets. We are interested in original works, that have not been produced in New York."

PRODUCTIONS *Harbor*, by Chad Beguelin; *Bronx Bombers*, by Fran Kirmser and Eric Simmonson; *The Model Apartment*, by Donald Margulies; *The Tribute Artist*, by Charles Busch.

PRINCE MUSIC THEATER

1412 Chestnut St., Philadelphia PA 19102. **E-mail:** info@princemusictheater.org. **Website:** www.prince-musictheater.org. "Professional musical productions. Drawing upon operatic and popular traditions, as well as European, African, Asian, and South American forms, new work, and new voices taking center stage." Play producer. Produces 4-5 musicals/year. "Our average audience member is in their mid-40s. We perform to ethnically diverse houses."

HOW TO CONTACT Submit 2-page synopsis with tape or CD of 4 songs. Include SASE. "May include complete script, but be aware that response is at least 10 months."

TIPS "Innovative topics and use of media, music, technology a plus. Sees trends of arts in technology (interactive theater, virtual reality, sound design); works are shorter in length (1-1 and 1/2 hours with no intermissions or 2 hours with intermission)."

THE REPERTORY THEATRE OF ST. LOUIS

130 Edgar Rd., P.O. Box 191730, St. Louis MO 63119. (314)968-7340. **Website:** www.repstl.org. **Contact:** Steven Woolf, artistic director.

HOW TO CONTACT Query with synopsis, character breakdown and set description. Does not return material. Responds in 2 years.

MUSICAL THEATER "We want plays with a small cast and simple setting. No children's shows or foul language. After a letter of inquiry we would prefer script and demo tape."

PRODUCTIONS *Almost September* and *Esmeralda*, by David Schechter and Steve Lutvak; *Jack*, by Barbara Field and Hiram Titus; and *Young Rube*, by John Pielmeier and Nattie Selman, *Ace* by Robert Taylor and Richard Oberacker.

THUNDER BAY THEATRE

400 N. Second Ave., Alpena MI 49707. (989)354-2267. **E-mail:** tbt@thunderbaytheatre.com; artisticdirector@thunderbaytheatre.com. **Website:** www.thunderbaytheatre.com. **Contact:** Jeffrey Mindock, artistic director.

HOW TO CONTACT Submit complete ms, score and tape of songs. Include SASE.

MUSICAL THEATER Small cast. Not equipped for large sets. Considers original background music for use in a play being developed or for use in a pre-existing play.

PLAY PUBLISHERS

HEUER PUBLISHING LLC

P.O. Box 248, Cedar Rapids IA 52406. (319)368-8008. **Fax:** (319)368-8011. **E-mail:** editor@hitplays.com. **E-mail:** editor@heuerpub.com. **Website:** www.hitplays.com. Publishes plays, musicals, operas/operettas and guides (choreography, costume, production/staging) for amateur and professional markets, including junior and senior high schools, college/university and community theaters. Focus includes comedy, drama, fantasy, mystery and holiday. Pays by percentage royalty or outright purchase. Pays by outright purchase or percentage royalty.

HOW TO CONTACT Query with musical CD or submit complete ms and score. Include SASE. Responds in 2 months.

MUSICAL THEATER "We prefer one, two or three act comedies or mystery-comedies with a large number of characters."

PUBLICATIONS *Happily Ever After*, by Allen Koepke (musical fairytale); *Brave Buckaroo*, by Renee J. Clark (musical melodrama); and *Pirate Island*, by Martin Follose (musical comedy).

TIPS "We are willing to review single-song submissions as a cornerstone piece for commissioned works. Special interest focus in multicultural, historic, classic literature, teen issues, and biographies."

CLASSICAL PERFORMING ARTS

Finding an audience is critical to the composer of orchestral music. Fortunately, baby boomers are swelling the ranks of classical music audiences and bringing with them a taste for fresh, innovative music. So the climate is fair for composers seeking their first performance.

Finding a performance venue is particularly important because once a composer has his work performed for an audience and establishes himself as a talented newcomer, it can lead to more performances and commissions for new works. Getting started, however, often can be difficult for those just trying to break in.

BEFORE YOU SUBMIT

Be aware that most classical music organizations are nonprofit groups that don't have a large budget for acquiring new works. It takes a lot of time and money to put together an orchestral performance of a new composition; therefore, these groups are quite selective when choosing new works to perform, so make sure you follow their submission guidelines to the letter. Also, don't be disappointed if the payment offered by these groups is small or even non-existent.

What you gain is the chance to have your music performed for an appreciative audience. Performing in front of that audience could eventually lead to more widespread recognition, reviews, and better opportunities. Sometimes the only way to get started is through word of mouth and local reviews.

Also, realize that many classical groups are understaffed, so it may take longer than expected to hear back on your submission. It pays to be patient, and employ diplomacy, tact and timing in your follow-up. Be courteous, prompt and appreciative in your interactions with staff. They can be some of your biggest champions and most important contacts should you work with them!

In this section you will find listings for classical performing arts organizations throughout the U.S. But if you have no prior performances to your credit, it's a good idea to begin with a small chamber orchestra, for example. Smaller symphony and chamber orchestras are usually more inclined to experiment with new works. A local university or conservatory of music, where you may already have contacts, is a great place to start.

Remember that like any other market in this book (and perhaps more so), you'll need time and patience to break into the classical performing arts.

All of the groups listed in this section are interested in hearing new works from contemporary classical composers. Pay close attention to the music needs of each group, and when you find one you feel might be interested in your music, follow the submission guidelines carefully. To locate classical performing arts groups in your area, consult the Geographic Index at the back of this book.

ACADIANA SYMPHONY ORCHESTRA

P.O. Box 53632, Lafayette LA 70505. (337)232-4277. **Website:** www.acadianasymphony.org. **Contact:** Jenny Krueger, executive director. Estab. 1984. Members are amateurs and professionals. Performs 20 concerts/year, including 1 new work. Commissions 1 new work/year. Performs in 2,230-seat hall with "wonderful acoustics." Pays "according to the type of composition."

HOW TO CONTACT Call first. Does not return material. Responds in 2 months.

MUSIC Full orchestra: 10 minutes at most. Reduced orchestra, educational pieces: short, up to 5 minutes.

PERFORMANCES Quincy Hilliard's *Universal Covenant* (orchestral suite); James Hanna's *In Memoriam* (strings/elegy); and Gregory Danner's *A New Beginning* (full orchestra fanfare).

THE AMERICAN BOYCHOIR

75 Mapleton Rd., Princeton NJ 08540. (609)924-5858. **Fax:** (609)924-5812. **E-mail:** admissions@american-boychoir.org. **Website:** www.americanboychoir.org. General Manager: Christie Starrett. Music Director: Fernando Malvar-Ruiz. Professional boychoir. Estab. 1937. Members are musically talented boys in grades 4-8. Performs 150 concerts/year. Commissions 1 new work approximately every 3 years. Actively seeks high-quality arrangements. Performs national and international tours, orchestral engagements, church services, workshops, school programs, local concerts, and at corporate and social functions.

HOW TO CONTACT Submit complete score. Include SASE. Responds in 1 year.

MUSIC Choral works in unison, SA, SSA, SSAA or SATB division; unaccompanied and with piano or organ; occasional chamber orchestra or brass ensemble. Works are usually sung by 28-60 boys. Composers must know boychoir sonority.

PERFORMANCES *Four Seasons*, by Michael Torke (orchestral-choral); *Garden of Light*, by Aaron Kernis (orchestral-choral); *Reasons for Loving the Harmonica*, by Libby Larsen (piano); and *Songs Eternity*, by Steven Paulus (piano).

ANDERSON SYMPHONY ORCHESTRA

1124 Meridian Plaza, Anderson IN 46016. **Website:** www.andersonsymphony.org. **Contact:** Dr. Richard Sowers, music director. Symphony orchestra. Estab. 1967. Members are professionals. Performs 7 concerts/year. Performs for typical Midwestern audience in a 1,500-seat restored Paramount Theatre. Pay negotiable.

HOW TO CONTACT Query first. Include SASE. Responds in several months.

MUSIC "Shorter lengths better; concerti OK; difficulty level: mod high; limited by typically 3 full-service rehearsals."

THE ATLANTA YOUNG SINGERS OF CALLANWOLDE

1085 Ponce de Leon Ave. NE, Atlanta GA 30306. (404)873-3365. **Fax:** (404)873-0756. **E-mail:** info@aysc.org. **Website:** www.aysc.org. **Contact:** Paige F. Mathis, music director. Children's chorus. Estab. 1975. Performs 3 major concerts/year, as well as invitational performances and co-productions with other Atlanta arts organizations. Audience consists of community members, families, alumni, and supporters. Performs most often at churches. Pay is negotiable.

HOW TO CONTACT Submit complete score and tape of piece(s). Include SASE. Responds in accordance with request.

MUSIC Subjects and styles appealing to 3rd- to 12th-grade boys and girls. Contemporary concerns of the world of interest. Unusual sacred, folk, classic style. Internationally and ethnically bonding. Medium difficulty preferred, with or without keyboard accompaniment.

TIPS "Our mission is to promote service and growth through singing."

AUGSBURG CHOIR

Augsburg College, 2211 Riverside Ave. S., Minneapolis MN 55454. (612)330-1265. **E-mail:** musicdept@augsburg.edu. **Website:** www.augsburg.edu. **Contact:** Peter A. Hendrickson, director of choral activities. Vocal ensemble (SATB choir). Members are amateurs. Performs 25 concerts/year, including 1-6 new works. Commissions 0-2 composers or new works/year. Audience is all ages, "sophisticated and unsophisticated." Concerts are performed in churches, concert halls and schools. Pays for outright purchase.

HOW TO CONTACT Query first. Include SASE. Responds in 1 month.

MUSIC Seeking "sacred choral pieces, no more than 5-7 minutes long, to be sung a cappella or with obbligato instrument. Can contain vocal solos. We have 50-60 members in our choir."

PERFORMANCES Carol Barnett's *Spiritual Journey*; Steven Heitzeg's *Litanies for the Living* (choral/orchestral); and Morton Lanriclsen's *O Magnum Mysteries* (a cappella choral).

BARDAVON

35 Market St., Poughkeepsie NY 12601. (845)473-5288. **Fax:** (845)473-4259. **Website:** www.bardavon.org. Symphony orchestra. Estab. 1969. Members are professionals. Performs 20 concerts/year including 1 new work. "Classical subscription concerts for all ages; pops concerts for all ages; New Wave concerts—crossover projects with a rock 'n' roll artist performing with an orchestra. HVP performs in 3 main theaters which are concert auditoriums with stages and professional lighting and sound." Pay is negotiable.
HOW TO CONTACT Query first. Include SASE. Responds only if interested.
MUSIC "HVP is open to serious classical music, pop music, and rock 'n' roll crossover projects. Desired length of work: 10-20 minutes. Orchestrations can be varied but should always include strings. There is no limit to difficulty since our musicians are professionals. The ideal number of musicians to write for would include up to a Brahms-size orchestra 2222, 4231, T, 2P, piano, harp, strings."
PERFORMANCES Joan Tower's *Island Rhythms* (serious classical work); Bill Vanaver's *P'nai El* (symphony work with dance); and Joseph Bertolozzi's *Serenade* (light classical, pop work).
TIPS "Don't get locked into doing very traditional orchestrations or styles. Our music director is interested in fresh, creative formats. He is an orchestrator, as well, and can offer good advice on what works well. Songwriters who are into crossover projects should definitely submit works. Over the past 4 years, HVP has done concerts featuring the works of Natalie Merchant, John Cale, Sterling Morrison, Richie Havens, and R. Carlos Naka (Native American flute player), all reorchestrated by our music director for small orchestra with the artist."

BILLING SYMPHONY

2721 Second Ave. N., Suite 350, Billings MT 59101. (406)252-3610. **Fax:** (406)252-3353. **E-mail:** symphony@billingssymphony.org. **Website:** www.billingssymphony.org. **Contact:** Darren Rich, executive director. Symphony orchestra, orchestra and chorale. Estab. 1950. Members are professionals and amateurs. Performs 12-15 concerts/year, including 6-7 new works. Traditional audience. Performs at Al-

berta Bair Theater (capacity 1,416). Pays by outright purchase (or rental).
HOW TO CONTACT Query first. Include SASE. Responds in 2 weeks.
MUSIC Any style. Traditional notation preferred.
PERFORMANCES 2013 Symphony in the Park includes Billings Community Band and Young Conductors' Contest (led by Maestra Anne Harrigan).
TIPS "Write what you feel (be honest) and sharpen your compositional and craftsmanship skills."

BIRMINGHAM-BLOOMFIELD SYMPHONY ORCHESTRA

P.O. Box 1925, Birmingham MI 48012. (248)352-2276. **E-mail:** info@bbso.org. **Website:** www.bbso.org. **Contact:** John Thomas Dodson, music director and conductor. Symphony orchestra. Estab. 1975. Members are professionals. Performs 5 concerts including 1 new work/year. Commissions 1 composer or new work/year "with grants." Performs for middle- to upper-class audience at Temple Beth El's Sanctuary. Pays per performance "depending upon grant received."
HOW TO CONTACT *Query first.* Does not return material. Responds in 6 months.
MUSIC "We are a symphony orchestra but also play pops. Usually 3 works on program (2 hours). Orchestra size 65-75. If pianist is involved, they must rent piano."
PERFORMANCES Brian Belanger's *Tuskegee Airmen Suite* (symphonic full orchestra); Larry Nazer & Friend's *Music from "Warm" CD* (jazz with full orchestra); and Mark Gottlieb's *Violin Concerto for Orchestra.*

THE BOSTON PHILHARMONIC

295 Huntington Ave., Suite 210, Boston MA 02116. (617)236-0999. **E-mail:** info@bostonphil.org. **Website:** www.bostonphil.org. **Contact:** Benjamin Zander, music director. Symphony orchestra. Estab. 1979. Members are professionals, amateurs and students. Performs 2 concerts/year. Audience is ages 30-70. Performs at New England Conservatory's Jordan Hall, Boston's Symphony Hall and Sanders Theatre in Cambridge. Both Jordan Hall and Sanders Theatre are small (approximately 1,100 seats) and very intimate.
HOW TO CONTACT Does not accept new music at this time.
MUSIC Full orchestra only.
PERFORMANCES Dutilleuxs' *Tout un monde lointain* for cello and orchestra (symphonic); Bernstein's

Fancy Free (symphonic/jazzy); Copland's *El Salon Mexico* (symphonic); Gershwin's *Rhapsody in Blue*; Shostakovitch's *Symphony No. 10*; Harbison's *Concerto for Oboe*; Holst's *The Planet Suite*; Schwantner's *New Morning for the World*; Berg's *Seven Early Songs*; and Ive's *The Unanswered Question*.

☪ CALGARY BOYS CHOIR

4825 Mt. Royal Gate SW, Calgary AB T3E 6K6 Canada. (403)440-6821. **Fax:** (403)440-6594. **E-mail:** gm.calgaryboyschoir@gmail.com. **Website:** levendis99.wix.com/calgaryboyschoir. **Contact:** Paul Grindlay, artistic director. Boys choir. Estab. 1973. Members are amateurs age 5 and up. Performs 5-10 concerts/year including 1-2 new works. Pay negotiable.

HOW TO CONTACT Query first. Submit complete score and tape of piece(s). Include SASE. Responds in 6 weeks. Does not return material.

MUSIC "Style fitting for boys choir. Lengths depending on project. Orchestration preferable a cappella/for piano/sometimes orchestra."

☪ CANADIAN OPERA COMPANY

227 Front St. E., Toronto ON M5A 1E8 Canada. (800)250-4653. **E-mail:** info@coc.ca; music@coc.ca. **Website:** www.coc.ca. **Contact:** Alexander Neef, general director. Opera company. Estab. 1950. Members are professionals. 68-72 performances, including a minimum of 1 new work/year. Pays by contract.

HOW TO CONTACT Submit complete CDs or DVDs of vocal and/or operatic works. "Vocal works please." Include SASE. Responds in 5 weeks.

MUSIC Vocal works, operatic in nature. "Do not submit works that are not for voice. Ask for requirements for the Composers-In-Residence program."

PERFORMANCES Dean Burry's *Brothers Grimm* (children's opera, 50 minutes long); Dean Burry's *Isis and the Seven Scorpions* (45-minute opera for children); James Rolfe's *Swoon*: James Rolfe's *Donna* (work title for forthcoming work); *Nixon in China* by John Adams; *L'Amour Do Loin* by Saariaho.

TIPS "We have a Composers-In-Residence program, which is open to Canadian composers or landed immigrants."

CANTATA ACADEMY

P.O. Box 1958, Royal Oak MI 48084. (313)248-7282. **E-mail:** cantata@cantataacademy.org. **E-mail:** director@cantataacademy.org. **Website:** cantataacademy.org. **Contact:** Susan Catanese, director. Vocal ensem-

ble. Estab. 1961. Members are professionals. Performs 10-12 concerts/year including 1-3 new works. "We perform in churches and small auditoriums throughout the metro Detroit area for audiences of about 500 people." Pays variable rate for outright purchase.

HOW TO CONTACT Submit complete score. Include SASE. Responds in 3 months.

MUSIC Four-part a cappella and keyboard accompanied works, two- and three-part works for men's or women's voices. Some small instrumental ensemble accompaniments acceptable. Work must be suitable for 40-voice choir. No works requiring orchestra or large ensemble accompaniment. No pop.

PERFORMANCES Libby Larsen's *Missa Gaia: Mass for the Earth* (SATB, string quartet, oboe, percussion, four-hand piano); Dede Duson's *To Those Who See* (SATB, SSA); and Sarah Hopkins' *Past Life Melodies* (SATB with Harmonic Overtone Singing); Eric Whiteacre *Five Hebrew Love Songs*; Robert Convery's *Songs of the Children*.

TIPS "Be patient. Would prefer to look at several different samples of work at one time."

CARMEL SYMPHONY ORCHESTRA

760 3rd Ave. SW, Suite 102, Carmel IN 46032. (317)844-9717. **Fax:** (317)844-9916. **E-mail:** info@carmelsymphony.org. **Website:** www.carmelsymphony.org. **Contact:** Alan Davis, president/CEO. Symphony orchestra. Estab. 1976. Members are paid and non-paid professionals. Performs 15 concerts/year, including 1-2 new works. Performs in a 1,600-seat Palladium at the Center for the Performing Arts.

HOW TO CONTACT *Query first.* Include SASE. Responds in 3 months.

MUSIC "Full orchestra works, 5-60 minutes in length. Parents are encouraged to bring a child. 85-piece orchestra, medium difficult to difficult.

PERFORMANCES Brahms' *Concerto in D Major for Violin and Orchestra*, Op. 77; Debussy's "La Mer"; Ravel's Second Suite from "Daphnis and Chloe"; Dvorak's *Carnival Overture*, Op. 92; and Sibelius' *Symphony No. 5 in E-flat Major*, Op. 82. Outstanding guest artists include Michael Feinstein, Sylvia McNair, Cameron Carpenter, Dale Clevenger, and Angela Brown.

CHATTANOOGA GIRLS CHOIR

1831 Hickory Valley Rd., Suite 400, Chattanooga TN 37421. (423)296-1006. **E-mail:** chattanoogagirlschoir@gmail.com. **Website:** chattanoogagirlschoir.com. **Contact:** Dale Dye, executive director. Vocal ensemble. Estab. 1986. Members are amateurs. Performs 2 concerts/year including at least 1 new work. Audience consists of cultural and civic organizations and national and international tours. Performance space includes concert halls and churches. Pays for outright purchase or per performance.

HOW TO CONTACT Query first. Include SASE. Responds in 6 weeks.

MUSIC Seeks renaissance, baroque, classical, romantic, twentieth century, folk and musical theater for young voices of up to 8 minutes. Performers include 5 treble choices: 4th grade (2 pts.); 5th grade (2 pts.) (SA); grades 6-9 (3 pts.) (SSA); grades 10-12 (3-4 pts.) (SSAA); and a combined choir: grades 6-12 (3-4 pts.) (SSAA). Medium level of difficulty. "Avoid extremely high Tessitura Sop I and extremely low Tessitura Alto II."

PERFORMANCES Jan Swafford's *Iphigenia Book: Meagher* (choral drama); Penny Tullock's *How Can I Keep from Singing* (Shaker hymn).

CHEYENNE SYMPHONY ORCHESTRA

1904 Thomes Ave., Cheyenne WY 82001. (307)778-8561. **E-mail:** administrative@cheyennesymphony.org. **Website:** www.cheyennesymphony.org. **Contact:** Elizabeth McGuire, executive director. Symphony orchestra. Estab. 1955. Members are professionals. Performs 5-6 concerts/year. "Orchestra performs for a conservative, mid-to-upper-income audience of 1,200 season members."

HOW TO CONTACT Query first to music director William Intriligator. Does not return material.

CIMARRON CIRCUIT OPERA COMPANY

P.O. Box 1085, Norman OK 73070. (405)364-8962. **Fax:** (405)321-5842. **E-mail:** info@cimarronopera.org. **Website:** www.cimarronopera.org. **Contact:** Kevin W. Smith, music director. Opera company. Estab. 1975. Members are semi professional. Performs 75 concerts/year including 1-2 new works. Commissions 1 or fewer new works/year. "CCOC performs for children across the state of Oklahoma and for a dedicated audience in central Oklahoma. As a touring company, we adapt to the performance space provided, ranging from a classroom to a full-raised stage." Pay is negotiable.

HOW TO CONTACT Query first. Does not return material. Responds in 6 months.

MUSIC "We are seeking operas or operettas in English only. We would like to begin including new, American works in our repertoire. Children's operas should be no longer than 45 minutes and require no more than a synthesizer for accompaniment. Adult operas should be appropriate for families, and may require either full orchestration or synthesizer. CCOC is a professional company whose members have varying degrees of experience, so any difficulty level is appropriate. There should be a small to moderate number of principals. Children's work should have no more than 4 principals. Our slogan is 'Opera is a family thing to do.' If we cannot market a work to families, we do not want to see it."

PERFORMANCES Menotti's *Amahl & the Night Visitors*; and Barab's *La Pizza Con Funghi*.

TIPS "45-minute fairy tale-type children's operas with possibly a 'moral' work well for our market. Looking for works appealing to K-8 grade students. No more than 4 principals."

CONNECTICUT CHORAL ARTISTS/CONCORA

233 Pearl St., Hartford CT 06103. **Website:** www.concora.org. **Contact:** Ann Drinan, executive director. City Arts on Pearl, 233 Pearl St., Hartford CT 06103. (860)293-0567. **Fax:** (860)244-0073. **E-mail:** contact@concora.org. **Website:** www.concora.org. Estab. 1974. Professional concert choir. Members are professionals. Performs 5 concerts per year, including 3-5 new works.

HOW TO CONTACT Query first. "No unsolicited submissions accepted." Include SASE. Responds in 1 year.

MUSIC Seeking "works for mixed chorus of 36 singers; unaccompanied or with keyboard and/or small instrumental ensemble; text sacred or secular/any language; prefers suites or cyclical works, total time not exceeding 15 minutes. Performance spaces and budgets prohibit large instrumental ensembles. Works suited for 750-seat halls are preferable. Substantial organ or piano parts acceptable. Scores should be very legible in every way."

PERFORMANCES Don McCullough's *Holocaust Contata* (choral with narration); Robert Cohen's *Sprig of Lilac: Peter Quince at the Clavier* (choral); Greg Bartholomew's *The 21st Century: A Girl Born in Afghanistan* (choral).

TIPS "Use conventional notation and be sure ms is legible in every way. Recognize and respect the vocal range of each vocal part. Work should have an identifiable rhythmic structure."

EUROPEAN UNION CHAMBER ORCHESTRA

Hollick, Yarnscombe, Devon EX31 3LQ United Kingdom. (44)1271-858249. **Fax:** (44)1271-858375. **E-mail:** eucorch1@aol.com. **Website:** www.euco.org.uk. Chamber orchestra. Members are professionals. Performs 70 concerts/year, including 6 new works. Commissions 2 composers or new works/year. Performs regular tours of Europe, Americas and Asia, including major venues. Pays per performance or for outright purchase, depending on work.

HOW TO CONTACT Query first. Does not return material. Responds in 6 weeks.

MUSIC Seeking compositions for strings, 2 oboes and 2 horns with a duration of about 8 minutes.

PERFORMANCES Tim Watts, "Bridge of Sighs;" Jane Wells, "Two wings and a prayer."

TIPS "Keep the work to less than 15 minutes in duration, it should be sufficiently 'modern' to be interesting but not too difficult as this could take up rehearsal time. It should be possible to perform without a conductor."

FONTANA CONCERT SOCIETY

359 S. Kalamazoo Mall, Suite 200, Kalamazoo MI 49007. (269)382-7774. **Fax:** (269)382-0812. **Website:** www.fontanachamberarts.org. Chamber music ensemble presenter. Estab. 1980. Members are professionals. Fontana Chamber Arts presents over 45 events, including the 6-week Summer Festival of Music and Art, which runs from mid-July to the end of August. Regional and guest artists perform classical, contemporary, jazz and nontraditional music. Commissions and performs new works each year. Fontana Chamber Arts presents 7 classical and 2 jazz concerts during the fall/winter season. Audience consists of well-educated individuals who accept challenging new works, but like the traditional, as well. Summer—180-seat hall; fall/winter—various venues, 400-1,500 seats.

HOW TO CONTACT Submit complete score, résumé and tapes of piece(s). Include SASE. Responds in approximately 1 month.

MUSIC Chamber music—any combination of strings, winds, piano. No "pop" music, New Age type. Special interest in composers attending premiere and speaking to the audience.

TIPS "Provide a résumé and clearly marked tape of a piece played by live performers."

FORT WORTH OPERA

1300 Gendy St., Ft. Worth TX 76107. (817)731-0833. **Fax:** (817)731-0835. **E-mail:** info@fwopera.org. **Website:** www.fwopera.org. **Contact:** Darren K. Woods, general director. Opera company. Estab. 1946. Members are professionals. Performs over 180 in-school performances/year. Audience consists of elementary school children; performs in major venues for district-wide groups and individual school auditoriums, cafetoriums and gymnasiums. Pays $40/performance.

HOW TO CONTACT Submit complete score and tape of piece(s). Include SASE. Responds in 6 months.

MUSIC "Familiar fairy tales or stories adapted to music of opera composers, or newly composed music of suitable quality. Ideal length: 40-45 minutes. Piano or keyboard accompaniment. Should include moral, safety, or school issues. Can be ethnic in subject matter and must speak to pre-K and grade 1-6 children. Prefer pieces with good, memorable melodies. Performed by young, trained professionals on 9-month contract. Requires work for 4 performers, doubled roles OK, SATB plus accompanist/narrator. Special interest in bilingual (Spanish/English) works."

GREATER GRAND FORKS SYMPHONY ORCHESTRA

P.O. Box 5302, Grand Forks ND 58206. (701)732-0579. **E-mail:** ggfso@ggfso.org. **Website:** www.ggfso.org. **Contact:** Director. Symphony orchestra. Estab. 1908. Members are professionals and/or amateurs. Performs 6 concerts/year. "New works are presented in 2-4 of our programs." Audience is "a mix of ages and musical experience. In 1997-98 we moved into a renovated, 420-seat theater." Pay is negotiable, depending on licensing agreements.

HOW TO CONTACT Submit complete score or complete score and tape of pieces. Include SASE. Responds in 6 months.

MUSIC "Style is open, instrumentation the limiting factor. Music can be scored for an ensemble up to but not exceeding: 3,2,3,2/4,3,3,1/3 perc./strings. Rehearsal time limited to 3 hours for new works."

PERFORMANCES Michael Harwood's *Amusement Park Suite* (orchestra); Randall Davidson's *Mexico Bolivar Tango* (chamber orchestra); and John Corigliano's *Voyage* (flute and orchestra); Linda Tutas Haugen's *Fable of Old Turtle* (saxophone concerto); Michael Wittgraf's *Landmarks*; Joan Tower's *Made in America*.

HEARTLAND MEN'S CHORUS

P.O. Box 32374, Kansas City MO 64171 United States. **Website:** www.hmckc.org. P.O. Box 32374, Kansas City MO 64171-5374. (816)931-3338. **Fax:** (816)531-1367. **E-mail:** hmc@hmckc.org. **Website:** www.hmckc.org. **Contact:** Dustin S. Cates, artistic director. Men's chorus. Estab. 1986. Members are professionals and amateurs. Performs 3 concerts/year; 9-10 are new works. Commissions 1 composer or new work/year. Performs for a diverse audience at the Folly Theater (1,100 seats). Pay is negotiable.

HOW TO CONTACT Query first. Include SASE. Responds in 2 months.

MUSIC "Interested in works for male chorus (ttbb). Must be suitable for performance by a gay male chorus. We will consider any orchestration, or a cappella."

PERFORMANCES Mark Hayes' *Two Flutes Playing* (commissioned song cycle); Andrew Lippa's *I Am Harvey Milk* (co-commissioned oratorio); Jake Heggie's *For a Look or a Touch* (chamber opera).

HELENA SYMPHONY

P.O. Box 1073, Helena MT 59624. (406)442-1860. **E-mail:** artisticplanning@helenasymphony.org. **Website:** www.helenasymphony.org. **Contact:** Allan R. Scott, music director and conductor. Symphony orchestra. Estab. 1955. Members are professionals and amateurs. Performs 7-10 concerts/year including new works. Performance space is an 1,800-seat concert hall. Payment varies.

HOW TO CONTACT Query first. Include SASE. Responds in 3 months.

MUSIC "Imaginative, collaborative, not too atonal. We want to appeal to an audience of all ages. We don't have a huge string complement. Medium to difficult OK—at frontiers of professional ability we cannot do."

PERFORMANCES Eric Funk's *A Christmas Overture* (orchestra); Donald O. Johnston's *A Christmas Processional* (orchestra/chorale); and Elizabeth Sellers' *Prairie* (orchestra/short ballet piece).

TIPS "Try to balance tension and repose in your works. New instrument combinations are appealing."

HENDERSONVILLE SYMPHONY ORCHESTRA

P.O. Box 1811, Hendersonville NC 28793. (828)697-5884. **E-mail:** info@hendersonvillesymphony.org. **Website:** www.hendersonvillesymphony.org. Symphony orchestra. Estab. 1971. Members are professionals and amateurs. Performs 6 concerts/year. "We would welcome a new work per year." Audience is a cross-section of retirees, professionals, and some children. Performance space is a 857-seat high school auditorium.

HOW TO CONTACT Query first. Include SASE. Responds in 1 month.

MUSIC "We use a broad spectrum of music (classical concerts and pops)."

PERFORMANCES Nelson's *Jubilee* (personal expression in a traditional method); Britten's "The Courtly Dances" from Glorina (time-tested); and Chip Davis' arrangement for Mannheim Steamroller's *Deck the Halls* (modern adaptation of traditional melody).

TIPS "Submit your work even though we are a community orchestra. We like to be challenged. We have the most heavily patronized fine arts group in the county. Our emphasis is on education."

HERSHEY SYMPHONY ORCHESTRA

P.O. Box 93, Hershey PA 17033. (717)533-8449. **Website:** www.hersheysymphony.org. **Contact:** Dr. Sandra Dackow, music director. Symphony orchestra. Estab. 1969. Members are professionals and amateurs. Performs 8 concerts/year, including 1-3 new works. Commissions "possibly 1-2" composers or new works/year. Audience is family and friends of community theater. Performance space is a 1,900 seat grand old movie theater. Pays commission fee.

HOW TO CONTACT Submit complete score and tape of piece(s). Include SASE. Responds in 3 months.

MUSIC "Symphonic works of various lengths and types which can be performed by a non-professional orchestra. We are flexible but like to involve all our players."

PERFORMANCES Paul W. Whear's *Celtic Christmas Carol* (orchestra/bell choir) and Linda Robbins Coleman's *In Good King Charlie's Golden Days* (overture).

TIPS "Please lay out rehearsal numbers/letter and rests according to phrases and other logical musical divisions rather than in groups of 10 measures, etc., which is very unmusical and wastes time and causes a surprising number of problems. Also, please do not send a score written in concert pitch; use the usual transpositions so that the conductor sees what the players see; rehearsal is much more effective this way. Cross-cue all important solos; this helps in rehearsal where instruments may be missing."

INDIANA UNIVERSITY NEW MUSIC ENSEMBLE

Indiana University Bloomington, School of Music, Bloomington IN 47405. **E-mail:** ddzubay@indiana.edu. **Website:** www.indiana.edu/~nme. **Contact:** David Dzubay, director. Performs solo, chamber and large ensemble works. Estab.1974. Members are students. Presents 4 concerts/year.

PERFORMANCES Peter Lieberson's *Free and Easy Wanderer*; Sven-David Sandstrom's *Wind Pieces*; Atar Arad's *Sonata*; and David Dzubay's *Dancesing in a Green Bay*.

LEXINGTON PHILHARMONIC SOCIETY

161 N. Mill St., Lexington KY 40507. (859)233-4226. **Website:** www.lexphil.org. **Contact:** Scott Terrell, music director. Symphony orchestra. Estab. 1961. Members are professionals. Series includes "8 serious, classical subscription concerts (hall seats 1,500); 3 concerts called Pops the Series; 3 Family Concerts; 10 outdoor pops concerts (from 1,500 to 5,000 tickets sold); 5-10 run-out concerts; and 10 children's concerts." Pays via ASCAP and BMI, rental purchase and private arrangements.

HOW TO CONTACT Submit complete score and tape of piece(s). Include SASE.

MUSIC Seeking "good current pops material and good serious classical works. No specific restrictions, but overly large orchestra requirements, unusual instruments and extra rentals help limit our interest."

PERFORMANCES "Visit our website for complete concert season listing."

TIPS "When working on large-format arrangement, use cross-cues so orchestra can be cut back if required. Submit good quality copy, scores and parts. Tape is helpful."

LIMA SYMPHONY ORCHESTRA

133 N. Elizabeth St., Lima OH 45801. (419)222-5701. **Fax:** (419)222-6587. **Website:** www.limasymphony.com. **Contact:** Crafton Beck, music conductor. Symphony orchestra. Estab. 1953. Members are professionals. Performs 17-18 concerts including at least 1 new work/year. Commissions at least 1 composer or new work/year. Middle to older audience; also Young People's Series. Mixture for stage and summer productions. Performs in Veterans' Memorial Civic & Convention Center, a beautiful hall seating 1,670; various temporary shells for summer outdoors events; churches; museums and libraries. Pays $2,500

for outright purchase (anniversary commission) or grants $1,500-5,000.

HOW TO CONTACT Submit complete score if not performed; otherwise submit complete score and tape of piece(s). Include SASE. Responds in 3 months.

MUSIC "Good balance of incisive rhythm, lyricism, dynamic contrast and pacing. Chamber orchestra to full (85-member) symphony orchestra." Does not wish to see "excessive odd meter changes."

PERFORMANCES Frank Proto's *American Overture* (some original music and fantasy); Werner Tharichen's *Concerto for Timpani and Orchestra*; and James Oliverio's *Pilgrimage—Concerto for Brass* (interesting, dynamic writing for brass and the orchestra).

TIPS "Know your instruments, be willing to experiment with unconventional textures, be available for in-depth analysis with conductor, be at more than 1 rehearsal. Be sure that individual parts are correctly matching the score and done in good, neat calligraphy."

LYRIC OPERA OF CHICAGO

20 N. Wacker Dr., Chicago IL 60606. (312)332-2244. **Fax:** (312)419-8345. **Website:** www.lyricopera.org. Opera company. Estab. 1953. Members are professionals. Performs 80 operas/year including 1 new work in some years. Commissions 1 new work every 4 or 5 years. "Performances are held in a 3,563-seat house for a sophisticated opera audience, predominantly 30-plus years old." Payment varies.

HOW TO CONTACT Query first. Does not return material. Responds in 6 months.

MUSIC "Full-length opera suitable for a large house with full orchestra. No musical comedy or Broadway musical style. We rarely perform one-act operas. We are only interested in works by composers and librettists with extensive theatrical experience. We have few openings for new works, so candidates must be of the highest quality. Do not send score or other materials without a prior contact."

PERFORMANCES William Bolcom's *View from the Bridge*; John Corigliano's *Ghosts of Versailles*; and Leonard Bernstein's *Candide*.

TIPS "Have extensive credentials and an international reputation."

MILWAUKEE YOUTH SYMPHONY ORCHESTRA

325 W. Walnut St., Milwaukee WI 53212. (414)267-2950. **Fax:** (414)267-2960. **E-mail:** general@myso.org.

Website: www.myso.org. **Contact:** Linda Edelstein, executive director. Multiple youth orchestras and other instrumental ensembles. Estab. 1956. Members are students. Performs 12-15 concerts/year including 1-2 new works. "Our groups perform in Uihlein Hall at the Marcus Center for the Performing Arts in Milwaukee, plus area sites. The audiences usually consist of parents, music teachers and other interested community members, with periodic reviews in the *Milwaukee Journal Sentinel*." Payment varies.

HOW TO CONTACT Query first. Include SASE. Does not return material. Responds in 1 month.

PERFORMANCES James Woodward's *Tuba Concerto*.

TIPS "Be sure you realize you are working with *students* (albeit many of the best in southeastern Wisconsin) and not professional musicians. The music needs to be on a technical level students can handle. Our students are 8-18 years of age, in 2 full symphony orchestras, a wind ensemble and 2 string orchestras, plus 2 flute choirs, advanced chamber orchestra and 15-20 small chamber ensembles."

MOORES OPERA CENTER

Moores School of Music, University of Houston, 120 School of Music Building, Houston TX 77204. (713)743-3009. **Fax:** (713)743-3166. **E-mail:** bross@uh.edu. **Website:** www.uh.edu/music/Mooresopera. **Director of Opera:** Buck Ross. Opera/music theater program. Members are professionals, amateurs, and students. Performs 12-14 concerts/year including 1 new work. Performs in a proscenium theater, which seats 800. Pit seats approximately up to 75 players. Audience covers wide spectrum, from first-time operagoers to very sophisticated. Pays per performance.

HOW TO CONTACT Submit complete score and tapes of piece(s). Include SASE. Responds in 6 months.

MUSIC "We seek music that is feasible for high graduate-level student singers. Chamber orchestras are very useful. No more than 2 1/2 hours. No children's operas."

PERFORMANCES *The Grapes of Wrath, Florencia en el Amazonas, Elmer Gantry, A Wedding*.

OPERA MEMPHIS

6745 Wolf River Pkwy., Memphis TN 38120. (901)257-3100. **Fax:** (901)257-3109. **E-mail:** info@operamemphis.org. **Website:** www.operamemphis.org. **Contact:** Ned Canty, general director. Opera company. Estab. 1956. Members are professionals. Performs 5 main stage shows/year including new works. Occasionally commissions composers. Audience is a mixture of long-time patrons and newcomers to opera drawn in through their "30 Days of Opera" program and Midtown Opera Festival. Pay is negotiable.

HOW TO CONTACT Query first. Include SASE. Responds in 1 year or less.

MUSIC "Accessible practical pieces for educational or second-stage programs. Educational pieces should not exceed 90 minutes or 4-6 performers. We encourage songwriters to contact us with proposals or work samples for theatrical works. We are very interested in works that crossover between musical genres."

PERFORMANCES Mike Reid's *Different Fields* (one act opera); David Olney's *Light in August* (folk opera); Sid Selvidge's *Riversongs* (one-act blues opera), and *Ghosts of Crosstown* (5 short operas).

TIPS "Spend many hours thinking about the synopsis (plot outline)."

ORCHESTRA SEATTLE/SEATTLE CHAMBER SINGERS

4759 15th Ave. NE, Box 2, Seattle WA 98105. (206)682-5208. **E-mail:** osscs@osscs.org. **Website:** www.osscs.org. **Contact:** Jeremy Johnsen, managing director. Symphony orchestra, chamber music ensemble, and community chorus. Estab. 1969. Members are amateurs and professionals. Performs 8 concerts/year including 2-3 new works. Commissions 1-2 composers or new works/year. "Our audience is made up of both experienced and novice classical music patrons. The median age is 45 with an equal number of males and females in the upper income range. Most concerts now held in Benaroya Hall."

HOW TO CONTACT Query first. Include SASE. Responds in 1 year.

PERFORMANCES Beyer's *The Turns of a Girl*; Bernstein's Choruses from *The Lark*; Edstrom's Concerto for Jazz Piano and Orchestra.

PALMETTO MASTERSINGERS

P.O. Box 7441, Columbia SC 29202. (803)765-0777. **E-mail:** info@palmettomastersingers.org. **Website:** www.palmettomastersingers.org. **Contact:** Walter Cuttino, music director. Eighty-voice male chorus. Estab. 1981 by the late Dr. Arpad Darasz. Members are professionals and amateurs. Performs 8-10 concerts/year. Commissions 1 composer of new works every other year (on average). Audience is generally older adults, "but it's a wide mix." Performance space for the season series is the Koger Center (approximately 2,000 seats) in Columbia, South Carolina.

More intimate venues also available. Fee is negotiable for outright purchase.

HOW TO CONTACT Query first. Include SASE. Or e-mail to info@palmettomastersingers.org.

MUSIC Seeking music of 10-15 minutes in length, "not too far out tonally. Orchestration is negotiable, but chamber size (10-15 players) is normal. We rehearse once a week and probably will not have more than 8-10 rehearsals. These rehearsals (2 hours each) are spent learning a 1-hour program. Only 1-2 rehearsals (max) are with the orchestra. Piano accompaniments need not be simplified, as our accompanist is exceptional."

PERFORMANCES Randal Alan Bass' *Te Deum* (12-minute, brass and percussion); Dick Goodwin's *Mark Twain Remarks* (40-minute, full symphony); and Randol Alan Bass' *A Simple Prayer* (a capella 6 minute).

TIPS "Contact us as early as possible, given that programs are planned by July. Although this is an amateur chorus, we have performed concert tours of Europe, performed at Carnegie Hall, The National Cathedral and the White House in Washington, DC. We are skilled amateurs."

PRINCETON SYMPHONY ORCHESTRA

P.O. Box 250, Princeton NJ 08542. (609)497-0020. **Fax:** (609)497-0904. **E-mail:** info@princetonsymphony.org. **Website:** www.princetonsymphony.org. **Contact:** Rossen Milanov, music director. Symphony orchestra. Estab. 1980. Members are professionals. Performs 6-10 concerts/year including some new works. Commissions 1 composer or new work/year. Performs in a "beautiful, intimate 800-seat hall with amazing sound." Pays by arrangement.

MUSIC "Orchestra usually numbers 40-60 individuals."

PRISM SAXOPHONE QUARTET

257 Harvey St., Philadelphia PA 19144. (215)438-5282. **E-mail:** info@prismquartet.com. **Website:** www.prismquartet.com. **Contact:** Matthew Levy. Chamber music ensemble. Estab. 1984. Members are professionals. Performs 80 concerts/year including 10-15 new works. Commissions 4 composers or new works/year. "Ours are primarily traditional chamber music audiences." Pays royalty per performance from BMI or ASCAP or commission range from $100 to $15,000.

HOW TO CONTACT Submit complete score (with parts) and tape of piece(s). Does not return material. Responds in 3 months.

MUSIC "Orchestration—sax quartet, SATB. Lengths—5-25 minutes. Styles—contemporary, classical, jazz, crossover, ethnic, gospel, avant-garde. No limitations on level of difficulty. No more than 4 performers (SATB sax quartet). No transcriptions. The Prism Quartet places special emphasis on crossover works which integrate a variety of musical styles."

PERFORMANCES David Liebman's *The Gray Convoy* (jazz); Bradford Ellis's *Tooka-Ood Zasch* (ethnic-world music); and William Albright's *Fantasy Etudes* (contemporary classical).

SACRAMENTO MASTER SINGERS

P.O. Box 417997, Sacramento CA 95841. (916)788-7464. **E-mail:** smsbusiness@surewest.net. **Website:** www.mastersingers.org. **Contact:** Dr. Ralph Edward Hughes, conductor/artistic director. Vocal ensemble. Estab. 1984. Members are professionals and amateurs. Performs 9 concerts/year including 5-6 new works. Commissions 2 new works/year. Audience is mainly made up of college-age and older patrons. Performs mostly in churches with 500-900 seating capacity. Pays $200 for outright purchase.

HOW TO CONTACT Submit complete score and tape of piece(s). Include SASE. Responds in 5 weeks.

MUSIC "A cappella works; works with small orchestras or few instruments; works based on classical styles with a 'modern' twist; multi-cultural music; shorter works probably preferable, but this is not a requirement. We usually have 38-45 singers capable of a high level of difficulty, but find that often simple works are very pleasing."

PERFORMANCES Joe Jennings' *An Old Black Woman, Homeless and Indistinct* (SATB, oboe, strings, dramatic).

TIPS "Keep in mind we are a chamber ensemble, not a 100-voice choir."

SAN FRANCISCO GIRLS CHORUS

44 Page St., Suite 200, San Francisco CA 94102. (415)863-1752. **E-mail:** info@sfgirlschorus.org. **Website:** www.sfgirlschorus.org. **Contact:** Lisa Bielawa, artistic director. Choral ensemble. Estab. 1978. Advanced choral ensemble of young women's voices. Performs 8-10 concerts/year including 3-4 new works. Commissions 2 composers or new works/year. Concerts are performed for "choral/classical music lovers, plus family audiences and audiences interested in international repertoire. Season concerts are performed in a 800-seat church with excellent acoustics and in San Francisco's Davies Symphony Hall, a 2,800-seat state-of-the-art auditorium." Pay negotiable for outright purchase.

HOW TO CONTACT Submit complete score and CD recording, if possible. Does not return material. Responds in 6 months.

MUSIC "Music for treble voices (SSAA); a cappella, piano accompaniment, or small orchestration; 3-10 minutes in length. Wide variety of styles; 45 singers; challenging music is encouraged."

PERFORMANCES See website under "Music/Commissions" for a listing of SFGC commissions. Examples: Jake Heggie's *Patterns* (piano, mezzo-soprano soloist, chorus); and Chen Yi's *Chinese Poems* (a cappella).

TIPS "Choose excellent texts and write challenging music. The San Francisco Girls Chorus has pioneered girls' choral music as an art form in the U.S. The Girls Chorus is praised for its 'stunning musical standard' (*San Francisco Chronicle*) in performances in the San Francisco Bay Area and on tour. SFGC's annual concert season showcases the organization's concert/touring ensemble, Chorissima, in performances of choral masterworks from around the world, commissioned works by contemporary composers, and 18th-century music from the Venetian Ospedali and Mexican Baroque, which SFGC has brought out of the archives and onto the concert stage. Chorissima tours through California with partial support provided by the California Arts Council Touring Program and has represented the U.S. and the city of San Francisco nationally and abroad. The chorus provides ensemble and solo singers for performances and recordings with the San Francisco Symphony and San Francisco Opera, Women's Philharmonic, and many other music ensembles. The Chorus has produced many solo CD recordings including: Voices of Hope and Peace, a recording that includes 'Anne Frank: A Living Voice' by an American composer Linda Tutas Haugen; Christmas, featuring diverse holiday selections; Crossroads, a collection of world folk music; and Music from the Venetian Ospedali, a disc of Italian Baroque music, which *The New Yorker* described as 'tremendously accomplished.'"

SOLI DEO GLORIA CANTORUM

3402 Woolworth Ave., Omaha NE 68105. (402)341-4111. **Fax:** (402)341-9381. **E-mail:** cantorum@berkey.com. **Website:** www.berkey.com. **Contact:** Linda Gardels, music director. Professional choir. Estab. 1988. Members are professionals. Performs 5-7 concerts/year; several are new works. Commissions 1-2 new works/year. Performance space: "cathedral, symphony hall, smaller intimate recital halls, as well."

Payment is "dependent upon composition and composer."

HOW TO CONTACT Submit complete score and tape of piece(s). Include SASE. Responds in 2 months.

MUSIC "Chamber music mixed with topical programming (e.g., all Celtic or all Hispanic programs, etc.). Generally a cappella compositions from very short to extended range (6-18 minutes) or multi-movements. Concerts are of a formal length (approximately 75 minutes) with 5 rehearsals. Difficulty must be balanced within program in order to adequately prepare in a limited rehearsal time. 28 singers. Not seeking orchestral pieces, due to limited budget."

PERFORMANCES Jackson Berkey's *Native Am Ambience* (eclectic/classical); John Rutter's *Hymn to the Creator of Light* (classical); and Arvo Part's *Te Deum* (multi-choir/chant-based classical).

ST. LOUIS CHAMBER CHORUS

P.O. Box 11558, Clayton MO 63105. **Website:** www.chamberchorus.org. **Contact:** Philip Barnes, artistic director. Vocal ensemble, chamber music ensemble. Estab. 1956. Members are professionals and amateurs. Performs 6 concerts/year including 5-10 new works. Commissions 3-4 new works/year. Audience is "diverse and interested in unaccompanied choral work and outstanding architectural/acoustic venues." Performances take place at various auditoria noted for their excellent acoustics—churches, synagogues, schools, and university halls. Pays by arrangement.

HOW TO CONTACT Query first. Does not return material. "Panel of 'readers' submit report to artistic director. Responds in 3 months. 'General Advice' leaflet available on request."

MUSIC *"Only a cappella writing!* No contemporary 'popular' works; historical editions welcomed. No improvisatory works. Our programs are tailored for specific acoustics—composers should indicate their preference."

PERFORMANCES Sir Richard Rodney Bennett's *A Contemplation Upon Flowers* (a cappella madrigal); Ned Rorem's *Ode to Man* (a cappella chorus for mixed voices); and Sasha Johnson Manning's *Requiem* (a cappella oratorio).

TIPS "We only consider a cappella works that can be produced in 5 rehearsals. Therefore, pieces of great complexity or duration are discouraged. Our seasons are planned 2-3 years ahead, so much lead time is required for programming a new work. We will accept handwritten mss, but we prefer typeset music."

SUSQUEHANNA SYMPHONY ORCHESTRA

P.O. Box 963, Abingdon MD 21009. **Fax:** (410)306-6069. **E-mail:** sheldon.bair@ssorchestra.org. **Website:** www.ssorchestra.org. **Contact:** Sheldon Bair, founder/music director. Symphony orchestra. Estab. 1978. Members are amateurs. Performs 6 concerts/year including 1-2 new works. Composers paid depending on the circumstances. "We perform in 1 hall, 600 seats with fine acoustics. Our audience encompasses all ages."

HOW TO CONTACT Query first. Include SASE. Responds in 3 or more months.

MUSIC "We desire works for large orchestra, any length, in a 'conservative 20th and 21st century' style. Seek fine music for large orchestra. We are a community orchestra, so the music must be within our grasp. Violin I to 7th position by step only; Violin II—stay within 5th position; English horn and harp are OK. Full orchestra pieces preferred."

PERFORMANCES Jazz Violin Concerto, by Scott Routenberg; Holiday music, by Toddy Hayden; plus, music by Russell Peck and Neil Anderson-Himmelspach.

☺ TORONTO MENDELSSOHN CHOIR

720 Bathurst St., Suite 404, Toronto ON M5S 2R4 Canada. (416)598-0422. **Fax:** (416)598-2992. **E-mail:** manager@tmchoir.org. **Website:** www.tmchoir.org. **Contact:** Cynthia Hawkins, executive director. Vocal ensemble. Members are professionals and amateurs. Performs 25 concerts/year including 1-3 new works. "Most performances take place in Roy Thomson Hall. The audience is reasonably sophisticated, musically knowledgeable but with moderately conservative tastes." Pays by commission and ASCAP/SOCAN.

HOW TO CONTACT Query first or submit complete score and tapes of pieces. Include SASE. Responds in 6 months.

MUSIC All works must suit a large choir (180 voices) and standard orchestral forces or with some other not-too-exotic accompaniment. Length should be restricted to no longer than 1/2 of a nocturnal concert. The choir sings at a very professional level and can sight-read almost anything. "Works should fit naturally with the repertoire of a large choir which performs the standard choral orchestral repertoire."

PERFORMANCES Holman's *Jezebel*; Orff's *Catulli Carmina*; and Lambert's *Rio Grande*.

☺ VANCOUVER CHAMBER CHOIR

1254 W. 7th Ave., Vancouver BC V6H 1B6 Canada. **E-mail:** info@vancouverchamberchoir.com. **Website:** www.vancouverchamberchoir.com. **Contact:** Jon Washburn, artistic director. Vocal ensemble. Members are professionals. Performs 40 concerts/year including 5-8 new works. Commissions 2-4 composers or new works/year. Pays SOCAN royalty or negotiated fee for commissions.

HOW TO CONTACT Submit complete score and CD of piece(s). Does not return material. Responds in 6 months if possible.

MUSIC Seeks "choral works of all types for small chorus, with or without accompaniment and/or soloists. Concert music only. Choir made up of 20 singers. Large or unusual instrumental accompaniments are less likely to be appropriate. No pop music."

PERFORMANCES The VCC has commissioned and premiered over 200 new works by Canadian and international composers, including Alice Parker's *That Sturdy Vine* (cantata for chorus, soloists and orchestra); R. Murray Schafer's *Magic Songs* (SATB a cappella); and Jon Washburn's *A Stephen Foster Medley* (SSAATTBB/piano).

TIPS "We are looking for choral music that is performable yet innovative, and which has the potential to become 'standard repertoire.' Although we perform much new music, only a small portion of the many scores submitted can be utilized."

VIRGINIA OPERA

P.O. Box 2580, Norfolk VA 23501. (757)627-9545. **Website:** www.vaopera.org. **Contact:** Alexandra Stacey, artistic coordinator. Opera company. Estab. 1974. Members are professionals. Performs more than 560 concerts/year. Commissions vary on number of composers or new works/year. Concerts are performed for school children throughout Virginia, grades K-5, 6-8, and 9-12 at the Harrison Opera House in Norfolk and at the Carpenter Theatre in Richmond. Pays on commission.

HOW TO CONTACT Query first. Include SASE. Response time varies.

MUSIC "Audience-accessible style approximately 45 minutes in length. Limit cast list to 3 vocal artists of any combination. Accompanied by piano and/or keyboard. Works are performed before school children of all ages. Pieces must be age-appropriate both aurally and dramatically. Musical styles are encouraged to be diverse, contemporary, as well as traditional. Works are produced and presented with sets, costumes, etc." Limitations: "Three vocal performers (any combination). One keyboardist. Medium to difficult acceptable, but prefer easy to medium. Seeking only pieces which are suitable for presentation as part of an opera education program for Virginia Opera's education and outreach department. Subject matter must meet strict guidelines relative to Learning Objectives, etc. Musical idiom must be representative of current trends in opera, musical theater. Extreme dissonance, row systems not applicable to this environment."

PERFORMANCES Seymour Barab's *Cinderella*; John David Earnest's *The Legend of Sleepy Hollow*; and Seymour Barab's *The Pied Piper of Hamelin*.

TIPS "Theatricality is very important. New works should stimulate interest in musical theater as a legitimate art form for school children with no prior exposure to live theatrical entertainment. Composer should be willing to create a product which will find success within the educational system."

WHEATON SYMPHONY ORCHESTRA

344 Spring Ave., Glen Ellyn IL 60137. (630)790-1430. **Fax:** (630)790-9703. **E-mail:** info@wheatonsymphony. org. **Website:** www.wheatonsymphony.org. **Contact:** Don Mattison, manager. Symphony orchestra. Estab. 1959. Members are professionals and amateurs. Performs 4 concerts/year in the summer. "No pay for performance but can probably record your piece."

HOW TO CONTACT Send a score and CD. Responds in 1 month.

MUSIC "This is a good amateur orchestra that wants pieces to be performed in the mode of John Williams or Samuel Barber, Corliango, etc. Large-scale works for orchestra only. No avant garde, 12-tone or atonal material. Pieces should be 20 minutes or less and must be prepared in 3 rehearsals. Instrumentation needed for woodwinds in 3s, full brass 4-3-3-1, 4 percussion and strings—full instrumentation only. Selections for full orchestra only. No pay for reading your piece, but we will record it at our expense. We will rehearse and give a world premiere of your piece if it is in the stated orchestration, probably with keyboard added."

PERFORMANCES Richard Williams's *Symphony in G Minor* (four-movement symphony); Dennis Johnson's *Must Jesus Bear the Cross Alone, Azon* (traditional); and Michael Diemer's *Skating* (traditional style).

TIPS "We want pops-type music only."

CONTESTS & AWARDS

Participating in contests is a great way to gain exposure for your music. Prizes vary from contest to contest, from cash to musical merchandise to studio time, and even publishing and recording deals. For musical theater and classical composers, the prize may be a performance of your work. Even if you don't win, valuable contacts can be made through contests. Many times, music publishers and other industry professionals judge contests, so your music may find its way into the hands of key industry people who can help further your career. Check the websites for any organizations or publishers hosting competitions—they'll often list the judges for the current competition.

And because your work could find its way into the hands of an industry professional, remember to always put your best work forward in any contest. Think of it as a tryout, because even if you don't win overall, there are plenty of success stories out there where a professional discovered someone through a competition that they were judging.

HOW TO SELECT A CONTEST

It's important to remember when entering any contest to do proper research before signing anything or sending any money. We have confidence in the contests listed in *Songwriter's Market*, but it pays to read the fine print. Contests can change from year to year, with different guidelines, judges, and even prizes. You'll want to make sure that you have all the available information before submitting. An incorrect submission, in terms of format or genre, will probably just leave you disqualified, no matter how good your work. It's especially important to double check the information if you've picked up this copy of *Songwriter's Market* some time after it was first released.

First, be sure you understand the contest rules and stipulations once you receive the entry forms and guidelines.

Then you need to weigh what you will gain against what they're asking you to give up. If a publishing or recording contract is the only prize a contest is offering, you may want to think twice before entering. Basically, the company sponsoring the contest is asking you to pay a fee for them to listen to your song under the guise of a contest, something a legitimate publisher or record company would not do. For those contests offering studio time, musical equipment or cash prizes, you need to decide if the entry fee you're paying is worth the chance to win such prizes.

Be wary of exorbitant entry fees, and if you have any doubts whatsoever as to the legitimacy of a contest, it's best to stay away. Songwriters need to approach a contest, award, or grant in the same manner as they would a record or publishing company. Make your submission as professional as possible; follow directions and submit material exactly as stated on the entry form.

Contests in this section encompass all types of music and levels of competition. Read each listing carefully and contact them if the contest interests you. Many contests now have websites that offer additional information and even entry forms you can print. Be sure to read the rules carefully and be sure you understand exactly what a contest is offering before entering.

AGO/ECS PUBLISHING AWARD IN CHORAL COMPOSITION

American Guild of Organists, 475 Riverside Dr., Suite 1260, New York NY 10115. (212)870-2310. **Fax:** (212)870-2163. **E-mail:** info@agohq.org; christian.lane@mac.com. **Website:** www.agohq.org/new-music-competitions-commissions/. **Contact:** Christian Lane, councilor for competitions. Biannual award.

REQUIREMENTS Composers are invited to submit a work for SATB choir and organ in which the organ plays a significant and independent role. Work submitted must be unpublished and usually no longer than 8 minutes in length. There is no age restriction. The deadline for the 2016 contest was in July 2014. Application information on the website; visit often to see when the next contest will open.

AWARDS Prize: $2,000 cash, publication by ECS Publishing, and premiere performance at the AGO National Convention. Further details are published in *The American Organist*.

AGO/MARILYN MASON AWARD IN ORGAN COMPOSITION

American Guild of Organists, 475 Riverside Dr., Suite 1260, New York NY 10115. (212)870-2310. **Fax:** (212)870-2163. **E-mail:** info@agohq.org; christian.lane@mac.com. **Website:** www.agohq.org. **Contact:** Christian Lane, councilor for competitions. For composers and performing artists. Biennial award.

REQUIREMENTS Organ solo.

AMERICAN SONGWRITER LYRIC CONTEST

113 19th Ave. S., Nashville TN 37203. (615)321 6096. **Fax:** (615)321-6097. **E-mail:** info@americansongwriter.com. **Website:** www.americansongwriter.com/lyric-contest/. For songwriters and composers. Award for each bimonthly issue of *American Songwriter* magazine, plus grand prize winner at year-end.

PURPOSE To promote and encourage the craft of lyric writing.

REQUIREMENTS Contest is open to any amateur songwriter. *AS* defines an amateur as one who has not earned more than $5,000 from songwriting related to royalties, advances, or works for hire. Lyrics must be typed and a check per entry must be enclosed. See website for exact dates.

AWARDS Grand Prize: The annual winner, chosen from the 6 contest winners, will receive round trip airfare to Nashville and a dream co-writing session.

TIPS "You do not have to be a subscriber to enter or win. You may submit as many entries as you like. All genres of music accepted."

ANNUAL NSAI SONG CONTEST

1710 Roy Acuff Place, Nashville TN 37203. (615)256-3354. **Fax:** (615)256-0034. **E-mail:** reception@nashvillesongwriters.com. **Website:** www.nashvillesongwriters.com.

PURPOSE "A chance for aspiring songwriters to be heard by music industry decision makers."

REQUIREMENTS In order to be eligible, contestants must not be receiving income from any work submitted—original material only. Mail-in submissions must be in CD form and include entry form, lyrics and melody. Online submissions available. Visit website for complete list of rules and regulations. Deadline is different each year; check website or send for application. Samples are required with application in the format of cassette or CD.

AWARDS Visit website for complete list of rules and prizes.

ARTISTS' FELLOWSHIPS

New York Foundation for the Arts, 20 Jay St., 7th Floor, Brooklyn NY 11201. (212)366-6900. **Fax:** (212)366-1778. **E-mail:** fellowships@nyfa.org. **Website:** www.nyfa.org. For songwriters, composers, and musical playwrights. Annual award, but each category is not funded annually. Check the website to see if songwriting/music is coming up.

PURPOSE Artists' Fellowships are $7,000 grants awarded by the New York Foundation for the Arts to individual originating artists living in the state of New York. The Foundation is committed to supporting artists from all over New York at all stages of their professional careers. Fellows may use the grant according to their own needs; it should not be confused with project support.

REQUIREMENTS Must be 18 years of age or older; resident of state of New York for 2 years prior to application; and cannot be enrolled in any graduate or undergraduate degree program.

AWARDS All Artists' Fellowships awards are for $7,000. Fellowships are awarded on the basis of the quality of work submitted. Applications are reviewed by a panel of 5 composers representing the aesthetic, ethnic, sexual and geographic diversity within the state of New York. The panelists change each year and review all allowable material submitted.

TIPS "Please note that musical playwrights may submit only if they write the music for their plays; librettists must submit in our playwriting category."

ARTIST TRUST FELLOWSHIP AWARD

1835 12th Ave., Seattle WA 98122. (209)467-8734, ext. 11. **Fax:** (866)218-7878. **E-mail:** info@artisttrust.org. **Website:** www.artisttrust.org. **Contact:** Miguel Guillen, program manager. Fellowships award $7,500 to practicing professional artists of exceptional talent and demonstrated ability. The Fellowship is a merit-based, not a project-based, award. Recipients present a Meet the Artist Event to a community in the state of Washington that has little or no access to the artist and their work. Awards 14 fellowships of $7,500 and 2 residencies with $1,000 stipends at the Millay Colony.

THE ASCAP DEEMS TAYLOR AWARDS

American Society of Composers, Authors & Publishers, One Lincoln Plaza, New York NY 10023. (212)621-6318. **E-mail:** jsteinblatt@ascap.com. **Website:** www.ascap.com/music-career/support/deems-taylor-guidelines.aspx. **Contact:** Jim Steinblatt. The ASCAP Deems Taylor Awards program recognizes books, articles, broadcasts, and websites on the subject of music selected for their excellence.

PURPOSE Honors the memory of composer/critic/commentator Deems Taylor.

TIPS "The website will answer all questions. Please call (212)621-6318 with any additional questions."

THE BLANK THEATRE COMPANY YOUNG PLAYWRIGHTS FESTIVAL

P.O. Box 38756, Hollywood CA 90038. (323)662-7734. **Fax:** (323)661-3903. **E-mail:** info@theblank.com. **E-mail:** submissions@youngplaywrights.com. **Website:** ypf.theblank.com. For both musical and non-musical playwrights. Annual award.

PURPOSE Purpose is to give young playwrights an opportunity to learn more about playwriting and to give them a chance to have their work mentored, developed, and presented by professional artists.

REQUIREMENTS Playwrights must be 19 years or younger at time of submission. Send legible, original plays of any length and on any subject (co-written plays are acceptable provided all co-writers meet eligibility requirements). Submissions must be postmarked by March 15 and must include a cover sheet with the playwright's name, date of birth, school (if any), home address, home phone number, e-mail address and production history. Pages must be numbered and submitted unbound (unstapled). For musicals, a tape or CD of a selection from the score should be submitted with the script. Mss will not be returned; do not send originals. Semi-finalists and winners will be contacted in May.

AWARDS Winning playwrights receive a workshop presentation of their work.

CRS COMPETITION FOR COMPOSERS' RECORDINGS

724 Winchester Rd., Broomall PA 19008. (610)205-9897. **Fax:** (707)549-5920. **E-mail:** crsnews@verizon.net. **Website:** www.crsnews.org. For songwriters, composers, and performing artists. College faculty and gifted artists. Each annual competition is limited to the first 300 applicants—all fees beyond this limit will be returned.

REQUIREMENTS "Each category requires a separate application fee. The work submitted must be non-published (prior to acceptance) and not commercially recorded on any label. The work submitted must not exceed 9 performers. Each composer/performer may submit 1 work for each application submitted. (Taped performances by composers are additionally encouraged.) Composition must not exceed 16 minutes in length. CRS reserves the right not to accept a first-prize winner. Write with SASE for application or visit website. Add $5 for postage and handling. Must send a detailed résumé with application form available on our web page under 'Events' category. Samples of work required with application. Send score and parts with optional CD or DAT. Application fee: $50."

AWARDS First prize will consist of a commercially distributed new compact disc recording grant featuring 1 composition along with other distinguished composers and performing artists. Second and third prizes will be awarded honorable mention toward future recordings with CRS and honorary life membership to the society. Applications are judged by a panel determined each year.

DELTA OMICRON INTERNATIONAL COMPOSITION COMPETITION

418 West Main St., Georgetown KY 40324. (865)471-6155. **Fax:** (865)475-9716. **E-mail:** ninabdurr@bellsouth.net. **Website:** www.delta-omicron.org/?q=node/131. **Contact:** Nina Belle Durr, chair, Composition Competition. The 2015 award is for solo piano.

PURPOSE "To encourage composers worldwide to continually add to our wonderful heritage of musical creativity instrumentally and/or vocally."

REQUIREMENTS People who are college-aged or older (or someone younger who is enrolled in college). Work must be unpublished and unperformed in public. "View our website for specific submission guidelines such as instrument selection and deadline. Click on 'Composition Competition' on homepage." Mss should be legibly written in ink or processed, signed with *nom de plume*, and free from any marks that would identify the composer to the judges. Entry fee: $25 per composition. Send for application. Composition is required with application.

AWARDS Prize: 1st Place: $1,000 and world premiere at Delta Omicron Triennial Conference. Judged by 2-3 judges (performers, conductors, and/or composers).

EUROPEAN INTERNATIONAL COMPETITION FOR COMPOSERS/IBLA FOUNDATION

568 Grand St., Suite 2001, New York NY 10002. (212)387-0111. **E-mail:** iblanewyork@gmail.com. **Website:** www.ibla.org/comp.composer.eng.php4. **Contact:** Dr. Salvatore Moltisanti, president. For songwriters and composers. Annual award.

PURPOSE "To promote the winner's career through exposure, publicity, recordings with Athena Records, and nationwide distribution with the Empire Group."

REQUIREMENTS Music score and/or recording of 1 work are required with application. Application fee is refunded if not admitted into the program.

AWARDS Winners are presented in concerts in Europe, Japan, U.S.

GRASSY HILL KERRVILLE NEW FOLK COMPETITION

P.O. Box 291466, Kerrville TX 78029. (830)257-3600. **Fax:** (830)257-8680. **E-mail:** info@kerrville-music.com. **Website:** kerrville-music.com/newfolk.htm. For songwriters. Annual award.

PURPOSE "To provide an opportunity for emerging songwriters to be heard and rewarded for excellence."

AWARDS Thirty-two finalists invited to sing the 2 songs entered during The Kerrville Folk Festival in May. Six writers are chosen as award winners. Initial round of entries judged by the festival producer and a panel of online listeners from the music industry. Thirty-two finalists judged by panel of 3 performer/songwriters.

TIPS "Do not allow instrumental accompaniment to drown out lyric content. Don't enter without complete copy of the rules. Former winners and finalists include Lyle Lovett, Nanci Griffith, Hal Ketchum, John Gorka, David Wilcox, Lucinda Williams and Robert Earl Keen, Tish Hinojosa, Carrie Newcomer, and Jimmy Lafave."

GREAT AMERICAN SONG CONTEST

PMB 135, 6327-C SW Capitol Hill Hwy., Portland OR 97239-1937. **E-mail:** info@greatamericansong.com. **Website:** www.greatamericansong.com. For songwriters, composers and lyricists. Annual award.

Also see the listing for Songwriters Resource Network in the Organizations section of this book.

PURPOSE To help songwriters get their songs heard by music-industry professionals; to generate educational and networking opportunities for participating songwriters; to help songwriters open doors in the music business.

AWARDS Winners receive a mix of cash awards and prizes. The focus of the contest is on networking and educational opportunities. (All participants receive detailed evaluations of their songs by industry professionals.) Songs are judged by knowledgeable music-industry professionals, including prominent hit songwriters, producers and publishers.

TIPS "Focus should be on the song. The quality of the demo isn't important. Judges will be looking for good songwriting talent. They will base their evaluations on the song—not the quality of the recording or the voice performance."

IAMA (INTERNATIONAL ACOUSTIC MUSIC AWARDS)

2881 E. Oakland Park Blvd., Suite 414, Fort Lauderdale FL 33306. **E-mail:** info@inacoustic.com. **Website:** www.inacoustic.com. For singer-songwriters, musicians, performing musicians in the acoustic genre.

PURPOSE "The purpose is to promote the excellence in acoustic music performance and songwriting." Genres include: folk, alternative, bluegrass, etc.

REQUIREMENTS Visit website for entry form and details. "All songs submitted must be original. There must be at least an acoustic instrument (voice) in any song. Electric and electronic instruments, along with loops, is allowed, but acoustic instruments (or voice) must be clearly heard in all songs submitted. Contestants may enter as many songs in as many categories as desired but each entry requires a separate CD, entry form, lyric sheet, and entry fee. CDs and lyrics will not be returned. Winners will be chosen by a Blue Ribbon judging committee composed of music industry professionals including A&R managers from record labels, publishers and producers. Entries are judged equally on music performance, production, originality, lyrics, melody and composition. Songs may be in any language. Winners will be notified by e-mail and must sign and return an affidavit confirming that winner's song is original and he/she holds rights to the song.

TIPS "Judging is based on music performance, music production, songwriting, and originality/artistry."

KATE NEAL KINLEY MEMORIAL FELLOWSHIP

University of Illinois, College of Fine and Applied Arts, 100 Architecture Bldg., 608 E. Lorado Taft Dr., Champaign IL 61820. (217)333-1661. **E-mail:** faa@illinois.edu. **Website:** faa.illinois.edu/kate_neal_kinley_memorial_fellowship. For students of architecture, art or music. Annual award.

PURPOSE For the advancement of study in the fine arts.

REQUIREMENTS "The fellowship will be awarded upon the basis of unusual promise in the fine arts. Open to college graduates whose principal or major studies have been in the fields of architecture, art or music." Deadline: December 6. Call or visit website for application. Samples of work are required with application.

AWARDS "One major fellowship yielding the sum of $20,000 to be used by the recipient toward defraying the expenses of advanced study of the fine arts in America or abroad." Two or 3 smaller fellowships may also be awarded upon committee recommendations. Good for 1 year. Grant is nonrenewable.

THE JOHN LENNON SONGWRITING CONTEST

180 Brighton Rd., Suite 801, Clifton NJ 07012. (888)884-5572. **E-mail:** info@jlsc.com; tiana@jlsc.com. **Website:** www.jlsc.com. **Contact:** Tiana Lewis, assistant director.

PURPOSE "The purpose of the John Lennon Songwriting Contest is to promote the art of songwriting by assisting in the discovery of new talent, as well as providing more established songwriters with an opportunity to advance their careers."

REQUIREMENTS "Each entry must consist of the following: completed and signed application; audio cassette, CD or MP3 containing 1 song only, 5 minutes or less in length; lyric sheet typed or printed legibly (English translation is required when applicable); $30 entry fee per song. Applications can be found in various music-oriented magazines, as well as on our website. Prospective entrants also can send for an application by e-mailing Tiana Lewis at tiana@jlsc.com."

AWARDS Entries are accepted in the following 12 categories: rock, country, jazz, pop, world, gospel/inspirational, R&B, hip-hop, Latin, electronic, folk and children's music. Winners will receive EMI Publishing Contracts, studio equipment from Brian Moore Guitars, Roland, Edirol and Audio Technica, 1,000 CDs in full color with premium 6-panel Digipaks courtesy of Discmakers, and gift certificates from Musiciansfriend.com. One entrant will be chosen to tour and perform for 1 week on the Warped Tour. One Lennon Award-winning song will be named "Song of the Year" and take home an additional $20,000 in cash.

MID-ATLANTIC SONG CONTEST

Songwriters Association of Washington, 4200 Wisconsin Ave., NW, PMB 106-137, Washington DC 20016. **E-mail:** contact@saw.org. **Website:** masc.saw.org. For songwriters and composers. Annual award.

PURPOSE "This is one of the longest-running contests in the nation; SAW has organized 27 contests since 1982. The competition is designed to afford rising songwriters (in a wide variety of genres) the opportunity to receive awards and exposure in an environment of peer competition."

REQUIREMENTS Amateur status is important. Applicants should request a brochure/application using the contact information above. Rules and procedures are clearly explained in the brochure and also online. CD and 3 copies of the lyrics are to be submitted with an application form and fee for each entry, or submit MP3 entries by applying online or through Sonicbids. Reduced entry fees are offered to members of Songwriters' Association of Washington; membership can be arranged simultaneously with entering. Multiple song discounts are also offered.

TIPS "Enter the song in the most appropriate category. Make the sound recording the best it can be (even though judges are asked to focus on melody and lyric and not on production.) Avoid clichés, extended introductions, and long instrumental solos."

THELONIOUS MONK INTERNATIONAL JAZZ COMPETITION

5225 Wisconsin Ave. NW, Suite 605, Washington DC 20015. (202)364-7272. **Fax:** (202)364-0176. **E-mail:** info@monkinstitute.org. **Website:** www.monkinstitute.org. For songwriters and composers. Check the website for current and up-to-date details on the most recent contest.

PURPOSE "This is the world's most prestigious jazz competition, recognized for discovering the next generation of jazz masters." The competition focuses on a different instrument each year and features an all-star judging panel.

REQUIREMENTS Deadline: See website. Send for application. Submission must include application form, résumé of musical experience, CD or MP3, entry, 4 copies of the full score, and a photo. The composition features a different instrument each year.

NACUSA YOUNG COMPOSERS' COMPETITION

Box 49256 Barrington Station, Los Angeles CA 90049. (541)765-2406. **E-mail:** nacusa@music-usa.org; membership@mail.music-usa.org. **Website:** www.music-usa.org/nacusa/contest.html.

PURPOSE Encourages the composition of new American concert hall music.

PULITZER PRIZE IN MUSIC

Columbia University, 709 Pulitzer Hall, 2950 Broadway, New York NY 10027. (212)854-3841. **Fax:** (212)854-3342. **E-mail:** pulitzer@pulitzer.org. **Website:** www.pulitzer.org; www.pulitzer.org/bycat/Music. For composers and musical playwrights. Annual award.

REQUIREMENTS "For distinguished musical composition by an American who has had his first performance or recording in the U.S. during the year." Entries should reflect current creative activity. Works that receive their American premiere between January 1 and December 31 of the contest year are eligible. A public performance or the public release of a recording shall constitute a premiere. Deadline: December 31. Samples of work are required with application, biography and photograph of composer, date and place of performance, score or ms and recording of the work, entry form, and $50 entry fee.

AWARDS Prize: $10,000. Applications are judged first by a nominating jury, then by the Pulitzer Prize board.

RICHARD RODGERS AWARDS FOR MUSICAL THEATER

American Academy of Arts and Letters, 633 W. 155 St., New York NY 10032. (212)368-5900. **Fax:** (212)491-4615. **E-mail:** academy@artsandletters.org. **Website:** www.artsandletters.org/awards2_rodgers.php. **Contact:** Jane Bolster, coordinator. "The Richard Rodgers Awards subsidize staged reading, studio productions, and full productions by nonprofit theaters in New York of works by composers and writers who are not already established in the field of musical theater. The awards are only for musicals—songs by themselves are not eligible. The authors must be citizens or permanent residents of the U.S."

ROCKY MOUNTAIN FOLKS FESTIVAL SONGWRITER SHOWCASE

Folks Showcase Contest, P.O. Box 769, Lyons CO 80540. (800)624-2422; (303)823-0848. **Fax:** (303)823-0849. **E-mail:** planet@bluegrass.com. **Website:** www.bluegrass.com. For songwriters, composers, and performers. Annual award.

PURPOSE Award based on having the best song and performance.

REQUIREMENTS Rules available on website. Samples of work are required with application. Send CD with $10/song entry fee. Can now submit online at www.sonicbids.com. "Contestants cannot be signed to a major label or publishing deal. No backup musicians allowed."

ROME PRIZE COMPETITION FELLOWSHIP

American Academy in Rome, 7 E. 60th St., New York NY 10022-1001. (212)751-7200. **Fax:** (212)751-7220. **E-mail:** info@aarome.org. **Website:** www.aarome.org. For composers. Annual award.

PURPOSE "Through its annual Rome Prize competition, the academy awards up to 30 fellowships in 11 disciplines, including musical composition. Winners of the Rome Prize pursue independent projects while residing at the Academy's 11-acre center in Rome."

REQUIREMENTS "Applicants for 11-month fellowships must be U.S. citizens and hold a bachelor's degree in music, musical composition, or its equivalent." Deadline: November 1. Entry fee: $60. Application guidelines are available through the Academy's website.

AWARDS "Up to 2 fellowships are awarded annually in musical composition. Fellowship consists of room, board, and a studio at the Academy facilities in Rome, as well as a stipend. In all cases, excellence is the primary criterion for selection, based on the quality of the materials submitted. Winners are announced in mid-April and fellowships generally begin in early September."

TELLURIDE TROUBADOUR CONTEST

ATTN: Troubadour Competition, P.O. Box 769, Lyons CO 80540. (303)823-0848; (800)624-2422. **Fax:** (303)823-0849. **E-mail:** planet@bluegrass.com. **Website:** www.bluegrass.com/telluride/contests. html. The Telluride Troubadour Competition is a nationally recognized songwriter competition open to anyone who writes and performs original music and who is not currently signed to a major recording or publishing deal. Contestants are judged on the quality of the song's composition, vocal delivery, and the overall performance. Finalists are awarded cash and prizes, as well as critical acclaim, well-deserved recognition, and a chance to perform on the festival main stage.

USA SONGWRITING COMPETITION

2881 E. Oakland Park Blvd., Suite 414, Ft. Lauderdale FL 33306. (954)537-3127. **Fax:** (954)537-9690. **E-mail:** info@songwriting.net. **Website:** www.songwriting.net. **Contact:** Contest Manager. For songwriters, composers, performing artists, and lyricists. Annual award.

PURPOSE "To honor good songwriters/composers all over the world, especially the unknown ones."

REQUIREMENTS Open to professional and beginner songwriters. No limit on entries. Each entry must include an entry fee, a CD, MP3, or audio cassette tape of song(s) and lyric sheet(s). Judged by music industry representatives. Past judges have included record label representatives and publishers from Arista Records, EMI and Warner/Chappell. Deadline: See website. Entry fee: $35 per song. See website or e-mail for entry forms at any time. Samples of work are not required. Deadline: May 29.

AWARDS Prizes include cash and merchandise in 15 different categories: pop, rock, country, Latin, R&B, gospel, folk, jazz, "lyrics only" category, instrumental, and many others.

TIPS "Judging is based on lyrics, originality, melody, and overall composition. CD-quality production is great but not a consideration in judging."

U.S.-JAPAN CREATIVE ARTISTS EXCHANGE FELLOWSHIP PROGRAM

Japan-U.S. Friendship Commission, 1201 15th St. NW, Suite 330, Washington DC 20005. (202)418-9800. **Fax:** (202)418-9802. **E-mail:** jusfc@jusfc.gov; pcottinghamstreater@jusfc.gov. **Website:** www.jusfc. gov/faqs/creative-artists-programs/. For all creative artists. Annual award.

PURPOSE "For artists to go as seekers, as cultural visionaries, and as living liaisons to the traditional and contemporary life of Japan."

REQUIREMENTS "Artists' works must exemplify the best in U.S. arts." Deadline: See website. Send for application and guidelines. Applications available on website. Samples of work are required with application. Requires 2 pieces on CD or DVD. The 2016 deadline was February 2, 2015.

AWARDS Five artists are awarded a 3-month residency anywhere in Japan. Awards monthly stipend for living expenses, housing, and professional support services; up to $2,000 for round-trip transportation will be provided for the artist.

TIPS "Applicants should anticipate a highly rigorous review of their artistry and should have compelling reasons for wanting to work in Japan."

WESTERN WRITERS OF AMERICA

271CR 219, Encampment WY 82325. (307)329-8942. **Fax:** (307)327-5465 (call first). **E-mail:** wwa. moulton@gmail.com. **Website:** www.westernwriters.org. **Contact:** Candy Moulton, executive director. 17 Spur Award categories in various aspects of the American West.

PURPOSE The nonprofit Western Writers of America has promoted and honored the best in Western literature with the annual Spur Awards, selected by panels of judges. Awards, for material published last year, are given for works whose inspirations, image and literary excellence best represent the reality and spirit of the American West.

Y.E.S. FESTIVAL OF NEW PLAYS

Northern Kentucky University, Department of Theatre and Dance, Nunn Dr., Highland Heights KY 41099-1007. (859)572-6303. **Fax:** (859)572-6057. **E-mail:** forman@nku.edu. **Contact:** Sandra Forman, project director. For musical playwrights. Biennial award (odd numbered years).

PURPOSE "The festival seeks to encourage new playwrights and develop new plays and musicals. Three plays or musicals are given full productions."

REQUIREMENTS "No entry fee. Submit a script with a completed entry form. Musicals should be submitted with a piano/conductor's score and/or a vocal parts score. Scripts may be submitted May 1 through September 30, for the New Play Festival occurring in April of the following year. Send SASE for application."

AWARDS Three awards of $500. "The winners are brought to NKU at our expense to view late rehearsals and opening night." Submissions are judged by a panel of readers.

TIPS "Plays/musicals which have heavy demands for mature actors are not as likely to be selected as an equally good script with roles for 18-30 year olds."

ORGANIZATIONS

One of the first places a beginning songwriter should look for guidance and support is a songwriting organization. Offering encouragement, instruction, contacts, and feedback, these groups of professional and amateur songwriters can help an aspiring songwriter hone the skills needed to compete in the ever-changing music industry. Having a community of support, with relevant information and contacts, is one of the most important things a songwriter can have.

The type of organization you choose to join depends on what you want to get out of it. Local groups can offer a friendly, supportive environment where you can work on your songs and have them critiqued in a constructive way by other songwriters, providing valuable feedback for your work. They're also great places to meet collaborators for projects where you might want a co-writer. Larger, national organizations can give you access to music business professionals and other songwriters across the country. The leaders of both local and national organizations may also be able to help you develop contacts, whether it's someone they know and have worked with directly, or a professional they know from one of their own contacts.

JOINING A SONGWRITING OR-GANIZATION

Most of the organizations listed in this book are nonprofit groups with membership open to specific groups of people—songwriters, musicians, classical composers, etc. They can be local groups with a membership of fewer than 100 people, or large national organizations with thousands of members from all over the country. In addition to regular meetings, most organizations occasionally sponsor events such as seminars and workshops to which music industry personnel are invited to talk about the business, and perhaps listen to and critique demo tapes.

Check the following listings, bulletin boards at local music stores, and your local newspapers for area organizations. If you are unable to locate an organization within an easy distance of your home, you may want to consider joining one of the national groups. These groups, based in New York, Los Angeles, and Nashville, keep their members involved and informed through newsletters, regional workshops, and large yearly conferences. They can help a writer who feels isolated in his hometown get his music heard by professionals in the major music centers.

In these listings, organizations describe their purpose and activities, as well as how much it costs to join. Before joining any organization, consider what it has to offer and how becoming a member will benefit you. Also, remember to look up each listing online before joining. While we are confident that all of the information in *Songwriter's Market* is accurate, information can change, and often changes quickly. Remember to fact-check membership fees, activities, and the types of songwriters that join these organizations. To locate an organization close to home, see the Geographic Index at the back of this book.

ACADEMY OF COUNTRY MUSIC

5500 Balboa Blvd., Encino CA 91316. (818)788-8000. **Fax:** (818)788-0999. **E-mail:** info@acmcountry.com. **Website:** www.acmcountry.com. There is a contact form for the group on the website. Serves country music industry professionals. Eligibility for professional members is limited to those individuals who derive some portion of their income directly from country music. Each member is classified by one of the following categories: artist/entertainer, club/venue operator, musician, on-air personality, manager, talent agent, composer, music publisher, public relations, publications, radio, TV/motion picture, record company, talent buyer or affiliated (general). The purpose of ACM is to promote and enhance the image of country music. The Academy is involved year-round in activities important to the country music community. Some of these activities include charity fundraisers, participation in country music seminars, talent contests, artist showcases, assistance to producers in placing country music on TV and in motion pictures and backing legislation that benefits the interests of the country music community. The ACM is governed by directors and run by officers elected annually. Applications are accepted throughout the year online. Membership: $75/year.

AMERICAN MUSIC CENTER, INC.)

90 John St., Suite 312, New York NY 10038. (212)645-6949. **Fax:** (212)490-0998. **E-mail:** info@newmusicusa.org; library@newmusicusa.org. **Website:** www.amc.net. The American Music Center, founded by a consortium led by Aaron Copland in 1939, is the first-ever national service and information center for new classical music and jazz by American composers. The Center has a variety of innovative new programs and services, including a monthly Internet magazine (www.newmusicbox.org) for new American music, online databases of contemporary ensembles and ongoing opportunities for composers, an online catalog of new music for educators specifically targeted to young audiences, a series of professional development workshops, and an online listening library. Each month, AMC provides its more than 2,500 members with a listing of opportunities including calls for scores, competitions, and other new music performance information. The AMC Collection at the New York Public Library for the Performing Arts presently includes over 60,000 scores and recordings, many un-

available elsewhere. "AMC also continues to administer several grant programs: the Aaron Copland Fund for Music; the Henry Cowell Performance Incentive Fund; and its own programs Live Music for Dance and the Composer Assistance Program." Members also receive a link their sites on www.amc.net. The American Music Center is not-for-profit and has an annual membership fee.

AMERICAN SOCIETY OF COMPOSERS, AUTHORS AND PUBLISHERS (ASCAP)

One Lincoln Plaza, New York NY 10023. (212)621-6000 (administration). **Fax:** (212)621-8453. **Website:** www.ascap.com. **Regional offices—West Coast:** 7920 W. Sunset Blvd., 3rd Floor, Los Angeles CA 90046, (323)883-1000; **Nashville:** Two Music Square W., Nashville TN 37203, (615)742-5000; **Atlanta:** 950 Joseph E. Lowery Blvd. NW, Suite 23, Atlanta GA 30318, (404)685-8699; **Miami:** 420 Lincoln Rd., Suite 385, Miami Beach FL 33139, (305)673-3446; **London:** 8 Cork St., London W1S 3LJ England, 011-44-207-439-0909; **Puerto Rico:** Ave. Martinez Nadal, c/ Hill Side 623, San Juan, Puerto Rico 00920, (787)707-0782. ASCAP is a membership association of over 240,000 composers, lyricists, songwriters, and music publishers whose function is to protect the rights of its members by licensing and collecting royalties for the nondramatic public performance of their copyrighted works. ASCAP licensees include radio, TV, cable, live concert promoters, bars, restaurants, symphony orchestras, new media, and other users of music. ASCAP is the leading performing rights society in the world. All revenues, less operating expenses, are distributed to members (about $.86 of each dollar). ASCAP was the first U.S.-performing rights organization to distribute royalties from the Internet. Founded in 1914, ASCAP is the only society created and owned by writers and publishers. The ASCAP board of directors consists of 12 writers and 12 publishers, elected by the membership. ASCAP's member card provides exclusive benefits geared towards working music professionals. Among the benefits are health, musical instrument and equipment, tour and studio liability, term life and long-term care insurance, discounts on musical instruments, equipment and supplies, access to a credit union, and much more. ASCAP hosts a wide array of showcases and workshops throughout the year, and offers grants, special awards, and networking opportunities in a variety of genres. Visit their website listed above for more information.

ARIZONA SONGWRITERS ASSOCIATION

428 E. Thunderbird Rd. #737, Phoenix AZ 85022. **E-mail:** azsongwriters@cox.net. **Website:** www.azsongwriters.org. **Contact:** John Iger, president. Members are all ages; all styles of music, novice to pro; many make money placing their songs in film and TV. Most members are residents of Arizona. Purpose is to educate about the craft and business of songwriting and to facilitate networking with business professionals and other songwriters, musicians, singers and studios. Offers instruction, e-newsletter, workshops, performance, and song pitching opportunities. Applications accepted year-round for membership (for a nomimal fee).

☼ ASSOCIATION DES PROFESSIONEL. LE.S DE LA CHANSON ET DE LA MUSIQUE

450 Rideau St., Suite 401, Ottawa ON K1N 5Z4 Canada. (613)745-5642. **Fax:** (613)745-9715. **E-mail:** communications@apcm.ca. **Website:** www.apcm.ca. **Contact:** Mathilde Hountchegnon, head of communications and promotion. Members are French Canadian singers and musicians. Members must be French singing and may have a CD to be distributed. Purpose is to gather French-speaking artists (outside of Quebec, mainly in Ontario) to distribute their material, other workshops, instructions, lectures, etc. Offers instruction, newsletter, lectures, workshops, and distribution. Applications accepted year-round. Membership fee: $60 (Canadian).

ASSOCIATION OF INDEPENDENT MUSIC PUBLISHERS

P.O. Box 69473, Los Angeles CA 90069. (818)771-7301. **E-mail:** LAinfo@aimp.org; NYinfo@aimp.org; NAinfo@aimp.org. **Website:** www.aimp.org. The organization's primary focus is to educate and inform music publishers about the most current industry trends and practices by providing a forum for the discussion of the issues and problems confronting the music publishing industry. Offers monthly panels and networking events. Applications accepted year-round. Professional membership fee: $75/year. Online only: $60/year.

AUSTIN SONGWRITERS GROUP

P.O. Box 2578, Austin TX 78768. (512)698-4237. **E-mail:** info@austinsongwritersgroup.com; leeduffy@austinsongwritersgroup.com. **Website:** www.austinsongwritersgroup.com. **Contact:** Lee Duffy, executive director. The Austin Songwriters Group is a nonprofit organization created by songwriters for songwriters. Serves all ages and all levels, from just beginning to advanced. "Prospective members should have an interest in the field of songwriting, whether it be for profit or hobby. The main purpose of this organization is to educate members in the craft and business of songwriting; to provide resources for growth and advancement in the area of songwriting; and to provide opportunities for performance and contact with the music industry." The primary benefit of membership to a songwriter is exposed to music industry professionals, which increases contacts and furthers the songwriter's education in both craft and business aspects. Offers competitions, instruction, lectures, library, newsletter, performance opportunities, evaluation services, workshops and contact with music industry professionals through special guest speakers at meetings, plus our yearly Austin Songwriters Symposium, which includes instruction, song evaluations, and song pitching direct to those pros currently seeking material for their artists, publishing companies, etc." Applications accepted year-round.

TIPS "Our newsletter is top-quality packed with helpful information on all aspects of songwriting-craft, business, recording and producing tips, and industry networking opportunities. Go to our website and sign up for e-mails to keep you informed about ongoing and upcoming events!"

BALTIMORE SONGWRITERS ASSOCIATION

P.O. Box 22496, Baltimore MD 21203. **E-mail:** info@baltimoresongwriters.org. **Website:** www.baltimoresongwriters.org. "The BSA is an inclusive organization with all ages, skill levels and genres of music welcome. We are trying to build a musical community that is more supportive and less competitive. We are dedicated to helping songwriters grow and become better in their craft." Offers instruction, newsletter, lectures, workshops, performance opportunities. Applications accepted year-round; membership not limited to location or musical status. There are meetings every month, as well as (performance) songwriting showcases.

THE BLACK ROCK COALITION

P.O. Box 1054, Cooper Station, New York NY 10276. **E-mail:** brcmembersinfo@gmail.com. **Website:** www.blackrockcoalition.org. **Contact:** Darrell M. McNeil, director of operations. Serves musicians, songwriters—male and female ages 18-40 (average). Also engineers, entertainment attorneys and producers. Looking for members who are "mature and serious about music as an artist or activist willing to help fellow musicians. The BRC independently produces, promotes and distributes black alternative music acts as a collective and supportive voice for such musicians within the music and record business. The main purpose of this organization is to produce, promote, and distribute the full spectrum of black music along with educating the public on what black music is. The BRC is now soliciting recorded music by bands and individuals for Black Rock Coalition Records. Please send copyrighted and original material only." Offers instruction, newsletter, lectures, free seminars and workshops, monthly membership meeting, quarterly magazine, performing opportunities, evaluation services, business advice, full roster of all members. Applications accepted year-round. Bands must submit a tape, bio with picture and a SASE before sending their membership fee. Membership fee: $25. A lifetime fee is $250.

BROADCAST MUSIC, INC. (BMI)

7 World Trade Center, 250 Greenwich St., New York NY 10007. (212)220-3000. **E-mail:** newyork@bmi.com. **Website:** www.bmi.com. **Los Angeles:** 8730 Sunset Blvd., 3rd Floor W., Los Angeles CA 90069. (310)659-9109. **E-mail:** losangeles@bmi.com. **Nashville:** 10 Music Square E., Nashville TN 37203. (615)401-2000. **E-mail:** nashville@bmi.com. **Miami:** 1691 Michigan Ave., Miami FL 33139. (305)673-5148. **E-mail:** miami@bmi.com. **Atlanta:** 3340 Peachtree Rd. NE, Suite 570, Atlanta GA 30326. (404)261-5151. **E-mail:** atlanta@bmi.com. **Puerto Rico:** 1250 Ave. Ponce de Leon, San Jose Building Santurce PR 00907. (787)754-6490. **United Kingdom:** 84 Harley House, Marylebone Rd., London NW1 5HN United Kingdom. 011-44-207-486-2036. **E-mail:** london@bmi.com. President and CEO: Del R. Bryant. Senior vice presidents: Phillip Graham, New York, writer/publisher relations; Alison Smith, performing rights. Vice presidents: Charlie Feldman, New York; Barbara Cane and Doreen Ringer Ross, Los Angeles; Paul Corbin, Nashville; Diane J. Almodovar, Miami; Catherine Brewton, Atlanta. Senior executive, London: Brandon Bakshi. BMI is a performing rights organization representing approximately 300,000 songwriters, composers and music publishers in all genres of music, including pop, rock, country, R&B, rap, jazz, Latin, gospel and contemporary classical.

"Applicants must have written a musical composition, alone or in collaboration with other writers, which is commercially published, recorded or otherwise likely to be performed." Purpose: BMI acts on behalf of its songwriters, composers and music publishers by insuring payment for performance of their works through the collection of licensing fees from radio stations, Internet outlets, broadcast and cable TV stations, hotels, nightclubs, aerobics centers and other users of music. This income is distributed to the writers and publishers in the form of royalty payments, based on how the music is used. BMI also undertakes intensive lobbying efforts in Washington D.C. on behalf of its affiliates, seeking to protect their performing rights through the enactment of new legislation and enforcement of current copyright law. In addition, BMI helps aspiring songwriters develop their skills through various workshops, seminars and competitions it sponsors throughout the country. Applications accepted year-round. There is no membership fee for songwriters; a one-time fee of $150 is required to affiliate, an individually owned publishing company; $250 for partnerships, corporations and limited-liability companies. "Visit our website for specific contacts, e-mail addresses and additional membership information."

CALIFORNIA LAWYERS FOR THE ARTS

Fort Mason Center, C-265, San Francisco CA 94123. (415)775-7200. **Fax:** (415)775-1143. **E-mail:** support@calawyersforthearts.org; sanfrancisco@calawyersforthearts.org. **Website:** www.calawyersforthearts.org. CLA's mission is to empower the creative community by providing education, representation and dispute resolution. CLA's vision is that creative artists and arts organizations serve as agents of democratic involvement, innovation, and positive social change, and the growth of an empowered arts sector is essential to healthy communities. CLA's leadership and services strengthen the arts for the benefit of communities throughout California. CLA serves creative artists of all disciplines, skill levels, and ages, supporting individuals, businesses, inventors, and creative arts organizations. CLA also serves groups and individuals who support the arts. CLA works most closely with the California arts and innovation community. Offers online education, newsletters, in-person workshops and seminars, library, mediation and arbitration service, attorney referral service, publications and arts advocacy. Membership fees: $20 for senior citizens and full-time students, $30 for working artists, $45 for general individual, $70 for non-panel attorney, $75 for panel attorney, $100 for patrons; organizations: $50 for small organizations (budget under $100,000), $90 for large organizations (budget of $100,000 or more), $100 for corporate sponsors.

☺ CANADA COUNCIL FOR THE ARTS/ CONSEIL DES ARTS DU CANADA

150 Elgin St., P.O. Box 1047, Ottawa ON K1P 5V8 Canada. (800)263-5588 or (613)566-4414, ext. 5060. **Fax:** (613)566-4390. **Website:** www.canadacouncil. ca. An independent agency that fosters and promotes the arts in Canada by providing grants and services to professional artists including songwriters and musicians. "Individual artists must be Canadian citizens or permanent residents of Canada, and must have completed basic training and/or have the recognition as professionals within their fields. The Canada Council offers grants to professional musicians to pursue their individual artistic development and creation. There are specific deadline dates for the various programs of assistance. Visit our website for more details."

☺ CANADIAN ACADEMY OF RECORDING ARTS AND SCIENCES (CARAS)

345 Adelaide St. W., 2nd Floor, Toronto ON M5V 1R5 Canada. (416)485-3135. **Fax:** (416)485-4978. **E-mail:** info@carasonline.ca; jaclyn@junoawards.ca. **Website:** www.carasonline.ca. Membership is open to all employees (including support staff) in broadcasting and record companies, as well as producers, personal managers, recording artists, recording engineers, arrangers, composers, music publishers, album designers, promoters, talent and booking agents, record retailers, rack jobbers, distributors, recording studios, and other music industry-related professions (on approval). Applicants must be affiliated with the Canadian recording industry. Offers newsletter, nomination and voting privileges for Juno Awards and discount tickets to Juno Awards show. "CARAS strives to foster the development of the Canadian music and recording industries and to contribute toward higher artistic standards." Applications accepted year-round. Membership fee: $75/year (Canadian) + HST. Applications accepted from individuals only, not from companies or organizations.

☺ CANADIAN COUNTRY MUSIC ASSOCIATION

120 Adelaide St. E., Suite 200, Toronto ON M5C 1K9 Canada. (416)947-1331. **Fax:** (416)947-5924. **E-mail:** country@ccma.org. **Website:** www.ccma.org. Members are artists, songwriters, musicians, producers, radio station personnel, managers, booking agents, and others. Offers newsletter, workshops, performance opportunities, and the CCMA Awards every September. "Through our newsletters and conventions, we offer a means of meeting and associating with artists and others in the industry. The CCMA is a federally chartered nonprofit organization, dedicated to the promotion and development of Canadian country music throughout Canada and the world and to providing a unity of purpose for the Canadian country music industry." See website for membership information and benefits. Membership dues start at $75 for 1 year.

CENTRAL CAROLINA SONGWRITERS ASSOCIATION (CCSA)

131 Henry Baker Rd., Zebulon NC 27597. (919)727-6647. **Website:** www.ccsa-raleigh.com. There is a contact form on the site. "CCSA welcomes songwriters of all experience levels, from beginner to professional, within the local RDU/Triad/Eastern area of North Carolina to join our group. Our members' musical background varies, covering a wide array of musical genres. CCSA meets monthly in Raleigh. We are unable to accept applications from incarcerated persons or those who do not reside in the local area, as our group's primary focus is on songwriters who are able to attend the monthly meetings-to ensure members get the best value for their yearly dues." CCSA strives to provide each songwriter and musician a resourceful organization where members grow musically by networking and sharing with one another. Offers annual songwriters forum, periodic workshops, critiques at the monthly meetings, opportunities to perform and network with fellow members. Applications are accepted year-round. Dues are $24/year (pro-rated for new members at $2/month by date of application) with annual renewal each January.

THE COLLEGE MUSIC SOCIETY

312 E. Pine St., Missoula MT 59802. (406)721-9616. **Fax:** (406)721-9419. **E-mail:** cms@music.org. **Website:** www.music.org. **Contact:** Shannon Devlin, member services. The College Music Society pro-

motes music teaching and learning, musical creativity and expression, research and dialogue, and diversity and interdisciplinary interaction. A consortium of college, conservatory, university, and independent musicians and scholars interested in all disciplines of music, the Society provides leadership and serves as an agent of change by addressing concerns facing music in higher education." Offers an online journal, newsletter, lectures, workshops, performance opportunities, job listing service, databases of organizations and institutions, music faculty, and mailing lists. Applications accepted year-round. Membership fees: $70 (regular dues), $35 (student dues), $35 (retiree dues).

CONNECTICUT SONGWRITERS ASSOCIATION

P.O. Box 511, Mystic CT 06355. **E-mail:** info@ct-songs.com. **Website:** www.ctsongs.com. **Contact:** Bill Pere, president and executive director. "We are an educational, nonprofit organization dedicated to improving the art and craft of original music. Founded in 1979, CSA has had almost 2,000 active members and has become one of the best-known and respected songwriters' associations in the country. Membership in the CSA admits you to 12-18 seminars/workshops/song critique sessions per year throughout Connecticut and surrounding region. Out-of-state members may mail in songs for free critiques at our meetings. Noted professionals deal with all aspects of the craft and business of music including lyric writing, music theory, music technology, arrangement and production, legal and business aspects, performance techniques, song analysis and recording techniques." CSA offers song screening sessions for members and songs that pass become eligible for inclusion on the CSA sampler anthology through various retail and online outlets and are brought to national music conferences. CSA is well connected in both the independent music scene and the traditional music industry. CSA also offers showcases and concerts that are open to the public and designed to give artists a venue for performing their original material for an attentive, listening audience. CSA benefits help local soup kitchens, group homes, hospice, world hunger, libraries, nature centers, community centers and more. CSA encompasses ballads to bluegrass and Bach to rock. Membership fee: $45/year (there are student and senior discounts).

DALLAS SONGWRITERS ASSOCIATION

Sammons Center for the Arts, 3630 Harry Hines Blvd. #20, Dallas TX 75219. (214)750-0916. **E-mail:** info@dallassongwriters.org. **Website:** dallassongwriters.blogspot.com. DSA is a nonprofit organization dedicated to providing learning opportunities on the craft and business of songwriting. All styles of music are welcome in the DSA, and membership includes writers of all ages. DSA monthly activities include meetings with guest speakers, song critiques and performance showcases that are open to the public. In addition, the DSA supports and promotes workshops and contests and publishes a monthly newsletter. Check the website for open mic information, as well as workshops and more. New membership is $50.

THE DRAMATISTS GUILD OF AMERICA, INC.

1501 Broadway, Suite 701, New York NY 10036. (212)398-9366. **Fax:** (212)944-0420. **E-mail:** rtec@dramatistsguild.com. **Website:** www.dramatistsguild.com. **Contact:** Roland Tec, director of membership. For over 3/4 of a century, The Dramatists Guild has been the professional association of playwrights, composers and lyricists, with more than 6,000 members across the country. All theater writers, whether produced or not, are eligible for associate membership ($90/year); students enrolled in writing degree programs at colleges or universities are eligible for student membership ($45/year); writers who have been produced on Broadway, Off-Broadway or on the main stage of a LORT theater are eligible for active membership ($130/year). The Guild offers its members the following activities and services: use of the Guild's contracts (including the Approved Production Contract for Broadway, the Off-Broadway contract, the LORT contract, the collaboration agreements for both musicals and drama, the 99-Seat Theatre Plan contract, the Small Theatre contract, commissioning agreements, and the Underlying Rights Agreements contract; advice on all theatrical contracts including Broadway, Off-Broadway, regional, showcase, equity-waiver, dinner theater and collaboration contracts); a nationwide toll-free number for all members with business or contract questions or problems; advice and information on a wide spectrum of issues affecting writers; free and/or discounted ticket service; symposia led by experienced professionals in major cities nationwide; access to health insurance programs; and a spacious meeting room that can accommodate up to 50 people for readings and auditions on a rental basis. The Guild's publications are: *The Dramatist*, a bimonthly journal containing articles on all aspects of the theater (which includes The Dramatists Guild Newsletter, with announcements of all Guild activities and current information of interest to dramatists); and an annual resource directory with up-to-date information on agents, publishers, grants, producers, playwriting contests, conferences and workshops, and an interactive website that brings our community of writers together to exchange ideas and share information.

THE FIELD

75 Maiden Lane, Suite 906, New York NY 10038. (212)691-6969. **E-mail:** claire@thefield.org. **Website:** www.thefield.org. **Contact:** Claire Baum, artist services associate. "Founded by artists for artists, The Field has been dedicated to providing impact services to thousands of performing artists in New York and beyond since 1986. From fostering creative exploration to stewarding innovative fundraising strategies, we are delighted to help artists reach their fullest potential. More than 1,900 performing artists come to The Field annually to build their businesses, 2,000-plus new artworks are developed under our stewardship each year, and our services are replicated in 11 cities across the U.S. and in Europe. At the same time, we remain true to our grassroots origin and artist-centered mission: to strategically and comprehensively serve the myriad artistic and administrative needs of independent performing artists and companies who work in the fields of dance, theater, music, text, and performance art. Our core values of affordability, accessibility and rigorous delivery infuse all of our interactions. Field services include career-building workshops (grant writing, touring, Internet strategies, etc.), fiscal sponsorship, creative residences in New York and out of town, an 'Artists' Kinkos' resource center, and membership benefits." Offers fiscal sponsorship, arts management and creative workshops, residencies, and performance opportunities. Applications accepted year-round. Membership fee: $100/year.

TIPS "The Field offers the most affordable and accessible fiscal sponsorship program in New York. The Sponsored Artist Program offered by The Field enables performing artists and groups to accumulate the funds they need to make their artistic and career goals a reality. Fiscal sponsorship provides independent performing artists and groups with: eligibility to apply for most government, foundation, and corporate grants that require a 501(c)(3), not-for-profit status; eligibility to receive tax-deductible donations of both money and goods from individuals; and other services where 501(c)(3) status is necessary."

⊛ FILM MUSIC NETWORK

13101 Washington Blvd., Suite 466, Los Angeles CA 90066. **Website:** www.filmmusic.net. "The Film Music Network, established in 1997, is a leading worldwide professional association of composers, songwriters, bands, recording artists, and more who are seeking to place their music or compose custom music for film or television projects. One of the Film Music Network's most popular member benefits is providing leads for projects seeking music or composers, including film projects, television projects, corporate videos, music libraries, and more. Additional member benefits include a free introductory legal consultation, discounted move theater and event tickets, resources including a directory of film music agents and managers, our Film Music Salary and Rate survey, and more." Full membership fee: $11.95/month. Audio-only fee: $4.95/month.

There is a contact form online. Responds to inquiries within 24 hours.

FLORIDA SONGWRITERS ASSOCIATION

200 South Harbor City Blvd., Suite 403, Melbourne FL 32901. **E-mail:** info@flsw.org. **Website:** www.flsw.org. Florida Songwriters Association is a collaboration of several companies in the industry. We all share the common goal of helping to further educate, motivate, and elevate songwriters. More information online. Annual memberships start at $100 per year.

TIPS "Learn what it takes to be a songwriter. Not just how to write songs, but how to protect your works, as well. Register with a Performing Rights Organization (PRO) and do your research on how the business works. This will go a long way when dealing with industry professionals."

FORT WORTH SONGWRITERS' ASSOCIATION

P.O. Box 330233, Fort Worth TX 76163. (817)654-5400. **E-mail:** fwsanewsletter@gmail.com. **Website:** www. fwsa.com. Members are beginners up to and including published writers. Interests cover gospel, country, western swing, rock, pop, bluegrass, and blues. Purpose is to allow songwriters to become more proficient at songwriting; to provide an opportunity for their efforts to be performed before a live audience; to provide songwriters an opportunity to meet co-writers. "We provide our members free critiques of their efforts. We provide a monthly newsletter outlining current happenings in the business of songwriting. We offer competitions and mini-workshops with guest speakers from the music industry. We promote a weekly open mic for singers of original material, and hold invitational songwriter showcase events at various times throughout the year. Each year, we hold a Christmas Song Contest, judged by independent music industry professionals. We also offer free web pages for members or links to member websites." Applications accepted year-round. Membership fee: $40 as of 2015.

○ There is a contact form on the website.

GLOBAL SONGWRITERS CONNECTION

P.O. Box 140623, Nashville TN 37214. (615)732-8832. **E-mail:** info@globalsongwriters.com. **Website:** www. globalsongwriters.com. Global Songwriters Connection is an association for singer/songwriters founded by music industry professional, career coach, mentor, motivational speaker, and teacher Sheree Spoltore. Sheree is passionate about encouraging, equipping, and empowering songwriters around the world to be their personal best. "GSC's personalized career mentoring services provide singers, songwriters, and artists in all genres and at every level with industry connections and an individualized plan to help the artist reach the next step. Whether it is song crafting, career, or artist development, GSC's mentoring services focus on personal songwriter development first." Mermbership fee: $50.

○ Mention this book in an e-mail to Sheree (sheree@globalsongwriters.com) and receive a free PDF of one of her classes on earning additional income through indie artist cuts.

GOSPEL MUSIC ASSOCIATION

4012 Granny White Pike, Nashville TN 37204-3924. (615)242-0303. **Fax:** (615)254-9755. **E-mail:** jackie@gospelmusic.org. **E-mail:** info@gospelmusic.org. **Website:** www.gospelmusic.org. Serves songwriters, musicians and anyone directly involved with or supportive of gospel music. Professional members include advertising agencies, musicians, songwriters, agents/managers, composers, retailers, music publishers, print and broadcast media, and other members of the recording industry. Associate members include supporters of gospel music and those whose involvement in the industry does not provide them with income. The primary purpose of the GMA is to expose, promote, and celebrate the Gospel through music. A GMA membership offers newsletters, performance experiences and workshops, as well as networking opportunities. Applications accepted year-round. Membership fees: $95/year for professionals; $25/year for iMembers (supporters of gospel music and those whose involvement in the industry does not provide them a source of income).

● THE GUILD OF INTERNATIONAL SONGWRITERS & COMPOSERS

Ebrel House, 2a Penlee Close, Praa Sands, Penzance, Cornwall TR20 9SR United Kingdom. (01) (736)762826. **Fax:** (01)(736)763328. **E-mail:** songmag@aol.com; gisc@btconnect.com. **Website:** www. songwriters-guild.co.uk. The Guild of International Songwriters & Composers is an international music industry organization based in England. Guild members are songwriters, composers, lyricists, poets, performing songwriters, musicians, music publishers, studio owners, managers, independent record companies, music industry personnel, etc., from many countries throughout the world. The Guild of International Songwriters & Composers has been publishing *Songwriting and Composing Magazine* since 1986, which is issued free to all Guild members throughout their membership. The Guild offers advice, guidance, assistance, copyright protection service, information, encouragement, contact information, Intellectual property/copyright protection of members' works through the Guild's Copyright Registration Centre along with other free services and more to Guild members with regard to helping members achieve their aims, ambitions, progression, and advancement in respect to the many different aspects of the music industry. Information, advice and services available to Guild members throughout their membership includes assistance, advice and help on many matters and issues relating to the music industry in general.

INTERNATIONAL BLUEGRASS MUSIC ASSOCIATION (IBMA)

608 W. Iris Dr., Nashville TN 37204. (615)256-3222 or (888)438-4262. **Fax:** (615)256-0450. **E-mail:** info@ibma.org. **Website:** www.ibma.org. Serves songwriters, musicians and professionals in bluegrass music.

"IBMA is a trade association composed of people and organizations involved professionally and semiprofessionally in the bluegrass music industry, including performers, agents, songwriters, music publishers, promoters, print and broadcast media, local associations, recording manufacturers, and distributors. Voting members must be currently or formerly involved in the bluegrass industry as full- or part-time professionals. A songwriter attempting to become professionally involved in our field would be eligible. Our mission statement reads: *IBMA: Working together for high standards of professionalism, a greater appreciation for our music, and the success of the worldwide bluegrass music community.* IBMA holds an annual trade show/convention with a songwriters' showcase in the fall, represents our field outside the bluegrass music community, and compiles and disseminates databases of bluegrass-related resources and organizations. Market research on the bluegrass consumer is available and we offer "Bluegrass in the Schools" information and matching grants. The primary value in this organization for a songwriter is having current information about the bluegrass music field and contacts with other songwriters, publishers, musicians and record companies." Offers workshops, liability insurance, rental car discounts, consultation and databases of record companies, radio stations, press, organizations and gigs. Applications accepted year-round. Membership fee: for a non-voting patron, $40/year; for an individual voting professional, $75/year; for an organizational voting professional, $205/year.

⦿ INTERNATIONAL SONGWRITERS ASSOCIATION LTD.

P.O. Box 46, Limerick City, Ireland 00-353-61-228837 United Kingdom. (01)(71)486-5353. **E-mail:** jliddane@songwriter.iol.ie. **Website:** www.songwriter.co.uk. **Contact:** Bill Miller, Ray Coleman, membership department. Serves songwriters and music publishers. "The ISA headquarters is in Limerick City, Ireland, and from there it provides its members with assessment services, copyright services, legal and other advisory services, and an investigations service, plus a magazine for 1 yearly fee. Our members are songwriters in more than 60 countries worldwide, of all ages." There are conditions for membership—see the website. "We provide information and assistance to professional or semiprofessional songwriters. Our publication, *Songwriter*, which was founded in 1967,

features detailed exclusive interviews with songwriters and music publishers, as well as directory information of value to writers." Applications accepted year-round. Membership fee for European writers is £19.95; for non-European writers, $30.

JUST PLAIN FOLKS MUSIC ORGANIZATION

5327 Kit Dr., Indianapolis IN 46237. **E-mail:** JPFolksPro@aol.com. **Website:** www.justplainfolks.org. "Just Plain Folks is among the world's largest music organizations. Our members cover nearly every musical style and professional field, from songwriters, artists, publishers, producers, record labels, entertainment attorneys, publicists and PR experts, performing rights organization staffers, live and recording engineers, educators, music students, musical instrument manufacturers, TV, radio and print media, and almost every major Internet music entity. Representing all 50 U.S. states and more than 160 countries worldwide, we have members of all ages, musical styles and levels of success, including winners and nominees of every major music industry award, as well as those just starting out. A complete demographics listing of our group is available on our website. Whether you are a No. 1 hit songwriter or artist, or the newest kid on the block, you are welcome to join. Membership *does* require an active e-mail account." The purpose of this organization is "to share wisdom, ideas and experiences with others who have been there, and to help educate those who have yet to make the journey. Just Plain Folks provides its members with a friendly networking and support community that uses the power of the Internet and combines it with good old-fashioned human interaction. We help promote our members ready for success and educate those still learning." Membership is free.

THE LAS VEGAS SONGWRITERS ASSOCIATION

P.O. Box 42683, Las Vegas NV 89116-0683. (702)223-7255. **E-mail:** lasvegassongwriters@yahoo.com; betty_miller@mcgraw-hill.com. **Website:** www.facebook.com/lasvegassongwriters. "We are an educational, nonprofit organization dedicated to improving the art and craft of the songwriter. We want members who are serious about their craft. We want our members to respect their craft and to treat it as a business. Members must be at least 18 years of age. We help turn amateur writers into professionals. Several of our songwriters have had their songs recorded on both independent and major labels."

LOS ANGELES MUSIC NETWORK

P.O. Box 2446, Toluca Lake CA 91610. (818)769-6095. **E-mail:** info@lamn.com. **Website:** www.lamn.com. "Our emphasis is on sharing knowledge and information, giving you access to top professionals and promoting career development. LAMN is an association of music industry professionals, i.e., artists, singers, songwriters, and people who work in various aspects of the music industry with an emphasis on the creative. Members are ambitious and interested in advancing their careers. LAMN promotes career advancement, communication and education among artists and creatives. LAMN sponsors industry events and educational panels held at venues in the Los Angeles area and now in other major music hubs around the country (New York, Las Vegas, Phoenix, and San Francisco). LAMN Jams are popular among our members. Experience LAMN Jams in Los Angeles or New York by performing your original music in front of industry experts who can advance your career by getting your music in the hands of hard-to-reach music supervisors. The singer-songwriter contest gives artists an opportunity to perform in front of industry experts and receive instant feedback on their music, lyrics, and performance. Offers performance opportunities, instruction, newsletter, lectures, seminars, music industry job listings, career counseling, résumé publishing, mentor network, and many professional networking opportunities. See our website for current job listings and a calendar of upcoming events." Applications accepted year-round. Annual membership fee as of 2015: $25.

LOUISIANA SONGWRITERS ASSOCIATION

P.O. Box 82009, Baton Rouge LA 70884. **E-mail:** info@louisianamusichalloffame.org. **Website:** louisianamusichalloffame.org/content/view/154/168/. Membership fee: $25/year. "The purposes of the registration and membership process are simply to create a database of Louisiana's songwriters and other industry people, to organize songwriters as part of our efforts to help build the music industry of Louisiana, provide a verifiable actual number of interested, dues-paying songwriters to seek programs and business partners to aid the musicians of Louisiana, and to create a verifiable 'force' in the music business by doing the following: showing

the number of songwriters with legitimate interest in the business, providing a path for communications to, from and between songwriters, musicians and other industry workers, helping to network for bookings, gigs, etc., and giving songwriters an advocate and voice to help build our music industry."

☺ MANITOBA MUSIC

1-376 Donald St., Winnipeg MB R3B 2J2 Canada. (204)942-8650. **Fax:** (204)942-6083. **E-mail:** info@manitobamusic.com. **Website:** www.manitobamusic.com. Organization consists of "songwriters, producers, agents, musicians, managers, retailers, publicists, radio, talent buyers, media, record labels, etc. (no age limit, no skill level minimum). Must have interest in the future of Manitoba's music industry." The main purpose of Manitoba Music is to foster growth in all areas of the Manitoba music industry primarily through education, promotion and lobbying. Offers newsletter, extensive website, directory of Manitoba's music industry, workshops, and performance opportunities. Manitoba Music also is involved with the Western Canadian Music Awards festival, conference and awards show. Applications accepted year-round. Membership fee: $50 (Canadian). Other membership levels, such as Band ($75) and Youth ($35) available, as well.

MEMPHIS SONGWRITERS' ASSOCIATION

P.O. Box 343106, Memphis TN 38184. (901)577-0906. **E-mail:** membership@memphissongwriters.org; songkindler@memphissongwriters.org. **Website:** www.memphissongwriters.org. "MSA is a nonprofit songwriters organization serving songwriters nationally. Our mission is to dedicate our services to promote, advance, and help songwriters in the composition of music, lyrics and songs; to work for better conditions in our profession; and to secure and protect the rights of MSA songwriters. The Memphis Songwriters Association is an organizational member of the Folk Alliance (FA.org). We also supply copyright forms. We offer critique sessions for writers at our monthly meetings. We also have monthly open-mic songwriters' nights to encourage creativity, networking and co-writing. We host an annual songwriters' seminar and an annual songwriters' showcase, as well as a bimonthly guest speaker series, which provides education, competition and entertainment for the songwriter. In addition, our members receive a bimonthly newsletter to keep them informed of MSA activities, demo services, and opportunities in the songwriting field." Membership fees: $50/year; $35/year for students and seniors; $75 for corporate.

⬭ There is a contact form on the website.

MINNESOTA ASSOCIATION OF SONGWRITERS

P.O. Box 4262, St. Paul MN 55104. **E-mail:** info@mnsongwriters.org. **Website:** www.mnsongwriters.org. "Includes a wide variety of members, ranging in age from 18 to 80; type of music is very diverse, ranging from alternative rock to folk, blues, theatrical and contemporary Christian; skill levels range from beginning songwriters to writers with recorded and published material. Main requirement is an interest in songwriting. Although most members come from the Minneapolis-St. Paul area, others come from nearby Wisconsin and other parts of the country. Some members are full-time musicians, but most represent a wide variety of occupations. MAS is a nonprofit community of songwriters that informs, educates, inspires, and assists its members in the art and business of songwriting." Offers instruction, workshops with pro songwriters, public performance opportunities, online and in-meeting evaluation services, Internet radio, and a public-access TV show being aired around the nation. Applications accepted year-round. Membership fee: $35. Student membership: $20. Other membership options listed online.

TIPS "Members are kept current on resources and opportunities. Original works are played at meetings or submitted via e-mail, then reviewed by involved members. Through this process, writers hone their skills and gain experience and confidence in refining their works and putting them into the music market."

⚙ MUSIC BC INDUSTRY ASSOCIATION

#100-938 Howe St., Vancouver BC V6Z 1N9 Canada. (604)873-1914. **Fax:** (604)873-9686. **E-mail:** info@musicbc.org. **Website:** www.musicbc.org. Music BC (formerly PMIA) is a nonprofit society that supports and promotes the spirit, development, and growth of the British Columbia music community provincially, nationally, and internationally. Music BC provides education, resources, advocacy, opportunities for funding, and a forum for communication. Visit website for membership benefits. There are several levels of membership (all with different pricing). A basic individual membership is $56.

MUSICIANS CONTACT

29684 Masters Dr., Murrieta CA 92563. (818)888-7879. **E-mail:** information@musicianscontact.com. **Website:** www.musicianscontact.com. "The primary source of paying jobs for musicians and vocalists nationwide. Job opportunities are posted daily on the Internet. Also offers exposure to the music industry for solo artists and complete acts seeking representation." Offers a newsletter.

NASHVILLE SONGWRITERS ASSOCIATION INTERNATIONAL (NSAI)

1710 Roy Acuff Place, Nashville TN 37203. (615)256-3354. **E-mail:** nsai@nashvillesongwriters.com. **Website:** www.nashvillesongwriters.com. Purpose: a not-for-profit service organization for both aspiring and professional songwriters in all fields of music. Membership: spans the U.S. and several foreign countries. Songwriters may apply in 1 of 3 annual categories: *active* ($200 for songwriters are actively working to improve in the craft of writing and/or actively pursing a career within the songwriting industry); *professional* ($100 for songwriters who are staff writers for a publishing company or earn 51% of their annual income from songwriting, whether from advances, royalties, or performances, or are generally regarded as a professional songwriter within the music industry); *lifetime* (please contact NSAI for details). Membership benefits: music industry information and advice, song evaluations, eNews, access to industry professionals through weekly Nashville workshops and several annual events, regional workshops, use of office facilities, and discounts on books and NSAI's 3 annual events. There are also "branch" workshops of NSAI. Workshops must meet certain standards and are accountable to NSAI.

⬭ There is a contact form on the website.

THE NATIONAL ASSOCIATION OF COMPOSERS/USA (NACUSA)

P.O. Box 49256, Barrington Station, Los Angeles CA 90049. **E-mail:** nacusa@music-usa.org; gregsteinke@mail.music-usa.org **Website:** www.music-usa.org/nacusa. **Contact:** Greg A. Steinke, Ph.D., membership coordinator. "We are of most value to the concert hall composer. Members are serious music composers of all ages and from all parts of the country who have a real interest in composing, performing, and listening to modern concert hall music. The main purpose of our organization is to perform, publish, broadcast and write news about composers of serious concert hall music—mostly chamber and solo pieces. Composers may achieve national notice of their work through our newsletter and concerts, and the fairly rare feeling of supporting a non-commercial music enterprise dedicated to raising the musical and social position of the serious composer. Ninety-nine percent of the money earned in music is earned, or so it seems, by popular songwriters who might feel they owe the art of music something, and this is one way they might help support that art. It's a chance to foster fraternal solidarity with their less prosperous, but wonderfully interesting classical colleagues at a time when the very existence of serious art seems to be questioned by the general populace." Offers competitions, lectures, performance opportunities, library and newsletter. Applications accepted year-round. Membership fee: National (regular): $30; National (students/seniors): $15. **TIPS** Also see the listing for NACUSA Young Composers' Competition in the Contests section of this book.

NEW MUSIC USA

90 John St., Suite 312, New York NY 10038. (212)645-6949. **Fax:** (646)490-0998. **E-mail:** info@newmusicusa.org. **Website:** www.newmusicusa.org. "New Music USA was formed by the merger of the American Music Center and Meet the Composer. We provide over $1 million each year in grant support for the creation and performance of new work and community building throughout the country. We amplify the voice of the new music community through New-MusicBox, profiling the people and ideas that energize and challenge music makers today. We stream a wide-ranging catalog of new music around the clock on Counterstream Radio and provide an online home for composers to feature their own music. This is not a membership organization; all musicians are eligible for support." Offers grant programs and information services. Deadlines vary for each grant program.

OPERA AMERICA

330 Seventh Ave., New York NY 10001. (212)796-8620. **Fax:** (212)796-8631. **E-mail:** info@operaamerica.org; SSnook@operaamerica.org. **Website:** www.operaamerica.org. Members are composers, librettists, musicians, singers, and opera/music theater producers. Offers conferences, workshops, and seminars for artists. Publishes online database of opera/music theater companies in the U.S. and Canada, database of opportunities for performing and creative artists, online directory of opera and musical performances worldwide and U.S., and an online directory of new works created and being developed by current-day composers and librettists, to encourage the performance of new works. Applications accepted year-round. Publishes quarterly magazine and a variety of electronic newsletters. Membership fees are on a sliding scale by membership level. 2015 Opera Conference is May 6-9.

🖰 There is a contact form on the website.

OUTMUSIC

1206 Pacific St., Suite 3D, New York NY 11216. **E-mail:** info@outmusicfoundation.org. **Website:** www.outmusicfoundation.org. "OUTMUSIC—The LGBT Academy of Recording Artists (LARA) is a 501(c)(3) nonprofit, charitable foundation that serves as an advocacy and awareness platform, and offers programming to support its mission to promote the advancement and appreciation of LGBT music culture and heritage, create opportunities to support the development of young aspiring artists, increase the viability and visibility of the LGBT music and entertainment platform, and honor, document and archive the contributions and achievements of out and proud LGBT music artists." Offers newsletter, lectures, workshops, performance opportunities, networking, industry leads. Sponsors OUTMUSIC Awards. Applications accepted year-round. Membership: $100 for individual artist; $150 for duo or group; $100 for individual patrons; $150 for business patrons.

PORTLAND SONGWRITERS ASSOCIATION

P.O. Box 28355, Portland OR 97228. **E-mail:** info@portlandsongwriters.org. **Website:** portlandsongwriters.org. "The PSA is a nonprofit organization providing education and opportunities that will assist writers in creating and marketing their songs. The PSA offers an annual National Songwriting Contest, monthly workshops, songwriter showcases, special performance venues, quarterly newsletter, mail-in critique service, discounted seminars by music industry pros." Membership fee: $25 (no eligibility requirements).
TIPS "Although most of our members are from the Pacific Northwest, we offer services that can assist songwriters anywhere. Our goal is to provide information and contacts to help songwriters grow artistically and gain access to publishing, recording and related mu-

sic markets. For more information, please check the website or e-mail."

RHODE ISLAND SONGWRITERS' ASSOCIATION

P.O. Box 9246, Warwick RI 02889. **E-mail:** generalinformation@risongwriters.com; memberships@risongwriters.com. **Website:** www.risongwriters.com. "Membership consists of novice and professional songwriters. RISA provides opportunities to the aspiring writer or performer, as well as the established regional artists who have recordings, are published and perform regularly. The only eligibility requirement is an interest in the group and the group's goals. Non-writers are welcome, as well." The main purpose is to "encourage, foster and conduct the art and craft of original musical and/or lyrical composition through education, information, collaboration and performance." Offers instruction, a newsletter, lectures, workshops, performance opportunities, and evaluation services. Applications accepted year-round. Membership fees: $25/year (individual); $35/year (family/band). "The group holds twice-monthly critique sessions; twice-monthly performer showcases (1 performer featured) at a local coffeehouse; songwriter showcases (usually 6-8 performers); weekly open mics; and a yearly songwriter festival called 'Hear In Rhode Island,' featuring approximately 50 Rhode Island acts, over 2 days."

SAN DIEGO SONGWRITERS GUILD

3952 Clairemont Mesa Blvd., D413, San Diego CA 92117. (858)376-7374. **Website:** sdsongwriters.org. There is a contact form on the website. Use it to e-mail them. "Members range with a variety of skill levels. Several members perform and work full time in music. Many are published and have songs recorded. Some are getting major artist record cuts. Most members are from San Diego County. New writers are encouraged to participate and meet others. All musical styles are represented." The purpose of this organization is to "serve the needs of songwriters and artists, especially helping them in the business and craft of songwriting through industry guest appearances." Offers competitions, newsletter, workshops, performance opportunities, discounts on services offered by fellow members, in-person song pitches and evaluations by publishers, producers and A&R executives. Applications accepted year-round. Individual membership dues: $50/year.

SESAC INC.

55 Music Square E., Nashville TN 37203. (615)320-0055. **Fax:** (615)963-3527. **Website:** www.sesac.com. There is a contact form on the website. "SESAC is a selective organization taking pride in having a repertory based on quality rather than quantity. Serves writers and publishers in all types of music who have their works performed by radio, television, nightclubs, cable TV, etc. Purpose of organization is to collect and distribute performance royalties to all active affiliates. As a SESAC affiliate, the individual may obtain equipment insurance at competitive rates. Music is reviewed upon invitation by the Writer/Publisher Relations department."

☉ SOCAN

41 Valleybrook Dr., Toronto ON M3B 2S6 Canada. (866)307-6226. **E-mail:** info@socan.ca; members@socan.ca. **Website:** www.socan.ca. "SOCAN is the Canadian copyright collective for the communication and performance of musical works. We administer these rights on behalf of our members (composers, lyricists, songwriters, and their publishers) and those of affiliated international organizations by licensing this use of their music in Canada. The fees collected are distributed as royalties to our members and to affiliated organizations throughout the world. We also distribute royalties received from those organizations to our members for the use of their music worldwide. SOCAN has offices in Toronto, Montreal, Vancouver, and Dartmouth."

SOCIETY OF COMPOSERS & LYRICISTS

8447 Wilshire Blvd., Suite 401, Beverly Hills CA 90211. (310)281-2812. **Fax:** (310)284-4861. **E-mail:** execdir@thescl.com; office@thescl.com. **Website:** www.thescl.com. The professional nonprofit trade organization for members actively engaged in writing music/lyrics for films, TV, and/or video games, or are students of film composition or songwriting for film. Primary mission is to advance the interests of the film and TV music community. Offers an award-winning quarterly publication, educational seminars, screenings, special member-only events, and other member benefits. Applications accepted year-round. Membership fees: $150 full membership (composers, lyricists, songwriters—film/TV music credits must be submitted); $85 associate/student membership for composers, lyricists, songwriters without credits only; $150 sponsor/special friend membership (music editors, music supervisors, music attorneys, agents, etc.).

☯ ◎ SODRAC INC.

Tower B, Suite 1010, 1470 Peel, Montreal QC H3A 1T1 Canada. (514)845-3268. **Fax:** (514)845-3401. **E-mail:** sodrac@sodrac.ca; members@sodrac.ca. **Website:** www.sodrac.ca. "SODRAC is a reproduction rights collective society facilitating the clearing of rights on musical and artistic works based on the Copyright Board of Canada tariffs or through collective agreements concluded with any users. It is responsible for the distribution of royalties to its national and international members. The society counts more than 6,000 Canadian members and represents musical repertoire originating from nearly 100 foreign countries and manages the right of 25,000 Canadian and foreign visual artists. SODRAC is the only reproduction rights society in Canada where both songwriters and music publishers are represented, equally and directly." Serves those with an interest in songwriting and music publishing no matter what their age or skill level is. "Members must have written or published at least one musical work that has been reproduced on an audio (CD, cassette, or LP) or audio-visual support (TV, DVD, video), or published 5 musical works that have been recorded and used for commercial purposes. The new member will benefit from a society working to secure his reproduction rights (mechanicals) and broadcast mechanicals." Applications accepted year-round.

SONGWRITERS' ASSOCIATION OF WASHINGTON

4200 Wisconsin Ave. NW, PMB 106-137, Washington DC 20016. **E-mail:** contact@SAW.org. **Website:** www. saw.org. The Songwriters' Association of Washington (SAW) is a nonprofit organization established in 1979 to benefit aspiring and professional songwriters. "Our mission: Strengthen the craft of songwriting; foster the talents of our members; provide an active forum for songwriters and their work; celebrate the power of music." Membership: $35/year, $20/year for students.

THE SONGWRITERS GUILD OF AMERICA

5120 Virginia Way, Suite C22, Brentwood TN 37027. (615)742-9945. **Fax:** (615)630-7501. **E-mail:** membership@songwritersguild.com. **Website:** www.songwritersguild.com. "The Songwriters Guild of America Foundation offers a series of workshops with discounts for some to SGA members, including online classes and song critique opportunities. There is a charge for some songwriting classes and seminars; however, online classes and some monthly events may be included with an SGA membership. Charges vary depending on the class or event. Current class offerings and workshops vary. Visit website to sign up for the newsletter and e-events, and for more information on current events and workshops. Some current events in Nashville are the Ask-a-Pro and ProCritique sessions that give SGA members the opportunity to present their songs and receive constructive feedback from industry professionals. Various performance opportunities are also available to members, including an SGA Showcase at the Bluebird. The New York office hosts a weekly Pro-Shop, which is coordinated by producer/musician/award-winning singer Ann Johns Ruckert. For each of 6 sessions, an active publisher, producer or A&R person is invited to personally screen material from SGA writers. Participation is limited to 10 writers and an audit of 1 session. Audition of material is required. Various performance opportunities and critique sessions are also available from time to time. SGAF Week is held periodically and is a week of scheduled events and seminars of interest to songwriters that includes workshops, seminars and showcases."

SONGWRITERS HALL OF FAME (SONGHALL)

330 W. 58th St., Suite 411, New York NY 10019. (212)957-9230. **Fax:** (212)957-9227. **E-mail:** info@songhall.org. **Website:** www.songhall.org. **Contact:** Jimmy Webb, chairman. "SongHall membership consists of songwriters of all levels, music publishers, producers, record company executives, music attorneys, and lovers of popular music of all ages. There are different levels of membership, all able to vote in the election for inductees, except supporters and associates, who pay only $15 and $25 in dues (respectively), but are unable to vote. SongHall's mission is to honor the popular songwriters who write the soundtrack for the world, as well as providing educational and networking opportunities to our members through our workshop and showcase programs." Offers: newsletter, workshops, performance opportunities, networking meetings with industry pros and scholarships for excellence in songwriting. Applications accepted year-round. Membership fees: $15 and up.

SONGWRITERS OF WISCONSIN INTERNATIONAL

P.O. Box 1027, Neenah WI 54957. **E-mail:** sowi2012@gmail.com. **Website:** www.SongwritersOfWisconsin.org. Serves songwriters. "Membership is open to songwriters writing all styles of music. Residency in Wisconsin is recommended but not required. Members are encouraged to bring tapes and lyric sheets of their songs to the meetings, but it is not required. We are striving to improve the craft of songwriting in Wisconsin. Living in Wisconsin, a songwriter would be close to any of the workshops and showcases offered each month at different towns. The primary value of membership for a songwriter is in sharing ideas with other songwriters, being critiqued and helping other songwriters." Offers competitions, field trips, instruction, lectures, newsletter, performance opportunities, social outings, workshops, and critique sessions. Applications accepted year-round. Membership dues: $30/year.

SONGWRITERS RESOURCE NETWORK

Portland OR **E-mail:** info@songwritersresourcenetwork.com. **Website:** www.SongwritersResourceNetwork.com. "For songwriters and lyricists of every kind, from beginners to advanced." No eligibility requirements. "Purpose is to provide free information to help songwriters develop their craft, market their songs, and learn about songwriting opportunities. We provide leads to publishers, producers and other music industry professionals." Visit website for more information.

SOUTHWEST VIRGINIA SONGWRITERS ASSOCIATION

P.O. Box 698, Salem VA 24153. **E-mail:** info@svsasongs.com. **Website:** www.svsasongs.com. Accepts members of all ages and skill levels in all genres of music. SVSA helps regional members improve their songwriting knowledge and skills through song critiques, workshops and discussions of related topics in an encouraging and supportive environment. SVSA offers performance opportunities, instruction, monthly meetings and a monthly newsletter. Applications accepted year-round. Membership fee: $20/year.

TEXAS ACCOUNTANTS & LAWYERS FOR THE ARTS

P.O. Box 144722, Austin TX 78714. (512)459-8252. **E-mail:** info@talarts.org; centraltexas@talarts.org. **Website:** www.talarts.org. TALA's members include accountants, attorneys, museums, theater groups, dance groups, actors, artists, musicians, and filmmakers. Our members are of all age groups and represent all facets of their respective fields. TALA is a non-

profit organization that provides pro bono legal and accounting services to income-eligible artists from all disciplines and to nonprofit arts organizations. TALA also provides mediation services for resolving disputes as a low-cost, non-adversarial alternative to litigation. Offers newsletter, lectures, library, and workshops. Applications accepted year-round. Annual membership fees: students, $30; artists, $50; bands, $100; nonprofit organizations, $200.

TIPS TALA's speaker's program presents low-cost seminars on topics such as the music business, copyright and trademark, and the business of writing. These seminars are held annually at a location in Houston. TALA's speaker's program also provides speakers for seminars by other organizations.

TEXAS MUSIC OFFICE

P.O. Box 13246, Austin TX 78711. (512)463-6666. **Fax:** (512)463-4114. **E-mail:** music@governor.state.tx.us. **Website:** governor.state.tx.us/music. **Contact:** Casey J. Monahan, director. "The Texas Music Office (TMO) is a state-funded business promotion office and information clearing house for the Texas music industry. The TMO assists more than 14,000 individual clients each year, ranging from a new band trying to make statewide business contacts to BBC journalists seeking information on "down-south hip hop." The TMO is the sister office to the Texas Film Commission, both of which are within the governor's office. The TMO serves the Texas music industry by using its Business Referral Network: Texas Music Industry (7,880 Texas music businesses in 96 music business categories); Texas Music Events (625 Texas music events); Texas Talent Register (8,036 Texas recording artists); Texas Radio Stations (942 Texas stations); U.S. Music Contacts; Classical Texas (detailed information for all classical music organizations in Texas); and International (1,425 foreign businesses interested in Texas music). Provides referrals to Texas music businesses, talent, and events in order to attract new business to Texas and/or to encourage Texas businesses and individuals to keep music business in-state. Serves as a liaison between music businesses and other government offices and agencies. Publicizes significant developments within the Texas music industry."

There is a contact form on the website.

TORONTO MUSICIANS' ASSOCIATION

15 Gervais Dr., Suite 500, Toronto ON M3C 1Y8 Canada. (416)421-1020. **Fax:** (416)421-7011. **E-mail:** info@

tma149.ca; rsinnaeve@tma149.ca. **Website:** www.torontomusicians.org. "Local 149 of the American Federation of Musicians of the U.S. and Canada is the professional association for musicians in the greater Toronto Area. A member-driven association of 3,500 members, the TMA represents professional musicians in all facets of music in the greater Toronto area. Dedicated to the development of musical talent and skills, the Toronto Musicians' Association has for the past 100 years fostered the opportunity through the collective efforts of our members for professional musicians to live and work in dignity while receiving fair compensation." Joining fee: $225; thereafter, members pay $63.75 per quarter.

VOLUNTEER LAWYERS FOR THE ARTS

1 E. 53rd St., 6th Floor, New York NY 10022. (212)319-2787, ext. 1. **Fax:** (212)752-6575. **E-mail:** vlany@vlany.org. **Website:** www.vlany.org. Purpose of organization: Volunteer Lawyers for the Arts is dedicated to providing free arts-related legal assistance to low-income artists and not-for-profit arts organizations in all creative fields. Over 1,000 attorneys in the New York area donate their time through VLA to artists and arts organizations unable to afford legal counsel. Everyone is welcome to use VLA's Art Law Line, a legal hotline for any artist or arts organization needing quick answers to arts-related questions. VLA also provides clinics, seminars, and publications designed to educate artists on legal issues that affect their careers. Members receive discounts on publications and seminars, as well as other benefits. Some of the many publications we carry are *All You Need to Know About the Music Business*; *Business and Legal Forms for Fine Artists, Photographers & Authors & Self-Publishers*; *Contracts for the Film & TV Industry*, plus many more.

WASHINGTON AREA MUSIC ASSOCIATION

6263 Occoquan Forest Dr., Manassas VA 20112. (703)368-3300. **Fax:** (703)393-1028. **E-mail:** dcmusic@wamadc.com. **Website:** www.wamadc.com. Serves songwriters, musicians and performers, managers, club owners and entertainment lawyers; "all those with an interest in the Washington music scene." The organization is designed to promote the Washington, D.C., scene and increase its visibility. Its primary value to members is seminars and networking opportunities. Offers lectures, newsletter, performance opportunities, and workshops. WAMA sponsors the annual Washington Music Awards (The Wammies; the 2015 awards were held in February) and The Crosstown Jam or annual showcase of artists in the DC area. Applications accepted year-round. Membership fee: $35/year.

WEST COAST SONGWRITERS

1724 Laurel St., Suite 120, San Carlos CA 94070. (650)654-3966. **E-mail:** info@westcoastsongwriters.org; ian@westcoastsongwriters.org. **Website:** www.westcoastsongwriters.org. "Our 1,200 members are lyricists and composers from ages 16-80, from beginners to professional songwriters. No eligibility requirements. Our purpose is to provide the education and opportunities that will support our writers in creating and marketing outstanding songs. WCS provides support and direction through local networking and input from Los Angeles and Nashville music industry leaders, as well as valuable marketing opportunities. Most songwriters need some form of collaboration, and by being a member they are exposed to other writers, ideas, critiquing, etc." Offers annual West Coast Songwriters Conference, "the largest event of its kind in northern California. This 2-day event held the second weekend in September features 16 seminars, 50 screening sessions (over 1,200 songs listened to by industry professionals) and a sunset concert with hit songwriters performing their songs." Also offers monthly visits from major publishers, songwriting classes, competitions, seminars conducted by hit songwriters (online), song-screening service for members who cannot attend due to time or location, a monthly e-newsletter, monthly performance opportunities and workshops Applications accepted year-round. Membership fees: $40/year for students; $90/year, regular individual; $119, bands; $150+, contributing members. The 2015 dates of the conference are September 26-27.

TIPS "WCS's functions draw local talent and nationally recognized names together. This is of a tremendous value to writers outside a major music center. We are developing a strong songwriting community in Portland, and in northern and southern California. We serve the San Jose, Monterey Bay, East Bay, San Francisco, Los Angeles, Sacramento and Portland, Washington areas.

RETREATS & COLONIES

///

This section provides information on retreats and artists' colonies. These are places for creatives, including songwriters, to find solitude and spend concentrated time focusing on their work. While a residency at a colony may offer participation in seminars, critiques, or performances, the atmosphere of a colony or retreat is much more relaxed than that of a conference or workshop. Also, a songwriter's stay at a colony is typically anywhere from one to twelve weeks (sometimes longer), while time spent at a conference may only run from one to fourteen days.

Like conferences and workshops, however, artists' colonies and retreats span a wide range. Yaddo, perhaps the most well-known colony, limits its residencies to artists "working at a professional level in their field, as determined by a judging panel of professionals in the field." The Brevard Music Center offers residencies only to those involved in classical music. Despite differ-ent focuses, all artists' colonies and retreats have one thing in common: They are places where you may work undisturbed, usually in nature-oriented, secluded settings.

SELECTING A COLONY OR RETREAT

When selecting a colony or retreat, the primary consideration for many songwriters is cost, and you'll discover that arrangements vary greatly. Some colonies provide residencies, as well as stipends for personal expenses. Some suggest donations of a certain amount. Still others offer residencies for substantial sums but have financial assistance available.

When investigating the various options, consider meal and housing arrangements and your family obligations. Some colonies provide meals for residents, while others require residents to pay for meals. Some colonies house artists in one main building; others provide separate cottages. A few have provisions for spouses and families. Others prohibit families altogether.

Overall, residencies at colonies and retreats are competitive. Since only a handful of spots are available at each place, you often must apply months in advance for the time period you desire. A number of locations are open year-round, and you may find planning to go during the "off-season" lessens your competition. Other colonies, however, are only available during certain months. In any case, be prepared to include a sample of your best work with your application. Also, know what project you'll work on while in residence and have alternative projects in mind in case the first one doesn't work out once you're there.

Each listing in this section details fee requirements, meal and housing arrangements, and space and time availability, as well as the retreat's surroundings, facilities and special activities. Of course, before making a final decision, send a SASE to the colonies or retreats that interest you to receive their most up-to-date details. Costs, application requirements, and deadlines are particularly subject to change.

MUSICIAN'S RESOURCE

For other listings of songwriter-friendly colonies, see *Musician's Resource* (available from Watson-Guptill—www.watsonguptill.com), which not only provides information about conferences, workshops, and academic programs but also residencies and retreats. Also check the Publications of Interest section in this book for newsletters and other periodicals providing this information.

THE TYRONE GUTHRIE CENTRE

Annaghmakerrig, Newbliss, County Monaghan Ireland. **E-mail:** info@tyroneguthrie.ie. **Website:** www.tyroneguthrie.ie. Offers year-round residencies. Artists may stay for anything from 1 week to 3 months in the Big House, or for up to 6 months at a time in one of the 5 self-catering houses in the old farmyard. Open to artists of all disciplines (music, dance, performing arts). For Irish and European artists. To qualify for a residency, it is necessary to show evidence of a significant level of achievement in the relevant field.

THE HAMBIDGE CENTER

105 Hambidge Court, Rabun Gap GA 30568. (706)746-5718. **Fax:** (706)746-9933. **E-mail:** center@hambidge.org; director@hambidge.org. **Website:** www.hambidge.org. **Contact:** Debra Sanders, office manager; Jamie Badoud, executive director. Hambidge provides a residency program that empowers talented artists to explore, develop, and express their creative voices. Situated on 600 acres in the mountains of north Georgia, Hambidge is a sanctuary of time and space that inspires artists working in a broad range of disciplines to create works of the highest caliber. Hambidge's Residency Program opens the first week of February and closes mid-to late-December through the month of January. Application deadlines are: January 15 for May-August; April 15 for September-December; September 15 for March-April of the following year.
COSTS Several scholarships are available.

ISLE ROYALE NATIONAL PARK ARTIST-IN-RESIDENCE PROGRAM

800 E. Lakeshore Dr., Houghton MI 49931. (906)482-0984. **Fax:** (906)482-8753. **E-mail:** Greg_Blust@nps.gov. **Website:** www.nps.gov/getinvolved/artist-in-residence.htm. Offers 2–3-week residencies from mid-June to mid-September. Open to all art forms. Accommodates 1 artist with 1 companion at 1 time. Personal living quarters include cabin with shared outhouse. A canoe is provided for transportation. Offers a guest house at the site that can be used as a studio. The artist is asked to contribute a piece of work representative of their stay at Isle Royale, to be used by the park in an appropriate manner. During their residency, artists will be asked to share their experience (1 presentation per week of residency, about 1 hour/week) with the public by demonstration, talk, or other means.

REQUIREMENTS Deadline: applications should be postmarked or delievered by February 16. Send for application forms and guidelines. Accepts inquiries via fax or e-mail. A panel of professionals from various disciplines and park representatives will choose the finalists. The selection is based on artistic integrity, ability to reside in a wilderness environment, a willingness to donate a finished piece of work inspired on the island, and the artist's ability to relate and interpret the park through his work.

KALANI OCEANSIDE RETREAT

RR2, Box 4500, Pahoa HI 96778. (808)965-7828. **Fax:** (808)965-0527. **Website:** www.kalani.com.

"Kalani Honua means harmony of heaven and earth, and this is what we aspire to. We welcome all in the spirit of aloha and are guided by the Hawai'ian tradition of `ohana (extended family), respecting our diversity yet sharing in unity. We invite you to open your heart to the Big Island of Hawaii at Kalani Oceanside Retreat."

SITKA CENTER FOR ART & ECOLOGY

56605 Sitka Dr., Otis OR 97368. (541)994-5485. **Fax:** (541)994-8024. **E-mail:** info@sitkacenter.org. **Website:** www.sitkacenter.org.
COSTS Residency and housing provided. The resident is asked to provide some form of community service on behalf of Sitka.

VIRGINIA CENTER FOR THE CREATIVE ARTS

154 San Angelo Dr., Amherst VA 24521. (434)946-7236. **Fax:** (434)946-7239. **E-mail:** vcca@vcca.com. **Website:** www.vcca.com. Offers residencies year-round, typical residency lasts 2 weeks to 2 months. Open to originating artists: composers, writers, and visual artists. Accommodates 25 at one time.
COSTS Application fee: $40. Deadline as of 2015: May 15 for October-January residency; September 15 for February-May residency; January 15 for June-September residency. For application form, download from website. Applications are reviewed by panelists. "Artists are accepted at VCCA without consideration for their financial situation. We ask Fellows to contribute according to their ability. The actual cost to us of a residency is $180 per day."

WORKSHOPS & CONFERENCES

For a songwriter just starting out, conferences and workshops can provide valuable learning opportunities. At conferences, songwriters can have their songs evaluated, hear suggestions for further improvement, and receive feedback from music business experts. They also are excellent places to make valuable industry contacts. Workshops can help a songwriter improve his craft and learn more about the business of songwriting. They may involve classes on songwriting and the business, as well as lectures and seminars by industry professionals.

Each year, hundreds of workshops and conferences take place all over the country. Songwriters can choose from small regional workshops held in someone's living room to large national conferences such as South by Southwest in Austin, Texas, which hosts more than 6,000 industry people, songwriters and performers. Many songwriting organizations—national and local—host workshops that offer instruction on just about every songwriting topic imaginable, from lyric writing and marketing strategy to contract negotiation. Conferences provide songwriters the chance to meet one-on-one with publishing and record company professionals and give performers the chance to showcase their work for a live audience (usually consisting of industry people) during the conference. There are conferences and workshops that address almost every type of music, offering programs for songwriters, performers, musical playwrights and much more.

This section includes national and local workshops and conferences with a brief description of what they offer, when they are held and how much they cost to attend. Write or call any that interest you for further information. To find out what workshops or conferences take place in specific parts of the country, see the Geographic Index at the end of this book.

ASCAP I CREATE MUSIC EXPO

1 Lincoln Plaza, New York NY 10023. **E-mail:** expo@ascap.com. **Website:** www.ascap.com. "The ASCAP I Create Music EXPO puts you face-to-face with some of the world's most successful songwriters, composers, producers and music business leaders, all who willingly share their knowledge and expertise and give you the know-how to take your music to the next level." For more info and to register, visit the website.

ASCAP LESTER SILL SONGWRITERS WORKSHOP

7920 Sunset Blvd., 3rd Floor, Los Angeles CA 90046. **Website:** www.ascap.com/music-career/workshops.aspx. Annual workshop for advanced songwriters sponsored by the ASCAP Foundation. Re-named in 1995 to honor ASCAP's late board member and industry pioneer Lester Sill, the workshop takes place over a four-week period and features prominent guest speakers from various facets of the music business. Workshop dates and deadlines vary from year to year. Applicants must submit 2 songs on a CD (cassette tapes not accepted), lyric sheets, brief bio and short explanation as to why they would like to participate, e-mail address, and telephone number. Limited number of participants are selected each year. This is one of many ASCAP workshops.

ASCAP MUSICAL THEATRE WORKSHOP

1 Lincoln Plaza, New York NY 10023. (212)621-6264. **Website:** www.ascap.com/music-career/workshops.aspx. Workshop is for musical theater composers and lyricists only. Its purpose is to nurture and develop new musicals for the theater. Offers programs for songwriters. Offers programs annually, usually April through May. Event takes place in New York. Four musical works are selected. Others are invited to audit the workshop. Participants are amateur and professional songwriters, composers and musical playwrights. Participants are selected by demo CD submission. Deadline: see website. Also available: the annual ASCAP/Disney Musical Theatre Workshop in Los Angeles. It takes place in January and February. Deadline is late November. Details similar to New York workshop as above.

BILLBOARD & THE HOLLYWOOD REPORTER FILM & TV MUSIC CONFERENCE

Sofitel LA, 8555 Beverly Blvd., Los Angeles CA 90048. (212)493-4026. **E-mail:** conferences@billboard.com. **Website:** www.billboardevents.com/filmtv. Promotes all music for film and TV. Offers programs for songwriters and composers. Held annually in November. More than 350 songwriters/musicians participate in each event. Participants are professional songwriters, composers, producers, directors, etc. Conference panelists are selected by invitation. For registration information, including fees, see the website.

THE BMI LEHMAN ENGEL MUSICAL THEATRE WORKSHOP

7 World Trade Center, 250 Greenwich St., New York NY 10007. (212)230-3000. **Fax:** (212)262-2824. **E-mail:** theatreworkshop@bmi.com. **Website:** www.bmi.com/genres/entry/the_bmi_lehman_engel_musical_theatre_workshop. **Contact:** Patricia Cook, director. "BMI is a music licensing company that collects royalties for affiliated writers and publishers. We offer programs to musical theater composers, lyricists and librettists. The BMI-Lehman Engel Musical Theatre Workshops were formed in an effort to refresh and stimulate professional writers, as well as to encourage and develop new creative talent for the musical theater. Each workshop meets 1 afternoon a week for 2 hours at BMI, New York. Participants are professional songwriters, composers and playwrights. The BMI Lehman Musical Theatre Workshop Showcase presents the best of the workshop to producers, agents, record and publishing company execs, press and directors for possible option and production. Visit the website for application. Tape and lyrics of 3 compositions required with applications."

TIPS BMI also sponsors a jazz composers workshop. For more information, contact Raette Johnson at rjohnson@bmi.com.

CMJ MUSIC MARATHON & FILM FESTIVAL

1201 Broadway, Suite 706, New York NY 10001. (212)277-7120. **Fax:** (212)719-9396. **E-mail:** marketing@cmj.com; editorial@cmj.com. **Website:** www.cmj.com/marathon. "Premier annual alternative music gathering of more than 9,000 music business and film professionals. Fall, New York; 2015 dates are Oct. 13-17. Features 5 days and nights of more than 75 panels and workshops focusing on every facet of the industry; exclusive film screenings; keynote speeches by the world's most intriguing and controversial voices; exhibition area featuring live performance stage; over 1,000 of music's brightest and most visionary talents (from the unsigned to the legendary) performing over

5 evenings at more than 80 of New York's most important music venues." Participants are selected by submitting demonstration tape.

CUTTING EDGE C.E.

(Formerly the Cutting Edge Music Business Conference), New Orleans LA 70116. (504)945-1800. E-mail: eric@cuttingedgenola.com. **Website:** www.cuttingedgenola.com. Cutting Edge C.E. will again discuss "Hot Topics" and "Current Trends" in today's entertainment business. Attend conference sessions on Entertainment law, music business, film financing and tax credits, roots music, and the new works showcases. Check out the NOLA Downtown Festival and Cruisin' New Orleans Pro Gear Show at the Historic Carver Theater. Held at the InterContinental Hotel & the Historic Carver Theater in New Orleans. 2015 dates: August 27-29. Schedule and speaker lineup are available online.

FOLK ALLIANCE ANNUAL CONFERENCE

509 Delaware St. #101, Kansas City MO 64105. (816)221-3655. **Fax:** (816)221-3658. **E-mail:** fai@folk.org. **Website:** www.folkalliance.org/conference. Conference/workshop topics change each year. Conference takes place late February and lasts 4 days at a different location each year. Two-thousand-plus attendees include artists, agents, arts administrators, print/broadcast media, folklorists, folk societies, merchandisers, presenters, festivals, recording companies, etc. Artists wishing to showcase should contact the office for a showcase application form. The February 2016 event will open to submissions for showcases, volunteering, and scholarships on July 1, 2015.

INDEPENDENT MUSIC CONFERENCE

304 Main Ave., PMB 287, Norwalk CT 06851. (203)606-4649. **E-mail:** IMC@intermixx.com. **Website:** www.independentmusicconference.com. "The purpose of the IMC is to bring together rock, hip-hop and acoustic music for of panels and showcases. Offers programs for songwriters, composers and performers. Two-hundred-fifty showcases at 20 clubs around the city. Also offer a DJ cutting contest." Held annually in the fall. Three-thousand amateur and professional songwriters, composers, individual vocalists, bands, individual instrumentalists, attorneys, managers, agents, publishers, A&R, promotions, club owners, etc., participate each year. Check the website for an application.

◗   Formerly the Philadelphia Music Conference.

KERRVILLE FOLK FESTIVAL

Kerrville Festivals, Inc., P.O. Box 291466, Kerrville TX 78029. **E-mail:** info@kerrville-music.com. **Website:** www.kerrvillefolkfestival.com. Hosts 3-day songwriters' school, a 4-day music business school and New Folk concert competition. Festival produced in late spring and early summer. Spring festival lasts 18 days and is held outdoors at Quiet Valley Ranch. One-hundred-ten or more songwriters participate. Performers are professional songwriters and bands. Participants selected by submitting demo, by invitation only. Send cassette, or CD, promotional material and list of upcoming appearances. "Songwriter and music schools include lunch, experienced professional instructors, camping on ranch and concerts. Rustic facilities. Food available at reasonable cost. Audition materials accepted at above address. These three-day and four-day seminars include noon meals, handouts and camping on the ranch. Usually held during Kerrville Folk Festival, first and second week in June. Write or check the website for contest rules, schools and seminars information, and festival schedules. Also establishing a Phoenix Fund to provide assistance to ill or injured singer/songwriters who find themselves in distress."

◗   This organization also organizes the Kerrville Fall Music Festival.

LAMB'S RETREAT FOR SONGWRITERS

P.O. Box 304, Royal Oak MI 48068-0304. (248)589-3913. **E-mail:** johndlamb@ameritech.net; info@springfed.org. **Website:** www.springfed.org. **Contact:** John D. Lamb, director. Lamb's Retreat for Songwriters is presented by Springfield Arts, a nonprofit organization. Offers programs for songwriters on annual basis; 2015 dates are November 5-8, and November 12-15, at The Birchwood Inn, Harbor Springs, Michigan. Sixty songwriters/musicians participate in each event. Participants are amateur and professional songwriters. Anyone can participate. Send for registration or e-mail. Deadline: 2 weeks before event begins. Faculty are noted songwriters.

MANCHESTER MUSIC FESTIVAL

P.O. Box 33, 42 Dillingham Ave., Manchester VT 05254. (802)362-1956. **Fax:** (802)362-0711. **E-mail:** info@mmfvt.org. **Website:** www.mmfvt.org. **Contact:** Joana Genova, education director. Offers classical music education and performances. Summer program for young professional musicians offered in tandem with a professional concert series in the mountains of Manchester, Vermont. Up to 23 young professionals, age 19 and up, are selected by audition for the Young Artists Program, which provides instruction, performance and teaching opportunities, with full scholarship for all participants. Commissioning opportunities for new music, and performance opportunities for professional chamber ensembles and soloists for both summer and fall/winter concert series. 2015 dates: August 19-22.

THE NEW HARMONY PROJECT

P.O. Box 441062, Indianapolis IN 46244-1062. (317)464-1103. **E-mail:** mhunter@newharmonyproject.org; jgrynheim@newharmonyproject.org. **Website:** www.newharmonyproject.org. **Contact:** Mead Hunter, artistic director; Joel Grynheim, project director.

O "The purpose of The New Harmony Project shall be to create, nurture, and promote new works for stage, television and film that sensitively and truthfully explore the positive aspects of life. Our goal is to bring the writers who seek to produce uplifting, high-quality entertainment alternatives to our conference, surround them with professional resources, provide them with the opportunity to develop these works in a supportive and life-affirming environment that further enables their writing creativity and helps each writer to tell their story well." 2015 dates: May 22-31.

NEWPORT FOLK FESTIVAL

New Festival Productions, LLC, P.O. Box 3865, Newport RI 02840. **E-mail:** info@newportfolk.org. **Website:** www.newportfolk.org. An annual folk festival. 2015 dates: July 24-26.

NEWPORT JAZZ FESTIVAL

New Festival Productions, LLC, Newport RI **E-mail:** jazz@newportjazzfest.org. **Website:** www.newportjazzfest.org. An annual jazz festival. 2015 dates: July 31 - August 2. "Hailed by *The New York Times* as the festival that put jazz festivals on the map, the Newport Jazz Festival was founded by jazz pianist George Wein in 1954 as the first outdoor music festival of its kind devoted entirely to jazz, and is now universally acknowledged as the grandfather of all jazz festivals. During the last half-century, the name Newport has become synonymous with the best in jazz music. In its long illustrious history, the Newport jazz Festival

has presented a virtual pantheon of Jazz immortals alongside an array of rising young artists: Duke Ellington's 1956 rebirth framing Paul Gonzalves' epic solo; subject of the classic 1958 documentary, *Jazz on a Summer's Day*; origin of famous recordings by Thelonious Monk, John Coltrane and Miles Davis; showcase for emerging young masters including Wynton Marsalis, Diana Krall, Joshua Redman and Esperanza Spalding. Referred to as a mecca of jazz, the event draws thousands of people from all over the world to its uniquely picturesque outdoor stages at the International Tennis Hall of Fame and Fort Adams State Park."

NORFOLK CHAMBER MUSIC FESTIVAL

P.O. Box 208246, New Haven CT 06520. **E-mail:** norfolk@yale.edu. **Website:** www.yale.edu/norfolk. Festival season of chamber music. Offers programs for composers and performers. Offers programs in summer only. Approximately 45 fellows participate. Participants are up-and-coming composers and instrumentalists. Participants are selected by following a screening round. Auditions are held in New Haven, Connecticut. "Held at the Ellen Battell Stoeckel Estate, the Festival offers a magnificent Music Shed with seating for 1,000, practice facilities, music library, dining hall, laundry and art gallery. Nearby are hiking, bicycling and swimming."

○ NORTH BY NORTHEAST MUSIC FESTIVAL AND CONFERENCE

189 Church St., Lower Level, Toronto ON M5B 1Y7 Canada. (416)863-6963. **Fax:** (416)863-0828. **E-mail:** info@nxne.com; alice@nowtoronto.com. **Website:** www.nxne.com. 2015 dates: June 17-21. "Our festival takes place mid-June at over 30 venues across downtown Toronto, drawing over 2,000 conference delegates, 500 bands and 50,000 music fans. Musical genres include everything from folk to funk, roots to rock, polka to punk and all points in between, bringing exceptional new talent, media front-runners, music business heavies and music fans from all over the world to Toronto." Participants include emerging and established songwriters, vocalists, composers, bands and instrumentalists. Festival performers are selected by submitting a CD and accompanying press kit or applying through sonicbids.com. Application forms are available by website or by calling the office. Submission period each year is from November 1 to the third weekend in January.

NSAI SONG CAMPS

1710 Roy Acuff Place, Nashville TN 37023. (800)321-6008; (615)256-335. **Fax:** (615)256-0034. **E-mail:** events@nashvillesongwriters.com; reception@nashvillesongwriters.com. **Website:** www.nashvillesongwriters.com. 2015 dates: July 24-26. Offers programs strictly for songwriters. Events held in late July in Nashville. "We provide most meals and lodging is available. We also present an amazing evening of music presented by the faculty." Camps are 3-4 days long, with 36-112 participants, depending on the camp. "There are different levels of camps, some having preferred prerequisites. Each camp varies. Please call, e-mail or refer to website. It really isn't about the genre of music, but the quality of the song itself. Song Camp strives to strengthen the writer's vision and skills, therefore producing the better song. Song Camp is known as 'boot camp' for songwriters. It is guaranteed to catapult you forward in your writing! Participants are all aspiring songwriters led by a pro faculty. We do accept lyricists only and composers only with the hopes of expanding their scope." Participants are selected through submission of 2 songs with lyric sheet. Song Camp is open to NSAI members, although anyone can apply and, upon acceptance, join the organization.
COSTS $410 for members; $510 for nonmembers.

☺ ORFORD FESTIVAL

Orford Arts Centre, 3165 chemin du Parc, Orford QC J1X 7A2 Canada. (819)843-9871; (800)567-6155. **Fax:** (819)843-7274. **E-mail:** info@arts-orford.org. **Website:** www.arts-orford.org. The Orford Arts Centre plays host to a world-class Academy of Music, which offers advanced training to particularly gifted young musicians who are at the beginning of a professional career in classical music. Together with internationally renowned professors and artists who are devoted to training the next generation, we are committed to providing our students with pedagogical activities that are as unique as they are enriching. In pursuit of its mission, the Centre abides by the following values: excellence, discipline, dedication, open-mindedness, respect and the will to surpass individual expectations.

☻ REGGAE SUMFEST

Shops 9 & 10 Parkway Plaza, Rose Hall, Montego Bay Jamaica. (876)953-8360. **Website:** reggaesumfest.com. **Contact:** Tina Mae Davis, festival coordinator. 2015 dates: July 12-18. "Reggae Sumfest is a musical event to which we welcome 30,000-plus patrons each year. The festival showcases the best of dance hall and reggae music, as well as top R&B/hip-hop performers. The festival also offers delicious Jamaican cuisine, as well as arts and crafts from all over the island. The main events of the festival are held at Catherine Hall, Montego Bay, Jamaica, over a three-day period, which usually falls in the third week of July, from Sunday to Saturday." Reggae Sumfest is presented by Summerfest Productions and accepts press kit submissions for persons wishing to perform at the festival between November and January each year.

THE SONGWRITERS GUILD OF AMERICA FOUNDATION

5120 Virginia Way, Suite C22, Brentwood TN 37027. (800)524-6742; (615)742-9945. **E-mail:** membership@songwritersguild.com. **Website:** www.songwritersguild.com. "For the professional songwriter and songwriters' heirs, SGA helps protect your copyrights, pitch your catalog and collect on royalties." The Foundation is in charge of many events, including workshops in the New York, Nashville, and Los Angeles areas.

SOUTH BY SOUTHWEST MUSIC CONFERENCE

SXSW Headquarters, P.O. Box 685289, Austin TX 78768. **E-mail:** sxsw@sxsw.com. **Website:** sxsw.com/music/about. 2015 dates: March 17-22. South by Southwest (SXSW) is a private company based in Austin, Texas, with a year-round staff of professionals dedicated to building and delivering conference and festival events for entertainment and related media industry professionals. Since 1987, SXSW has produced the internationally recognized music and media conference and festival (SXSW). As the entertainment business adjusted to issues of future growth and development in 1994, SXSW added conferences and festivals for the film industry (SXSW Film), as well as for the blossoming interactive media (SXSW Interactive Festival). Now 3 industry events converge in Austin during a Texas-sized week, mirroring the ever-increasing convergence of entertainment/media outlets. The next SXSW Music Conference and Festival will be held in March. Offers panel discussions, "Crash Course" educational seminars and nighttime showcases. SXSW Music seeks out speakers who have developed unique ways to create and sell music. The conference includes over 50 sessions including a panel of label heads discussing strategy, interviews with notable artists, topical discussions, demo listening sessions and the mentor program. And when the sun goes down, a multitude of performances by musicians and songwriters from across the country and around the world populate the SXSW Music Festival, held in venues in central Austin." Write, e-mail or visit website for dates and registration instructions.

TIPS "Visit the website in August to apply for showcase consideraton. SXSW is also involved in North by Northeast (NXNE), held in Toronto, Canada in late spring."

THE SWANNANOA GATHERING—CONTEMPORARY FOLK WEEK

Warren Wilson College, P.O. Box 9000, Asheville NC 28815-9000. (828)298-3434. **Fax:** (828)298-3434. **E-mail:** gathering@warren-wilson.edu. **Website:** www.swangathering.com. "For anyone who ever wanted to make music for an audience, we offer a comprehensive week in artist development, including classes in songwriting, performance, and vocal coaching." For a brochure or other info, contact The Swannanoa Gathering. There are several programs that happen in the summer (July and August), such as Celtic Week, Fiddle Week, and Guitar Week. Annual program of The Swannanoa Gathering Folk Arts Workshops.

WEST COAST SONGWRITERS CONFERENCE

(formerly Northern California Songwriters Association), 1724 Laurel St., Suite 120, San Carlos CA 94070. (650)654-3966. **E-mail:** info@westcoastsongwriters.org; ian@westcoastsongwriters.org. **Website:** www.westcoastsongwriters.org. 2015 dates: September 26-27. "Conference offers opportunity and education; 16 seminars, 50 song-screening sessions (1,500 songs reviewed), performance showcases, one-on-one sessions and concerts." Offers programs for lyricists, songwriters, composers and performers. "During the year we have competitive live songwriter competitions. Winners go into the playoffs. Winners of the playoffs perform at the sunset concert at the conference." Event

takes place second weekend in September at Foothill College, Los Altos Hills, California. More than 500 songwriters/musicians participate in this event. Participants are songwriters, composers, musical playwrights, vocalists, bands, instrumentalists and those interested in a career in the music business."

WESTERN WIND WORKSHOP IN ENSEMBLE SINGING

263 W. 86th St., New York NY 10024. (212)873-2848. **E-mail:** workshops@westernwind.org; info@westernwind.org. **Website:** www.westernwind.org/workshops.html. Participants learn the art of ensemble singing—no conductor, one on-a-part. Workshops focus on blend, diction, phrasing, and production. Offers programs for performers. Limited talent-based scholarship available. Offers programs annually. Takes place June and August in the music department at Smith College, Northampton, Massachusetts. Seventy to 80 songwriters and/or musicians participate in each event. Participants are amateur and professional vocalists. Anyone can participate. Send for application or register at their website. (2015 dates: Session 1 is June 26–28 and June 29–July 4. Session 2 is July 31–August 2 and August 3–8.)

WINTER MUSIC CONFERENCE INC.

3450 NE 12 Terrace, Ft. Lauderdale FL 33334. (954)563-4444. **Fax:** (954)563-1599. **E-mail:** info@wintermusicconference.com. **Website:** www.wintermusicconference.com. Features educational seminars and showcases for dance, hip-hop, alternative, and rap. Offers programs for songwriters and performers. Offers programs annually. Event takes place March of each year in Miami, Florida. Three-thousand songwriters/musicians participate in each event. Participants are amateur and professional songwriters, composers, musical playwrights, vocalists, bands and instrumentalists. Participants are selected by submitting demo tape. Send SASE, visit website or call for application. Deadline: February. Event held at either nightclubs or hotel with complete staging, lights and sound. 2015 dates were March 24–28.

VENUES

THE 4TH AVENUE TAVERN
210 E. 4th Ave., Olympia WA 98501. (360)951-7887.
E-mail: the4thave@gmail.com. **Website:** www.the4t-
have.com. Music: indie, alternative, funk, rock, punk.
"The 4th Ave is home to one of the largest stages in
Olympia. Booking is very selective. Only contact if
you have a large draw in the South Sound area."

40 WATT CLUB
285 W. Washington St., Athens GA 30601. (706)549-
7871. **E-mail:** velenavego@gmail.com. **Website:**
www.40watt.com. **Contact:** Velena Vego, talent buyer.
Music: indie, rock, alternative.

123 PLEASANT STREET
123 Pleasant St., Morgantown WV 26505. (304)292-
0800. **Fax:** (304)292-2700. **E-mail:** 123pleasantstreet@
gmail.com. **Website:** www.123pleasantstreet.com.
"An eclectic crowd can be expected any given night
and is as diverse as the bands that grace our stage,
whether it be rock, bluegrass, punk, jazz, reggae, salsa,
country, DJs, indie, hardcore, old time, or some mixture of some or all or the above." To book, send media,
press kits, 8x10 glossies, etc., via postal mail.

ABG'S BAR
190 W. Center St., Provo UT 84601. (801)373-1200. E-
mail: bigdanet@gmail.com. **Website:** abgsbar.com.
Music: rock, alt-country, alternative, folk, blues, jazz.

ACL LIVE AT THE MOODY THEATER
310 W. Willie Nelson Blvd., Austin TX 78701.
(512)225-7999. **E-mail:** info@acl-live.com. **Web-**
site: www.acl-live.com. Austin City Limits Live at
the Moody Theater (ACL Live) is a state-of-the-art,
2,750-person capacity live-music venue that hosts approximately 100 concerts a year.

ANDERSON FAIR RETAIL RESTAURANT
(832)767-2785. **Website:** andersonfair.net. Features
original, eclectic music performed largely by Texas
singer/songwriters.

ANTONE'S
2015 E. Riverside Dr., Austin TX 78741. (512)800-
4628. **Website:** www.antonesnightclub.com. "Antone's Nightclub, the first club on 6th St., opened its
doors in the summer of 1975 with the great Clifton
Chenier. The venue, now located at the corner of 5th
and Lavaca streets, was founded by legendary promoter Clifford Antone and has hosted such blues 'greats'
as Muddy Waters, B.B. King, Buddy Guy, John Lee
Hooker, Pinetop Perkins, James Cotton, and countless others."

ARLENE'S GROCERY
95 Stanton St., New York NY 10002. (212)358-1633.
Fax: (212)995-1719. **E-mail:** booking@arlenesgrocery.
net. **Website:** www.arlenesgrocery.net. "For booking,
write the name of your band and any requested dates/
time frame for the show in the subject line of an e-
mail. The body of the e-mail should contain a brief
description of your music and instrumentation; links
to your band's website, streaming music, an EPK, and
social media pages; show history in New York and

estimated draw; and requested dates or time frame." Shows usually booked at least 6 weeks out. Music: rock, alternate, indie, old school, new school, etc.

ARMADILLO'S BAR & GRILL

132 Dock St., Annapolis MD 21401. (410)280-0028; (410)756-4665. **E-mail:** socialpub25@gmail.com. **Website:** www.armadillosannapolis.com. **Contact:** Chad Byers. "Armadillo's is the top choice for nightlife in downtown Annapolis. We are the only venue in town to provide 2 levels of live entertainment. Upstairs, Armadillo's brings you the hottest local and national bands, in a casual, intimate setting, while DJs keep the crowd moving downstairs." Music: rock, acoustic, reggae, soul, pop, indie, alternative.

ART BAR

1211 Park St., Columbia SC 29201. (803)929-0198. **Website:** artbarsc.com. Booking guidelines available on website. Music: rock, alternative, indie, punk, hard rock, hip-hop.

TIPS Booking via online submissions form: artbarsc. com/music/booking.

ASHLAND COFFEE & TEA

100 N. Railroad Ave., Ashland VA 23005. (804)798-1702. **Fax:** (804)798-2573. **Website:** ashlandcoffeeandtea.com. "Join us most Thursdays, Fridays, and Saturdays in our intimate 'Listening Room' for an evening of Americana, bluegrass, folk, blues, jazz, pop—you never know what we'll have on tap with our wide range of performers. Don't miss 'Homegrown Wednesday,' featuring local Virginia talent, or the 'Songwriter's Showdown,' a songwriting and vocal performance competition every Tuesday."

BACKBOOTH

37 W. Pine St., Orlando FL 32801. (407)999-2570. **E-mail:** booking@backbooth.com. **Website:** www.backbooth.com. "BackBooth's reputation as a music venue has grown to it being named one of the best live-music venues in the city, according to *Orlando Weekly*, and still boasts the most impressive draft selection in downtown. With a capacity of 350, a large stage, a powerful sound/lighting system, balcony, and back bar area, the club still maintains a very comfortable and inviting, almost pub-like, atmosphere with Old English décor, including woodwork and dark curtains throughout. As a venue, BackBooth continues to play host to many popular national and regional acts, while remaining a favorite among locals. The club is also known for its dance parties, which are among the most popular and recognized in town. Whether it be for an intimate live performance, a rousing rock show, or a night of dancing and drinks, BackBooth is established in the heart of the central Florida community as a favorite destination." Music: reggae, acoustic, alternative, indie, pop, hip-hop, jam, roots, soul, gospel, funk, dubstep, country, rock, metal.

BACK EAST BAR & GRILL

9475 Briar Village Point, Colorado Springs CO 80920. (719)264-6161. **Website:** www.backeastbarandgrill.com/briargate/index.cfm. "We have created the perfect place for you to watch your favorite game and enjoy the incredible food and flavors that we have brought from home. We know you will enjoy every minute that you share with us. So sit back and have a drink, eat some great food, and enjoy your favorite team on one of our many TVs." Music: rock, alternative, R&B, blues, country, pop.

THE BARLEY STREET TAVERN

2735 N. 62nd St., Omaha NE 68104. (402)408-0028. **E-mail:** bradhoshawbooking@gmail.com; bookings@barleystreet.com. **Website:** www.barleystreet.com. **Contact:** Brad Hoshaw, booking agent. "We have live music performances on scheduled nights, featuring some great local and regional performers, as well as national touring acts. This is the music venue to find the best in all music styles." Music: rock, alternative, folk, indie, country, pop, Americana.

THE BELL HOUSE

149 7th St., Brooklyn NY 11215. (718)643-6510. **E-mail:** info@thebellhouseny.com. **E-mail:** booking@thebellhouseny.com. **Website:** www.thebellhouseny.com. "In fall 2008, a 1920s warehouse was converted into The Bell House. Called 'a welcome oasis' by TimeOut, The Bell House is a magnificent two-room music and events venue located in the Gowanus section of Brooklyn. The Main Room boasts 25-foot wooden arched ceilings, a 450-square-foot stage, and unobstructed views from any part of the room."

BELLY UP

143 S. Cedros Ave., Solana Beach CA 92075. (858)481-8140. **E-mail:** booking@bellyup.com. **Website:** bellyup.com. "The Belly Up is a live-music venue located in Solana Beach, California. We have all types of music almost every night and serve bar food and alcohol (and some tasty soft drinks), as well."

BERKELEY CAFE

217 W. Martin St., Raleigh NC 27601. (919)828-9190. **E-mail:** lakeboonee@bellsouth.net. **Contact:** Jim Shires. Music: rock, bluegrass, alternative, blues, punk, folk.

BILLY'S LOUNGE

1437 Wealthy St. SE, Grand Rapids MI 49506. (616)459-5757. **E-mail:** booking@billyslounge.com. **Website:** www.billyslounge.com. **Contact:** Lyndi Charles, booking manager. "Billy's Lounge is a local hot spot in the Eastown community. With our live music, a fully stocked bar, and dirt-cheap drink specials on a nightly basis, you can see why! Billy's has a strong history in keeping with the tradition of service and entertainment. We pride ourselves on our support of local music, our ability to drink, and the atmospheres we produce." Music: blues, rock, R&B, Americana, hip-hop, jazz.

BIMBO'S 365 CLUB

1025 Columbus Ave., San Francisco CA 94133. (415)474-0365. **E-mail:** info@bimbos365club.com. **E-mail:** booking@bimbos365club.com. **Website:** www.bimbos365club.com. Has featured Adele, 10,000 Maniacs, A Tribe Called Quest, Air, Ben Harper, Black Eyed Peas, Brian McKnight, Brian Setzer Orchestra, Coldplay, Iron and Wine, Jack Johnson, Jewel, Nelly Furtado, Pink Martini, She & Him, The Raconteurs, The Strokes, The Wallflowers, Van Morrison, and many more.

BLUE

650A Congress St., Portland ME 04101. (207)774-4111. **E-mail:** booking@portcityblue.com. **Website:** portcityblue.com. Mailing address for standard press kits and CDs: P.O. Box 4254, Portland, ME 04101. "Located in the heart of Portland's Arts District, Blue is Portland's most intimate live music venue. We present an array of music such as Celtic, Middle Eastern, blues, old time, jazz, folk, and more."

THE BLUE DOOR

2805 N. McKinley Ave., Oklahoma City OK 73106. (405)524-0738. **E-mail:** bluedoorokc@gmail.com. **Website:** www.bluedoorokc.com. **Contact:** Greg Johnson. "We have grown to become Oklahoma's premiere venue for performing songwriters, hosting such legends as Jimmy Webb, Joe Ely, Ramblin' Jack Elliott, David Lindley, and Tom Rush. We love working with new songwriters who are developing their audience and always welcome the best in bluegrass, folk, rock, country, and blues."

BLUE WHALE BAR

123 Astronaut E. S. Onizuka St., Suite 301, Los Angeles CA 90012. (213)538-8038. **Website:** bluewhalemusic.com. Blue Whale is a live jazz bar located in the heart of Little Tokyo, Los Angeles.

BOGART'S

2621 Vine St., Cincinnati OH 45219. (513)872-8801. **Fax:** (513)872-8805. **Website:** www.bogarts.com. The venue holds approximately 1,500 people, has 6 bars, 3 levels for concert viewing, 2 entrances, and an elevated stage. Bogart's has been recognized on the international stage for bringing the newest and best music and entertainment to the public for over 2 decades. Today, it is operated by Live Nation Inc., and continues the tradition of quality live entertainment that has been its forté since the building was built in 1890.

BOOTLEG BAR & THEATER

2220 Beverly Blvd., Los Angeles CA 90057. (213)908-5344. **E-mail:** sterling@foldsilverlake.com. **E-mail:** buyer@foldsilverlake.com. **Website:** oldsilverlake.com. **Contact:** Kelsey Mitchell, talent buyer. "For booking inquiries, please provide your name, the band's name, a phone number, and e-mail address in all correspondences. Please list your targeted show dates, or even some details on how you got referred. Please don't e-mail MP3s and such as attachments; just e-mail the appropriate URL or sound-clip address."

THE BOTTLENECK

737 New Hampshire, Lawrence KS 66044. (785)841-5483. **E-mail:** booking@pipelineproductions.com. **Website:** www.thebottlenecklive.com. "The Bottleneck is considered by many to be a rock 'n' roll historical landmark. The Bottleneck cemented its status as a scheduled stop on many major-city, national tours, giving nearby University of Kansas students access to some of the best names in modern music." Music: indie, rock, alternative, folk, country, jazz, blues, funk, dance, ska, psychedelic.

THE BOTTLETREE

3719 3rd Ave. S., Birmingham AL 35222. (205)533-6288. **Fax:** (205)533-7565. **E-mail:** info@thebottletree.com. **E-mail:** booking@thebottletree.com. **Website:** www.thebottletree.com. **Contact:** Merrilee Challiss. Music: punk, indie, folk, rock, country, soul, alternative.

TIPS All booking is done via e-mail.

BOTTOM OF THE HILL

1233 17th St., San Francisco CA 94107. (415)626-4455. **E-mail:** booking@bottomofthehill.com. **Website:** bottomofthehill.com. **Contact:** Ramona Downey; Ursula Rodriguez, bookers. "Chosen by *Rolling Stone* magazine as 'the best place to hear live music in San Francisco,' the Bottom of the Hill presents some of the finest original artists, 7 nights a week. Featuring up-and-coming acts from around the globe, as well as in our own backyard, the music spans the spectrum from alternative, rockabilly, punk, and hard rock to folk and funk and pop." Music: alternative, rock, rockabilly, punk, hard rock.

BOWERY BALLROOM

6 Delancey St., New York NY 10002. **E-mail:** info@bowerypresents.com. **Website:** www.boweryballroom.com. **Contact:** Eddie Brusier. "The best way to get a show at a Bowery Presents club is to send your press pack to: The Bowery Presents, c/o Eddie Bruiser, 156 Ludlow St., New York, NY 10002. Please list a New York show history and allow 4-6 weeks before following up with an e-mail."

THE BRASS RAIL

1121 Broadway, Ft. Wayne IN 46802. (260)267-5303. **E-mail:** corey@brassrailfw.com. **Website:** www.brassrailfw.com. Music: rock, garage punk, metal, country, rockabilly, surf, 1960s soul, indie rock, ska, reggae. **TIPS** "All booking is conducted through the website; do not call the bar."

THE BRICKYARD

129 N. Rock Island Rd., Wichita KS 67202. (316)263-4044. **E-mail:** booking@brickyardoldtown.com. **Website:** www.brickyardoldtown.com. Music: rock, indie, alternative, punk, classic rock, country.

BROOKLYN BOWL

61 Wythe Ave., Brooklyn NY 11249. (718)963-3369. **E-mail:** rock.androll@brooklynbowl.com. **E-mail:** booking@brooklynbowl.com. **Website:** www.brooklynbowl.com. "Brooklyn Bowl redefines the entertainment experience for the 21st century. Centered around a 16-lane bowling alley, 600-capacity performance venue with live music 7 nights a week, and food by Blue Ribbon, Brooklyn Bowl stakes out expansive new territory, literally and conceptually, in the 23,000-square-foot former Hecla Iron Works (1882), 1 block from the burgeoning waterfront." Music: rock, indie, hip-hop, R&B, alternative, punk, funk, folk, reggae, soul.

THE BROTHERHOOD LOUNGE

119 Capitol Way N., Olympia WA 98501. (360)352-4153. **Website:** thebrotherhoodlounge.com. Music: soul, funk, rock, pop, hip-hop, R&B.

THE CACTUS CLUB

2496 S. Wentworth Ave., Milwaukee WI 53207. (414)897-0663. **E-mail:** cactuscl@execpc.com. **Website:** cactusclub.dostuff.info. "Milwaukee's Cactus Club has been among the finest live-music venues in the Midwest, featuring such acts as The White Stripes, Queens of the Stone Age, Interpol, Death Cab for Cutie, The Sword, High On Fire, The Faint, Bright Eyes, Eyedea & Abilities, Red Fang, Sylvan Esso, Redd Kross, Sharon Van Etten, Polica, Russian Circles, King Tuff, and countless other national, international, and local bands." Music: punk, rock, alternative, indie, funk, psychedelic.

CAFE 939

939 Boylston St., Boston MA 02115. **E-mail:** 939booking@berklee.edu. **Website:** www.cafe939.com. "Cafe 939 showcases Berklee's emerging student performers and local Boston artists, as well as national acts seeking a more intimate, personal space in which to connect with their fans. The venue is open to the general public and aims to attract musicians and music fans from all walks of life." Music: rock, jazz, folk, Americana, bluegrass, hip-hop, electronica, pop, indie.

CAFE NINE

250 State St., New Haven CT 06510. (203)789-8281. **E-mail:** bookcafenine@gmail.com. **Website:** www.cafenine.com. **Contact:** Paul Mayer, booker. "Cafe Nine features live music from national, regional, and local acts 7 nights a week. Catch some of your favorites getting back to their roots in our intimate setting, or see tomorrow's stars on their way to the stadiums." Music: indie, rock, alternative, jazz, punk, garage, alt-country.

CALEDONIA LOUNGE

256 W. Clayton St., Athens GA 30601. **E-mail:** booking@caledonialounge.com. **Website:** caledonialounge.com. Music: indie, rock, alternative, folk.

THE CANOPY CLUB

708 S. Goodwin Ave., Urbana IL 61801. (217)344-2263. **E-mail:** mikea@jaytv.com. **Website:** www.canopyclub.com. **Contact:** Mike Armintrout. "In striving to

VENUES

achieve the highest level of entertainment, the Canopy Club prides itself on being able to offer entertainment for all walks of life. Whether you like rock, country, hip-hop, jazz, funk, indie, or anything in between, the Canopy Club has something to offer you. If you're a fan of live music and entertainment, the Canopy Club is your home in central Illinois!"

CASSELMAN'S BAR & VENUE

2620 Walnut St., Denver CO 80205. (720)242-8923. **Fax:** (877)667-7572. **Website:** www.casselmans.com. "Casselman's is a multi-use live music and special events venue located in NoDo (North Downtown) Denver. Casselman's opened in 2009 and started to brand 'NoDo' as the new entertainment and arts district of Denver. The name 'Casselman' is the maiden name of our great-grandmother and was carried as the middle name down to 3 members of the family business. Casselman's is a proud recipient of the Westword's 2010 Best New Club award!" Bookings should be completed electronically through the website (www.casselmans.com/page/booking). Music: pop, rock, R&B, hip-hop, alternative.

THE CAVE

452 1/2 W. Franklin St., Chapel Hill NC 27516. (919)968-9308. **E-mail:** cavencbooking@gmail.com. **Website:** caverntavern.com. Music: pop, rock, country, twang, folk, acoustic, funk, indie, punk, blues, bluegrass.
TIPS Use online booking form.

CHELSEA'S CAFE

2857 Perkins Rd., Baton Rouge LA 70808. (225)387-3679. **E-mail:** dave@chelseascafe.com. **Website:** www.chelseascafe.com. "Chelsea's Cafe is Baton Rouge's favorite place to relax, offering good food, drinks, and live music in an intimate, casual atmosphere." Music: rock, indie, alternative, soul.

CHILKOOT CHARLIES

1068 W. Fireweed Lane, Suite A, Anchorage AK 99503. (907)279-1692. **E-mail:** promo@koots.com. **Website:** www.koots.com. "Chilkoot Charlie's features a rustic Alaskan atmosphere with sawdust-covered floors, 3 stages, 3 dance floors, and 10 bars (11 in the summertime!) with padded tree stumps and beer kegs for seating. Literally filled to the rafters with such things as famous band photos and autographs, huge beer can collections, hilarious gags, and tons of Alaska memorabilia, Chilkoot Charlie's is the type of place a person

could walk around in for days and still not see everything." Music: rock, punk, metal, ska.

CHURCHILL'S

5501 NE 2nd Ave., Miami FL 33137. (305)757-1807. **Website:** www.churchillspub.com. Music: rock, alternative, indie, pop, jazz, hip-hop, electronica, acoustic. **TIPS** Book through online booking form: www.churchillspub.com/page/contact.

CITY TAVERN

1402 Main St., Dallas TX 75201. **E-mail:** info@citytaverndowntown.com. **E-mail:** booking@citytaverndowntown.com. **Website:** www.citytaverndowntown.com. Music: country, rock, jam, pop, alternative.

CLUB 209

209 N. Boulder Ave., Tulsa OK 74103. (918)584-9944. **E-mail:** thegang@club209tulsa.com. **Website:** www.club209tulsa.com. Music: indie, Americana, alt-country, folk.

CLUB CONGRESS

311 E. Congress St., Tucson AZ 85701. (520)622-8848. **Fax:** (520)792-6366. **E-mail:** bookingashow@hotelcongress.com. **Website:** www.hotelcongress.com. **Contact:** David Slutes, entertainment and booking director. "From its 1985 inception as a once-weekly showcase for downtown Tucson's creative community to its current status as 'One of the 10 best rock clubs in the U.S.,' Club Congress has continuously striven to be a catalyst for art. In addition to showcasing music's cutting edge, the Club Congress has earned repeated accolades as the city's best dance club." Music: rock, alternative, indie, folk, Americana.

THE CLUBHOUSE

1320 E. Broadway Rd., Tempe AZ 85282. (460)968-3238. **E-mail:** clubhousegigs@hotmail.com. **Website:** www.clubhousemusicvenue.com. "A club that features the best in local, touring, and regional acts. Voted Best Local Music Venue by *The New Times Magazine*, we host shows for all age groups on a nightly basis." Music: rock, punk, metal, alternative.

D.B.A.

618 Frenchmen St., New Orleans LA 70116. (504)942-3731. **E-mail:** booking@dbaneworleans.com. **Website:** www.dbaneworleans.com. "We are proud to present some of New Orleans' and the region's greatest musicians and are privileged to have had appearances on our stage by greats such as Clarence 'Gatemouth' Brown, David 'Honeyboy' Edwards, Jimmy

Buffet, and Stevie Wonder. When in New Orleans, get away from the tourist traps of Bourbon Street and head down to the 'Marigny,' just downriver from the French Quarter, voted with Williamsburg, Brooklyn, and the Inner Mission in San Francisco as one of the hippest neighborhoods in the country." Music: blues, jazz, R&B, Cajun.

TIPS "We currently have a heavy rotation of local and regional bands that play d.b.a. On occasion we will add new bands to that rotation or need a late fill-in."

THE DOGFISH BAR & GRILLE

128 Free St., Portland ME 04101. (207)772-5483. **E-mail:** michele@thedogfishcompany.com. **Website:** www.thedogfishcompany.com. **Contact:** Michele Arcand. "Great food, drink, and service in a casual and unpretentious atmosphere and a great place to hear live local artists. The Dogfish Bar and Grille is an intimate, informal restaurant with a great dinner menu and daily specials. We have 2 very comfortable decks for those who enjoy eating outside, a dining room upstairs, and a friendly tavern on the ground floor. The Dogfish Bar and Grille books local, regional, and national talent most evenings of the week. The music is mostly acoustic, blues, and jazz. There is never a cover charge" Music: jazz, bebop, blues, soul, jam, acoustic.

THE DOUBLE DOOR INN

1218 Charlottetowne Ave., Charlotte NC 28204. (704)376-1446. **E-mail:** maxxmusic2@gmail.com. **Website:** www.doubledoorinn.com. **Contact:** Gregg McCraw, talent buyer/promoter. "Established in 1973 and recognized as the 'Oldest Live Music Venue East of the Mississippi,' the Double Door Inn oozes musical tradition. Looking at our walls, packed with 35 years of autographed photos, has been described as 'viewing a timeline for live music in the Queen City.' Also holding the title 'Oldest Blues Club in the U.S. Under Original Ownership,' the Double Door Inn strives to bring the best in local, regional, and national touring and recording artists to the discriminating music lover. Legendary performers like Eric Clapton, Stevie Ray Vaughn, Dave Alvin, Leon Russell, Buddy Guy, Junior Brown, Bob Margolin, and others have graced the stage of our historic and intimate venue." Music: blues, rock, soul, pop, funk, jazz, bluegrass, acoustic, folk, alt-country, R&B, Americana, reggae.

DOUG FIR LOUNGE

830 E. Burnside St., Portland OR 97214. (503)231-9663. **E-mail:** inquiries@dougfirlounge.com. **E-mail:**

booking@dougfirlounge.com. **Website:** www.dougfirlounge.com. Music: rock, alternative, indie, funk, garage, pop, dance, folk, bluegrass, soul, Americana.

DUFFY'S TAVERN

1412 O St., Lincoln NE 68508. (402)474-3543. **E-mail:** duffysmusic@gmail.com. **Website:** www.duffyslincoln.com. **Contact:** Jeremy Buckley, booking and promotions. "We're known for a lot of things, but if you ask any of us, we will tell you that we're a music venue. Many national acts have graced our stage, including Nirvana, 311, Bright Eyes, the Boss Martians, Slobberbone, Wesley Willis, and many others. A lot of us think some of the local acts are even better, and on any Sunday or Wednesday night, you can be assured Duffy's stage will be jumping with some of the best original music around." Music: rock, folk, Americana, indie, psychedelic, pop, hard rock.

THE ECHO

1822 Sunset Blvd., Los Angeles CA 90026. (213)413-8200. **Website:** www.attheecho.com. Music: funk, punk, rock, indie, folk, hip-hop, electronica, Mexicana, pop.

ELBOW ROOM

1855 Stephens, Missoula MT 59801. **E-mail:** paffer17@yahoo.com. **Website:** www.elbowroombar.com. **Contact:** Josh Paffhausen, owner and general manager. "Features entertainment at least 5 nights a week, ranging from karaoke and red-hot DJs to favorite local bands and major headliners." Music: rock, alternative, country.

EL REY THEATRE

5515 Wilshire Blvd., Los Angeles CA 90036. (323)936-6400. **E-mail:** booking@theelrey.com. **Website:** www.theelrey.com. "The El Rey Theatre is an original art deco theater in the heart of the Miracle Mile, one of Los Angeles' preserved art deco districts. After over 50 years as a first-run movie house, the El Rey was converted into a live-music venue in 1994."

THE EMPTY BOTTLE

1035 N. Western Ave., Chicago IL 60622. (773)276-3600. **E-mail:** christen@emptybottle.com; brent@emptybottle.com. **Website:** www.emptybottle.com. **Contact:** Christen Thomas, talent buyer. Music: rock, indie, psychedelic, anti-pop, garage, metal, country, dance, electronica, soul, blues, folk.

TIPS "We strongly prefer electronic booking requests to physical packages."

THE EMPTY GLASS

410 Elizabeth St., Charleston WV 25311. (304)345-3914. **E-mail:** booking@emptyglass.com. **Website:** www.emptyglass.com. "Located under a three-story house in Charleston, West Virginia's historically diverse East End. Here you will find delicious food, great conversation, friendly spirits, and live original music from all over the planet!" Music: blues, jazz, rock, folk, bluegrass, indie.

EXIT/IN

2208 Elliston Place, Nashville TN 37203. (615)321-3340. **Website:** www.exitin.com. "The Exit/In began its role as a Nashville music venue back in 1971. Since then, countless shows and great memories have happened within these walls." Music: rock, country, alt-country, folk, punk, pop, psychedelic.

TIPS Booking via online submissions form: www.exitin.com/contact.

FAT CATZ MUSIC CLUB

440 Bourbon St., New Orleans LA 70130. (504)525-0303. **E-mail:** info@fatcatzmusicclub.com. "When you are looking for a great place to hang out in New Orleans, look no further! Stop by for a great time any day of the week. We have awesome music all the time, and our staff is second to none. Kick back, relax, and enjoy quality music with us! We have live bands EVERY night of the week that feature a large variety of music styles." Music: R&B, rock, alternative, jazz, hip-hop, pop, blues.

THE FINELINE MUSIC CAFE

318 1st Ave., Minneapolis MN 55401. (612)338-8100. **Fax:** (612)337-8416. **E-mail:** info@finelinemusic.com. **E-mail:** localbookings@finelinemusic.com; nationalbooking@finelinemusic.com. **Website:** www.finelinemusic.com. Music: rock, acoustic, indie, folk, alternative.

FIREHOUSE SALOON

5930 Southwest Freeway, Houston TX 77057. (281)513-1995. **E-mail:** info@firehousesaloon.com. **E-mail:** rebecca@firehousesaloon.com. **Website:** firehousesaloon.com. **Contact:** Rebecca Harrington, talent buyer. "Our musical guests range from up-and-coming artists in the country scene to renowned favorites. You can discover new stars here before anyone else! Miranda Lambert played the Firehouse stage more than 17 times before being catapulted to superstardom. We not only showcase country music, but ALL types of music, because we are first and foremost a music venue."

TIPS "An opening band must be able to draw at least 50 people. In order to get a headlining spot, the band must be able to draw 150 people."

FREIGHT & SALVAGE COFFEEHOUSE

2020 Addison St., Berkeley CA 94704. (510)644-2020, ext. 118. **E-mail:** folk@freightandsalvage.org. **E-mail:** renee@freightandsalvage.org. **Website:** www.thefreight.org. **Contact:** Renee Gaumond. Music: folk, bluegrass, acoustic, jazz, Celtic, experimental.

FREIGHT HOUSE DISTRICT

250 Evans Ave., Reno NV 89501. (775)334-4700. **Website:** www.freighthousereno.com. Includes: Duffy's Ale House, 205 Lounge, Bugsy's Sports Bar and Grill, Arroyo Mexican Grill. Music: funk, rock, Latin, pop, dance, alternative, soul, reggae, blues.

TIPS Contact through online submission form: freighthousereno.com/book-an-event.

THE FREQUENCY

121 W. Main St., Madison WI 53703. (608)819-8777. **Fax:** (608)819-8778. **E-mail:** madisonfrequency@gmail.com. **Website:** www.madisonfrequency.com. "A live-music venue and night club located in downtown Madison near the capitol square. We host a wide variety of live music 7 nights a week, featuring local, regional, national, and international acts playing rock, punk, metal, bluegrass, jazz, and indie."

GEORGE'S MAJESTIC LOUNGE

519 W. Dickson St., Fayetteville AR 72701. (479)527-6618. **E-mail:** saxsafe@aol.com. **Website:** www.georgesmajesticlounge.com. **Contact:** Brian Crowne, owner/operator/booking; Harold Weities, general manager. "George's is perhaps best known for the incredible musicians that have graced our stages, bringing the best in local, regional, and national acts through our doors. Some artists of note that have performed at George's through the years include Robert Cray, Leon Russell, Little River Band, Delbert McClinton, Eddie Money, Pat Green, Derek Trucks, Sam Bush, Tower of Power, Leftover Salmon, Bob Margolin, Chubby Carrier, Tommy Castro, Coco Montoya, Anthony Gomes, Bernard Allison, Michael Burks, Charlie Robison, Cross Canadian Ragweed, Jason Boland, Dark Star Orchestra, Steve Kimock, Martin Fierro, North Mississippi Allstars, Robert Randolph, David Lindley, Big Smith, Cate Brothers, Oteil Burbridge, and so many more." Music: rock, folk, alternative, country, bluegrass, punk.

THE GOLDEN FLEECE TAVERN

132 W. Loockerman St., Dover DE 19904. (302)674-1776. **E-mail:** info@goldenfleecetavern.com. **Website:** www.thegoldenfleecetavern.com. Music: rock, indie, classic rock, pop, alternative.

THE GRAMOPHONE

4243 Manchester Ave., St. Louis MO 63110. (314)531-5700. **E-mail:** gramophonestl@gmail.com. **Website:** thegramophonelive.com. "The Gramophone features an eclectic schedule of live music and DJs in an intimate concert setting." Music: hip-hop, funk, soul, indie, rock, Americana.

GREAT AMERICAN MUSIC HALL

859 O'Farrell St., San Francisco CA 94109. (415)885-0750. **E-mail:** dana@slims-sf.com. **Website:** www.slimspresents.com. **Contact:** Dana Smith, booking. "The past 3 decades at the Great American Music Hall have been full of music, with artists ranging from Duke Ellington, Sarah Vaughan, and Count Basie to Van Morrison, the Grateful Dead, and Bobby McFerrin." Music: contemporary pop, indie, jazz, folk, rock, alternative, Americana.

THE GREAT NORTHERN BAR & GRILL

27 Central Ave., Whitefish MT 59937. (406)862-2816. **E-mail:** info@greatnorthernbar.com. **Website:** www.greatnorthernbar.com. "The Great Northern Bar & Grill is the premiere destination in the Flathead Valley for good food, good music, and good times." Music: rock, alternative.

GREAT SCOTT

1222 Commonwealth Ave., Allston MA 02134. (617)566-9014. **E-mail:** submissions@greatscottboston.com. **Website:** www.greatscottboston.com. **Contact:** Carl Lavin, booking agent. Music: rock, metal, alternative, indie.

GREEK THEATRE

2700 N. Vermont Ave., Los Angeles CA 90027. (323)665-5857. **Fax:** (323)666-8202. **E-mail:** yourcontact@greektheatrela.com. **Website:** www.greektheatrela.com. Music: theatrical, pop, family, rock, ethnic, comedy. Has booked Bruce Springsteen, Dave Matthews Band, Crosby, Stills, Nash & Young, James Taylor, Journey, and more.

THE GREEN LANTERN

497 W. 3rd St., Lexington KY 40508. (859)252-9539. **E-mail:** greenlanternbooking@gmail.com. **Website:** greenlanternlexington.tumblr.com. "Making the best neighborhood bar in Lex a reality." Music: rock, alternative, indie, folk, punk, metal.

GUNPOWDER LODGE

10092 Bel Air Rd., Kingsville MD 21087. (410)256-2626. **E-mail:** info@thegunpowderlodge.com. **Website:** www.thegunpowderlodge.com. Music: rock, indie, acoustic, classic rock.

HAL & MAL'S

200 S. Commerce St., Jackson MS 39204. (601)948-0888. **E-mail:** booking@halandmals.com. **Website:** www.halandmals.com. "The most talked-about, upscale honky tonk in all of Mississippi. Here, art is made, music is played, and locals gather to share community and celebrate the very best of Mississippi's creative spirit." Music: honky-tonk, country, rock, blues, classic rock, alternative.

HANK'S CAFE

1038 Nuuanu Ave., Honolulu HI 96817. (808)526-1411. **Website:** hankscafehawaii.com. Music: rock, doo-wop, dance, country, pop.

THE HAVEN

6700 Aloma Ave., Winter Park FL 32792. (407)673-2712. **E-mail:** maniacal_mojo_records@yahoo.com. **Website:** www.thehavenrocks.com. **Contact:** John "Clint" Pinder. The Haven is a 350-plus capacity venue with a full-liquor bar located in the Aloma Square Shopping Center in Winter Park, FL. Music: alternative, classic rock, cover band, funk, jam band, metal, punk, reggae, rock, and singer/songwriter—all types of live music with local, regional, and national bands, and most shows are age 18 and up.

TIPS See House P.A., Stage and Lighting Specs, Mains, Monitors, Microphones, Stage Dimensions, and Lighting Specs at: www.thehavenrocks.com/specs.

HEADLINERS MUSIC HALL

1386 Lexington Rd., Louisville KY 40206. (502)584-8088. **E-mail:** booking@headlinerslouisville.com. **Website:** headlinerslouisville.com. "Locally owned and operated, Headliners Music Hall is the premiere live entertainment venue of Louisville, Kentucky. We bring the best local and national acts to our stage, with fantastic sound and a fun atmosphere. We've had the privilege of hosting some amazing rock, metal, acoustic, hip-hop, and alternative bands such as My Morning Jacket, Jimmy Eat World, Neko Case, Clutch, Sharon Jones & The Dap Kings, Umphrey's McGee, Old Crow Medicine Show, Kings of Leon, Talib Kweli,

Girl Talk, and more." Music: rock, indie, punk, folk, reggae, soul, R&B, psychedelic.

THE HIDEOUT

1354 W. Wabansia, Chicago IL 60642. (773)227-4433. **Fax:** (773)227-3650. **Website:** www.hideoutchicago. com. "The Hideout is music, art, performance, plays, poetry, rock, and rebellion." Music: indie, folk, rock, alternative, country.

HIGHLANDS TAP ROOM

1058 Bardstown Rd., Louisville KY 40204. (502)584-5222. **Website:** www.highlandstaproom.com. "Fun, friendly neighborhood bar in the heart of the Highlands in Louisville, Kentucky. Live entertainment 7 days a week." Music: rock, acoustic, hip-hop, folk, blues, bluegrass, alt-country.
TIPS Book online using contact form: www.highlandstaproom.com/bookings.html.

HIGH NOON SALOON

701A E. Washington Ave., Madison WI 53703. (608)268-1122. **Fax:** (608)268-1121. **E-mail:** info@high-noon.com. **E-mail:** booking@high-noon.com. **Website:** www.high-noon.com. **Contact:** Cathy Dethmers, owner/manager. "Founded in 2004 in downtown Madison, Wisconsin, High Noon Saloon is a live-music venue that features many different styles of music, including rock, alternative, metal, indie, alt-country, pop, punk, bluegrass, folk, jam, world music, and more. We host large national acts, smaller touring bands from around the world, and lots of local music."

HI-TONE CAFE

412-414 N. Cleveland St., Memphis TN 38104. (901)725-9999. **E-mail:** thehitonecafe@gmail.com. **Website:** www.hitonememphis.com. **Contact:** Brian McCabe. Music: rock, alternative, indie, pop, alt-country, Americana, psych, metal, hip-hop, rap.
TIPS All booking is handled via e-mail; do not call.

HODI'S HALF NOTE

167 N. College Ave., Fort Collins CO 80524. (970)472-2034. **E-mail:** booking@hodishalfnote.com. **Website:** www.hodishalfnote.com. **Contact:** Eric Imbrosciano, talent buyer.

HOTEL CAFE

1623 1/2 N. Cahuenga Blvd., Los Angeles CA 90028. (323)461-2040. **E-mail:** marko@hotelcafe.com. **Website:** www.hotelcafe.com. "For booking, e-mail a link to your website or online press kit. Include where you are from, other places you've played in Los Angeles,

and your current draw in the Los Angeles area. Allow up to several weeks for a response and at least 1-2 months for a booking."

HOT TUNA

2817 Shore Dr., Virginia Beach VA 23451. (757)481-2888. **E-mail:** rstreet@hottunavb.com. **Website:** www.hottunavb.com. Music: rock, acoustic, alternative, dance, pop.

HOUSE OF ROCK

511 Starr St., Corpus Christi TX 78401. (361)882-7625. **E-mail:** casey@texashouseofrock.com. **Website:** www.texashouseofrock.com. **Contact:** Casey Lain.
TIPS "House of Rock was established on July 28, 2005, in the heart of downtown Corpus Christi. Since our early years we have supported a wide range of entertainment, including live music, art shows, and many other cultural events. In addition to entertainment, we host private events, corporate events, and fundraisers."

HOWLER'S PITTSBURGH

4509 Liberty Ave., Pittsburgh PA 15224. (412)682-0320. **E-mail:** booking@howlerspittsburgh.com. **Website:** www.howlerspittsburgh.com. "Howler's Pittsburgh is an independent mid-level music venue and bar in Pittsburgh's east end, hosting local and national acts of all genres 5 days a week." Music: rock, alternative, pop, dance, blues, alt-country, punk, jam, psychedelic, folk, indie.

HUMPY'S

610 W. 6th Ave., Anchorage AK 99501. (907)276-2337. **Website:** www.humpys.com. Music: folk, rock, metal, blues, Americana.

JEREMIAH BULLFROGS LIVE

2940 SW Wanamaker Rd., Topeka KS 66614. (785)272-3764. **E-mail:** bullfrogslive@gmail.com. **Website:** www.bullfrogslive.com. Music: blues, soul, rock, alternative, dance.

JUANITA'S PARTY ROOM

614 President Clinton Ave., Little Rock AR 72201. (501)681-7552. **E-mail:** jsnyder@juanitas.com. **Website:** www.juanitas.com. **Contact:** James Snyder, general manager. Music: rock, reggae, alternative, country, alt-country, indie.

KILBY COURT

741 S. Kilby Ct., Salt Lake City UT 84101. **Fax:** (801)364-3538. **E-mail:** will@sartainandsaunders.

com. **Website:** www.kilbycourt.com. **Contact:** Will Sartain, owner/talent buyer. Music: rock, alternative, Americana, indie, pop, ska, punk.

KNICKERBOCKERS

901 O St., Lincoln NE 68508. (402)476-6865. **Fax:** (402)420-2787. **E-mail:** mail@knickerbockers.net. **Website:** www.knickerbockers.net. Music: alternative, rock, metal, punk, indie, folk, electronica, Americana.

LARIMER LOUNGE

2721 Larimer St., Denver CO 80205. (303)296-1003. **E-mail:** bart@larimerlounge.com. **Website:** www.larimerlounge.com; www.booklarimer.com. **Contact:** Bart Dahl, booking manager. Music: rock, pop, electronica, indie, garage, alternative.

LAST CONCERT CAFÉ

1403 Nance St., Houston TX 77003. (713)226-8563; (832)422-5561. **E-mail:** booking@havinaballproductions.com. **Website:** www.lastconcert.com. "Last Concert Café is Houston's favorite place to see live music 7 days a week. From world-class bands to local residents participating in our Sunday Jam Circle, you're sure to find your favorite entertainment at Last Concert Café!"

LAUNCHPAD

618 Central Ave. SW, Albuquerque NM 87102. (505)764-8887. **Website:** www.launchpadrocks.com. Music: rock, punk, reggae, alternative.

LEADBETTERS TAVERN

1639 Thames St., Baltimore MD 21231. (410)675-4794. **E-mail:** leadbetterstavern2@gmail.com. **Website:** www.leadbetterstavern.com. Music: blues, rock, soul, jazz, punk, alternative, funk, pop, indie.

LIQUID LOUNGE

405 S. 8th St., Boise ID 83702. (208)941-2459. **E-mail:** liquidbooking@gmail.com. **Website:** www.liquidboise.com. Music: rock, reggae, funk, ska, bluegrass, dance, soul, folk, punk.

THE LOFT

2506 W. Colorado Ave. #C, Colorado Springs CO 80904. (719)445-9278. **Website:** www.loftmusicvenue.com. "We are here to bring you the best musical experience in Colorado Springs with an intimate atmosphere, amazing sound, and GREAT music. We hope you come often and tell your friends about our place." Music: rock, pop, country, acoustic, indie, blues, jazz, bluegrass, folk.

THE LOST LEAF BAR & GALLERY

914 N. 5th St., Phoenix AZ 85004. (602)481-4004. **E-mail:** solnotes@hotmail.com. **Website:** www.thelostleaf.org. **Contact:** Tato Caraveo. Music: Latin, blues, salsa, hip-hop, R&B, funk, outlaw country, Americana.

THE LOUNGE AT HOTEL DONALDSON

101 Broadway, Fargo ND 58102. (701)478-1000; (888)478-8768. **E-mail:** info@hoteldonaldson.com. **Website:** www.hoteldonaldson.com. Music: Americana, folk, indie, country, bluegrass.

LOW SPIRITS

2823 2nd St. NW, Albuquerque NM 87107. **Website:** www.lowspiritslive.com. Music: rock, indie, blues, alternative, folk.

LUCKEY'S CLUB CIGAR STORE

933 Olive St., Eugene OR 97401. (541)687-4643. **Website:** www.luckeysclub.com. "Today, Luckey's combines art nouveau décor, saloon sensibilities, serious pool players, cutting-edge music, and a chair for everyone in the community. It still has echoes of the sounds, smells, pool games, and conversations from the past 100 years. It's like a time capsule with a hip twist." Music: folk, acoustic, blues, indie, Americana, rock.

MAD ANTHONY BREWING CO.

2002 Broadway, Ft. Wayne IN 46802. (260)426-2537. **E-mail:** madbrew@msn.com. **Website:** www.madbrew.com. "A cool, laid-back atmosphere, full food menu, and weekly live music." Music: rock, jam, jazz, blues, funk, soul, pop.

THE MAJESTIC/MAGIC STICK

4140 Woodward Ave., Detroit MI 48201. (313)833-9700. **E-mail:** ryan@majesticdetroit.com. **Website:** www.majesticdetroit.com. "The Majestic Theatre is steeped in history. Designed by C. Howard Crane, it opened in 1915 as the largest theater in the world of its kind. Since the mid 1980s, The Majestic Theatre has been the site of memorable concerts featuring live music and entertainment from touring indie rock, blues, jazz, folk, hip-hop and worldbeat artists. The Majestic has produced shows for The Black Keys, George Clinton, Black Eyed Peas, Flaming Lips, Wilco, Sheryl Crow, Dr. John, Yo La Tengo, Patti Smith, Sublime, Matt & Kim, Drake, Fleet Foxes, The Decemberists, Yeah Yeah Yeahs, Foster The People, Jimmy Cliff, 311, Sonic Youth, Fela Kuti, and many more."

VENUES

MAJESTIC THEATRE

115 King St., Madison WI 53703. (608)255-0901. E-mail: majesticinfo2014@gmail.com. **Website:** www.majesticmadison.com. Estab. 1906. The Majestic Theatre is a world-class venue located in Madison, Wisconsin, that hosts major national touring acts. Seeks established local and regional acts to open for high-profile headlining acts. Music: acoustic, alternative, Americana, classic rock, country, electronic/dance/DJ, folk, funk, hip-hop/rap, jam band, metal, pop, punk, reggae, rock, singer/songwriter, spoken word, urban/R&B.

TIPS Contact/submit online at website.

THE MANGY MOOSE RESTAURANT & SALOON

PO Box 590, Teton Village WY 83025. (307)733-4913. **E-mail:** management@mangymoose.com. **E-mail:** booking@mangymoose.com. **Website:** mangymoose.com. Music: funk, punk, electronica, indie, folk, rock, bluegrass.

MARTIN'S DOWNTOWN BAR & GRILL

413 1st St. SW, Roanoke VA 24015. **E-mail:** jason@martinsdowntown.com. **E-mail:** booking@martinsdowntown.com. **Website:** www.martinsdowntown.com. Estab. 2005. Music: rock, jam band, reggae, grass, funk, ska.

MAXWELL'S

1039 Washington St., Hoboken NJ 07030. (201)653-7777. **E-mail:** bookings@maxwellsnj.com. **Website:** www.maxwellsnj.com. "We're about music, arts, a friendly atmosphere, great food and drink, and an exceptional Hoboken neighborhood experience. Come join us!" Music: rock, alternative, blues, punk, indie.

MELODY INN

3826 N. Illinois St., Indianapolis IN 46208. (317)923-4707. **E-mail:** melodyinn2001@gmail.com. **Website:** www.melodyindy.com. Music: punk, rock, metal, indie, pop, rockabilly, bluegrass.

MEMPHIS ON MAIN

55 E. Main St., Champaign IL 61820. (217)398-1097. E-mail: info@memphisonmain.com. **Website:** memphisonmain.com. Music: rock, classic rock, R&B, blues, soul, funk, folk, country, metal, rockabilly, punk, reggae.

MERCURY LOUNGE

1747 S. Boston Ave., Tulsa OK 74119. (918)382-0012. **Website:** www.mercurylounge918.com. Music: country, alt-country, Americana, blues, jazz, rock, reggae, rockabilly, pop.

TIPS Booking is completed through online submissions form: www.mercurylounge918.com/contact-us.

MERCY LOUNGE/CANNERY BALLROOM

One Cannery Row, Nashville TN 37203. (615)251-3020. **E-mail:** info@mercylounge.com. **E-mail:** booking@mercylounge.com. **Website:** www.mercylounge.com. **Contact:** Todd Ohlhauser, owner. "Since the doors to the Mercy Lounge first opened back in January of 2003, the cozy little club on Cannery Row has been both locally favored and nationally renowned. Building a reputation for showcasing the best in burgeoning buzz-bands and renowned national talents, the club has maintained its relevance by consistently offering reliable atmosphere and entertainment." Music: pop, country, rock, folk, Americana, indie, funk, soul, psychedelic.

THE MET

1005 Main St., Pawtucket RI 02860. (401)729-1005. **E-mail:** info@themetri.com. **Website:** themetri.com. Music: rock, funk, folk, blues, soul, punk, alternative.

THE MIDDLE EAST NIGHTCLUB

472 Massachusetts Ave., Cambridge MA 02139. (617)864-3278. **E-mail:** booking@mideastclub.com. **Website:** www.mideastclub.com. Downstairs room capacity is 575. Upstairs is 194. Parking garage is attached to the Meridian Hotel. Music: funk, rock, alternative, dance, pop, hip-hop, punk, Americana.

MILLER THEATRE

Columbia University School of the Arts, 2960 Broadway, MC 1801, New York NY 10027. (212)854-6205. **Website:** www.millertheatre.com. **Contact:** Melissa Smey, executive director. "Miller Theatre's mission is to develop the next generation of cultural consumers, to reinvigorate public enthusiasm in the arts nationwide by pioneering new approaches to programming, to educate the public by presenting specialized, informative programs inviting to a broad audience, to discover new and diverse repertoire and commission new works, and to share Columbia University's intellectual riches with the public." Music: dance, contemporary and early music, jazz, opera, performance.

MILLY'S TAVERN

500 Commercial St., Manchester NH 03101. (603)625-4444. **E-mail:** info@millystavern.com. **Website:** www.millystavern.com. "There is always something hap-

pening in our lounge. Whether it's from 4-7 p.m. or all night, you are bound to have a good time. We offer live music every Tuesday, Thursday, Friday, and Saturday." Music: blues, rock, retro, funk, dance.

MISSISSIPPI STUDIOS

3939 N. Mississippi, Portland OR 97227. (503)288-3895. **E-mail:** info@mississippistudios.com. **E-mail:** booking@mississippistudios.com. **Website:** www.mississippistudios.com. **Contact:** Matt King, senior talent buyer. "Portland's premier concert venue, offering guests the best sound and an intimate concert experience." Music: indie, folk, rock, Americana, alternative, pop, blues.

MOHAWK

912 Red River St., Austin TX 78701. **E-mail:** cody@mohawkaustin.com. **E-mail:** patrick@mohawkaustin.com. **Website:** mohawkaustin.com. **Contact:** Cody R. Cowan, general manager; Patrick Waites, booking and events. Venue known for rock shows. Values creative expression, originality, and work ethic. Contact Patrick Waites with MP3 links only to be considered for booking.

THE MOHAWK PLACE

47 E. Mohawk Place, Buffalo NY 14203. (716)465-2368. **E-mail:** buffalosmohawkplace@gmail.com. **Website:** www.buffalosmohawkplace.com. Music: indie, rock, alternative, punk.

 "We book shows predominantly through e-mail. Please understand we get a high volume of e-mails daily. In most cases, local bands get priority. If we are interested, we will get back to you."

MOJO 13

1706 Philadelphia Ave., Wilmington DE 19809. (302)746-7033. **E-mail:** mojo13booking@gmail.com. "We play host to local and touring music acts, as well as a whole host of other forms of entertainment that cater to the rock 'n' roll lifestyle. We're looking to become the home-away-from-home for the alternative-minded music community here in Delaware and beyond ... so if you've got a band, are a musician, entertainer, or just a fan ... please join us." Music: punk, rock, alternative, indie.

THE MONKEY HOUSE

30 Main St., Winooski VT 05404. (802)655-4563. **E-mail:** monkeybarmusic@gmail.com. **Website:** monkeyhousevt.com. Music: folk, indie, hard rock, punk, rock, alternative, Americana, funk, blues.

MOTR PUB

1345 Main St., Cincinnati OH 45202. (513)381-6687. **Website:** www.motrpub.com. Music: rock, alternative, folk, indie, Americana.

THE MUSIC HALL AT CAPITAL ALE HOUSE

623 E. Main St., Richmond VA 23219. (804)780-2537. **E-mail:** booking@capitalalehouse.com. **Website:** capitalalehouse.com. Music: indie, rock, jazz, blues, pop.

MUSIC HALL OF WILLIAMSBURG

The Bowery Presents, 66 N. 6th St., Brooklyn NY 11211. **E-mail:** info@bowerypresents.com. **Website:** www.musichallofwilliamsburg.com. **Contact:** Eddie Bruiser. "The best way to get a show at a Bowery Presents club is to send your press pack to: The Bowery Presents, c/o Eddie Bruiser, 156 Ludlow St., New York, NY 10002. Please list a New York show history and allow 4-6 weeks before following up with an e-mail."

NATASHA'S BISTRO & BAR

112 Esplanade Alley, Lexington KY 40507. (888)259-6873; (859)259-2754. **Website:** bistro.beetnik.com. **Contact:** Matt Gibson. "Natasha's has hosted a wide variety of acts, including jazz, rock, world, comedy, pop, country, Americana, folk, singer/songwriter, indie, and blues. Over the Rhine, Punch Brothers, Vienna Teng, Sara Watkins, Michelle Shocked, Richard Shindell, Patty Larkin, and Nellie McKay have all played recently on our stage."

NECTAR'S

188 Main St., Burlington VT 05401. (802)658-4771. **E-mail:** booking@liveatnectars.com. **Website:** liveatnectars.com. "A long-standing landmark on Main Street in Burlington, Nectar's restaurant and bar has been the headquarters for thousands of local (and not-so-local) music acts. From Phish to Led Loco, from reggae to rock, Nectar's Bar and Lounge is THE place to see live music in downtown Burlington." Music: blues, Americana, folk, rock, alternative, punk, indie, jazz, pop, dance, funk, psychedelic.

NEUMOS

925 E. Pike St., Seattle WA 98122. (206)709-9442. **Fax:** (206)219-5644. **E-mail:** steven@neumos.com; jason@neumos.com; eli@neumos.com. **Website:** neumos.com. "The showroom side of the business has always been our priority and the lifeline to all other things that surround it. We pride ourselves on our always relevant and carefully curated music calendar, lighting production, and state-of-the-art sound system. The Neumos show-

room has 3 full-service bars and a second floor with a nicely seated mezzanine and balcony overlooking the stage. The showroom is fitted with an ample-size stage, merch area, and superior unobstructed sight lines. We play host to several musical genres, by national and local artists alike, including indie rock, hip-hop, punk rock, DJ's, metal, singer/songwriters, country, and much more. Downstairs, below Neumos, is Barboza, a second, more intimate showroom."

NEUROLUX
111 N. 11th St., Boise ID 83702. (208)343-0886. **Fax:** (208)336-5034. **Website:** www.neurolux.com. Music: funk, indie, rock, reggae, folk, country, bluegrass.

THE NICK ROCKS
2514 10th Ave. S., Birmingham AL 35205. (205)252-3831. **Website:** www.thenickrocks.com. **Contact:** Dan Nolen, talent buyer. "The music heard almost every night of the week includes local, regional, and national acts. The diverse range of acts adds to the appeal of an evening at the Nick. One can hear blues, rock, punk, emo, pop, country, metal, bluegrass, rockabilly, roots rock, or whatever your genre of choice. The Nick has it all. It is an up-close-and personal room voted 3 times in a row as Birmingham's best live music venue by *Birmingham Weekly*."

To contact, use online form at www.thenick-rocks.com/info/contact/book-your-band.

NIETZSCHE'S
248 Allen St., Buffalo NY 14201. (716)886-8539. **Website:** www.nietzsches.com. Call for information regarding booking. Music: blues, jazz, rock, alternative, funk, soul.

NORTHSIDE TAVERN
4163 Hamilton Ave., Cincinnati OH 45223. (513)542-3603. **E-mail:** northsidetavern@gmail.com. **Website:** www.northside-tavern.com. Neighborhood tavern and free, original, live music venue in Cincinnati.

NORTH STAR BAR & RESTAURANT
2639 Poplar St., Philadelphia PA 19130. **Website:** www.northstarbar.com. Music: rock, indie, psychedelic, pop, funk, jam, ska, punk, alternative.
TIPS Contact via online submissions form: www.northstarbar.com/contact.

THE OLD ROCK HOUSE
1200 S. 7th St., St. Louis MO 63104. (314)588-0505. **E-mail:** info@oldrockhouse.com. **Website:** oldrock-house.com. **Contact:** Tim Weber, co-owner. Music: rock, indie, alternative, punk, folk, pop.

ONE TRICK PONY GRILL & TAPROOM
136 E. Fulton, Grand Rapids MI 49503. (616)235-7669. **Website:** www.onetrick.biz. **Contact:** Dan Verhil, owner. Music: acoustic, rock, country, blues.

ON STAGE DRINKS & GRINDS
802 Kapahulu Ave., Honolulu HI 96816. (808)738-0004. **Website:** www.onstagedrinksandgrinds.com. "On Stage is our ultimate living room. A cool, 'off the beaten path,' fun, and comfortable spot to hang and chill. Equipped with a stage area complete with sound system, guitars, congas, and drums. We feature live music and, at times, surprise jams by well-known local artists who pop in. A kind of neat, underground music scene." Music: blues, rock, Hawaiian, acoustic.

PAPER TIGER
E-mail: papertigersa@gmail.com. **Website:** paper-tiger.queueapp.com. Music: punk, hardcore.

PARADISE ROCK CLUB
967 Commonwealth Ave., Boston MA 02115. (617)547-0620. **E-mail:** informationdise@crossroad-spresents.com. **E-mail:** bookinginquiriesparadise@crossroadspresents.com. **Website:** crossroadspresents.com/paradise-rock-club. **Contact:** Lee Zazofsky, general manager. Music: pop, reggae, alternative, rock, indie, punk, hip-hop, Americana.
TIPS "Booking is handled by Crossroads Presents."

PARAMOUNT CENTER FOR THE ARTS
518 State St., Bristol TN 37620. (423)274-8920. **E-mail:** paramountcenter@btes.tv. **Website:** www.thepara-mountcenter.com. "Built in 1931 and restored to its original splendor in 1991, the Paramount continues to grow as the Mountain Empire's premier performing arts center. Listed on the National Register of Historic Places, the Paramount is an excellent example of the art deco motion picture palaces built in the late 1920s and early 1930s. The restoration retained the Paramount's opulent, richly embellished interior. The original Venetian-styled murals and the art deco ambience were faithfully re-created. The auditorium holds 756."

PARISH
214 E. 6th St., Austin TX 78701. **E-mail:** austen@theparishaustin.com. **Website:** www.theparishaustin.com. **Contact:** Austen Bailey, director of entertainment/booking. "Located in the heart of downtown Aus-

tin, in the historic district of 6th Street, The Parish is arguably the best indoor live-music venue in Austin that offers the highest-quality production for artists and events alike. With a 450 capacity, The Parish has hosted musical legends such as Pete Townshend, Slash, and Perry Farrell, as well as independent artists such as Grizzly Bear and Yeasayer. It is an all-genres venue that provides an intimate, live-music experience for all music fans."

PARISH UNDERGROUND

214 E. 6th St., Suite B, Austin TX 78701. (512)494-6078. **E-mail:** booking@parishunderground.com. **Website:** www.parishunderground.com. Parish Underground is a beautiful room located directly below the world-renowned venue, Parish (see separate listing). At night, patrons can enjoy a live performance on stage featuring the best local and national acts.

PETE'S CANDY STORE

709 Lorimer St., Brooklyn NY 11211. **E-mail:** booking@petescandystore.com. **Website:** www.petescandystore.com. **Contact:** Jake Silver.
TIPS "We listen to all submissions and contact those acts that we are planning on booking. This follow-up may take anywhere from a week to a month. We do not confirm submissions, nor follow up with acts that we are not planning on booking. Please do not contact us to see if we received your submission, as the volume is quite high.We prefer to receive links to websites with songs/videos. Please do not include links to Myspace sites. *Please do not send audio files.*"

PJ'S LAGER HOUSE

1254 Michigan Ave., Detroit MI 48226. (313)961-4668. **E-mail:** info@pjslagerhouse.com. **E-mail:** lagerhousebooking@yahoo.com. **Website:** www.pjslagerhouse.com. "PJ's features the best of Detroit's original rock 'n' roll. Up-and-coming and established acts, along with a variety of touring bands, occupy PJ's stage most nights." Music: rock, alternative, hard rock, pop, folk, indie, punk.

PLOUGH AND STARS

912 Massachusetts Ave., Cambridge MA 02139. (617)576-0032. **Website:** www.ploughandstars.com. "The Plough and Stars Irish pub and restaurant in Cambridge has become a favorite of locals and visitors alike. With its warm, cozy atmosphere and great music scene, The Plough has become a staple of the Cambridge community. There is live music nearly ev-

ery night." Music: alternative, pop, rock, indie, psychedelic, acoustic, folk.

PLUSH

340 E. Sixth St., Tucson AZ 85705. (502)798-1298. **E-mail:** booking@plushtucson.com. **Website:** www. plushtucson.com. "Dynamic and comfy! Plush, yet affordable! Come hither and partake. PLUSH is dedicated to Tucson's live music scene. Yes, we book 'em live! Talented local, regional, and national touring acts 5-7 nights a week. And our rooms and sound system were designed to sound good and look good so you feeeeel good!" Music: rock, indie, garage, electronica, alt-country, rockabilly.
TIPS Contact via e-mail only; do not call the venue.

POSITIVE PIE

22 State St., Montpelier VT 05602. (802)229-0453. **E-mail:** music@positivepie.com. **Website:** www.positivepie.com. Music: hip-hop, pop, R&B.

THE POUR HOUSE

1977 Maybank Hwy., Charleston SC 29412. (843)571-4343. **E-mail:** alexharrispoho@gmail.com. **Website:** www.charlestonpourhouse.com. **Contact:** Alex Harris, owner/booking. Music: bluegrass, classic rock, indie, rock, funk, folk, country.

THE QUARTER

2504 13th St., Gulfport MS 39501. (228)863-2650. **E-mail:** info@thequarterbar.com. **E-mail:** manager@thequarterbar.com. "Our goal is to provide the coast with live music up to 5 nights a week or more in a relaxing French Quarter-like atmosphere." Music: metal, pop, rock, country, blues, classic rock.

RECORD BAR

1020 Westport Rd., Kansas City MO 64111. (816)753-5207. **Website:** www.therecordbar.com. "We strive to provide our guests with diverse live entertainment, special events, and gourmet food in a comfortable atmosphere. You'll see the best of the Kansas City music scene, as well as nationally known touring artists." Music: rock, punk, indie, jazz, swing, folk, pop, alternative,
TIPS Book your band through the online submission form: www.therecordbar.com/booking.

RED SQUARE

136 Church St., Burlington VT 05401. (802)859-8909. **E-mail:** info@redsquarevt.com. **E-mail:** booking@redsquarevt.com. **Website:** www.redsquarevt.com. Music: jazz, blues, rock, reggae.

RHYTHM & BREWS

2308 4th St., Tuscaloosa AL 35401. (205)750-2992. **Website:** www.rhythmnbrews.com. "Rhythm & Brews first opened in Tuscaloosa, Alabama. The club has the reputation of being the premier location for the best live bands in the region. From dance music to performances by Nashville recording artists, the music you find at Rhythm & Brews will please all. We are committed to bringing you a fun and friendly atmosphere by offering a wide variety of drinks, great service, and great entertainment." Music: pop, rock, country, blues.

RICK'S BAR

2721 Main Ave., Fargo ND 58103. (701)232-8356. **Fax:** (701)232-1095. **E-mail:** meghanc@ricks-bar.com. **Website:** www.ricks-bar.com. **Contact:** Meghan Carik. Music: rock, metal, alternative.

ROCK ISLAND LIVE

101 N. Rock Island, Wichita KS 67202. **E-mail:** rockislandlivemusic@gmail.com. **Website:** rockislandlive.tumblr.com. "Rock Island Live is a nationally recognized music venue in historic old town." Music: rock, alternative, pop, indie, dance.

ROCKWOOD MUSIC HALL

196 Allen St., New York NY 10002. (212)477-4155. **E-mail:** info@rockwoodmusichall.com. **Website:** www.rockwoodmusichall.com. "Those interested in booking should send an e-mail with links to your Web pages, official and social, audio and video. Do not include attachments, only links. Each submission is reviewed, and responses are sent if/when there is an opening."

SAINT VITUS BAR

1120 Manhattan Ave., Brooklyn NY 11222. **E-mail:** saintvitusbar@gmail.com. **E-mail:** bookingsaintvitusbar@gmail.com. **Website:** www.saintvitusbar.com. "Saint Vitus, a Gothic-themed bar in Greenpoint, Brooklyn, named after a Black Sabbath song, is actually a welcoming spot for downing cheap beers and listening to Pantera."

SAM BONDS GARAGE

407 Blair, Eugene OR 97402. (541)431-6603. **E-mail:** booking@sambonds.com. **Website:** www.sambonds.com. "Since opening in 1995, we've strived to represent the uniqueness of the neighborhood with a warm, laid-back atmosphere, always-changing local and regional microbrew selection, a full bar, quality vittles, and, of course, one of the West Coast's best places to see diverse local, regional, and worldly entertainment." Music: bluegrass, rock, Irish jam, funk, alternative, folk, Americana.

SANTA FE SOL

37 Fire Place, Santa Fe NM 87508. **Website:** www.sol-santafelive.com. Music: rock, Mexicana, Latin, alternative.

SCHUBAS TAVERN

3159 N. Southport, Chicago IL 60657. (773)525-2508. **E-mail:** demos@schubas.com. **Website:** www.schubas.com. **Contact:** Matt Rucins, talent buyer; Sam Andolsen, production manager. Schubas presents a diverse lineup of live music 7 nights a week, from honky-tonk to indie rock, from Americana to jazz, from pop to country.

The building is a brick and masonry neo-Gothic neighborhood landmark built in 1903.

TIPS "Have a confirmed show? Use the Media List link on the website to help better promote your show. Advance your show with our Production Manager Sam Andolsen. Send any promotional materials (posters, CDs, bios, photos) to Jud Eakin."

SHANK HALL

1434 N. Farwell Ave., Milwaukee WI 53202. (414)276-7288. **E-mail:** shank@wi.rr.com. **Website:** www.shankhall.com. **Contact:** Peter Jest. Music: indie, rock, alternative, Americana, pop, folk, bluegrass.

THE SHED

15094 Mills Rd., Gulfport MS 39503. (228)875-8577. **E-mail:** admin.gulfport@theshedbbq.com. **Website:** theshedbbq.com. Music: blues, folk, country, bluegrass, rock, alternative.

SILVER DOLLAR

478 King St., Charleston SC 29403. (843)722-7223. **Website:** www.charlestoncocktail.com/silverdollar.html. Music: rock, pop, dance, hip-hop, R&B, funk.

THE SLOWDOWN

729 N. 14th St., Omaha NE 68102. (402)345-7569. **Website:** www.theslowdown.com. Music: rock, indie, alternative, psychedelic, punk, folk, pop.

TIPS "Send us a demo of your music (CD, vinyl, or tape is fine; we have all sorts of players). Your package should contain pertinent information about your band: contact name/number, where you have played, and whatever else you think we should know." Accepts mail or drop-off submissions.

THE SMILING MOOSE

1306 E. Carson St., Pittsburgh PA 15203. (412)431-4668. **Website:** www.smiling-moose.com. Music: rock, alt-country, indie, country, acoustic, pop, garbage, funk, hip-hop, metal.

TIPS Booking via online submissions form: www.smiling-moose.com/contact/index.php#.

SMITH'S OLDE BAR

1578 Piedmont Ave. NE, Atlanta GA 30307. (404)875-1522. **E-mail:** seanmcphrsn@yahoo.com; office@nolenreevesmusic.com. **Website:** www.smithsoldebar.com. **Contact:** Sean McPherson, talent buyer; Brittany Burdett, assistant talent buyer. "Smith's Olde Bar is an Atlanta institution, offering some of the best music to be found anywhere in the city. Our atmosphere is very relaxed, and you can find something good to eat and something fun to do almost every night." Music: rock, indie, punk, hip-hop, alternative, garage, bluegrass, reggae, jazz, funk.

THE SPACE

295 Treadwell St., New Haven CT 06514. (203)288-6400. **E-mail:** spacebooking@gmail.com. **Website:** www.thespacect.com. **Contact:** Nicholas Firine, promoter and talent buyer. "The Space (since 2003) exists to build a safe, positive community for people of all ages through music and the arts. Physically, we are a listening room venue located in an unlikely industrial park in a sleepy suburb of New Haven." Music: alternative, rock, blues, Latin, folk, pop, indie, dance, hip-hop, Americana.

THE SPANISH MOON

1109 Highland Rd., Baton Rouge LA 70802. (225)383-6666. **E-mail:** moonbooking@hotmail.com. **Website:** www.thespanishmoon.com. **Contact:** Aaron Scruggs, talent buyer/booking manager. Music: rock, pop, dubstep, indie, alternative, Americana.

THE SPOT UNDERGROUND

101 Richmond St., 2nd Floor, Providence RI 02903. (401)383-7133. **E-mail:** 725@thespotprovidence.com. **E-mail:** thespotunderground@gmail.com. **Website:** www.thespotunderground.com. Music: rock, indie, world, hip-hop, R&B, funk, dance, jam, pop.

STRANGE BREW TAVERN

88 Market St., Manchester NH 03101. (603)666-4292. **E-mail:** bookings@strangebrewtavern.net. **Website:** strangebrewtavern.net. Music: blues, acoustic, rock, alternative.

SULLY'S PUB

2071 Park St., Hartford CT 06106. (860)231-8881. **E-mail:** sully@sullyspub.com; rob@sullyspub.com. **Website:** www.sullyspub.com. **Contact:** Darrel "Sully" Sullivan, owner; Rob Salter, manager. "This mantra is an important one in any community: Original music must be supported on every level of society. Sully's is proud to stand on the front lines of musical evolution, blazing a trail with the very musicians composing and performing." Music: pop, rock, alternative, indie.

SWEETWATER MUSIC HALL

19 Corte Madera Ave., Mill Valley CA 94941. (415)388-3850. **E-mail:** info@swmh.com. **E-mail:** booking@swmh.com. **Website:** www.sweetwatermusichall.com. "The much-anticipated Sweetwater Music Hall—a community gathering place and live-music venue dedicated to bringing back the Sweetwater's musical legacy to Mill Valley—opened in late January 2012. The opening of Sweetwater Music Hall marked a rebirth of the landmark roots music venue and Bay Area treasure originally opened on November 17, 1972. The Sweetwater Music Hall is a state-of-the-art nightclub and café that not only presents nationally recognized, top-quality entertainment but also provides a comfortable home venue for local and emerging talent to perform and experiment."

THE BIG EASY SOCIAL AND PLEASURE CLUB

5731 Kirby Dr., Houston TX 77005. (713)523-9999. **E-mail:** bigeasyblues@pando.org. **Website:** www.thebigeasyblues.com. Music: rhythm, blues.

THE COMET

4579 Hamilton Ave., Cincinnati OH 45223. (513)541-8900. **E-mail:** cometbarbooking@gmail.com. **Website:** cometbar.com. Estab. 1996. "Rooted in drink, rock 'n' roll, and shared ideas between persons of original thought."

THE DRINKERY

1150 Main St., Cincinnati OH 45202. (513)827-9357. **E-mail:** drinkerybooking@icloud.com. **Website:** www.drinkeryotr.com. **Contact:** Matt Ogden, booking. The Drinkery OTR is a music venue featuring local draft beer, quality craft bottles, and soothing, warm bourbons.

THE FILLMORE

1805 Geary Blvd., San Francisco CA 94115. (415)346-3000. **E-mail:** thefillmore@livenation.com. **Website:**

thefillmore.com. Has featured The Smashing Pumpkins, Gin Blossoms, Brian Setzer Orchestra, Huey Lewis and the News, Blues Traveler and Soul Hat, Tom Petty and the Heartbreakers, and more.

THE MINT

6010 W. Pico Blvd., Los Angeles CA 90035. (323)954-9400. **Fax:** (323)938-2994. **E-mail:** booking@themint-la.com. **Website:** themintla.com. "In a city where history is measured in months instead of decades, the Mint is a real cultural treasure. The bar has been presenting live music ever since it opened in 1937, and Stevie Wonder, Macy Gray, Ray Charles, Zigaboo Modeliste, Leo Nocentelli, Royal Crown Revue, and the Wallflowers are among the many notable musicians who've performed on its small stage."

THE REDMOOR

(513)871-6789. **Website:** www.theredmoor.com. "Some venues demand performance. In an intimate, acoustically engineered atmosphere, musicians connect with their audiences with distinctive energy. From blue notes to chords that swing, live music lives here."

THE SOUTHGATE HOUSE REVIVAL

111 E. 6th St., Newport KY 41071. (859)431-2201. **E-mail:** sghbooking@gmail.com. **Website:** www.southgatehouse.com. **Contact:** Morrella. "The Southgate House Revival is a three-in-one music venue, with the Sanctuary, the Revival Room, and the Lounge serving audiences from 85-500. Located in a renovated historic church, the venue presents an eclectic lineup of independent music (and other events) up to 7 nights a week."

TIN ROOF

160 Freedom Way, Suite 150, Cincinnati OH 45202. (513)381-2176. **Website:** www.tinroofbars.com/home/cincinnati. Tin Roof is a live-music restaurant and bar with a laid-back atmosphere.

TOAD

1912 Massachusetts Ave., Cambridge MA 02140. (617)497-4950. **E-mail:** info@toadcambridge.com. **E-mail:** bookagig@toadcambridge.com. **Website:** www.toadcambridge.com. **Contact:** Billy Beard. "Toad is a small neighborhood bar and music club featuring live music 7 nights a week." Music: folk, alternative, rock, acoustic, Americana, indie.

TRACTOR TAVERN

5213 Ballard Ave. NW, Seattle WA 98107. (206)789-3599. **E-mail:** booking@tractortavern.com. **Website:** www.tractortavern.com. "The Tractor hosts live shows 5-7 nights a week featuring a wide range of local and national acts. Check out all of your favorite rock, alternative country, rockabilly, groove and psychedelia, Celtic, cajun and zydeco, folk, blues, jazz, and bluegrass acts, to name a few."

THE TREE BAR

887 Chambers Rd., Columbus OH 43212. (614)725-0955. **E-mail:** booking@treebarcolumbus.com. **Website:** treebarcolumbus.com. Music: rock, classic rock, alternative, indie, Americana, folk, pop.
TIPS "You must include in your e-mail: the date you're interested in, the lineup you propose for the night, and links to your music."

TRIPLE CROWN

206 N. Edward Gary St., San Marcos TX 78666. (512)396-2236. **E-mail:** booking@triplecrownlive.com. **Website:** www.triplecrownlive.com. **Contact:** Eric Shaw. Music: rock, country, Americana, jazz, blues, bluegrass, punk, hip-hop, folk.

TRIPLE ROCK SOCIAL CLUB

629 Cedar Ave., Minneapolis MN 55454. (612)333-7399. **Fax:** (612)333-7703. **E-mail:** booking.triplerock@gmail.com. **Website:** www.triplerocksocialclub.com. Estab. 2003. The Triple Rock has become one of the big destination punk, indie rock, and underground hip-hop clubs in the Twin Cities—a good-sized music venue with a capacity of 400. The Triple Rock is owned and operated by the members of punk rock band Dillinger Four. Music: acoustic, alternative, blues, classic rock, country, cover band, electronic/dance/DJ, folk, funk, Goth, hip-hop/rap, jam band, metal, pop, punk, reggae, rock, singer/songwriter, soul, and urban/R&B.

TROCADERO

1003 Arch St., Philadelphia PA 19107. (215)922-6888. **E-mail:** trocadero@thetroc.com. **Website:** www.thetroc.com. Music: pop, indie, Americana, alternative, rock, hip-hop, rap, folk, bluegrass.

TROUBADOUR

9081 Santa Monica Blvd., West Hollywood CA 90069. **Website:** www.troubadour.com. Estab. 1958. "The Troubadour is rich with musical history. Elton John, Billy Joel, James Taylor, and Joni Mitchell have all made debuts at the Troubadour. The legendary musical lineups at the Troubadour continue until today. The Troubadour schedule features a wide arrangement of musical performances. Nada Surf, Bob Schneider, The Morning Benders, and Manchester Orchestra were some of the performances featured on the Troubadour schedule for 2010." Music: pop, indie, alternative, rock, hip-hop, Americana, jazz, blues.

 To contact, use form online at www.troubadour.com/contact-booking. See also lighting plot, stage layout, technical rider links at same site.

TURF CLUB

1601 University Ave., St. Paul MN 55104. (651)647-0486. **E-mail:** booking@turfclub.net. **Website:** www.turfclub.net. "Turf Club is a perfect setting for rock. The long, prominent bar scales one side of the narrow interior, the stage is at the back, and the entire space is enveloped in dark woods. The music is loud, the crowd is devoted." Music: rock, indie, alternative, punk, classic rock.

UNDERGROUND 119

119 S. President St., Jackson MS 39201. (601)352-2322. **E-mail:** underground119music@gmail.com. **Website:** www.underground119.com. Music: blues, jazz, bluegrass, country, funk, rock, alternative.

UNION POOL

484 Union Ave., Brooklyn NY 11211. **E-mail:** booking@union-pool.com. **Website:** www.union-pool.com. Music: rock, indie, alternative, Americana. **TIPS** Venue guidelines and tech specs on website.

UPSTATE CONCERT HALL

1208 NY-146, Clifton Park NY 12065. (518)371-0012. **Website:** www.upstateconcerthall.com. **TIPS** "To book your own show, please e-mail dave@upstateconcerthall.com. To get booked on an existing bill, please e-mail: tetoll@nycap.rr.com.

URBAN LOUNGE

241 S. 500 E., Salt Lake City UT 84102. (801)746-0557. **E-mail:** will@sartainandsaunders.com. **Website:** www.theurbanloungeslc.com. **Contact:** Will Sartain. "The Urban Lounge has been a staple in the Salt Lake City, Utah, music community for more than a decade. What started off as a local live-music bar has flourished into a regular stop for headlining national acts, hosting a variety of music from independent artists of all genres, including rock, hip-hop, folk, electronic, reggae, and experimental. Nearly every night of the week you can find a fresh take on a familiar scene."

VAUDEVILLE MEWS

212 4th St., Des Moines IA 50309. **E-mail:** booking@vaudevillemews.com. **Website:** www.vaudeville-mews.com. Music: folk, pop, blues, rock, alternative, Americana, hip-hop, soul, rap, country, hard rock, electronica.

THE VISULITE THEATRE

1615 Elizabeth Ave., Charlotte NC 28204. (704)358-9200. **Fax:** (704)358-9299. **E-mail:** boxoffice@visulite.com. **Website:** www.visulite.com. Music: rock, pop, funk, Americana, indie, blues, folk.

THE WAY STATION

683 Washington Ave., Brooklyn NY 11238. (347)627-4949. **E-mail:** bookingtws@gmail.com. **Website:** way-stationbk.blogspot.com. **Contact:** Andy Heidel, proprietor. "For booking, send an e-mail with a short introduction and a link to hear your music or watch videos. Looking for 1 set of 40-45 minutes. Books 3 months in advance. If your band has already played at The Way Station, contact gailaheidel@yahoo.com with 2-3 dates to rebook."

THE WEBSTER UNDERGROUND

31 Webster St., Hartford CT 06114. (860)246-8001. **E-mail:** booking@webstertheater.com. **Website:** www.webstertheater.com. "The Main Theater is a great room for sizeable events or concerts. Book now and share the same stage that launched careers such as Staind, Marilyn Manson, Sevendust, Incubus, 311, Jay Z, Method Man, Godsmack, Fall Out Boy, and many more. The Underground is our intimate room equipped for shows and more—perfect for national, regional, and locals that are looking to create their own show in a historic room." Music: rock, reggae, punk, alternative, pop, soul, indie, funk, hard rock.

WHISKY A GO-GO

8901 W. Sunset Blvd., West Hollywood CA 90069. (310)652-4202, ext. 11; (310)652-4202, ext. 17. **E-mail:** mproductionsrocks@gmail.com; erika@whiskyagogo.com. **Website:** www.whiskyagogo.com. **Contact:** Luke Iblings and Jake Perry, national talent buyers; Erika Gimenes, booking agent. "As long as there has been a Los Angeles rock scene, there has been the Whisky A Go-Go. An anchor on the Sunset Strip since its opening in 1964, the Whisky A Go-Go has played host to rock 'n' roll's most important bands, from the Doors, Janis Joplin, and Led Zeppelin to today's up-and-coming new artists." Music: hip-hop, rock, punk, metal, alternative, reggae, pop, classic rock, indie, Americana.

WHITE WATER TAVERN

2500 W. 7th St., Little Rock AR 72205. **E-mail:** white-waterbooking@gmail.com. **Website:** www.whitewatertavern.com. Music: rock, country, alternative, Americana, punk.

THE WILTERN

3790 Wilshire Blvd., Los Angeles CA 90010. (213)388-1400. **Website:** www.thewiltern.net. Music: rock, pop.

WOODLANDS TAVERN

1200 W. 3rd Ave., Columbus OH 43212. (614)299-4987. **Website:** woodlandstavern.com. Music: blue-grass, acoustic, psychedelic, reggae, jam, funk, rock, classic rock, jazz, blues.

TIPS Submit booking inquiries through online submission form: woodlandstavern.com/find-contact-us.

WORMY DOG SALOON

311 E. Sheridan Ave., Oklahoma City OK 73104. (405)601-6276. **E-mail:** booking@wormydog.com. **Website:** www.wormydog.com. Music: country, blue-grass, rock, Americana, rockabilly, folk.

YOUNG AVENUE DELI

2119 Young Ave., Memphis TN 38104. (901)278-0034; (901)274-7080. **Website:** www.youngavenuedeli.com. Music: rock, country, pop, folk.

TIPS Booking via online submissions form: www.youngavenuedeli.com/contact.

STATE & PROVINCIAL GRANTS

//

Arts councils in the U.S. and Canada provide assistance to artists (including songwriters) in the form of fellowships or grants. These grants can be substantial and confer prestige upon recipients; however, **only state or province residents are eligible**. Because deadlines and available support vary annually, query first or check websites for updated guidelines.

UNITED STATES ARTS AGENCIES

ALABAMA STATE COUNCIL ON THE ARTS, 201 Monroe St., Montgomery AL 36130-1800. (334)242-4076. Website: www.arts.state.al.us.

ALASKA STATE COUNCIL ON THE ARTS, 161 Klevin St., Suite 102, Anchorage AK 99508-1506. (907)269-6610 or (888)278-7424. E-mail: aksca.info@alaska.gov. Website: www.eed. state.ak.us/aksca.

ARIZONA COMMISSION ON THE ARTS, 417 W. Roosevelt St., Phoenix AZ 85003-1326. (602)771-6501. E-mail: info@azarts.gov, Website: www.azarts.gov.

ARKANSAS ARTS COUNCIL, 323 Center St., Suite 1500, Little Rock AR 72201-2606. (501)324-9766. Website: www.arkansasarts. org.

CALIFORNIA ARTS COUNCIL, 1300 I St., Suite 930, Sacramento CA 95814. (916)322-6555 or (800)201-6201. E-mail: info@arts.ca.gov. Website: www.cac.ca.gov.

CONNECTICUT COMMISSION ON CULTURE & TOURISM, Arts Division, One Constitution Plaza, Kinsley St., Hartford CT 06103. (860)256-2800. Website: www.cultureand-tourism.org.

COLORADO CREATIVE INDUSTRIES, 1625 Broadway, Suite 2700, Denver CO 80202. (303)892-3840. E-mail: online form. Website: www.coloradocreativeindustries.org.

DELAWARE DIVISION OF THE ARTS, Carvel State Office Bldg., 4th Floor, 820 N. French St., Wilmington DE 19801. (302)577-8278 (New Castle Co.) or (302)739-5304 (Kent or Sussex Counties). E-mail: delarts@state.de.us. Website: www.artsdel.org.

DISTRICT OF COLUMBIA COMMISSION ON THE ARTS AND HUMANITIES, 200 I St., SE, Washington, DC 20003. (202)724-5613. E-mail: cah@dc.gov. Website: www.dcarts. dc.gov.

"FLORIDA DIVISION OF CULTURAL AFFAIRS," 329 N. Meridian St., Tallahassee FL 32308. (850)245-6470. E-mail: info@florida-arts. org. Website: www.florida-arts.org.

GEORGIA COUNCIL FOR THE ARTS, 75 Fifth St., NW, Suite 1200, Atlanta GA 30308. E-mail: gaarts@gaarts.org. Website: www. gaarts.org.

GUAM COUNCIL ON THE ARTS & HUMANITIES AGENCY, P.O. Box 2950, Hagatna GU 96932. (671)300-1204. Website: www. guamcaha.org.

HAWAII STATE FOUNDATION ON CULTURE AND THE ARTS, 250 S. Hotel St., 2nd Floor, Honolulu HI 96813. (808)586-0300. Website: sfca.hawaii.gov.

IDAHO COMMISSION ON THE ARTS, 2410 N. Old Penitentiary Rd., Boise ID 83712. (208)334-2119 or (800)278-3863. E-mail: info@arts.idaho.gov. Website: www.arts. idaho.gov.

"ILLINOIS ARTS COUNCIL AGENCY," James R. Thompson Center, 100 W. Randolph, Suite 10-500, Chicago IL 60601. (312)814-6750 or (800)237-6994. E-mail: iac.info@illinois.gov. Website: www.arts.illinois.gov.

INDIANA ARTS COMMISSION, 100 N. Senate Ave., Room N505, Indianapolis IN 46204. (317)232-1268. E-mail: IndianaArtsCommission@iac.in.gov. Website: www.in.gov/arts.

IOWA ARTS COUNCIL, 600 E. Locust, Des Moines IA 50319-0290. (515)242-6194. Website: www.iowaartscouncil.org.

KANSAS CITY - ARTSKC - REGIONAL ARTS COUNCIL, 106 Southwest Blvd., Kansas City MO 64108. (816)221-1777. Website: www. artskc.org.

KENTUCKY ARTS COUNCIL, 21st Floor, Capital Plaza Tower, 500 Mero St., Frankfort KY 40601-1987. (502)564-3757 or (888)833-2787. E-mail: kyarts@ky.gov. Website: www. artscouncil.ky.gov.

LOUISIANA DIVISION OF THE ARTS, 1051 N. 3rd St., Room 405, Baton Rouge LA 70802. (225)342-8180. E-mail: arts@crt.la.gov. Website: www.crt.state.la.us/cultural-development/arts/.

MAINE ARTS COMMISSION, 193 State St., 25 State House Station, Augusta ME 04333-0025. (207)287-2724. E-mail: MaineArts. info@maine.gov. Website: www.mainearts. maine.gov.

MARYLAND STATE ARTS COUNCIL, 175 W. Ostend St., Suite E, Baltimore MD 21230. (410)767-6555. Website: www.msac.org.

MASSACHUSETTS CULTURAL COUNCIL, 10 St. James Ave., 3rd Floor, Boston MA 02116-3803. (617)858-2700 or (800)232-0960. E-mail: mcc@art.state.ma.us. Website: www. massculturalcouncil.org.

MICHIGAN COUNCIL FOR ARTS AND CULTURAL AFFAIRS, 300 N. Washington Square, Lansing MI 48913. (888)522-0103. E-mail: Online form. Website: www.michiganbusiness.org/community/council-arts-cultural-affairs.

MINNESOTA STATE ARTS BOARD, Park Square Court, 400 Sibley St., Suite 200, St. Paul MN 55101-1928. (651)215-1600 or (800)866-2787. E-mail: msab@arts.state. mn.us. Website: www.arts.state.mn.us.

MISSISSIPPI ARTS COMMISSION, 501 N. West St., Suite 1101A, Woolfolk Bldg., Jackson MS 39201. (601)359-6030. Website: www.arts.state.ms.us.

MISSOURI ARTS COUNCIL, 815 Olive St., Suite 16, St. Louis MO 63101-1503. (314)340-6845 or (866)407-4752. E-mail: moarts@ded.mo.gov. Website: www.missouri-artscouncil.org.

MONTANA ARTS COUNCIL, P.O. Box 202201, Helena MT 59620-2201. (406)444-6430. E-mail: mac@mt.gov. Website: www.art. mt.gov.

NATIONAL ASSEMBLY OF STATE ARTS AGENCIES, 1200 18th St. NW, Suite 1100, Washington, DC 20036. (202)347-6352. E-mail: nasaa@nasaa-arts.org. Website: www. nasaa-arts.org.

THE NATIONAL MUSEUM OF PUERTO RICAN ARTS & CULTURE, 3015 W. Division St., Chicago IL 60622. (773)486-8345. E-mail: info@NMPRAC.org. Website: www. iprac.org.

NEBRASKA ARTS COUNCIL, 1004 Farnam St., Plaza Level, Burlington Bldg., Omaha NE 68102. (402)595-2122 or (800)341-4067. Website: www.nebraskaartscouncil.org.

NEVADA ARTS COUNCIL, 716 N. Carson St., Suite A, Carson City NV 89701. (775)687-6680. E-mail: infonvartscouncil@nevada-culture.org. Website: www.nac.nevadaculture.org.

NEW HAMPSHIRE STATE COUNCIL ON THE ARTS, 19 Pillsbury St., 1st Floor, Concord NH 03301. (603)271-2789. Website: www. nh.gov/nharts.

NEW JERSEY STATE COUNCIL ON THE ARTS, 225 W. State St., 4th Floor, Trenton NJ 08608. (609)292-6130. Website: www. artscouncil.nj.gov.

NEW MEXICO ARTS, Bataan Memorial Bldg., 407 Galisteo St., Suite 270, Santa Fe NM 87501-2641. (505)827-6490 or (800)879-4278. Website: www.nmarts.org.

NEW YORK STATE COUNCIL ON THE ARTS, 300 Park Ave. S, 10th Floor, New York NY 10010. (212)459-8800. Website: www.nysca.org.

NORTH CAROLINA ARTS COUNCIL, 109 E. Jones St., Raleigh NC 27601. (919)807-6500. E-mail: ncarts@ncdcr.gov. Website: www. ncarts.org.

NORTH DAKOTA COUNCIL ON THE ARTS, 1600 E. Century Ave., Suite 6, Bismarck ND 58503-0649. (701)328-7590. Website: www. nd.gov/arts.

OHIO ARTS COUNCIL, 30 E. Broad St., 33rd Floor, Columbus OH 43215-3414. (614)466-2613. Website: www.oac.state.oh.us.

OKLAHOMA ARTS COUNCIL, Jim Thorpe Building, 2101 N. Lincoln Blvd., Suite 640, Oklahoma City OK 73105. (405)521-2931. E-mail: okarts@arts.ok.gov. Website: www. arts.ok.gov.

OREGON ARTS COMMISSION, 775 Summer St. NE, Suite 200, Salem OR 97301-1280. (503)986-0082. E-mail: oregon.artscomm@ state.or.us. Website: www.oregonartscom- mission.org.

PENNSYLVANIA COUNCIL ON THE ARTS, 216 Finance Bldg., Harrisburg PA 17120. (717)787-6883. E-mail: RA-arts@pa.gov Website: www.arts.pa.gov.

RHODE ISLAND STATE COUNCIL ON THE ARTS, One Capitol Hill, 3rd Floor, Provi- dence RI 02908. (401)222-3880. E-mail: info@arts.ri.gov. Website: www.arts.ri.gov.

SOUTH CAROLINA ARTS COMMISSION, 1026 Sumter St., Suite 200, Columbia SC 29201-3746. (803)734-8696. E-mail: info@ arts.sc.gov. Website: www.southcaroli- naarts.com.

SOUTH DAKOTA ARTS COUNCIL, 711 E. Wells Ave., Pierre SD 57501. (605)773-5977. E-mail: sdac@state.sd.us. Website: www. artscouncil.sd.gov.

TENNESSEE ARTS COMMISSION, 401 Charlotte Ave., Nashville TN 37243-0780. (615)741-1701. Website: www.tn.gov/arts.

TEXAS COMMISSION ON THE ARTS, E.O. Thompson Office Bldg., 920 Colorado, Suite 501, Austin TX 78701. (512)463-5535. E- mail: front.desk@arts.texas.gov. Website: www.arts.texas.gov.

UTAH DIVISION OF ARTS & MUSEUMS, 617 E. South Temple, Salt Lake City UT 84102. (801)236-7555. Website: www.heritage.utah. gov/utah-division-of-arts-museums.

VERMONT ARTS COUNCIL, 136 State St., Montpelier VT 05633-6001. (802)828-3291. E-mail: info@vermontartscouncil.org. Website: www.vermontartscouncil.org.

VIRGIN ISLANDS COUNCIL ON THE ARTS, 5070 Norre Gade, Suite 1, St. Thomas VI 00802-6762. (340)774-5984. Website: www. vicouncilonarts.org.

VIRGINIA COMMISSION FOR THE ARTS, 1001 E. Broad St., Suite 330, Richmond VA 23219. (804)225-3132. E-mail: arts@vca.virginia. gov. Website: www.arts.virginia.gov.

WASHINGTON STATE ARTS COMMISSION, P.O. Box 42675, Olympia WA 98504-2675. (360)753-3860. E-mail: online form. Web- site: www.arts.wa.gov.

WEST VIRGINIA COMMISSION ON THE ARTS, The Culture Center, Capitol Complex, 1900 Kanawha Blvd. E., Charleston WV 25305- 0300. (304)558-0220. Website: www.wvcul- ture.org/arts.

WISCONSIN ARTS BOARD, P.O. Box 8690, Madison WI 53708-8690. (608)266-0190. E-mail: artsboard@wisconsin.gov. Web- site: www.artsboard.wisconsin.gov.

WYOMING ARTS COUNCIL, 2301 Central Ave., Barrett Bldg., 2nd Floor, Cheyenne WV 82002. (307)777-7742. E-mail: online form. Website: wyoarts.state.wy.us.

CANADIAN PROVINCIAL ARTS AGENCIES

ALBERTA FOUNDATION FOR THE ARTS, 10708-105 Ave., Edmonton, AB T5H 0A1.

(780)427-9968. E-mail: online form. Website: www.affta.ab.ca.

ARTSNB, 634 Queen St., 2nd Floor, Fredericton, NB E3B 1C3. (506)444-4444 or (866)460-2787. Website: www.artsnb.ca.

BRITISH COLUMBIA ARTS COUNCIL, P.O. Box 9819, Stn. Prov. Govt., Victoria, BC V8W 9W3. (250)356-1718. E-mail: BCArtsCouncil@gov.bc.ca. Website: www. bcartscouncil.ca.

CANADA COUNCIL FOR THE ARTS, 150 Elgin St., P.O. Box 1047, Ottawa, ON K1P 5V8. (613)566-4414 or (800)263-5588 (within Canada). E-mail: info@canadacouncil.ca. Website: www.canadacouncil.ca.

MANITOBA ARTS COUNCIL, 525-93 Lombard Ave., Winnipeg, MB R3B 3B1. (204)945-2237 or (866)994-2787 (in Manitoba). E-mail: info@artscouncil.mb.ca. Website: www.artscouncil.mb.ca.

NEWFOUNDLAND AND LABRADOR ARTS COUNCIL, P.O. Box 98, St. John's, NL A1C 5H5. (709)726-2212 or (866)726-2212 (in Newfoundland and Labrador). E-mail: nlacmail@nlac.ca. Website: www.nlac.ca.

NOVA SCOTIA DEPARTMENT OF COMMUNITIES, CULTURE AND HERITAGE, 1741 Brunswick St., 3rd Floor, P.O. Box 456, STN Central, Halifax, NS B3J 2R5. (902)424-2170. E-mail: cch@novascotia.ca. Website: cch.novascotia.ca.

ONTARIO ARTS COUNCIL, 151 Bloor St. W., 5th Floor, Toronto, ON M5S 1T6. (416)961-1660 or (800)387-0058 (in Ontario). E-mail: info@arts.on.ca. Website: www.arts.on.ca.

THE PRINCE EDWARD ISLAND COUNCIL OF THE ARTS, 115 Richmond St., Charlottetown, PE C1A 1H7. (902)368-4410 or (888)734-2784 (within Prince Edward Island). E-mail: info@prica.ca. Website: www. peiartscouncil.com.

QUÉBEC COUNCIL FOR ARTS & LITERATURE, 79 boul. René-Lévesque Est, 3e étage, Québec, QC G1R 5N5. (418)643-1707 or (800)608-3350 (in Québec). E-mail: info@ calq.gouv.qc.ca. Website: www.calq. gouv. qc.ca.

THE SASKATCHEWAN ARTS BOARD, 1355 Broad St., Regina, SK S4R 7V1. (306)787-4056 or (800)667-7526 (in Saskatchewan). E-mail: info@artsboard.sk.ca. Website: www.artsboard.sk.ca.

YUKON ARTS FUNDING PROGRAM, Cultural Services Branch, Dept. of Tourism and Culture, Government of Yukon, Box 2703, Whitehorse, YT Y1A 2C6. (867)667-3535 or (800)661-0408, ext. 3535 (in Yukon). E-mail: artsfund@gov.yk.ca. Website: www.tc.gov. yk.ca/af.

PUBLICATIONS OF INTEREST

//

Knowledge about the music industry is essential for both creative and business success, and staying informed requires keeping up with constantly changing information. Updates on the evolving trends in the music business are available to you in the form of music magazines, music trade papers, and books. There is a publication aimed at almost every type of musician, songwriter, and music fan, from the most technical knowledge of amplification systems to gossip about your favorite singer. These publications can enlighten and inspire you, and provide information vital in helping you become a more well-rounded, educated, and, ultimately, successful musical artist.

What follows is a cross-section of all types of magazines and books you may find interesting. From songwriters' newsletters and glossy music magazines to tip sheets and how-to books, there should be something listed here that you'll enjoy and benefit from.

PERIODICALS

ALTERNATIVE PRESS, 1305 W. 80th St., Suite 214, Cleveland OH 44102-3045. (216)631-1510. E-mail: editorial@altpress.com. Website: http://altpress.com. *Reviews, news, and features for alternative and indie music fans.*

AMERICAN SONGWRITER, 113 19th Ave. S., Nashville, TN 37203. (615)321-6096. E-mail: info@americansongwriter.com. Website: www.americansongwriter.com. *Bimonthly publication for and about songwriters.*

ARTROCKER, 43 Chute House, Stockwell Park Road, Brixton, SW9 0DW. E-mail: info@artrockermagazine.com. Website: http://artrockermagazine.com. *Monthly magazine involved in music promotion and publishing.*

BACK STAGE (NYC), 45 Main St., Brooklyn NY 11201. (212)493-4420. E-mail: Online form. Website: www.backstage.com.

BACK STAGE (LA), 5700 Wilshire Blvd., Los Angeles CA 90036. (323)525-2358. Website:

www.backstage.com. *Weekly East and West Coast performing-artist trade papers.*

BASS PLAYER, 28 E. 28th St., 12th Floor, New York NY 10016. (212)378-0400. Website: www.bassplayer.com. *Monthly magazine for bass players with lessons, interviews, articles, and transcriptions.*

BILLBOARD, P.O. Box 15, Congers NY 10920. (800)684-1873. E-mail: subscriptions@billboard.com. Website: www.billboard.com. *Weekly industry trade magazine.*

CANADIAN MUSICIAN, 4056 Dorchester Rd., Suite 202, Niagara Falls, ON L2E 6M9 Canada. (905)374-8878. E-mail: mail@nor.com. Website: www.canadianmusician.com. *Bimonthly publication for amateur and professional Canadian musicians.*

CCM MAGAZINE, 402 BNA Dr., Suite 400, Nashville TN 37217. (800)527-5226. E-mail: online form. Website: www.ccmmagazine.com. *Online magazine focusing on Christian singers and performers.*

CHART ATTACK, 200-41 Britain St., Toronto, ON M5A 1R7 Canada. E-mail: Online form. Website: www.chartattack.com. *Monthly magazine covering the Canadian and international music scenes.*

CMJ NEW MUSIC REPORT/CMJ NEW MUSIC MONTHLY, 115 E. 23rd St., 3rd Floor, New York NY 10113. Website: www.cmj.com. *Weekly college radio and alternative music tip sheet.*

COUNTRY LINE MAGAZINE, 9508 Chisholm Trail, Austin TX 78748. (512)292-1113. E-mail: sandra@countrylinemagazine.com. Website: www.countrylinemagazine.com. *Monthly Texas-only country music cowboy and lifestyle magazine.*

ENTERTAINMENT LAW & FINANCE, Website: www.lawjournalnewsletters.com/ljn_entertainment/. *Monthly newsletter covering music industry contracts, lawsuit filings, court rulings, and legislation.*

EXCLAIM!, 849A Bloor St. W., Toronto, ON M6G 1M3 Canada. (416)535-9735. E-mail: exclaim@exclaim.ca. Website: https://exclaim.ca. *Canadian music monthly covering all genres of non-mainstream music.*

"GAMUT: ONLINE JOURNAL OF THE MUSIC THEORY SOCIETY OF THE MID-ATLANTIC," Website: http://trace.tennessee.edu/gamut. *Peer-reviewed online journal of the Music Theory Society of the Mid-Atlantic. A journal of criticism, commentary, research, and scholarship.*

GUITAR PLAYER, 28 E. 28th St., 12th Floor, New York NY 10016. (212)378-0400. Website: www.guitarplayer.com. *Monthly guitar magazine with transcriptions, columns, and interviews, including occasional articles on songwriting.*

JAZZTIMES, 10801 Margate Rd., Silver Spring MD 20910. (617)315-9155. E-mail: Online form. Website: www.jazztimes.com. *Ten issues/year; magazine covering the American jazz scene.*

MOJO, Bauer Media, Endeavour House, 189 Shaftesbury Ave., London, England WC2H 8JG. E-mail: MOJO@bauermedia.co.uk. Website: www.mojo4music.com. *Monthly*

UK maagzine focusing on classic rock, acts as well as emerging rock and indie bands.

MUSIC CONNECTION MAGAZINE, 3441 Ocean View Blvd., Glendale CA 91208. (818)995-0101. E-mail: Online form. Website: www.musicconnection.com. *Monthy music industry trade publication.*

MUSIC ROW MAGAZINE, 1231 17th Ave. S, Nashville TN 37212. (615)349-2171. E-mail: info@musicrow.com. Website: www.musicrow.com. *Biweekly Nashville industry publication.*

MUSIC WEEK, Suncourt House, 18-26 Essex Road, Islington, London, United Kingdom N1 8LN. Website: www.musicweek.com. *UK industry publication with music news, data, analysis, and opinions.*

NEW MUSICAL EXPRESS (NME), NME, 8th Floor, Blue Fin Bldg., London, United Kingdom SE1 0SU. Website: www.nme.com. *UK weekly publication of music journalism.*

OFFBEAT MAGAZINE, 421 Frenchman St., Suite 200, New Orleans LA 70116. (504)944-4300. E-mail: offbeat@offbeat.com. Website: www.offbeat.com. *Monthly magazine covering Louisiana music and artists.*

PERFORMER MAGAZINE, P.O. Box 348, Somerville MA 02143. E-mail: editorial@performermag.com. (617) 627-9200. Website: www.performermag.com. *Focuses on independent musicians, those unsigned and on small labels, and their success in a DIY environment.*

THE PERFORMING SONGWRITER, Performing Songwriter Enterprises, LLC P.O. Box 158989, Nashville TN 37215. E-mail: lydia@performingsongwriter.com. Website: www.performingsongwriter.com. *Bimonthly songwriters' magazine.*

SING OUT!, P.O. Box 5460, Bethlehem PA 18015-0460. (610)865-5366 or (888)SING-OUT. Fax: (215)895-3052. E-mail: info@singout.org. Website: www.singout.org. *Quarterly folk music magazine.*

SONG CAST, SongCast, Inc., 2926 State Rd., Suite 111, Cuyahoga Falls OH 44223. E-mail: info@songcastmusic.com. *Offers assistance selling music through online retail sites like iTunes or Amazon.*

SONGLINK INTERNATIONAL, 23 Belsize Crescent, London NW3 5QY United Kingdom. +44(0)207-794-2540. Fax: +44(0)207-794-7393. E-mail: Online form. Website: www.songlink.com. *Ten issues/year; newsletter including details of recording artists looking for songs; contact details for industry sources; also news and features on the music business.*

SOUND ON SOUND, Media House, Trafalgar Way, Bar Hill, Cambridge, CB23 8SQ, United Kingdom. +44(0)1954 789888. Website: www.soundonsound.com. *Monthly music technology magazine with online forum.*

VARIETY, 11175 Santa Monica Blvd., Los Angeles CA 90025. (323)617-9100. Website: www.variety.com. *Weekly entertainment trade newspaper.*

WORDS AND MUSIC, 41 Valleybrook Dr., Toronto, ON M3B 2S6 Canada. (416)445-8700. Website: www.socan.ca. *Monthly songwriters' magazine.*

BOOKS & DIRECTORIES

1000 SONGWRITING IDEAS: MUSIC PRO GUIDES, by Lisa Aschmann, Hal Leonard Corp., P.O. Box 13819, Milwaukee WI 53213. E-mail: Online form. Website: www.halleonardbooks.com.

101 SONGWRITING WRONGS & HOW TO RIGHT THEM, by Pat & Pete Luboff, Writer's Digest Books, 10151 Carver Rd., Suite 200, Blue Ash OH 45242. (855)840-5124. Website: www.writersdigestshop.com.

THE A&R REGISTRY, by Ritch Esra, SRS Publishing, 7510 Sunset Blvd., Suite #1041, Los Angeles CA 90046-3400. (800)377-7411 or (800)552-7411. E-mail: musicregistry@compuserve.com.

THE BILLBOARD GUIDE TO MUSIC PUBLICITY, rev. ed., by Jim Pettigrew, Jr..

BREAKIN' INTO NASHVILLE, by Jennifer Ember Pierce, Madison Books, University Press of America, 4501 Forbes Road, Suite 200, Lanham MD 20706.

CMJ DIRECTORY, 1201 Broadway, Suite 706, New York, NY 10001. Website: www.cmj.com.

THE CRAFT AND BUSINESS OF SONGWRITING, by John Braheny, Writer's Digest Books, 10151 Carver Rd., Suite 200, Blue Ash OH 45242. (855)840-5124. Website: www.writersdigestshop.com.

THE CRAFT OF LYRIC WRITING, by Sheila Davis, Writer's Digest Books, 10151 Carver Rd., Suite 200, Blue Ash OH 45242. (855)840-5124. Website: www.writersdigestshop.com.

HOLLYWOOD CREATIVE DIRECTORY. *Lists producers in film and TV.*

THE HOLLYWOOD REPORTER, The Writers Store, 3510 W. Magnolia Blvd., Burbank CA, 91505. (800)272-8927. Website: www.writersstore.com.

HOW TO GET SOMEWHERE IN THE MUSIC BUSINESS FROM NOWHERE WITH NOTHING, by Mary Dawson, CQK Books, CQK Music Group, 2221 Justin Rd., Suite 119-142, Flower Mound TX 75028. (972)317-2760. Website: www.FromNowhereWithNothing.com.

HOW TO PROMOTE YOUR MUSIC SUCCESSFULLY ON THE INTERNET, by David Nevue, Midnight Rain Productions. Website: www.rainmusic.com.

HOW TO MAKE IT IN THE NEW MUSIC BUSINESS: LESSONS, TIPS, & INSPIRATIONS FROM MUSIC'S BIGGEST AND BEST, by Robert Wolff, Billboard Books, 1745 Broadway, New York NY 10019. Website: www.billboard.com.

HOW YOU CAN BREAK INTO THE MUSIC BUSINESS: WITHOUT BREAKING YOUR HEART, YOUR DREAM, OR YOUR BANK ACCOUNT, by Marty Garrett, Lonesome Wind Corp.

LOUISIANA MUSIC DIRECTORY, OffBeat, Inc., 421 Frenchmen St., Suite 200, New Orleans LA 70116. (504)944-4300. Website: www.louisianamusicdirectory.com.

LYDIAN CHROMATIC CONCEPT OF TONAL ORGANIZATION, VOLUME ONE: THE ART AND SCIENCE OF TONAL GRAVITY, by George Russell, Concept Publishing Co. E-mail: postmaster@lydiancromaticconcept.com. Website: www.lydian chromaticconcept.com.

MELODY IN SONGWRITING, by Jack Perricone, Berklee Press, 1140 Boylston St., Boston MA 02215. (617)747-2146. E-mail: support@online.berklee.com. Website: www. berkleepress.com.

MUSIC ATTORNEY LEGAL & BUSINESS AFFAIRS REGISTRY, by Ritch Esra and Steve Trumbull, SRS Publishing, 7510 Sunset Blvd., Suite #1041, Los Angeles CA 90046-3400. (800)552-7411. E-mail: musicregistry@compuserve.com or srspubl@aol.com.

THE MUSIC BUSINESS REGISTRY, by Ritch Esra, SRS Publishing, 7510 Sunset Blvd., Suite #1041, Los Angeles CA 90046-3400. (800)552-7411. E-mail: info@musicregistry. com. Website: www.musicregistry.com.

MUSIC DIRECTORY CANADA, Norris-Whitney Communications Inc., 4056 Dorchester Rd., Suite 202, Niagara Falls, ON L2E 6M9 Canada. (905)374-8878 or (877)RING-NWC. E-mail: mail@nor.com. Website: http://nor. com. www.musicdirectorycanada.com

MUSIC LAW: HOW TO RUN YOUR BAND'S BUSINESS, by Richard Stim, Nolo Press, 950 Parker St., Berkeley CA 94710. (510)549-1976. Website: www.nolo.com.

MUSIC, MONEY AND SUCCESS: THE INSIDER'S GUIDE TO THE MUSIC INDUSTRY, by Jeffrey Brabec and Todd Brabec, Schirmer Trade Books, 257 Park Ave. S., Suite 20, New York NY 10010. (212) 254-2100.

THE MUSIC PUBLISHER REGISTRY, by Ritch Esra, SRS Publishing, 7510 Sunset

Blvd. #1041, Los Angeles CA 90046-3400. (800)552-7411. E-mail: info@musicregistry. com.

MUSIC PUBLISHING: A SONGWRITER'S GUIDE, rev. ed., by Randy Poe, Writer's Digest Books, 10151 Carver Rd., Suite 200, Blue Ash OH 45242. (855)840-5124. Website: www.writersdigestshop.com.

THE MUSICIAN'S GUIDE TO MAKING & SELLING YOUR OWN CDS & CASSETTES, by Jana Stanfield, Writer's Digest Books, 10151 Carver Rd., Suite, 200, Blue Ash OH 45242. (855)840-5124. Website: www.writersdigestshop.com.

MUSICIANS PHONE BOOK, THE LOS ANGELES MUSIC INDUSTRY DIRECTORY, Get Yourself Some Publishing, 28336 Simsalido Ave., Canyon Country CA 91351.

NASHVILLE MUSIC BUSINESS DIRECTORY, by Mark Dreyer, NMBD Publishing, 9 Music Square S., Suite 210, Nashville TN 37203. (615)826-4141. E-mail: Online form. Website: www.nashvilleconnection.com.

NASHVILLE'S UNWRITTEN RULES: INSIDE THE BUSINESS OF COUNTRY MUSIC, by Dan Daley, Overlook Press, 141 Wooster St., New York NY 10012. (212) 673-2210. E-mail: sales@overlookny.com. Website: www.overlookpress.com

THE REAL DEAL—HOW TO GET SIGNED TO A RECORD LABEL FROM A TO Z, by Daylle Deanna Schwartz, Billboard Books.

RECORDING INDUSTRY SOURCEBOOK, Music Books Plus, 4600 Witmer Industrial Estates, Suite 6, Niagara Falls NY 14305.

(800)265-8481. Website: www.musicbook-splus.com.

REHARMONIZATION TECHNIQUES, by Randy Felts, Berklee Press, 1140 Boylston St., Boston MA 02215. (617)747-2146. E-mail: support@online.berklee.edu. Website: www.berkleepress.com.

THE SONGWRITERS IDEA BOOK, by Sheila Davis, Writer's Digest Books, 10151 Carver Rd., Suite 200, Blue Ash OH 45242. (855)840-5124. Website: www.writersdigestshop.com.

SONGWRITER'S MARKET GUIDE TO SONG & DEMO SUBMISSION FORMATS, Writer's Digest Books, 10151 Carver Rd., Suite 200, Blue Ash OH 45242. (855)840-5124. Website: www.writersdigestshop.com.

SONGWRITER'S PLAYGROUND—INNOVATIVE EXERCISES IN CREATIVE SONGWRITING, by Barbara L. Jordan, BookSurge Publishing. Website: www.songwritersplayground.com

THE SONGWRITER'S WORKSHOP: HARMONY, by Jimmy Kachulis, Berklee Press, 1140 Boylston St., Boston MA 02215. (617)747-2146. E-mail: support@online.berklee.edu. Website: www.berkleepress.com.

THE SONGWRITER'S WORKSHOP: MELODY, by Jimmy Kachulis, Berklee Press, 1140 Boylston St., Boston MA 02215. (617)747-2146. E-mail: support@online.berklee.edu. Website: www.berkleepress.com.

SONGWRITING AND THE CREATIVE PROCESS, by Steve Gillette, Sing Out! Publications, P.O. Box 5460, Bethlehem PA 18015-

0460. (610)865-5366 or (888)SING-OUT. E-mail: singout@libertynet.org.

SONGWRITING: ESSENTIAL GUIDE TO LYRIC FORM AND STRUCTURE, by Pat Pattison, Berklee Press, 1140 Boylston St., Boston MA 02215. (617)747-2146. E-mail: support@online.berklee.edu. Website: www.berkleepress.com.

SONGWRITING: ESSENTIAL GUIDE TO RHYMING, by Pat Pattison, Berklee Press, 1140 Boylston St., Boston MA 02215. (617)747-2146. E-mail: support@online.berklee.edu. Website: www.berkleepress.com.

THE SONGWRITING SOURCEBOOK: HOW TO TURN CHORDS INTO GREAT SONGS, by Rikky Rooksby, Hal Leonard Corp., P.O. Box 13819, Milwaukee WI 53213. E-mail: Online form. Website: www.halleonardbooks.com.

SONGWRITING STRATEGIES: A 360-DEGREE APPROACH, by Mark Simos, Berklee Press, 1140 Boylston St., Boston MA 02215. (617)747-2146. E-mail: support@online.berklee.edu. Website: www.berkleepress.com.

SONGWRITING WITHOUT BOUNDARIES, by Pat Pattison, 10151 Carver Rd., Suite 200, Blue Ash OH 45242. (855)840-5124. Website: www.writersdigestshop.com.

THE SOUL OF A WRITER, by Susan Tucker with Linda Lee Strother, Journey Publishing Co.

SUCCESSFUL LYRIC WRITING, by Sheila Davis, Writer's Digest Books, 10151 Carver Rd.,

Suite 200, Blue Ash OH 45242. (855)840-5124. Website: www.writersdigestshop.com.

THIS BUSINESS OF MUSIC MARKETING AND PROMOTION, by Tad Lathrop, Billboard Books, The Crown Publishing Group, 1745 Broadway, New York NY 10019. (212)782-9000. E-mail: crownosm@penguinrandomhouse.com.

TIM SWEENEY'S GUIDE TO RELEASING INDEPENDENT RECORDS, by Tim Sweeney, TSA Books, 31805 Temecula Pkwy., Suite 351, Temecula CA 92592. (951)303-9506. E-mail: sweeney@timsweeney.com. Website: www.timsweeney.com.

TEXAS MUSIC INDUSTRY DIRECTORY, Texas Music Office, Office of the Governor, P.O. Box 13246, Austin TX 78711. (512)463-6666. E-mail: Online form. Website: gov.texas.gov/musicdirectory/.

TUNESMITH: INSIDE THE ART OF SONGWRITING, by Jimmy Webb, Hachette Book Group, 1290 Avenue of the Americas, New York NY 10104. (800)759-0190.

VOLUNTEER LAWYERS FOR THE ARTS GUIDE TO COPYRIGHT FOR MUSICIANS AND COMPOSERS, by Timothy JensenOne E. 53rd St., 6th Floor, New York NY 10022. (212)319-2787.

WRITING BETTER LYRICS, by Pat Pattison, Writer's Digest Books, 10151 Carver Rd., Suite 200, Blue Ash OH 45242. (855)840-5124. Website: www.writersdigestshop.com.

WRITING MUSIC FOR HIT SONGS, by Jai Josefs, Schirmer Trade Books, 257 Park Ave. S., Suite 20, New York NY 10010. (212)254-2100.

THE YELLOW PAGES OF ROCK, The Album Network, 120 N. Victory Blvd., Burbank CA 91502. Fax: (818)955-9048. E-mail: ypinfo@yprock.com.

WEBSITES OF INTEREST

The Internet provides a wealth of information for songwriters and performers, and the number of sites devoted to music grows each day. Below is a list of websites that can offer you information, links to other music sites, contact with other songwriters, and places to showcase your songs. Due to the dynamic nature of the online world, this is certainly not a comprehensive list, but it gives you a place to start on your Internet journey as you search for opportunities to get your music heard.

ABOUT.COM MUSICIANS' EXCHANGE

www.musicians.about.com
Site features headlines and articles of interest to independent musicians and songwriters, as well as links and label profiles.

ABSOLUTE PUNK

www.absolutepunk.net
Searchable online community focusing on punk and rock music, including news, reviews, articles, interviews, and forums to discuss music and pop culture.

AMERICAN SOCIETY OF COMPOSERS, AUTHORS AND PUBLISHERS (ASCAP)

www.ascap.com

Database of works in ASCAP's repertoire. Includes performer, songwriter, and publisher information, as well as membership information and industry news.

AMERICAN SONGWRITER MAGAZINE HOMEPAGE

www.americansongwriter.com
This is the official homepage for _American Songwriter_ magazine. Features an online article archive, e-mail newsletter, and links.

BANDCAMP

www.bandcamp.com
An online music store and platform for artist promotion that caters mainly to independent artists.

BEAIRD MUSIC GROUP DEMOS

www.beairdmusicgroup.com
Nashville demo service that offers a variety of demo packages.

BILLBOARD

www.billboard.com
Industry news and searchable online database of music companies by subscription.

THE BLUES FOUNDATION

www.blues.org
Nonprofit organization located in Memphis, Tennessee; website contains information on the foundation, membership, and events.

BROADCAST MUSIC, INC. (BMI)

www.bmi.com
Offers lists of song titles, writers, and publishers of the BMI repertoire. Includes membership information and general information on songwriting and licensing.

THE BUZZ FACTOR

www.thebuzzfactor.com
Website offers free tips on music marketing and self-promotion.

BUZZNET

www.buzznet.com
Searchable networking and news site featuring music, pop culture, photos, videos, concert reviews, and more.

CDBABY

www.cdbaby.com
An online CD store dedicated to the sales of independent music.

CADENZA

www.cadenza.org
Online resource for contemporary and classical music and musicians, including methods of contacting other musicians.

CHORUS AMERICA

www.chorusamerica.org
The website for Chorus America, a national organization for professional and volunteer choruses. Includes job listings and professional development information.

FILM MUSIC NETWORK

www.filmmusicworld.com or www.filmmusic.net
Network of links, news, and job listings within the film music world.

GET SIGNED

www.getsigned.com
Interviews with musicians, songwriters, and industry veterans, how-to business information, and more.

GOVERNMENT LIAISON SERVICES

www.trademarkinfo.com
An intellectual property research firm. Offers a variety of trademark searches.

GUITAR NINE RECORDS

www.guitar9.com
Offers articles on songwriting, music theory, guitar techniques, etc.

GOOGLE

www.google.com

Online search engine can be used to look up music, information, lyrics.

HARMONY CENTRAL

www.harmony-central.com

Online community for musicians with in-depth reviews and discussions.

HARRY FOX AGENCY

www.harryfox.com

Offers a comprehensive FAQ about licensing songs for use in recording, performance, and film.

INDEPENDENT DISTRIBUTION NETWORK

www.idnmusic.com

Website of independent bands distributing their music with advice on everything from starting a band to finding labels.

INDEPENDENT SONGWRITER
WEB MAGAZINE

www.independentsongwriter.com

Independent music reviews, classifieds, message board, and chat sessions.

INDIE-MUSIC.COM

www.indie-music.com

Website of how-to articles, record label directory, links to musicians and venue listings.

JAZZ CORNER

www.jazzcorner.com

Portal for the websites of jazz musicians and organizations. Includes the jazz video share, jukebox, and the "Speak-easy" bulletin board.

JUST PLAIN FOLKS

www.jpfolks.com or www.justplain-folks.org

Website for songwriting organization featuring message boards, lyric feedback forums, member profiles, music, contact listings, chapter homepages, and more.

LAST.FM

www.last.fm

Music tracking and social networking site.

HAL'S GUIDE FOR SONGWRITERS IN L.A.

www.halsguide.com

Website for songwriters with information on clubs, publishers, books, etc. Links to other songwriting sites.

LIVE365

www.live365.com/index.live

Internet radio/audio stream search engine.

LIVEJOURNAL

www.livejournal.com

Social networking community using open-source technology, music communities providing news, interviews, and reviews.

LOS ANGELES GOES UNDERGROUND

www.lagu.somaweb.org

Website dedicated to underground rock bands from Los Angeles and Hollywood.

LYRIC IDEAS FOR SONGWRITERS

www.lyricideas.com

Offers songwriting prompts, themes, and creative techniques for songwriting.

MI2N (MUSIC INDUSTRY NEWS NETWORK)

www.mi2n.com

Offers news on happenings in the music industry and career postings.

THE MUSE'S MUSE

www.musesmuse.com

Classifieds, catalog of music samples, songwriting articles, newsletter, and chat room.

MOG

www.mog.com

Internet radio/streaming audio. Contains music news and concert reviews, personalized recommendations.

MUSIC BOOKS PLUS

www.musicbooksplus.com

Online bookstore dedicated to music books on every music-related topic, plus a free newsletter.

MUSIC PUBLISHERS ASSOCIATION

www.mpa.org

Ofers directories for music publishers and imprints, copyright resource center, and information on the organization.

MUSIC YELLOW PAGES

www.musicyellowpages.com

Listings of music-related businesses.

MYSPACE

www.myspace.com

Social networking site featuring music web pages for musicians and songwriters.

NASHVILLE SONGWRITERS ASSOCIATION INTERNATIONAL (NSAI)

www.nashvillesongwriters.com

Official NSAI homepage. Offers news, links, online registration, and message board for members.

NATIONAL ASSOCIATION OF COMPOSERS/ USA (NACUSA)

www.music-usa.org/nacusa

A nonprofit organization devoted to the promotion and performance of American concert hall music.

NATIONAL MUSIC PUBLISHERS ASSOCIATION

www.nmpa.org

Organization's online site filled with information about copyright, legislation, and other concerns of the music publishing world.

NEW MUSIC USA ONLINE LIBRARY

library.newmusicusa.org

Classical and jazz archives. Includes a list of organizations and contacts for composers.

ONLINE ROCK

www.onlinerock.com

Range of membership options including a free option, offers web page services, articles, chat rooms, links, and more.

OPERA AMERICA

www.operaamerica.org
Website of OPERA America features information on advocacy and awareness programs, publications, conference schedules, and more.

PANDORA

www.pandora.com
A site created by the founders of the Music Genome Project; a searchable music radio/streaming audio site.

PERFORMER MAG

www.performermag.com
Offers articles, music, industry news, classifieds, and reviews.

PERFORMING SONGWRITER MAGAZINE HOMEPAGE

www.performingsongwriter.com
Official home page for the magazine features articles and links.

PITCHFORK

www.pitchforkmedia.com
Offers indie news, reviews, media, and features.

PUBLIC DOMAIN MUSIC

www.pdinfo.com
Articles on public domain works and copyright, including public domain song lists, research sources, tips, and FAQs.

PUMP AUDIO

www.pumpaudio.com
License music for film and television on a non-exclusive basis. No submission fees, rights retained by songwriter.

PUREVOLUME

www.purevolume.com
Music hosting site with searchable database of songs by signed and unsigned artists. Musicians and songwriters can upload songs and events.

THE RECORDING PROJECT

www.recordingproject.com
Online community for musicians and recording artists, every level welcome.

RECORD PRODUCER.COM

www.record-producer.com
Extensive site dedicated to audio engineering and record production. Offers a free newsletter, online instruction, and e-books on various aspects of record production and audio engineering.

ROCK AND ROLL HALL OF FAME + MUSEUM

www.rockhall.com
Website for the Rock and Roll Hall of Fame and Museum, including events listings, visitor info, and more.

SESAC INC.

www.sesac.com
Website for performing rights organization with songwriter profiles, industry news updates, licensing information, and links to other sites.

SLACKER

www.slacker.com

Internet radio/streaming audio. User can create personalized channels and playlists online.

SOMA FM

www.somafm.com
Internet underground/alternative radio with commercial-free broadcasting from San Francisco.

SONGLINK INTERNATIONAL

www.songlink.com
Offers opportunities to pitch songs to music publishers for specific recording projects and industry news.

SONGRAMP

www.songramp.com
Online songwriting organization with message boards, blogs, news, and streaming music channels. Offers variety of membership packages.

SONGSALIVE!

www.songsalive.org
Online songwriters organization and community.

SONGWRITER 101

www.songwriter101.com
Offers articles, industry news, and message boards.

SONGWRITER'S GUILD OF AMERICA (SGA)

www.songwritersguild.com
Industry news, member services information, newsletters, contract reviews, and more.

SONGWRITER'S RESOURCE NETWORK

www.songwritersresourcenetwork.com
News and education resource for songwriters, lyricists, and composers.

SONGWRITERUNIVERSE

www.songwriteruniverse.com
In-depth articles, business information, education, and recommended reading.

SONIC BIDS

www.sonicbids.com
Features an online press kit with photos, bio, music samples, date calendar. Free trial period first month for artists/bands to sign up, newsletter.

SOUNDCLOUD

www.soundcloud.com
An online audio distribution platform that allows collaboration, promotion, and distribution of audio recordings.

SOUNDPEDIA

www.soundpedia.com
Internet radio/streaming audio. User can create personalized channels and playlists online.

STARPOLISH

www.starpolish.com
Features articles and interviews about the music industry.

SUMMERSONGS SONGWRITING CAMPS

www.summersongs.com
Information about songwriting camps, staff, and online registration.

TAXI

www.taxi.com
Independent A&R vehicle that shops demos to A&R professionals.

TUNECORE

www.tunecore.com
Service that allows musicians to sell their music digitally via online retailers such as iTunes, Amazon, Spotify, and more.

UNITED STATES COPYRIGHT OFFICE

www.copyright.gov
Homepage for the US Copyright Office. Offers information on registering songs.

WEIRDO MUSIC

www.weirdomusic.com
Online music magazine with articles, reviews, downloads, and links to Internet radio shows.

YAHOO!

www.news.yahoo.com
Search engine with radio station guide, music industry news, and listings.

YOUTUBE

www.youtube.com
Social networking site which hosts audiovisual content. Searchable database provides links to music videos, interviews, and more.

GLOSSARY

A CAPPELLA. Choral singing without accompaniment.

AAA FORM. A song form in which every verse has the same melody, often used for songs that tell a story.

AABA, ABAB. A commonly used song pattern consisting of two verses, a bridge, and a verse, or a repeated pattern of verse and bridge, where the verses are musically the same.

A&R DIRECTOR. Record company executive in charge of the Artists and Repertoire Department who is responsible for finding and developing new artists and matching songs with artists.

A/C. Adult contemporary music.

ADVANCE. Money paid to the songwriter or recording artist, which is then recouped before regular royalty payment begins. Sometimes called "up front" money, advances are deducted from royalties.

AFIM. Association for Independent Music (formerly NAIRD). Organization for independent record companies, distributors, retailers, manufacturers, etc.

AFM. American Federation of Musicians. A union for musicians and arrangers.

AFTRA. American Federation of Television and Radio Artists. A union for performers.

AIMP. Association of Independent Music Publishers.

AIRPLAY. The radio broadcast of a recording.

AOR. Album-Oriented Rock. A radio format that primarily plays selections from rock albums as opposed to hit singles.

ARRANGEMENT. An adaptation of a composition for a recording or performance, with consideration for the melody, harmony, instrumentation, tempo, style, etc.

ASCAP. American Society of Composers, Authors, and Publishers. A performing rights society. (See the "Organizations" section.)

ASSIGNMENT. Transfer of song rights from writer to publisher.

AUDIO VISUAL INDEX (AVI). A database containing title and production information for cue sheets which are available from a performing rights organization. Currently, BMI, ASCAP, SOCAN, PRS, APRA, and SACEM contribute their cue-sheet listings to the AVI.

AUDIOVISUAL. Refers to presentations that use audio backup for visual material.

BACKGROUND MUSIC. Music used that creates mood and supports the spoken dialogue of a radio program or visual action of an audiovisual work. Not feature or theme music.

B&W. Black and white.

BED. Prerecorded music used as background material in commercials. In rap music, often refers to the sampled and looped drums and music over which the rapper performs.

BLACK BOX. Theater without fixed stage or seating arrangements, capable of a variety of formations. Usually a small space, often attached to a major theater complex, used for workshops or experimental works calling for small casts and limited sets.

BMI. Broadcast Music, Inc. A performing rights society. (See the "Organizations" section.)

BOOKING AGENT. Person who schedules performances for entertainers.

BOOTLEGGING. Unauthorized recording and selling of a song.

BUSINESS MANAGER. Person who handles the financial aspects of artistic careers.

BUZZ. Attention an act generates through the media and word of mouth.

B/W. Backed with. Usually refers to the B-side of a single.

C&W. Country and western.

CATALOG. The collected songs of one writer or all songs handled by one publisher.

CD. Compact Disc.

CD-R. A recordable CD.

CD-ROM. Compact Disc-Read Only Memory. A computer information storage medium capable of holding enormous amounts of data. Information on a CD-ROM cannot be deleted. A computer user must have a CD-ROM drive to access a CD-ROM.

CHAMBER MUSIC. Any music suitable for performance in a small audience area or chamber.

CHAMBER ORCHESTRA. A miniature orchestra usually containing one instrument per part.

CHART. The written arrangement of a song.

CHARTS. The trade magazines' lists of the best-selling records.

CHR. Contemporary Hit Radio. Top-40 pop music.

COLLABORATION. Two or more artists, writers, etc., working together on a single project; for instance, a playwright and a songwriter creating a musical together.

COMPACT DISC. A small disc (about 4.7 inches in diameter) holding digitally encoded music that is read by a laser beam in a CD player.

COMPOSERS. The men and women who create musical compositions for motion pictures and other audiovisual works or the creators of classical music compositions.

COPUBLISH. Two or more parties own publishing rights to the same song.

COPYRIGHT. The exclusive legal right giving the creator of a work the power to control the publishing, reproduction, and sales of the work. Although a song is technically copyrighted at the time it is written, the best legal protection of that copyright comes through registering the copyright with the Library of Congress.

COPYRIGHT INFRINGEMENT. Unauthorized use of a copyrighted song or portions thereof.

COVER RECORDING. A new version of a previously recorded song.

CROSSOVER. A song that becomes popular in two or more musical categories (e.g., country and pop).

CUT. Any finished recording; a selection from an LP. Also, to record.

DAT. Digital Audio Tape. A professional and consumer audiocassette format for recording and playing back digitally encoded material. DAT cassettes are approximately one-third smaller than conventional audiocassettes.

DCC. Digital Compact Cassette. A consumer audio cassette format for recording and playing back digitally encoded tape. DCC tapes are the same size as analog cassettes.

DEMO. A recording of a song submitted as a demonstration of a writer's or artist's skills.

DERIVATIVE WORK. A work derived from another work, such as a translation, musical arrangement, sound recording, or motion-picture version.

DISTRIBUTOR. Wholesale marketing agent responsible for getting records from manufacturers to retailers.

DONUT. A jingle with singing at the beginning and end and an instrumental background in the middle. Ad copy is recorded over the middle section.

E-MAIL. Electronic mail. Computer address where a company or individual can be reached via modem.

ENGINEER. A specially trained individual who operates recording studio equipment.

ENHANCED CD. General term for an audio CD that also contains multimedia computer information. It is playable in both standard CD players and CD-ROM drives.

EP. Extended-Play record, CD, or cassette containing more selections than a standard single, but fewer than a standard album.

EPK. Electronic press kit. Usually contains photos, sound files, bio information, reviews, tour dates, etc., posted online. Sonicbids.com is a popular EPK hosting website.

FINAL MIX. The art of combining all the various sounds that take place during the recording session into a two-track stereo or mono tape. Reflects the total product and all of the energies and talents the artist, producer, and engineer have put into the project.

FLY SPACE. The area above a stage from which set pieces are lowered and raised during a performance.

FOLIO. A softcover collection of printed music prepared for sale.

FOLLOWING. A fanbase committed to going to gigs and buying albums.

FOREIGN RIGHTS SOCIETIES. Performing rights societies other than domestic that have reciprocal agreements with ASCAP and BMI for the collection of royalties accrued by foreign radio, television airplay, and other public performance of the above groups' writer members.

HARRY FOX AGENCY. Organization that collects mechanical royalties.

GRAMMY. Music industry awards presented by the National Academy of Recording Arts and Sciences.

HIP-HOP. A dance-oriented musical style derived from a combination of disco, rap, and R&B.

HIT. A song or record that achieves Top-40 status.

HOOK. A memorable "catch" phrase or melody line that is repeated in a song.

HOUSE. Dance music created by remixing samples from other songs.

HYPERTEXT. Words or groups of words in an electronic document that are linked to other text, such as a definition or a related document. Hypertext also can be linked to illustrations.

INDIE. An independent record label, music publisher, or producer.

INFRINGEMENT. A violation of the exclusive rights granted by the copyright law to a copyright owner.

INTERNET. A worldwide network of computers that offers access to a wide variety of electronic resources.

IPS. Inches per second, a speed designation for tape recording.

IRC. International reply coupon, necessary for the return of materials sent out of the country. Available at most post offices.

JINGLE. Usually a short verse set to music, designed as a commercial message.

LEAD SHEET. Written version (melody, chord symbols, and lyric) of a song.

LEADER. Plastic (non-recordable) tape at the beginning and between songs for ease in selection.

LIBRETTO. The text of an opera or any long choral work. The booklet containing such text.

LISTING. Block of information in this book about a specific company.

LP. Designation for long-playing record played at 33⅓ rpm.

LYRIC SHEET. A typed or written copy of a song's lyrics.

MARKET. A potential song or music buyer. Also a demographic division of the record-buying public.

MASTER. Edited and mixed tape used in the production of records; the best or original copy of a recording from which copies are made.

MD. MiniDisc. A 2.5-inch disk for recording and playing back digitally encoded music.

MECHANICAL RIGHT. The right to profit from the physical reproduction of a song.

MECHANICAL ROYALTY. Money earned from record, tape, and CD sales.

MIDI. Musical instrument digital interface. Universal standard interface that allows musical instruments to communicate with each other and computers.

MINI DISC. (see MD above.)

MIX. To blend a multi-track recording into the desired balance of sound, usually to a two-track stereo master.

MODEM. MOdulator/DEModulator. A computer device used to send data from one computer to another via telephone line.

MOR. Middle of the road. Easy-listening popular music.

MP3. File format of a relatively small size that stores audio files on a computer. Music saved in MP3 format can be played only with an MP3 player (which can be downloaded onto a computer).

MS. Manuscript.

MULTIMEDIA. Computers and software capable of integrating text, sound, photographic-quality images, animation, and video.

MUSIC BED. (see Bed above.)

MUSIC JOBBER. A wholesale distributor of printed music.

MUSIC LIBRARY. A business that purchases canned music, which can then be bought by producers of radio and TV commercials, films, videos, and audiovisual productions to use however they wish.

MUSIC PUBLISHER. A company that evaluates songs for commercial potential, finds artists to record them, finds other uses (such as TV or film) for the songs, collects income generated by the songs, and protects copyrights from infringement.

MUSIC ROW. An area of Nashville, Tennessee, encompassing Sixteenth, Seventeenth and Eighteenth avenues where most of the major publishing houses, recording studios, mastering labs, songwriters, singers, promoters, etc., practice their trade.

NARAS. National Academy of Recording Arts and Sciences.

THE NATIONAL ACADEMY OF SONGWRITERS (NAS). The largest U.S. songwriters' association. (See the "Organizations" section.)

NEEDLE-DROP. Refers to a type of music library. A needle-drop music library is a licensed library that allows producers to borrow music on a rate schedule. The price depends on how the music will be used.

NETWORK. A group of computers electronically linked to share information and resources.

NMPA. National Music Publishers Association.

ONE-OFF. A deal between songwriter and publisher that includes only one song or project at a time. No future involvement is implicated. Many times a single-song contract accompanies a one-off deal.

ONE-STOP. A wholesale distributor who sells small quantities of records to "mom-and-pop" record stores, retailers, and jukebox operators.

OPERETTA. Light, humorous, satiric plot, or poem set to cheerful, light music with occasional spoken dialogue.

OVERDUB. To record an additional part (vocal or instrumental) onto a basic multitrack recording.

PARODY. A satirical imitation of a literary or musical work. Permission from the owner of the copyright is sometimes required before commercial exploitation of a parody.

PAYOLA. Dishonest payment to broadcasters in exchange for airplay.

PERFORMING RIGHTS. A specific right granted by U.S. copyright law protecting a composition from being publicly performed without the owner's permission.

PERFORMING RIGHTS ORGANIZATION. An organization that collects income from the public performance of songs written by its members and then proportionally distributes this income to the individual copyright holder based on the number of performances of each song.

PERSONAL MANAGER. A person who represents artists to develop and enhance their careers. Personal managers may negotiate contracts, hire and dismiss other agencies and personnel relating to the artist's career, review material, help with artist promotions, and perform many other services.

PIRACY. The unauthorized reproduction and selling of printed or recorded music.

PITCH. To attempt to solicit interest for a song by audition.

PLAYLIST. List of songs a radio station will play.

POINTS. A negotiable percentage paid to producers and artists for records sold.

PRODUCER. Person who supervises every aspect of a recording project.

PRODUCTION COMPANY. Company specializing in producing jingle packages for advertising agencies. May also refer to companies specializing in audiovisual programs.

PROFESSIONAL MANAGER. Member of a music publisher's staff who screens submitted material and tries to get the company's catalog of songs recorded.

PROSCENIUM. Permanent architectural arch in a theater that separates the stage from the audience.

PUBLIC DOMAIN. Any composition with an expired, lapsed, or invalid copyright, therefore belonging to everyone.

PURCHASE LICENSE. Fee paid for music used from a stock music library.

QUERY. A letter of inquiry to an industry professional soliciting his interest.

R&B. Rhythm and blues.

RACK JOBBER. Distributors who lease floor space from department stores and put in racks of albums.

RATE. The percentage of royalty as specified by contract.

RELEASE. Any record issued by a record company.

RESIDUALS. In advertising or television, payments to singers and musicians for use of a performance.

RIAA. Recording Industry Association of America.

ROYALTY. Percentage of money earned from the sale of records or use of a song.

RPM. Revolutions per minute. Refers to phonograph turntable speed.

SAE. Self-addressed envelope (with no postage attached).

SASE. Self-addressed stamped envelope.

SATB. The abbreviation for parts in choral music, meaning Soprano, Alto, Tenor, and Bass.

SCORE. A complete arrangement of all the notes and parts of a composition (vocal or instrumental) written out on staves. A full score, or orchestral score, depicts every orchestral part on a separate staff and is used by a conductor.

SELF-CONTAINED. A band or recording act that writes all its own material.

SESAC. A performing rights organization, originally the Society of European Stage Authors and Composers. (see the "Organizations" section.)

SFX. Sound effects.

SHOP. To pitch songs to a number of companies or publishers.

SINGLE. 45rpm record with only one song per side. A 12£ single refers to a long version of one song on a 12£ disc, usually used for dance music.

SKA. Up-tempo dance music influenced primarily by reggae and punk, usually featuring horns, saxophone, and bass.

SOCAN. Society of Composers, Authors and Music Publishers of Canada. A Canadian performing rights organization. (see the "Organizations" section.)

SOLICITED. Songs or materials that have been requested.

SONG PLUGGER. A songwriter representative whose main responsibility is promoting uncut songs to music publishers, record companies, artists, and producers.

SONG SHARK. Person who deals with songwriters deceptively for his own profit.

SOUNDSCAN. A company that collates the register tapes of reporting stores to track the actual number of albums sold at the retail level.

SOUNDTRACK. The audio, including music and narration, of a film, videotape, or audiovisual program.

SPACE STAGE. Open stage that features lighting and, perhaps, projected scenery.

SPLIT PUBLISHING. To divide publishing rights between two or more publishers.

STAFF SONGWRITER. A songwriter who has an exclusive agreement with a publisher.

STATUTORY ROYALTY RATE. The maximum payment for mechanical rights guaranteed by law that a record company may pay the songwriter and his publisher for each record, CD, or tape sold.

SUBPUBLISHING. Certain rights granted by a U.S. publisher to a foreign publisher in exchange for promoting the U.S. catalog in his terrItory.

SYNCHRONIZATION. Technique of timing a musical soundtrack to action on film or video.

TAKE. Either an attempt to record a vocal or instrumental part or an acceptable recording of a performance.

TEJANO. A musical form begun in the late 1970s by regional bands in south Texas, its style reflects a blended Mexican-American culture. Incorporates elements of rock, country, R&B, and jazz, and often features accordion and 12-string guitar.

THRUST STAGE. Stage with audience on three sides and a stagehouse or wall on the fourth side.

TOP 40. The first forty songs on the pop music charts at any given time. Also refers to a style of music which emulates that heard on the current Top 40.

TRACK. Divisions of a recording tape (e.g., 24-track tape) that can be individually recorded in the studio, and then mixed into a finished master.

TRADES. Publications covering the music industry.

12-SINGLE. A 12-inch record containing one or more remixes of a song, originally intended for dance club play.

UNSOLICITED. Songs or materials that were not requested and are not expected.

VOCAL SCORE. An arrangement of vocal music detailing all vocal parts and condensing all accompanying instrumental music into one piano part.

WEBSITE. An address on the World Wide Web that can be accessed by computer modem. It may contain text, graphics, and sound.

WING SPACE. The offstage area surrounding the playing stage in a theater, unseen by the audience, where sets and props are hidden, actors wait for cues, and stagehands prepare to change sets.

WORLD MUSIC. A general music category that includes most musical forms originating outside the U.S. and Europe, including reggae and calypso. World music finds its roots primarily in the Caribbean, Latin America, Africa, and the South Pacific.

WORLD WIDE WEB (WWW). An Internet resource that utilizes hypertext to access information. It also supports formatted text, illustrations, and sounds, depending on the user's computer capabilities.

GENERAL INDEX

CATEGORY INDEX

RECORD COMPANIES

RECORD PRODUCERS

MANAGERS & BOOKING AGENTS

GEOGRAPHIC INDEX